P9-DYE-865

From IT Pro to Cloud Pro: Microsoft Office 365 and SharePoint Online

Ben Curry
Brian Laws

PUBLISHED BY
Microsoft Press
A division of Microsoft Corporation
One Microsoft Way
Redmond, Washington 98052-6399

Copyright © 2016 by Yuri Diogenes, Jeff Gilbert, Robert Mazzoli

All rights reserved. No part of the contents of this book may be reproduced or transmitted in any form or by any means without the written permission of the publisher.

Library of Congress Control Number: 2016941108
ISBN: 978-1-5093-0414-1

Printed and bound in the United States of America.

1 16

Microsoft Press books are available through booksellers and distributors worldwide. If you need support related to this book, email Microsoft Press Support at mspinput@microsoft.com. Please tell us what you think of this book at http://aka.ms/tellpress.

This book is provided "as-is" and expresses the author's views and opinions. The views, opinions and information expressed in this book, including URL and other Internet website references, may change without notice.

Some examples depicted herein are provided for illustration only and are fictitious. No real association or connection is intended or should be inferred.

Microsoft and the trademarks listed at http://www.microsoft.com on the "Trademarks" webpage are trademarks of the Microsoft group of companies. All other marks are property of their respective owners.

Acquisitions Editor: Karen Szall
Developmental Editor: Karen Szall
Project Editor: Christian Holdener, S4Carlisle Publishing Services
Editorial Production: S4Carlisle Publishing Services
Technical Reviewer: Charlie Russell; Technical Review services provided by Content Master, a member of CM Group, Ltd.
Copyeditor: Roger LeBlanc
Indexer: Maureen Johnson, MoJo's Indexing
Cover: Twist Creative • Seattle

I dedicate this book to my family, Kimberly, Madison, and Bryce. They gave up time with "Hubby B" and Daddy to allow this book to make it to you. I love you all as high as the sky!

    —BEN CURRY

I dedicate this book to my incredible wife (Kathy) and kids (Daniel, Benjamin, and Isabella) for supporting me, giving me up for so long, picking up my slack, and loving me through all of it. They are my greatest blessing.

    —BRIAN LAWS

Contents

What do you think of this book? We want to hear from you!

Microsoft is interested in hearing your feedback so we can improve our books and learning resources for you. To participate in a brief survey, please visit:

http://aka.ms/tellpress

Chapter 3   Working with Azure Active Directory for Office 365   51

What do you think of this book? We want to hear from you!

Microsoft is interested in hearing your feedback so we can improve our books and learning resources for you. To participate in a brief survey, please visit:

http://aka.ms/tellpress

Introduction

From the beginning of this project, Brian and I wanted to create a book that would highlight how IT Pros would need to become Cloud Pros. At the same time, we wanted to give newer Microsoft Office 365 professionals a solid guide for implementation. We knew this book couldn't be a comprehensive guide, or it would turn into a large volume that would soon be outdated. Instead, we wanted to keep the book fresh and relevant, and only discuss topics that aren't likely to change or are brand new. Where technologies are likely to change, we referenced the best starting points for you, the reader. Some topics are very technical in nature and highlight the technical skill needed to transition from IT Pro to Cloud Pro. Others, such as migration, are more process-focused and underscore the need for Cloud Pros to be aware of proper project planning and methodologies. The cloud requires us to be both technical and business savvy.

Although it's focused on IT Pros, this book is for anyone who is responsible for designing, configuring, implementing, or managing an Office 365 deployment. This book will help you understand what your team is up against when it comes to your Microsoft SharePoint Online, OneDrive for Business, or hybrid deployment. Also, it will discuss additional technologies and concepts that underlie Office 365 but aren't readily apparent, such as Azure Active Directory (Azure AD), Security & Compliance, and lots of Windows PowerShell. However, this book rarely issues prescriptive guidance—you should use the online Microsoft resources for that. Our goal is to help you think through the various design points so that you can make the right decisions for your company.

This book assumes you have a working knowledge of SharePoint Server 2013 and SharePoint Online administration, or that you have access to that information. It also assumes you have a working knowledge of Office 365 fundamentals, such as how to work with users and navigate the administration centers. We assume you understand most networking concepts, such as DNS, firewalls, routing, and proxy servers, along with the how-to of those concepts. Newer areas of technology (many of which many IT Pros lack experience with or are weak in) are covered in more technical detail than other, better-known topics.

Finally, we often "deep dive" into a single, specific area to show the logic of being a Cloud Pro. Because there isn't room in any book to dive deeply into every area of Office 365, you should pay attention to how, in these deep dives, we go about solving problems and not just focus on how we solve that specific problem.

Acknowledgments

Writing a book requires support from many people. We had several people who were more than willing to help in areas in which we needed additional feedback. Sometimes, we simply wanted a top pro's advice. First, we want to thank the two contributing authors, Jason Batchelor and Jay Simcox. They have both contributed to Microsoft books before, and it was a pleasure to work with them again. They brought expertise in areas that weren't strengths for Brian and me, thus making those sections deeper and more relevant. Next, James Curry helped with developing some PowerShell for the book. As always, his code is stellar!

Matt Whitehorn provided valuable insights into governance and process management. Thanks, Matt. Also, we want to say thanks to Rob de Jong for his input into managing users and groups with Azure AD. We had some graphics advice from Summit 7 Systems' Robin Williams. Thanks to her for helping lay out some challenging sketches from me.

Last, but not least, thanks to Neil Hodgkinson and Manas Biswas for their expert insights into hybrid Office 365 design and configuration. If you ever get the chance to attend their sessions or read their books, you'll be very glad you did.

Free ebooks from Microsoft Press

From technical overviews to in-depth information on special topics, the free ebooks from Microsoft Press cover a wide range of topics. These ebooks are available in PDF, EPUB, and Mobi for Kindle formats, ready for you to download at:

http://aka.ms/mspressfree

Check back often to see what is new!

Errata, updates, & book support

We've made every effort to ensure the accuracy of this book and its companion content. You can access updates to this book—in the form of a list of submitted errata and their related corrections—at:

http://aka.ms/CloudPro/errata

If you discover an error that is not already listed, please submit it to us at the same page.

If you need additional support, email Microsoft Press Book Support at mspinput@microsoft.com.

Please note that product support for Microsoft software and hardware is not offered through the previous addresses. For help with Microsoft software or hardware, go to *http://support.microsoft.com*.

We want to hear from you

At Microsoft Press, your satisfaction is our top priority, and your feedback our most valuable asset. Please tell us what you think of this book at:

http://aka.ms/tellpress

The survey is short, and we read every one of your comments and ideas. Thanks in advance for your input!

Stay in touch

Let's keep the conversation going! We're on Twitter: *http://twitter.com/MicrosoftPress*.

CHAPTER 1

Getting started as an Office 365 cloud pro

Welcome to what we hope to be the first in a long line of books centered on the Microsoft cloud pro. The primary purpose of this book is to come alongside traditional IT pros and help them be prepared to manage Office 365, Microsoft's premier Software as a Service (SaaS). Quite often, an IT pro is thrust into the cloud after someone in their organization decided it was the right thing to do. "We're moving to Office 365, and you're going to manage it."

That can be a lot to swallow, so in this little book we're going to do what we can to help you get your arms around it and approach it from the right direction. By no means is this book comprehensive, nor is it overly deep. Sure, we'll dive deeply into some of the aspects we think you'll need to know, but a significant and important goal of this book is to simply make you aware of what you have available. Wouldn't it be great if you could not only deliver to the business the SharePoint Online you wanted but then also, for example, hand to them automatic data-loss protection or enterprise social through Yammer? As we enter the era of the cloud pro, you have tremendous opportunities to innovate for your business and add greater value. It's hard to do that if you don't know what's possible.

A fundamental premise of this book is that you are an IT pro and generally know what you're doing on-premises. Or you know enough to play an IT pro on TV. Regardless, you're smart, and you know how to find stuff on Bing or TechNet. We're not going to insult your intelligence by pretending you can't. As such, we'll assume you possess a certain amount of knowledge. For example, we'll assume you already know the fundamentals of Office 365, such as how to get it, how to create and license users, and how to navigate the admin portals. Don't worry, though, if you're completely new to Office 365. We'll provide you with some information at the end of the chapter to help you with some of the prerequisites if you're not familiar with Office 365 yet.

1

The purpose of this chapter is to address a couple of miscellaneous fundamental topics you should keep in mind as you start your journey as a cloud pro. These are the foundations upon which the rest can be built.

Becoming a cloud pro

"Cloud pro? What in the world is a cloud pro?" We used that term a bunch already. You might be scratching your head about it right now. You've heard of developers (or devs) and IT pros, but a *cloud pro*?

To "do" the cloud, someone working in IT must have a mix of skills that don't fit neatly into any one of the two traditional categories. They must be able to understand infrastructure, write scripts, understand authentication and authorization (OAuth vs. SAML vs. WS-FED), be comfortable in Visual Studio, and perform various other IT tasks. They're not devs, and they're not quite IT pros.

They're cloud pros.

Cloud pro is a term that describes the new category of professional who is focused on the cloud and cloud technologies. Although these professionals tend to have more of an IT-pro bent, they also have a lot of the skills traditionally plied by their dev colleagues as well. The mix of skills is similar to that of a DevOps practitioner. A cloud pro is someone who understands the underlying concepts of the cloud, like Infrastructure as a Service (IaaS), Platform as a Service (PaaS), and Software as a Service (SaaS). They know how authentication works and how to set up hybrid identities. They're comfortable with Microsoft Windows PowerShell and frequently think in terms of automation and scalability. They understand that the cloud is really all about disposable computing. Their focus is frequently on building a patchwork of cloud services that modern businesses need to be efficient, resilient, and cost conscious. They build the bridges that allow their customers to reap all those valuable cloud benefits.

But what about the IT pro?

Let's face it: the days of the traditional IT pro *might* be numbered. It's uncomfortable to talk about, but we're your friends—we've got to. We're moving more and more into a world driven by PowerShell and configuration tools. Although scripting and light development was par for the course for IT pros "back in the day," many of the current IT pros would be lost if they didn't have a nice UI and lots of help from Bing. Because cloud work also frequently involves dev and even business analyst skills, many modern IT pros won't be able to do cloud. By no means do we intend to bash IT pros. We really think of ourselves as IT pros at heart. They're our tribe. However, IT pros unwilling to modernize their skills will find themselves put out to pasture as the cloud comes rolling in. There still are COBOL programmers out there who are gainfully and comfortably employed, but opportunities for them are few and far between.

The good news, though, is that it's definitely possible for them to prepare for the cloudy future—and they'll have fun doing so!

Cloud pro diversity

One hallmark of the cloud is that, at its most basic level, it's a set of services that can be consumed to solve a problem. Those services are many and varied. One layer of the stack comprises the vendors: Microsoft, Amazon, Google, and others. Beneath the vendor layer are the main cloud categories: Infrastructure as a Service (IaaS), Platform as a Service (PaaS), and Software as a Service (SaaS). Inside each of these categories are the individual vendor-specific products. A cloud pro might specialize in any tier or component in the stack. One cloud pro might have a particular focus on Microsoft Azure PaaS offerings, while another might be focused on AWS' IaaS, while yet another might be focused on Salesforce and SaaS. Some cloud pros might be focused on Office 365. Others might not specialize at all and be open to any and all cloud services, tying them together (including across vendors).

The tremendous diversity in cloud services will result in great diversity among cloud pros. With the cloud vendors' rapid pace of innovation, the options will only grow, providing even more opportunities to learn and potentially specialize further. For someone who loves technology and is always interested in learning something new, all this diversity and innovation will be delightful. However, if you're unwelcoming of continual challenge and aren't looking for more personal growth, this might be a daunting field for you. Don't get us wrong—it doesn't mean you can't or shouldn't be a cloud pro. You certainly can pick and stick with a few specialties. However, the speed at which a vendor can iterate in your specialty will likely mean an increased need for you to stay current in your niche.

Cloud pro skills

Although it's still early in the age of the cloud pro, we'll try to outline some primary skills and technologies a cloud pro likely needs. You'll see that a lot of these skills apply to a traditional IT pro. However, they have a different bent or context, and they'll be needed in conjunction with the other skills listed.

Technologies:

- **IaaS, PaaS, and SaaS** Understand each of these types of services and when and where each is appropriate.
- **Know the major Microsoft cloud services** Stay familiar with the planned roadmaps, and know how to calculate costs (at least roughly).
- **PowerShell or other scripting (including best practices)**
- **Identity Management (SAML, OAuth, and WS-Fed) and identity sync tools** Be especially familiar with Microsoft Azure Active Directory Connect.
- **Performance profiling and monitoring in the cloud**
- **Microsoft Visual Studio, other IDEs, or both** Develop some comfort with code and the tools of the dev trade. At a minimum, at least learn how to read the primary development languages used by your organization.

- **Networking, at least at a medium level** The cloud needs lots of connections, so at least be able to talk at an intermediate level with a network professional. Build relationships with them—you'll need them on your side!

- **Cloud security**

- **JSON and XML**

- **Know the basic concepts of working with public-key infrastructure (PKI) services** This includes issuing, installing, renewing, and revoking certificates.

- **Desired State Configuration (or other declarative configuration technologies like Chef) if you're doing IaaS** Ideally, instead of bespoke servers which are manually configured, VMs should be disposable and thus be configured through declarative technologies like Desired State Configuration (DSC). In the cloud space, we use the term "cattle, not pets" to describe this philosophy of managing servers.

- **Source control** We really should be using it.

- **Azure Active Directory**

- **Storage, networking, and compute** Know how to make them performant and fault tolerant.

- **Azure Resource Manager (ARM)**

- **Azure Recovery Services**

"Soft skills" will be just as important as the technology (and sometimes more so). They can actually be harder than the technology. Here are just a few skills that serve the cloud pro well:

- Understand the whole concept of disposable computing.

- Understand loosely coupled architectures.

- Understand scaling strategies.

- Be able to perform workload analysis. (Is it even fit for the cloud?)

- Be able to perform cost analysis.

- Understand most of the concepts in DevOps.

- Understand workload migration (lots of planning and testing).

- Be able to do strategic planning.

- Develop the ability to collaborate well with business users to define such things as goals and requirements.

- Be able to perform testing.

- Understand application life-cycle management (ALM) and the software development life-cycle (SDLC).

Again, these are just a few of the skills required by the cloud pro. The challenge for the cloud pro is that, unlike a traditional IT pro or Dev, you really need to have the large majority of these skills to succeed.

The Office 365 cloud pro

So far, everything has been generic and applicable to cloud pros in the broad sense. However, this book is focused on Office 365. What do those of us who work with Office 365 need to be concerned with?

Office 365 is SaaS that's hosted and supported by Microsoft. It's a subset of the Microsoft cloud. Because it's SaaS, a lot of the work of administration and configuration has been done for you. You don't have to worry about servers, patching Microsoft SharePoint, and keeping it all running. Sure, it's IaaS under the cover, but it's nothing you need to care about. Nevertheless, you need to understand and maintain most of the same skills, such as working with PowerShell, cloud networking, cloud security, Azure Active Directory, identity management, and change management. Hybrid configurations are the cloud pro's bread and butter, so it will be important that you understand each component in a hybrid architecture. Additionally, as the use of Office 365 grows and companies become more and more familiar with the cloud and its advantages, opportunities to bring together Office 365 and Azure services will likely grow as well. Advanced capabilities of Azure Active Directory, the Power BI platform, provider-hosted add-ins, Power Apps, and Microsoft Flow—all of these (and more!)—can be leveraged to extend the capabilities you get out of the box with Office 365.

Living in a tenant world

One of the most important concepts of the public cloud (and even sometimes in private clouds) is that of the *tenant*. If you truly understand this concept and its implications, you're well on your way to understanding why the services are the way they are and why certain limitations are in place. In our opinion, it's the key to understanding the cloud.

Merriam-Webster defines *tenant* as follows: "a person, business, group, etc., that pays to use another person's property: someone who rents or leases a house, apartment, etc., from a landlord" (*http://www.merriam-webster.com/dictionary/tenant*). This is an excellent description of a tenant in the cloud, too. Let's elaborate.

Let's take the example of living in an apartment. If you do so, you're paying for the right to use a portion of the space. Every month, you pay somebody (either the owner or a management company) for the amount of space you occupy. Some apartments are more expensive than others because they're larger or have more amenities. You're paying for the temporary right to live there; you have no ownership stake in the property except for what you brought into the apartment. The stuff that was already in there (such as the carpet and cabinets) is owned by the landlord, and that landlord was responsible for making sure it was in good order when it was delivered to you. Although you're responsible for what's inside the apartment, the landlord is responsible for everything else: the building itself, maintaining the grounds, keeping the stairwell in good repair, making sure utilities can be delivered to your apartment, and so forth. You tap into those utilities—like water, sewage, cable, and electricity—with other tenants of the building, and you either pay for what you use or pay a flat fee that the landlord hopes will average out over time. You might have an individual agreement with the cable company, but it comes in over a common infrastructure.

In an apartment, you have limited options and there are boundaries. You can't go into another apartment, for example. You don't have full say over what goes on in the complex. However, you don't have the responsibility of the mortgage, paying people to take care of the grounds, or maintaining the building. By paying rent, you absolve yourself from all of that and are responsible only for the services you paid for.

This is an almost-perfect analogy for the cloud as well. Microsoft is the owner of its cloud services. It owns the servers as well as the buildings and grounds holding them. It makes sure everything is maintained and ready for use, including hiring staff to manage it all. The company makes sure the points of ingress and egress are safe and that you can only get to where you're allowed to go. Microsoft also makes sure all the "utilities" are available, such as networking, storage, and all the Office 365 and Azure services. Microsoft is the landlord, and the cloud is the apartment complex along with everything in it.

As for you? You're renting a piece of the cloud, like you do an apartment. A little chunk of the whole is carved out for your use, and you can do whatever you want with what you're given. But rules are in place to ensure you stay in that space and don't interfere with the space of others. You give up some of your rights and options when you choose to live in an apartment, just as you do in a cloud tenant. For example, in an apartment complex, we can't bash down a wall to our neighbor's unit and we can't play loud music late at night. In the same way, Microsoft ensures that how you use your space doesn't negatively affect another tenant's use of it, either in terms of security or user experience. That's why you can't deploy farm solutions in SharePoint Online. Instead of an apartment, you have a *tenant*. You get the freedom of not having to worry about everything it takes to make the services work. You're paying Microsoft to do that. You pay for what you use, and you have the luxury of walking away once your lease is done.

If you don't like the restrictions, you can look for other options, such as hosting a service yourself in IaaS, subscribing to a dedicated service, or running servers in your data center. You can buy a house if you need to play your music loudly at night. But along with this comes a lot of responsibility. When the plumbing springs a leak in the middle of the night, it's up to you to fix it. In the same way, if you run your own service and you lose the network or your code causes an outage, you are responsible for bringing the system back online.

So when you're working in your tenant and wondering why something is the way that it is or you're frustrated with a restriction, remember that you have neighbors and they have a right to the same quality of service as you do.

The rapid pace of change

Most on-premises systems do not change much from week to week. It's quite common for them to not see any major changes at all for as many as three to five years, when the next version of the software is released. For many organizations, this lack of change can be quite comfortable because it creates a sense of stability, and users (and IT staff) don't have to be concerned with learning something new. It does come at a cost, though, because it decreases the chance for greater innovation (and thus greater value) in the system.

This scenario stands in stark contrast to the cloud. The cloud, especially Office 365 and Microsoft Azure, is continually growing and changing. Office 365 is massive, and Microsoft is continually adding to its already impressive capabilities. These cloud services are called *evergreen* because they're always growing and being refreshed. Although this structure provides tremendous opportunity, because the service provider can continue to add new value or quickly fix issues, it can be uncomfortable to users as they see the system change around them. Some might find this exciting, while others will find it worrisome and challenging. An opportunity for one can be a hindrance to another.

And the challenge isn't just for our end users. We also have to deal with that constant change. Cloud pros, far more than IT pros, live in a world where the ground is continually shifting beneath their feet and where the walls keep moving. We have to keep up, even more so than the end user. Again, this field can be exciting because working with ever-changing technology means there will always be things to learn. But it can also be exhausting—and for the exact same reason. Choosing the cloud as a career means choosing a life of continual learning.

So what are we supposed to do? How do we manage this, both for ourselves and for our users? To some degree, we simply need to accept it and adapt. We need to be realistic about the systems we use and manage, and we need to understand that frequent change is inevitable. Frankly, most of us have simply been lucky we've been able to avoid it for so long. The same goes for our end users as well. They also must come to grips with the new pace of change. There's a degree to which they must also sink or swim. At least we're all in the same boat together!

We think, however, we can take a few steps to make this reality a little easier to bear. Here are a couple of ideas:

- We can help our users by keeping them informed of the expected changes and, better yet, the opportunities those changes provide. If we control the message, we can cast the change as something to be excited about instead of something to worry over.

- We need to adopt a pattern of continual learning. In the past, we got away with learning new technology in large chunks with each major release. Now, we need to regularly set aside time for learning, either through blogs, podcasts, or in-classroom training. We need to sip, not just gulp.

- If needed, we can use features in the platform to minimize the amount of change or its impact. In Office 365, for example, you can choose whether or not to include your tenant (or a subset of users in your tenant) in the first-release program. Those in the program will receive updates sooner than others. This option can be used strategically to prepare key individuals for changes before the rest of the organization gets them. As will be discussed later in the book, you can also control the frequency of updates to Office applications through ProPlus. For SharePoint Online, although we wouldn't recommend it, you could potentially prohibit users from seeing changes by using a custom master page. Although this can delay changes to the interface, it comes at the high cost of continually managing the master page and ensuring it continues to work.

Change is a fact of life for the cloud pro, and we must come to terms with it. Instead of fighting it, we should embrace it. By doing so, we can turn what could be a negative into a strategic advantage.

Preparing the network

The fundamental nature of the public cloud is that it's entirely accessed over the network and that it's external to your company. It's hosted somewhere out on the internet. As such, your network—the wide area network (WAN) in particular—must be as prepared for the move to the cloud as possible. Take some time to ensure your WAN is solid and ready to go. Evaluate the bandwidth you have available, and monitor it to ensure it's sufficient. As Office 365 becomes increasingly critical to your company, you can even consider getting Azure ExpressRoute for Office 365 to give you dedicated bandwidth and reduced latency. Although that's a pricey option, it can really improve the user experience and help the service seem like it's on-premises.

If your organization uses a proxy, be sure you have access to everything needed to manage the tenant and that your users will be able to reach the service. We highly recommend you allow Office 365 traffic to bypass the proxy, because all transmitted data is encrypted via SSL/TLS. If you are unable to do so, you need to manually configure the proxy for the URLs, IP address ranges, and ports. The following links tell you what you need to know. Note that the endpoints change, requiring you to perform ongoing proxy maintenance. Microsoft has provided an RSS feed you can subscribe to that tells you when endpoints change. The link to the feed is on the first page listed here, as is an XML file, which includes a list of all the endpoints.

- "Office 365 URLs and IP address ranges" at *https://support.office.com/article/Office-365-URLs-and-IP-address-ranges-8548a211-3fe7-47cb-abb1-355ea5aa88a2*
- "Hybrid Identity Required Ports and Protocols" at *https://azure.microsoft.com/documen-tation/articles/active-directory-aadconnect-ports*

> **MORE INFO**   For additional network testing and tuning resources, see:
> - "Network planning and performance tuning for Office 365" at *https://support. office.com/article/Network-planning-and-performance-tuning-for-Office-365-e5f1228c-da3c-4654-bf16-d163daee8848*
> - Microsoft Ignite 2015 session "Planning for Internet Performance and Capacity" at *https://channel9.msdn.com/Events/Ignite/2015/BRK3166*

If after you deploy Office 365 things aren't working quite right, you can run the Microsoft Connectivity Analyzer to help you with the troubleshooting. It also is a little application you install from *https://portal.office.com/tools*. You can use it, for example, to troubleshoot Microsoft Outlook connectivity or federation. Figure 1-1 shows the Connectivity Diagnostics page.

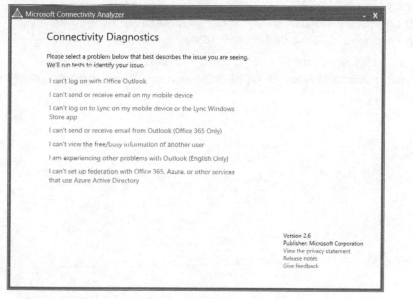

FIGURE 1-1 Connectivity Diagnostics page from the Microsoft Connectivity Analyzer

Getting started with Office 365

Again, in this book, we assume you have a base-level of knowledge about Office 365 and its services. We expect you to know fundamentals such as creating an Office 365 tenant, maintaining user licensing, navigating the Admin Centers, and performing basic user maintenance.

If you're not familiar with Office 365 and are just beginning to consider using it, we recommend taking some time to learn the basics. There are lots of great resources from Microsoft and the community to get you started. Additionally, any number of Microsoft partners can give you a hand. Consider taking instructor-led classes, as well.

Take a look at the following resources to get started:

- "How to sign up for Office 365 – Admin help" at *https://support.office.com/article/How-to-sign-up-for-Office-365-Admin-Help-9b23c065-eef9-4bf7-acf5-127eb46d5e67*

- "Get started with Office 365 for Business" at *https://support.office.com/article/Get-started-with-Office-365-for-business-d6466f0d-5d13-464a-adcb-00906ae87029*

- "Office help and training" at *https://support.office.com*

- Microsoft Virtual Academy "Office 365 Fundamentals" series at *https://channel9.msdn.com/Series/Office-365-Fundamentals*

- "About the Office 365 admin center" at *https://support.office.com/article/About-the-Office-365-admin-center-58537702-d421-4d02-8141-e128e3703547*
- "Users and passwords in Office 365 for business – Admin Help" at *https://support.office.com/article/Users-and-passwords-in-Office-365-for-business-%E2%80%93-Admin-Help-e4df7dbc-a98c-4bb4-9fa7-ab28a9c56b8e*
- "Get your organization ready for Office 365 Enterprise" at *https://support.office.com/article/Get-your-organization-ready-for-Office-365-Enterprise-712fced7-f9d0-4fde-8b79-286262a5d0bc*

PowerShell 101 for cloud pros

In this chapter, we talk about interacting with Microsoft Office 365 using Microsoft Windows PowerShell. For readers entirely new to PowerShell, we provide a brief introduction to PowerShell fundamentals. We then talk about how to configure your environment to use PowerShell with Office 365, followed by how to connect using it. There's a tremendous amount you can do in Office 365 using PowerShell—far more than we can include here. However, we provide examples of how you can use PowerShell to work inside of Office 365.

Beyond the browser with Office 365

With Office 365, Microsoft gives you a tremendous number of tools to support your business. It encompasses at least four major products (Exchange Online, SharePoint Online, Skype for Business, and Yammer), not to mention the fundamental platform itself. Add to that Azure Active Directory, Power BI, Information Rights Management, Intune/Mobile Device Management, Office ProPlus, the Add-In platform, Project Online, Dynamics CRM Online, and Parature—that's a lot to manage! Microsoft has done an extremely good job of providing in-browser management experiences through a collection of administration centers.

> **MORE INFO** Most admin center URLs for Microsoft products and features are predictable. The exception is Skype for Business, which you need to get from the Office 365 Admin Center. The following are the administration center URLs:
> - Office 365: *https://portal.office.com/AdminPortal*
> - Exchange: *https://outlook.office365.com/ecp*

- SharePoint: *https://<domain>-admin.sharepoint.com* (for example, *https://contoso-admin.sharepoint.com*)

- Yammer: *https://www.yammer.com/<domain>/admin* (for example, *https://www.yammer.com/contoso.com/admin*)

- Skype for Business: *https://admin<suffix>.online.lync.com/lscp* (for example, *https://admin0a.online.lync.com/lscp*)

- Security and Compliance: *https://protection.office.com*

- Azure Active Directory: *https://manage.windowsazure.com/<domain>* (for example, *https://manage.windowsazure.com/contoso.com*)

Microsoft continually makes improvements to the admin centers. Sometimes it seems like there's something new every day. Microsoft continues to bring into the browser experience more and more functionality and configuration options that previously were accessible only through a command line. However, not every option is available in the browser.

Some configurations or capabilities, such as repairing a SharePoint Online site collection or configuring hybrid search, require PowerShell. That's not necessarily a negative—often it's more efficient or expedient to step away from the browser. Updating users *en masse* (such as changing licenses or adding email addresses) can be far more efficient, and processes can be standardized and repeated simply by using PowerShell. You can also interact with the various Office 365 services all from a single command line or script. For example, you can create a user, assign licenses, update its properties, create and configure a mailbox, add the user to Share-Point Online sites, and assign a Skype for Business phone number in a matter of seconds all from the same user-onboarding script.

At this time, there really are two programmatic ways to configure Office 365: PowerShell and the REST APIs. Whereas you can normally operate on only a single item at a time in the browser, PowerShell gives you the opportunity to do something with a collection of items all at once. This task could be updating an attribute or taking a set of actions on each item (like a loop). Power-Shell is at its most powerful when it can reduce a manual, repetitive, time-consuming task into a couple of lines of code that executes in seconds.

Microsoft also makes available a collection of REST APIs. These are service endpoints Microsoft exposes that provide deeper, programmatic access to many of the Office 365 services. The center-piece of these is the Office Graph. The Office Graph provides a simple, consistent, unified, single point of entry to multiple APIs, making it simpler to interact with Office 365 through code. The Office Graph and the REST APIs are generally centered on a user, as opposed to the PowerShell cmdlets, which focus more on the services and their configurations. These APIs are really more of a developer topic, so we're not going to go further with them. However, it's important to know that they exist and, if you have the skills, provide an alternative mechanism for working with Office 365 from outside of the browser.

MORE INFO For more information on the Office 365 API, see the following:

- Office 365 API Reference: *https://msdn.microsoft.com/en-us/office/office365/api/api-catalog*

- Office 365 API Sandbox: *https://apisandbox.msdn.microsoft.com*

These techniques, both PowerShell and the REST APIs, are not just about being efficient. Although being efficient and productive is important, they're also about repeatability and having a consistent process with a consistent outcome. Browser-based processes are manual by their nature. You can miss steps and make mistakes easily in a manual process. A parameterized script in a runbook can help eliminate accidents, and it better guarantees completeness.

You also can use parameterized scripts to build a library or repository of scripts and code that you can then share with others, check into a source control system (like Team Foundation Server or Git), or both. Source control can help ensure your hard work isn't lost, and you can use it to roll back to previous versions of your scripts.

Scripting also can be critical in organizations with strict controls around implementing changes in a production environment. Change management is critical when you're responsible for a mission-critical system or for one that's being audited (such as one that's subject to the US Sarbanes-Oxley Act, also known as *SOX*). The scripts can be attached to the change record and then deployed by somebody with the authority to do so.

TRADE-OFFS You might hear the argument that creating and sharing scripts is bad for job security. To some degree, committing management procedures to a script or runbook might enable somebody else to do your job. However, we're willing to bet you're more valuable to your company than your ability to push a few buttons or navigate an admin center.

Automating the busy work enables you to move higher up the stack and contribute to the business in more valuable ways. It might allow you to address all those other issues that are clamoring for your attention. Perhaps it will allow you to bring more innovation to the table and solve more interesting problems. Heck, maybe it will give you the breathing room to finally take a day off. You're now a cloud pro, and you have the rest of the cloud to take on.

As PowerShell practitioners like to say, building a proficiency in scripting and automation enables you to become a tool maker, not just a tool user. Plus, it's a whole lot of fun.

Microsoft Windows PowerShell fundamentals

Before we get into using PowerShell with Office 365, let's do a high-level overview of PowerShell. If you already know PowerShell, feel free to skip ahead. Although this isn't intended to be a true instructional on PowerShell, we hope it provides the uninitiated with enough of an idea of how it works so that they can understand what follows.

If you want to go deeper, you can find all kinds of excellent resources online to get you started. We especially recommend anything by "The Scripting Guy," Ed Wilson. Check out "Hey, Scripting Guy! Blog" at *https://blogs.technet.microsoft.com/HeyScriptingGuy*, or take a look at his books, such as *Windows PowerShell 3.0 First Steps* (Microsoft Press, 2013).

So what is PowerShell? Here's the Microsoft definition from TechNet (*https://technet.microsoft.com/library/bb978526.aspx*):

> *Windows PowerShell is a task-based command-line shell and scripting language designed especially for system administration. Built on the .NET Framework, Windows PowerShell helps IT professionals and power users control and automate the administration of the Windows operating system and applications that run on Windows.*

This definition calls out its two most important aspects. First, it's a command-line shell. *Shells* have been around forever. They provide powerful, command-line access to the core of a system. In a shell, a set of commands are made available which you can use to interact with the system. Second, it's a scripting language. *Scripting languages* are similar to programming languages in that they have specific grammar, syntax, and methods for using multiple commands in a sequence. A scripting language, though, operates at a higher level in the stack and usually doesn't offer the full power and flexibility of a true programming language. However, scripts can provide an almost-just-in-time development experience, providing you with agility that can be difficult to get with a full, compiled programming language.

Finally, PowerShell is built on the Microsoft .NET Framework and can tap into its power. Because of the relationship between the two, you can go far past already-built cmdlets and use .NET libraries and objects directly in your scripts, bringing you quite close to a native .NET language. You can even dynamically write C# code in a script, load it into memory, and run it as you would a compiled library—but that's far outside the scope of this book. For now, just understand that PowerShell can make available to you a tremendous amount of power from a command line. It was well named.

Let's now talk about some fundamental elements of PowerShell. These will help you read the commands shown later and understand what's going on. Let's review cmdlets, the pipeline, objects and variables, and collections. Then we'll talk a little about discovering more information and capabilities by exploring the PowerShell objects.

Cmdlets

Cmdlets (pronounced *command-lets*) are the most foundational component. A cmdlet is a command you can use. They come in the form of [Verb]-[Noun], such as Get-Service, Set-ExecutionPolicy, and New-PSSession. For example, to get a list of all the running services and their status, you can run Get-Service at a PowerShell command prompt as shown in Figure 2-1.

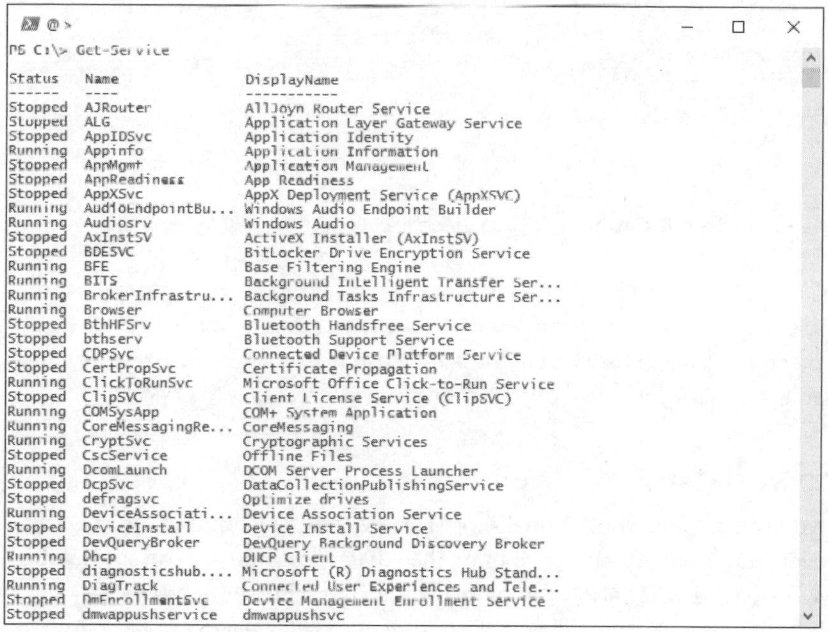

```
PS C:\> Get-Service

Status   Name               DisplayName
------   ----               -----------
Stopped  AJRouter           AllJoyn Router Service
Stopped  ALG                Application Layer Gateway Service
Stopped  AppIDSvc           Application Identity
Running  Appinfo            Application Information
Stopped  AppMgmt            Application Management
Stopped  AppReadiness       App Readiness
Stopped  AppXSvc            AppX Deployment Service (AppXSVC)
Running  AudioEndpointBu... Windows Audio Endpoint Builder
Running  Audiosrv           Windows Audio
Stopped  AxInstSV           ActiveX Installer (AxInstSV)
Stopped  BDESVC             BitLocker Drive Encryption Service
Running  BFE                Base Filtering Engine
Running  BITS               Background Intelligent Transfer Ser...
Running  BrokerInfrastru... Background Tasks Infrastructure Ser...
Running  Browser            Computer Browser
Stopped  BthHFSrv           Bluetooth Handsfree Service
Stopped  bthserv            Bluetooth Support Service
Stopped  CDPSvc             Connected Device Platform Service
Stopped  CertPropSvc        Certificate Propagation
Running  ClickToRunSvc      Microsoft Office Click-to-Run Service
Stopped  ClipSVC            Client License Service (ClipSVC)
Running  COMSysApp          COM+ System Application
Running  CoreMessagingRe... CoreMessaging
Running  CryptSvc           Cryptographic Services
Stopped  CscService         Offline Files
Running  DcomLaunch         DCOM Server Process Launcher
Stopped  DcpSvc             DataCollectionPublishingService
Stopped  defragsvc          Optimize drives
Running  DeviceAssociati... Device Association Service
Stopped  DeviceInstall      Device Install Service
Stopped  DevQueryBroker     DevQuery Background Discovery Broker
Running  Dhcp               DHCP Client
Stopped  diagnosticshub.... Microsoft (R) Diagnostics Hub Stand...
Running  DiagTrack          Connected User Experiences and Tele...
Stopped  DmEnrollmentSvc    Device Management Enrollment Service
Stopped  dmwappushservice   dmwappushsvc
```

FIGURE 2-1 Results from the Get-Service cmdlet

PowerShell verbs are fairly standard. The following are the primary ones you'll see:

- **Get** is self-explanatory. Use it to retrieve information and objects. A Get is a read-only operation and thus is pretty safe.
- **Set** is used to update something. It can be used to make configuration changes, change users, and to perform other similar tasks.
- **New** is also self-explanatory. It's used to create something, like a new user or a new site collection.
- **Add** is used to add an object to something else. For example, Add-MsolRoleMember is used to add a user to a role in the Office 365 tenant.
- **Remove** is effectively the opposite of Add and New and is used (not surprisingly) to remove something. PowerShell doesn't use the verb "delete"; it uses Remove instead.

> ***MORE INFO*** **For a list of approved PowerShell verbs, see "Approved Verbs for Windows PowerShell Commands" at *https://msdn.microsoft.com//library/ms714428(v=vs.85).aspx.***

Most of the time, a cmdlet has parameters. These provide input to the cmdlet. Some cmdlets have required parameters, and many have optional parameters. The parameters a cmdlet has are specified after the cmdlet name. For example, to see only the Print Spooler service, you use Get-Service -DisplayName "Print Spooler", as shown in Figure 2-2.

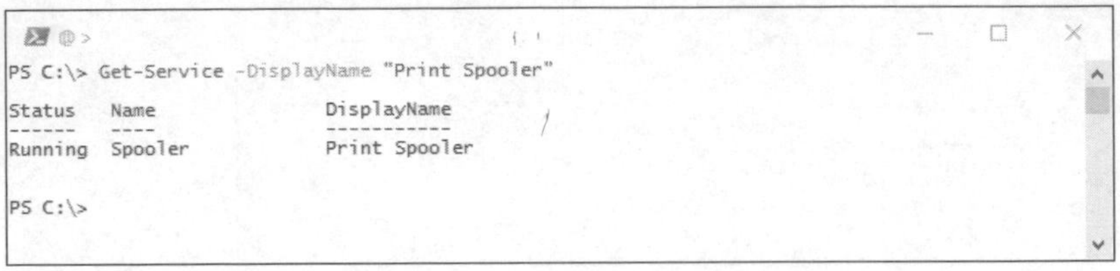

```
PS C:\> Get-Service -DisplayName "Print Spooler"

Status    Name          DisplayName
------    ----          -----------
Running   Spooler       Print Spooler

PS C:\>
```

FIGURE 2-2 Using Get-Service to retrieve the Print Spooler service

Again, cmdlets are at the core of PowerShell. You can also create your own custom functions, which act like cmdlets. Cmdlets and functions are often wrapped together into modules, which you can then load and use. Later in the chapter, we'll demonstrate how you can take advantage of modules to load the cmdlets you need for connecting to and working with Office 365.

Objects and variables

Cmdlets produce output of some kind. Normally, you just see the cmdlet output the results to the screen. However, most cmdlets actually do more than that. The output can be any number of things, such as a result (like true/false) or a complex set of data with lots of properties and other sets of data inside it. A set of data returned from a cmdlet is called an *object*. An object contains properties that hold the data, and the object usually also has commands (called *methods*) associated with it that you can use to act on it. An object encapsulates a thing and gives you ways to interact with it.

Objects are frequently stored in a variable. A *variable* is a type of object that stores something. It's a way to hold onto something for use later. You can store the result of a cmdlet in a variable, for example, and then display its properties. With PowerShell, you can put pretty much anything in a variable, from plain old text and numbers to entire scripts and collections of complex objects. A variable always begins with a dollar sign ($).

Let's go back to the example of the Print Spooler service. In Figure 2-3, we take the result of our previous command and stick it in a variable named *$service*. The *$service* variable contains an object that represents the Print Spooler service. We can then use that variable, for example, to view its properties, such as the internal name of the service and its status. We then use the *Stop* method to stop the service. We call Get-Service again to get an updated service object and then display the updated status of the Print Spooler service. Finally, we start it up again.

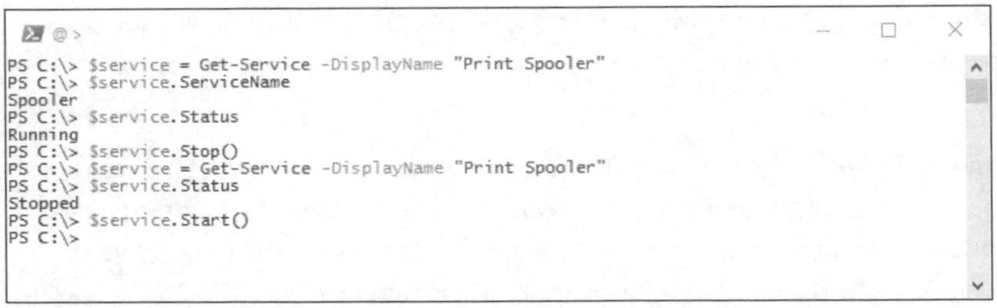

```
PS C:\> $service = Get-Service -DisplayName "Print Spooler"
PS C:\> $service.ServiceName
Spooler
PS C:\> $service.Status
Running
PS C:\> $service.Stop()
PS C:\> $service = Get-Service -DisplayName "Print Spooler"
PS C:\> $service.Status
Stopped
PS C:\> $service.Start()
PS C:\>
```

FIGURE 2-3 Stopping and starting the Print Spooler service

Again, the *$service* variable contains the object that represents the Print Spooler service. *ServiceName* and *Status* are just two properties of the object. As you can see in Figure 2-4, there are more properties available.

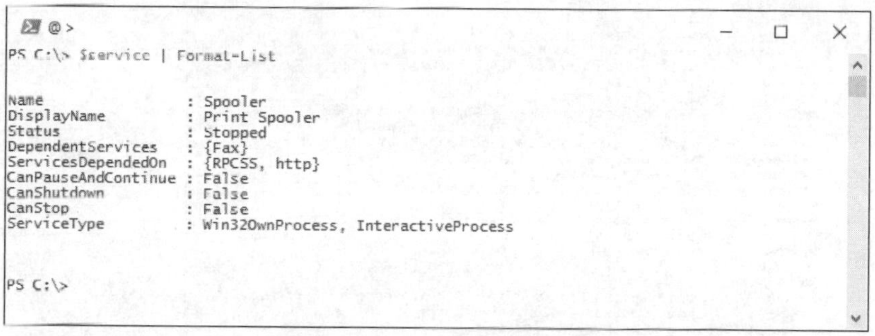

```
PS C:\> $service | Format-List

Name              : Spooler
DisplayName       : Print Spooler
Status            : Stopped
DependentServices : {Fax}
ServicesDependedOn : {RPCSS, http}
CanPauseAndContinue : False
CanShutdown       : False
CanStop           : False
ServiceType       : Win32OwnProcess, InteractiveProcess


PS C:\>
```

FIGURE 2-4 Viewing the default properties of the Print Spooler service

Normally, a default set of properties is returned in the output. If you want to see every property on the object or objects, use the asterisk (*) after Select-Object. (We'll say more about this usage in a moment.) For example, use $service | Select-Object * to see everything about the Print Spooler service. In this case, it does not reveal much extra that is interesting. (See Figure 2-5.) However, this technique can be helpful when you're working with more complex objects.

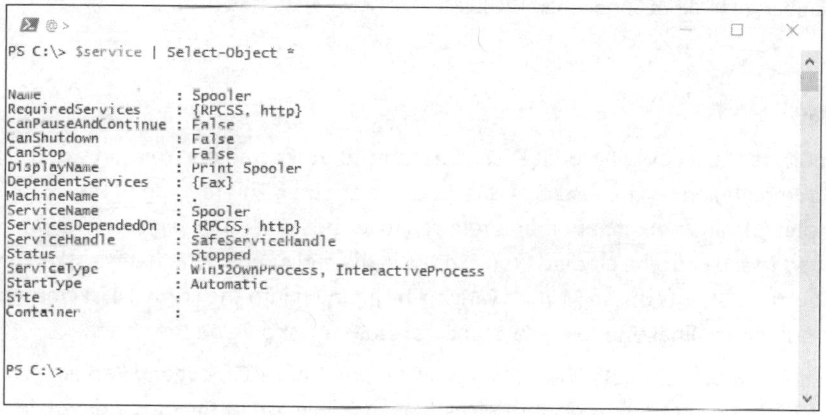

```
PS C:\> $service | Select-Object *

Name              : Spooler
RequiredServices  : {RPCSS, http}
CanPauseAndContinue : False
CanShutdown       : False
CanStop           : False
DisplayName       : Print Spooler
DependentServices : {Fax}
MachineName       : .
ServiceName       : Spooler
ServicesDependedOn : {RPCSS, http}
ServiceHandle     : SafeServiceHandle
Status            : Stopped
ServiceType       : Win32OwnProcess, InteractiveProcess
StartType         : Automatic
Site              :
Container         :


PS C:\>
```

FIGURE 2-5 Viewing all properties of the Print Spooler service

You can also use the Get-Member cmdlet to do something similar. Instead of actually giving you the values, it will output the various components available in the object, including its properties and methods (activities you can perform on the object). Use it to learn more about what's possible to do with the object at hand. Figure 2-6 shows the members available in the *$service* object.

```
PS C:\> $service | Get-Member


    TypeName: System.ServiceProcess.ServiceController

Name                      MemberType    Definition
----                      ----------    ----------
Name                      AliasProperty Name = ServiceName
RequiredServices          AliasProperty RequiredServices = ServicesDependedOn
Disposed                  Event         System.EventHandler Disposed(System.Object, System...
Close                     Method        void Close()
Continue                  Method        void Continue()
CreateObjRef              Method        System.Runtime.Remoting.ObjRef CreateObjRef(type r...
Dispose                   Method        void Dispose(), void IDisposable.Dispose()
Equals                    Method        bool Equals(System.Object obj)
ExecuteCommand            Method        void ExecuteCommand(int command)
GetHashCode               Method        int GetHashCode()
GetLifetimeService        Method        System.Object GetLifetimeService()
GetType                   Method        type GetType()
InitializeLifetimeService Method        System.Object InitializeLifetimeService()
Pause                     Method        void Pause()
Refresh                   Method        void Refresh()
Start                     Method        void Start(), void Start(string[] args)
Stop                      Method        void Stop()
WaitForStatus             Method        void WaitForStatus(System.ServiceProcess.ServiceCo...
CanPauseAndContinue       Property      bool CanPauseAndContinue {get;}
CanShutdown               Property      bool CanShutdown {get;}
CanStop                   Property      bool CanStop {get;}
Container                 Property      System.ComponentModel.IContainer Container {get;}
DependentServices         Property      System.ServiceProcess.ServiceController[] Dependen...
DisplayName               Property      string DisplayName {get;set;}
MachineName               Property      string MachineName {get;set;}
ServiceHandle             Property      System.Runtime.InteropServices.SafeHandle ServiceH...
ServiceName               Property      string ServiceName {get;set;}
ServicesDependedOn        Property      System.ServiceProcess.ServiceController[] Services...
ServiceType               Property      System.ServiceProcess.ServiceType ServiceType {get;}
Site                      Property      System.ComponentModel.ISite Site {get;set;}
StartType                 Property      System.ServiceProcess.ServiceStartMode StartType {...
Status                    Property      System.ServiceProcess.ServiceControllerStatus Stat...
ToString                  ScriptMethod  System.Object ToString();

PS C:\>
```

FIGURE 2-6 The members of the Print Spooler service object

The pipeline

Variables or the objects that a cmdlet produces can be inputs to other cmdlets. You can string together multiple cmdlets and let the results of one feed into another. This feeding of the results of one cmdlet (or variable) into another is referred to as the PowerShell *pipeline*. The pipe character (|) is used to separate the cmdlets. You can see in the earlier example that we asked PowerShell to show the contents of the *$service* variable by piping it into the Format-List cmdlet. The right-most cmdlet is the final one to execute, and its results are shown on the screen.

Two of the most important cmdlets PowerShell provides are Where-Object and ForEach-Object. You use Where-Object to filter results before they're passed on to the next element in the pipeline (or the screen). You use ForEach-Object to run a command for each object in the set of results (or pipeline). Both use a special variable to represent the object that the pipeline sent to it: *$_*. The *$_* variable holds whatever is to the left in the pipeline.

Let's see what some of this looks like. In our first example, shown in Figure 2-7, we filter the results of the Get-Service cmdlet so that only the started services are returned. We then pipe the results yet again, except this time we use the Select-Object cmdlet to limit the results to just the first five items. The result is that we get the first five running services.

```
PS C:\> Get-Service | Where-Object {$_.Status -eq "Running"} | Select-Object -First 5

Status    Name              DisplayName
------    ----              -----------
Running   Appinfo           Application Information
Running   AudioEndpointBu... Windows Audio Endpoint Builder
Running   Audiosrv          Windows Audio
Running   BFE               Base Filtering Engine
Running   BITS              Background Intelligent Transfer Ser...


PS C:\>
```

FIGURE 2-7 Using Where-Objects to return only running services

In the second example, seen in Figure 2-8, we use ForEach-Object to loop through the first five services and output their status to the screen (along with some extra text).

```
PS C:\> Get-Service| Select-Object -First 5 | ForEach-Object { Write-Host "The service $($_.DisplayName) is $($_.Status)" }
The service AllJoyn Router Service is Stopped
The service Application Layer Gateway Service is Stopped
The service Application Identity is Stopped
The service Application Information is Running
The service Application Management is Stopped
PS C:\>
```

FIGURE 2-8 Using ForEach-Object to display the status of the first five services

The pipeline is a powerful construct in PowerShell. You can use it to accomplish a tremendous amount in a single line of code. It can also be very dangerous. If you're not careful, instead of deleting a small handful of files, for example, you can end up deleting everything. Be very, very careful when you're acting against items in the pipeline. Make sure you really understand what's in the pipeline before you act.

> **TRADE-OFFS** Many people new to PowerShell are tempted to pack as much as they can into a single, epic line of code. These monster lines can be an accomplishment. However, consider whether or not it's wise to take this route.
>
> Is the command readable? Would someone looking at it after you know what it's supposed to do? How easy or hard would it be to modify that command? What is the risk if a mistake is made in the command?
>
> Instead of writing one long or complicated line of code, consider breaking up the one command into multiple commands by taking advantage of variables and other PowerShell constructs. Sure, it might not be quite as impressive, but you'll find multiple lines of code much easier to understand and maintain than a large single line.
>
> Lots of times you'll have a single command that's really long all by itself. This is common if many parameters are used. To make this more readable, you can use a backtick (`) at the end of a line in order to continue the command onto the next line. We'll use it in long commands later in this chapter.

Collections

A *collection* is a set of objects. The most common form of a collection is the output from a cmdlet that displays as multiple rows. Each row is its own object, and the set of all of them is a collection. An object also can have collections as properties. This arrangement is common in complex objects in which there are other objects nested inside of them. A good example is the *$service* variable/object. Again, take a look at the properties of the object shown in Figure 2-4.

The *DependentServices* and *ServicesDependedOn* properties are collections (as evidenced by the curly braces). If you interrogate these two properties, you'll see that they contain one or two rows. Each row is an object. In this case, these objects are, in the case of *ServicesDependedOn*, services that the Print Spooler service depends on. Each item is a full services object, just like the Print Spooler object. As an example, you can see in Figure 2-9 that the first of the *ServicesDependedOn* objects, Remote Procedure Call (RPC), also is a complete services object just like the Print Spooler one.

```
PS C:\> $service = Get-Service -DisplayName "Print Spooler"
PS C:\> $service.DependentServices

Status    Name          DisplayName
------    ----          -----------
Stopped   Fax           Fax


PS C:\> $service.ServicesDependedOn

Status    Name          DisplayName
------    ----          -----------
Running   RPCSS         Remote Procedure Call (RPC)
Running   http          HTTP Service


PS C:\> $service.ServicesDependedOn[0] | Format-List


Name                 : RPCSS
DisplayName          : Remote Procedure Call (RPC)
Status               : Running
DependentServices    :
ServicesDependedOn   : {DcomLaunch, RpcEptMapper}
CanPauseAndContinue  : False
CanShutdown          : False
CanStop              : False
ServiceType          : Win32ShareProcess



PS C:\>
```

FIGURE 2-9 Viewing the collections in the Print Spooler service object

Collections are an important concept because you can use them to work your way through an object or a dataset to gain additional information or functionality. They also provide you with a way to easily act on a set of data (such as a collection of users). In the pipeline, the cmdlet to the right of the pipe acts on each item in the result set, whether it's one or many. You can see that in the prior example, with the ForEach-Object cmdlet providing you with a way to act on each of the five services in the pipeline.

Prepare your environment for Office 365 PowerShell

Now that we've reviewed the PowerShell fundamentals, let's talk about Office 365 again. Before you can do anything with PowerShell and Office 365, you first need to prepare your environment.

> **MORE INFO** For more information on configuring your environment, including links to the software you need, visit "Connect to Office 365 PowerShell" at *https://technet.microsoft. com/library/dn975125.aspx.*

Office 365 PowerShell Requirements

As defined on the "Connect to Office 365 PowerShell" page referenced in the previous More Info link, you must first meet the following requirements in order to use PowerShell for Office 365:

- Any recent 64-bit version of Windows, starting from Windows 7 with Service Pack 1 (SP1), or any recent 64-bit version of Windows Server starting with Windows Server 2008 R2 Service Pack 1 (SP1)

> **MORE INFO** 64-bit Windows is required because the 32-bit version of the Windows Azure Active Directory Module for Windows PowerShell was discontinued in 2014. Although you still can download the 32-bit version, there will be no support or updates for it.

- Microsoft .NET Framework 3.5.x installed on the machine
- An Office 365 subscription
- Generally, an Office 365 account that is a member of the Global Admin role, although you don't need to be a Global Admin to use all cmdlets. For example, all you need to use most SharePoint Online cmdlets is to be a member of the SharePoint Administrators role.
- The PowerShell execution policy set to at least RemoteSigned. To do so, run the following from an elevated PowerShell command prompt:

```
Set-ExecutionPolicy RemoteSigned
```

Install the client components

If you meet all the preceding requirements, you can then connect to Office 365 after you install the client components. To manage the Office 365 platform, you must first install the MS Online Services Sign-In Assistant (which is available at *https://www.microsoft.com/download/details. aspx?id=41950*) and Windows Azure Active Directory Module for Windows PowerShell (which is available at *http://go.microsoft.com/fwlink/p/?linkid=236297*). After downloading them, step through the install wizard for each one.

Windows Azure Active Directory Module for Windows PowerShell adds an item to your Start menu that opens a PowerShell console with the Azure AD module loaded. However, you don't need to use this console because the Azure AD module will likely be automatically added to your PowerShell profile. As such, the Azure AD cmdlets should be available from any Power-Shell window you open. If they're not, you can run the following code in PowerShell to import the cmdlets:

```
Import-Module MsOnline
```

Optionally, if you intend to manage SharePoint Online or Skype for Business Online, you need to download and install the required modules for each. You can download them from the following sites:

- SharePoint Online Management Shell at *https://www.microsoft.com/download/details. aspx?id=35588*
- Skype for Business Online, Windows PowerShell Module at *https://www.microsoft.com/ download/details.aspx?id=39366*

Unlike with the other modules, a 32-bit SharePoint Online Management Shell is available and supported.

How to connect via PowerShell

After preparing your environment, you're now ready to connect to Office 365 via PowerShell.

First, open either a PowerShell console or the PowerShell Integrated Scripting Environment (ISE). You must open PowerShell in an elevated session (by right-clicking and selecting Run As Administrator). If you need to schedule a script using Window's Task Scheduler, ensure that the Run With Highest Privileges option is selected.

Credentials are needed to connect to each Office 365 service. Credentials securely encap-sulate your user name and password. We'll store the credentials used in this book in a variable so that they can be used multiple times. Don't worry—once you close your PowerShell session, the credential object is destroyed and no longer accessible. To create the credentials, simply use the following command:

```
$credential = Get-Credential
```

As shown in Figure 2-10, you are prompted for your user name and password. Your user name generally will be your email address.

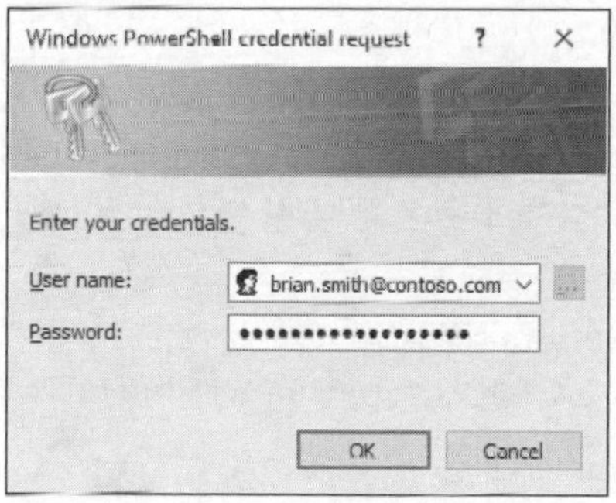

FIGURE 2-10 Enter PowerShell credentials

After you obtain your credentials, you can connect to each service by using the *credential* parameter. If you omit the *credential* parameter, the command to connect prompts you for your user name and password.

Connect to Office 365 (Azure Active Directory)

When you connect to the core of Office 365, you're really connecting to Azure Active Directory. You use the Azure Active Directory PowerShell module and connect to the tenant as if you were connecting to Azure Active Directory. To connect, simply use the Connect-MsolService cmdlet.

You'll also import the Azure Active Directory module just in case it hasn't already been loaded. You'll know whether or not you need it if the Connect-MsolService cmdlet isn't available.

To connect to Azure Active Directory, run the following:

```
Import-Module MsOnline
Connect-MsolService -Credential $credential
```

At this point, if your user name and password are correct and you have permissions to Office 365, you can start using the Office 365 Azure Active Directory cmdlets. All of these include "Msol" as the first part of the noun, as in Get-MsolUser.

> **TIP** At the time of this writing, the Azure Active Directory PowerShell Module version 2.0 is in preview. In Version 2.0, all the cmdlets have been renamed from "Msol" to "AzureAD." For example, Get-MsolUser becomes Get-AzureADUser. Expect some cmdlet behavior changes as well. However, don't let this stop you from working with Office 365 from PowerShell; PowerShell Version 1.0 will continue to be supported for quite some time. You will have plenty of time to transition your scripts and practices to Version 2.0 of the module.

Connect to SharePoint Online

To connect to SharePoint Online, you must be a member of the tenant's Global Admin or SharePoint Administrator role. Additionally, the SharePoint Online Management Shell must be installed. To connect to SharePoint Online, run the following, supplying the URL to your Share-Point Online admin center:

```
Import-Module Microsoft.Online.SharePoint.PowerShell -DisableNameChecking
Connect-SPOService -Url https://<domain>-admin.sharepoint.com -credential $credential
```

For example, to connect to the Contoso tenant, the command is

```
Import-Module Microsoft.Online.SharePoint.PowerShell -DisableNameChecking
Connect-SPOService -Url https://contoso-admin.sharepoint.com -credential $credential
```

At this point, if your user name and password are correct and you have permissions to SharePoint Online, you can start using the SharePoint Online cmdlets. These all include "SPO" as the first part of the noun, as in Get-SPOSite.

It's good practice to disconnect your session with the Disconnect-SPOService cmdlet after you finish. See the "Remove Sessions" section for more details.

Connect to Exchange Online

The technique for connecting to Exchange Online is different from the process for connecting to the other Office 365 products, because it requires you to first create a PowerShell session and then import it. This process downloads all the items needed to manage Exchange Online using PowerShell and places them in the computer's memory. The cmdlets will not be available in your session until they have been imported.

To connect to Exchange Online, run the following:

```
$exoSession = New-PSSession -ConfigurationName Microsoft.Exchange `
    -ConnectionUri "https://outlook.office365.com/powershell-liveid/" `
    -Credential $credential -Authentication "Basic" -AllowRedirection
Import-PSSession $exoSession -DisableNameChecking
```

At this point, if your user name and password are correct and you have permissions to Exchange Online, you can start using the Exchange Online cmdlets. These do not have a predictable naming pattern. A good way to verify that you're connected is to use the Get-Mailbox cmdlet. Use it with the *-Identity* parameter to only pull back one mailbox instead of potentially thousands.

It is a good practice to remove the session after you finish. To remove the session, run the following cmdlet:

```
Remove-PSSession $exoSession
```

Connect to Skype for Business Online

To connect to Skype for Business Online, you use the *SkypeOnlineConnector* module (which is installed with the Skype for Business Online Windows PowerShell Module). As before, you need to import the module first. When that is done, you create a new session using the New-CsOnlineSession cmdlet and then import it. This cmdlet operates the same way as the one you used for Exchange Online, where it downloads all the management objects needed and loads them into memory. As with Exchange Online, the cmdlets will not be available in your session until this happens.

To connect to Skype for Business Online, run the following:

```
Import-Module SkypeOnlineConnector
$sfbSession = New-CsOnlineSession -Credential $credential
Import-PSSession $sfbSession
```

At this point, if your user name and password are correct and the account is a member of the Global Admin or Skype for Business Administrator role, you can start using the Skype for Business cmdlets. These all include "Cs" as the first part of the noun, as in Get-CsOnlineUser.

It is a good practice to remove the session after you finish. To remove the session, run the following:

```
Remove-PSSession $sfbSession
```

Connect to the Security & Compliance Center

The process of connecting to the Security & Compliance Center is almost identical to that of connecting to Exchange Online. Again, you create a PowerShell session and import it. However, you need to give it a different URL:

```
$complianceSession = New-PSSession `
    -ConfigurationName Microsoft.Exchange `
    -ConnectionUri "https://ps.compliance.protection.outlook.com/powershell-liveid/" `
    -Credential $credential -Authentication Basic -AllowRedirection
Import-PSSession $complianceSession
```

At this point, if your user name and password are correct and you have permissions to the Security & Compliance Center, you can start using the cmdlets. As with Exchange Online, these cmdlets do not have a predictable naming pattern.

It is a good practice to remove the session after you finish. To remove the session, run the following:

```
Remove-PSSession $complianceSession
```

Remove sessions

When you're done working in PowerShell, you just close your console or ISE and go about your business. Normally, doing this isn't much of an issue. However, with Exchange Online, SharePoint Online, Skype for Business, and the Security & Compliance Center connections, an improperly closed session will remain open for some amount of time (around 15 minutes). The problem is that Microsoft limits the number of simultaneous connections to the services. For example, in Skype for Business, an administrator is allowed a maximum of three open sessions, and a tenant is allowed nine overall. In situations where multiple administrators are interacting with Office 365 through PowerShell or if several automated scripts are running around the same time, it's possible for the limit to be hit and for the connection to be rejected.

To avoid this situation, and to be a good citizen of the shared resources you consume, we recommend you explicitly close your sessions. For Exchange Online, Skype for Business Online, and the Security & Compliance Center, you can use Remove-PSSession to do this. Disconnect-SPOService is used for SharePoint Online. You don't need to explicitly disconnect from Azure Active Directory.

The following is an example of how to disconnect from all four services (assuming the variables used earlier):

```
Remove-PSSession $exoSession
Remove-PSSession $sfbSession
Remove-PSSession $complianceSession
Disconnect-SPOService
```

Connect to all Office 365 services in the same session

If you use Office 365 PowerShell heavily, or if you simply want the full breadth of cmdlets to be available to you at the same time, you might find it beneficial to connect to everything inside a single PowerShell window. This approach beats opening up a separate window for each Office 365 service. It also allows you to develop more comprehensive, cross-service scripts.

Microsoft has provided on TechNet an excellent resource that lays out how to connect to all four services in the same window. You can find it at *https://technet.microsoft.com/library/dn568015.aspx*. Not only is the script useful, the page also describes what the script is doing in great detail.

> **IMPORTANT** The Exchange Online and Security & Compliance Center modules use cmdlets with the same name. For example, both contain the Get-User cmdlet. It's not possible for two Get-User cmdlets to load at the same time. To work around this issue, the script prepends a prefix of "cc" to all the Security & Compliance Center cmdlets. This means you can use Get-User to refer to the Exchange Online cmdlet and Get-ccUser for the other cmdlet. If you choose to do this, you must remember to always use the "cc" cmdlets when working with the Security & Compliance Center. Existing scripts or scripts found online will need to be updated appropriately. Because of this, you might not want to load both modules in the same window.

For simplicity, the script on the webpage is reproduced here (although we updated it to use the variable names used earlier):

```
$credential = Get-Credential

Import-Module MsOnline
Connect-MsolService -Credential $credential

Import-Module Microsoft.Online.SharePoint.PowerShell -DisableNameChecking
Connect-SPOService -Url https://<domain> admin.sharepoint.com -credential $credential

Import-Module SkypeOnlineConnector
$sfbSession = New-CsOnlineSession -Credential $credential
Import-PSSession $sfbSession -DisableNameChecking

$exoSession = New-PSSession -ConfigurationName Microsoft.Exchange `
    -ConnectionUri "https://outlook.office365.com/powershell-liveid/" `
    -Credential $credential -Authentication "Basic" -AllowRedirection
Import-PSSession $exoSession -DisableNameChecking

$complianceSession = New-PSSession -ConfigurationName Microsoft.Exchange `
    -ConnectionUri "https://ps.compliance.protection.outlook.com/powershell-liveid/" `
    -Credential $credential -Authentication Basic -AllowRedirection
Import-PSSession $complianceSession -Prefix cc
```

Next level

Improve your session load time

If you frequently connect to Exchange Online or the Security & Compliance Center, you might find it time consuming to download and load the modules each time. You can save some time by avoiding these downloads.

To do so, you export the session's module (or modules) to a local directory and then import that module going forward. The downside to this method is that you need to enter your password the first time you use a cmdlet from the module. This eliminates the ability to use this technique in a script that runs unattended.

To export the session's module, first import the session and then export it to a directory of your choosing using the Export-PSSession command. If the directory already exists, the *-AllowClobber* parameter overwrites whatever is there. The following code connects and imports both. Unfortunately, this method doesn't work for Skype for Business. To import just one of the two, simply run the commands for the module you need. The following code outputs both to the C:\O365Modules directory:

```
$credential = Get-Credential
```

```
$exoSession = New-PSSession -ConfigurationName Microsoft.Exchange
    -ConnectionUri "https://outlook.office365.com/powershell-liveid/"
    -Credential $credential -Authentication "Basic" -AllowRedirection
Import-PSSession $exoSession -DisableNameChecking
Export-PSSession $exoSession -AllowClobber -OutputModule
    C:\O365Modules\ExchangeOnline -Force

$complianceSession = New-PSSession -ConfigurationName Microsoft.Exchange
-ConnectionUri "https://ps.compliance.protection.outlook.com/powershell-
liveid/" `
    -Credential $credential -Authentication Basic -AllowRedirection
Import-PSSession $complianceSession
Export-PSSession $complianceSession -AllowClobber `
    -OutputModule C:\O365Modules\ComplianceCenter -Force
```

You can then close your session whenever you need to. The exported sessions remain in the directory. To then use the Import-Module to load the exported modules, use the following commands:

```
Import-Module C:\O365Modules\ExchangeOnline -DisableNameChecking
Import-Module C:\O365Modules\ComplianceCenter -Prefix cc
```

As discussed earlier, if you want to connect to both Exchange Online and the Security & Compliance Center in the same session, you need to use the -Prefix parameter when you import the module. Then all Security & Compliance Center cmdlets will include "cc" in their name (for example, Get-ccGroup instead of Get-Group). If you will be working only with the Security & Compliance Center cmdlets and not Exchange Online, you can leave -Prefix cc off of the command.

You will be prompted for your password the first time you attempt to run a cmdlet from the module.

Work with Office 365 using PowerShell

Now that you at least know how to read PowerShell and you're connected to the tenant, let's get to work! There are way too many cmdlets to cover them all, but we'll cover the ones related to various activities you might need to perform as a cloud pro. As you get comfortable with these examples, you should start exploring the rest of the PowerShell cmdlets.

Because this book is focused on the root Office 365 service and the content management services, we look at tasks related to managing the tenant and its users. We also look at managing SharePoint Online and discuss the Security & Compliance Center. Exchange Online and Skype for Business Online will hopefully be covered in a subsequent book.

> **MORE INFO** For an excellent resource to get you started with Office 365 PowerShell, go to "Manage Office 365 with Office 365 PowerShell" at *https://technet.microsoft.com/library/dn568031.aspx*. This page is an excellent starting point for managing each Office 365 service with PowerShell.

Because PowerShell cmdlets often are self-descriptive, the list of cmdlets should provide you with a good sense of what is possible through PowerShell.

> **MORE INFO** Microsoft has made available a handy online tool that can help you craft Azure Active Directory and SharePoint Online PowerShell commands in a visual manner: *https://www.microsoft.com/resources/technet/en-us/office/media/windowspowershell/windowspowershellcommandbuilder.html*. To use it, select SharePoint Online or Office 365 in the drop-down menu at the top of the page. Then pick a verb and a noun and click the Send arrow to fill out the Design Surface. As you do so, the parameters for the cmdlets become available, allowing you to fill them out as you need to. The result is a PowerShell command you can then copy to your clipboard and paste into a PowerShell window.

Work with Office 365 and Azure Active Directory

Again, to begin working with the Office 365 tenant and Azure Active Directory, make sure the MsOnline module has been loaded:

```
Import-Module MsOnline
```

To get a list of the loaded cmdlets, run the following command:

```
Get-Command -Module MsOnline
```

> **MORE INFO** You can find the "Azure Active Directory Cmdlets" reference at *https://msdn.microsoft.com//library/jj151815.aspx*.

In this section, we'll show you some Azure Active Directory PowerShell examples for doing such things as:

- Working with the tenant
- Working with users
- Working with licenses

Working with the tenant

Although there's lots you can do, we'll use the following as examples of how to work with the tenant in PowerShell:

- Get basic information about your tenant
- Get domain information
- Get tenant role membership

GET BASIC INFORMATION ABOUT YOUR TENANT

To view basic information about your tenant, use the Get-MsolCompanyInformation cmdlet. Besides contact information, this cmdlet returns some important information, such as whether or not directory synchronization is enabled and, if it is, the time of the last sync. (See Figure 2-11.) This information is important when troubleshooting directory sync issues.

```
PS C:\> Get-MsolCompanyInformation

DisplayName                              : Contoso
PreferredLanguage                        : en
Street                                   : 11 Times Square
City                                     : New York
State                                    : NY
PostalCode                               : 10036
Country                                  :
CountryLetterCode                        : US
TelephoneNumber                          : 8006427676
MarketingNotificationEmails              : {}
TechnicalNotificationEmails              : {brian.smith@contoso.com}
SelfServePasswordResetEnabled            : True
UsersPermissionToCreateGroupsEnabled     : True
UsersPermissionToCreateLOBAppsEnabled    : True
UsersPermissionToReadOtherUsersEnabled   : True
UsersPermissionToUserConsentToAppEnabled : True
DirectorySynchronizationEnabled          : False
DirSyncServiceAccount                    :
LastDirSyncTime                          :
LastPasswordSyncTime                     :
PasswordSynchronizationEnabled           : False
DirSyncApplicationType                   :
DirSyncClientVersion                     :
DirSyncClientMachineName                 :

PS C:\>
```

FIGURE 2-11 Get-MsolCompanyInformation

GET DOMAIN INFORMATION

Use Get-MsolDomain to retrieve information about all the domains registered in the tenant. In Figure 2-12, there are two domains. One is awaiting verification.

```
PS C:\> Get-MsolDomain

Name                         Status      Authentication
----                         ------      --------------
MOD215415.onmicrosoft.com    Verified    Managed
contoso.com                  Unverified  Managed

PS C:\>
```

FIGURE 2-12 Get-MsolDomain

GET TENANT ROLE MEMBERSHIP

Use Get-MsolRole and Get-MsolRoleMember to view the various Office 365 security roles and their membership. Get-MsolRole returns a list of all the available roles. You can call Get-Msol-RoleMember to view the membership of a given role. In Figure 2-13, you can see all the roles and then the membership of the Company Administrator role.

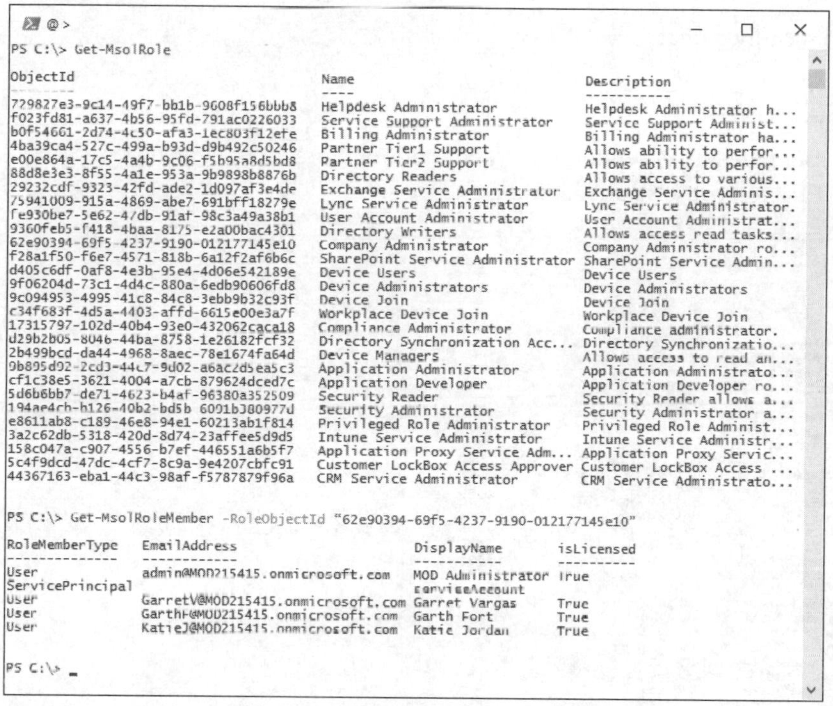

FIGURE 2-13 Get-MsolRole and Get-MsolRoleMember

Use Add-MsolRoleMember to add a user to a tenant role. (See Figure 2-14.) The following command adds Rob Young to the Password Administrator role (which used to be called Help-desk Administrator) and displays the membership for validation:

```
Add-MsolRoleMember -RoleName "Helpdesk Administrator" `
    RoleMemberEmailAddress roby@mod215415.onmicrosoft.com
Get-MsolRoleMember -RoleObjectId "729827e3-9c14-49f7-bb1b-9608f156bbb8"
```

FIGURE 2-14 Add-MsolRoleMember and Get-MsolRoleMember

Working with users

Next, we'll look at examples of working with users through PowerShell. We will:

- Get user information
- Create users
- Update users
- Work with security groups

GET USER INFORMATION

Get-MsolUser is your means to view information about one or more users. Running Get-MsolUser by itself will return all users. (See Figure 2-15.)

```
PS C:\> Get-MsolUser

UserPrincipalName                    DisplayName                isLicensed
-----------------                    -----------                ----------
Crystal@MOD215415.onmicrosoft.com    Conf Room Crystal          False
admin@MOD215415.onmicrosoft.com      MOD Administrator          True
AlexD@MOD215415.onmicrosoft.com      Alex Darrow                True
AziH@MOD215415.onmicrosoft.com       Aziz Hassouneh             True
KatieJ@MOD215415.onmicrosoft.com     Katie Jordan               True
JulianI@MOD215415.onmicrosoft.com    Julian Isla                True
DavidL@MOD215415.onmicrosoft.com     David Longmuir             True
victorf@MOD215415.onmicrosoft.com    Victor Freitas             True
BelindaN@MOD215415.onmicrosoft.com   Belinda Newman             True
AllieB@MOD215415.onmicrosoft.com     Allie Bellew               True
GarthF@MOD215415.onmicrosoft.com     Garth Fort                 True
BonnieK@MOD215415.onmicrosoft.com    Bonnie Kearney             True
MollyD@MOD215415.onmicrosoft.com     Molly Dempsey              True
PavelB@MOD215415.onmicrosoft.com     Pavel Bansky               True
Baker@MOD215415.onmicrosoft.com      Conf Room Baker            False
FabriceC@MOD215415.onmicrosoft.com   Fabrice Canel              True
martinw@MOD215415.onmicrosoft.com    Martin Weber               True
Adams@MOD215415.onmicrosoft.com      Conf Room Adams            False
RobinC@MOD215415.onmicrosoft.com     Robin Counts               True
AnneW@MOD215415.onmicrosoft.com      Anne Wallace               True
BrianJ@MOD215415.onmicrosoft.com     Brian Johnson (TAILSPIN)   False
JanetS@MOD215415.onmicrosoft.com     Janet Schorr               True
benm@MOD215415.onmicrosoft.com       Ben Miler                  True
GarretV@MOD215415.onmicrosoft.com    Garret Vargas              True
RobY@MOD215415.onmicrosoft.com       Rob Young                  True
Stevens@MOD215415.onmicrosoft.com    Conf Room Stevens          False
DorenaP@MOD215415.onmicrosoft.com    Dorena Paschke             True
Rainier@MOD215415.onmicrosoft.com    Conf Room Rainier          False
Hood@MOD215415.onmicrosoft.com       Conf Room Hood             False
DenisD@MOD215415.onmicrosoft.com     Denis Dehenne              True


PS C:\>
```

FIGURE 2-15 Get-MsolUser

You can use Where-Object to filter based on any property you need. For example, the following returns all licensed users:

```
Get-MsolUser | Where-Object {$_.isLicensed -eq $true}
```

Get-MsolUser includes the following set of parameters to make filtering a little simpler: *City*, *Country*, *Department*, *DomainName*, *State*, *Synchronized*, and *Title*. Adding the *ReturnDeletedUsers* switch brings back all deleted users, and the *UnlicensedUsersOnly* switch returns all unlicensed users.

To view all information about a user, use Select-Object *. (See Figure 2-16.) For example, the following command returns all information about the user Rob Young:

```
Get-MsolUser -UserPrincipalName "RobY@MOD215415.onmicrosoft.com" | Select-Object *
```

```
PS C:\> Get-MsolUser -UserPrincipalName "RobY@MOD215415.onmicrosoft.com" | Select-Object *

ExtensionData                        : System.Runtime.Serialization.ExtensionDataObject
AlternateEmailAddresses              : {}
AlternateMobilePhones                : {}
AlternativeSecurityIds               : {}
BlockCredential                      : False
City                                 : Bloomington
CloudExchangeRecipientDisplayType    : 1073741824
Country                              : United States
Department                           : Legal
DirSyncProvisioningErrors            : {}
DisplayName                          : Rob Young
Errors                               :
Fax                                  :
FirstName                            : Rob
ImmutableId                          :
IndirectLicenseErrors                : {}
IsBlackberryUser                     : False
IsLicensed                           : True
LastDirSyncTime                      :
LastName                             : Young
LastPasswordChangeTimestamp          : 5/24/2016 4:32:31 PM
LicenseReconciliationNeeded          : False
Licenses                             : {MOD215415:POWER_BI_PRO, MOD215415:ENTERPRISEPREMIUM}
LiveId                               : 10037FFE97C89916
MSExchRecipientTypeDetails           :
MSRtcSipDeploymentLocator            :
MSRtcSipPrimaryUserAddress           :
MobilePhone                          :
ObjectId                             : d05fcfc3-9162-4f1b-ad73-6802e6380c34
Office                               : 19/2109
OverallProvisioningStatus            : PendingInput
PasswordNeverExpires                 : True
PasswordResetNotRequiredDuringActivate :
PhoneNumber                          : +1 309 555 0104
PortalSettings                       :
PostalCode                           : 61704
PreferredLanguage                    : en-US
ProxyAddresses                       : {SMTP:RobY@MOD215415.onmicrosoft.com}
ReleaseTrack                         :
ServiceInformation                   : {}
SignInName                           : RobY@MOD215415.onmicrosoft.com
SoftDeletionTimestamp                :
State                                : IL
StreetAddress                        : 2203 E. Empire St., Suite J
StrongAuthenticationMethods          : {}
StrongAuthenticationPhoneAppDetails  : {}
StrongAuthenticationProofupTime      :
StrongAuthenticationRequirements     : {}
StrongAuthenticationUserDetails      :
StrongPasswordRequired               : True
StsRefreshTokensValidFrom            : 5/24/2016 4:32:31 PM
Title                                : CVP Legal
UsageLocation                        : US
UserLandingPageIdentifierForO365Shell :
UserPrincipalName                    : RobY@MOD215415.onmicrosoft.com
UserThemeIdentifierForO365Shell      :
UserType                             : Member
ValidationStatus                     : Healthy
```

FIGURE 2-16 Using Get-MsolUser and Select-Object * to get full information about a user

To export users to a comma-delimited file, add the ConvertTo-Csv and Out-File cmdlets to the pipeline. For example, the following command outputs all licensed users to C:\Temp\ LicensedUsers.csv:

```
Get-MsolUser | Where-Object {$_.isLicensed -eq $true} |
    ConvertTo-Csv -NoTypeInformation | Out-File "C:\Temp\LicensedUsers.csv"
```

CREATE USERS

Use New-MsolUser to create a new user in the tenant (really, in Azure Active Directory). The only required parameters are *DisplayName* and *UserPrincipalName*, but you'll likely want to add more. Some available parameters include *Password*, *FirstName*, *LastName*, *City*, *State*, *PostalCode*, *Department*, and *Title*. The *UserPrincipalName* is what the user will use to sign in. For example, the following basic command creates a user named Terry Adams and sets a password:

```
New-MsolUser -DisplayName "Terry Adams" `
    -UserPrincipalName "terrya@mod215415.onmicrosoft.com" -Password "pass@word1" `
    -FirstName "Terry" -LastName "Adams"
```

If a password is not supplied, a random password is generated for the user. The *ForceChangePassword* switch can be used to ensure that the user changes her password the next time she signs in.

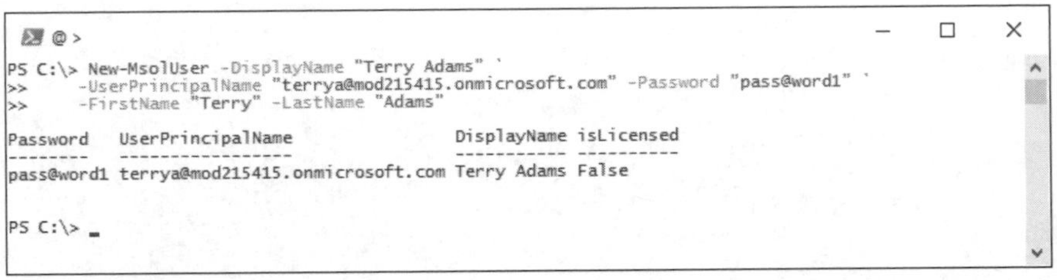

FIGURE 2-17 New-MsolUser

As a cloud pro, you'll likely need to create multiple users at the same time. Creating a single user at a time can be time consuming, especially if you do it from the browser. This is when PowerShell really shines. You can take advantage of the PowerShell pipeline to read information from a file and then pipe it into the New-MsolUser cmdlet. When you do this, the cmdlet runs against every row in the file.

To start, create a comma-separated-value (CSV) with all the users you want to add. We recommend just using Microsoft Excel and then saving the file as "CSV (Comma delimited) (*.csv)." In the spreadsheet, add as many columns for as many properties as you would like to set. Ensure that you at least add the DisplayName and UserPrincipalName columns. Although in theory you can call the columns anything you want, it might simplify management to maintain the same names as the parameters. The following example demonstrates how you might add five users using Excel to create the CSV file. (See Figure 2-18.) The file is called NewUsers.csv, and we set the *DisplayName*, *UserPrincipalName*, *Password*, *FirstName*, *LastName*, *Title*, and *Department* properties.

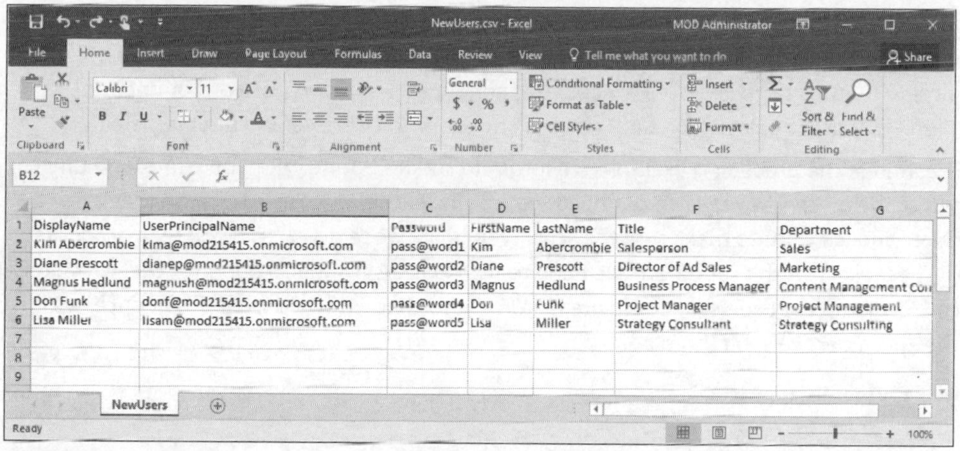
NewUsers.csv - Excel
DisplayName | UserPrincipalName | Password | FirstName | LastName | Title | Department
Kim Abercrombie | kima@mod215415.onmicrosoft.com | pass@word1 | Kim | Abercrombie | Salesperson | Sales
Diane Prescott | dianep@mod215415.onmicrosoft.com | pass@word2 | Diane | Prescott | Director of Ad Sales | Marketing
Magnus Hedlund | magnush@mod215415.onmicrosoft.com | pass@word3 | Magnus | Hedlund | Business Process Manager | Content Management Co
Don Funk | donf@mod215415.onmicrosoft.com | pass@word4 | Don | Funk | Project Manager | Project Management
Lisa Miller | lisam@mod215415.onmicrosoft.com | pass@word5 | Lisa | Miller | Strategy Consultant | Strategy Consulting
NewUsers
Ready

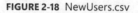

FIGURE 2-18 NewUsers.csv

After the file is saved as a CSV, it's ready to be used to create the users *en masse*. The following command demonstrates how to do this. Note that you use the *$_ special* variable to designate the row coming in from the pipeline. You use it to map parameters to each of the fields in the CSV file. (See Figure 2-19.)

```
$newUsers = Import-Csv -Path "C:\Temp\NewUsers.csv"
foreach ($user in $newUsers)
{
    New-MsolUser -DisplayName $user.DisplayName `
        -UserPrincipalName $user.UserPrincipalName -Password $user.Password `
        -FirstName $user.FirstName -LastName $user.LastName `
        -Department $user.Department
}
```

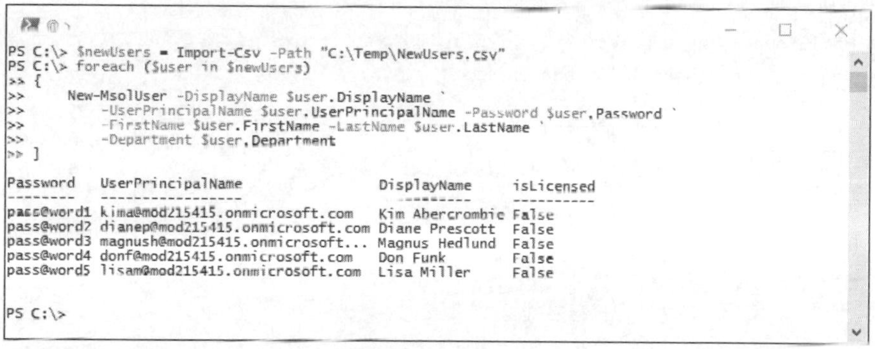
PS C:\> $newUsers = Import-Csv -Path "C:\Temp\NewUsers.csv"
PS C:\> foreach ($user in $newUsers)
>> {
>> New-MsolUser -DisplayName $user.DisplayName `
>> -UserPrincipalName $user.UserPrincipalName -Password $user.Password `
>> -FirstName $user.FirstName -LastName $user.LastName `
>> -Department $user.Department
>> }
Password UserPrincipalName DisplayName isLicensed
pass@word1 kima@mod215415.onmicrosoft.com Kim Abercrombie False
pass@word2 dianep@mod215415.onmicrosoft.com Diane Prescott False
pass@word3 magnush@mod215415.onmicrosoft... Magnus Hedlund False
pass@word4 donf@mod215415.onmicrosoft.com Don Funk False
pass@word5 lisam@mod215415.onmicrosoft.com Lisa Miller False
PS C:\>

FIGURE 2-19 Creating new users from a CSV file

As you can see, all five users were created. If the password was not included in the CSV file, the user's random password would have been available in the cmdlet's output.

UPDATE USERS

Users can be updated using the Set-MsolUser command. The list of parameters is almost identical to that of New-MsolUser, except you cannot use it to set a password or updated licensing. (You use the Set-MsolUserPassword and Set-MsolUserLicense cmdlets instead.)

To continue the preceding example, we forgot to set the Country/Region, State, and City of each of the users. They're all in our headquarters in Seattle, WA. Also, because they are new hires and we want to make sure they can't yet log in, we're going to block their accounts. Finally, because it wasn't set before, we need to set the users' *UsageLocation* to "US," which tells Office 365 where the user is (to configure features accordingly). To do all of this at once, we'll use the *$newUsers* variable from before:

```
foreach ($user in $newUsers)
{
    Set-MsolUser -UserPrincipalName $user.UserPrincipalName `
        -Country "United States" -State "WA" -City "Seattle" -BlockCredential $true `
        -UsageLocation "US"
}
```

WORK WITH SECURITY GROUPS

Office 365/Azure Active Directory includes the concept of *groups*. These include distribution lists, security groups, and mail-enabled security groups. Use the Get-MsolGroup cmdlet to view all of them:

```
Get-MsolGroup | Select-Object DisplayName, EmailAddress
```

Get-MsolGroupMember is used to determine which users are in a group. To use it, you need to have the ObjectID of the group you want to examine. In the following example (shown in Figure 2-20), we select the Big Wigs distribution list and then display its members using ForEach-Object:

```
$group = Get-MsolGroup | Where-Object { $_.DisplayName -eq "Big Wigs" }
Get-MsolGroupMember -GroupObjectId $group.ObjectId
```

```
⯈ @ >                                                          —   □   ×

PS C:\> $group = Get-MsolGroup | Where-Object { $_.DisplayName -eq "Big Wigs" }
PS C:\> Get-MsolGroupMember -GroupObjectId $group.ObjectId

GroupMemberType EmailAddress                      DisplayName
--------------- ------------                      -----------
User            admin@MOD215415.onmicrosoft.com   MOD Administrator
User            AnneW@MOD215415.onmicrosoft.com   Anne Wallace
User            BonnieK@MOD215415.onmicrosoft.com Bonnie Kearney
User            DorenaP@MOD215415.onmicrosoft.com Dorena Paschke
User            GarretV@MOD215415.onmicrosoft.com Garret Vargas
User            RobY@MOD215415.onmicrosoft.com    Rob Young


PS C:\>
```

FIGURE 2-20 Get-MsolGroupMember

Next, you create a new security group called "Seattle Staff" that will be used in SharePoint Online to secure the Seattle office site. This is done using New-MsolGroup. (See Figure 2-21.) To simplify the next line, store the results of New-MsolGroup in a variable. Next, add all the users in Seattle, WA, to the group using Add-MsolGroupMember. You use ForEach-Object to loop through the collection of Seattle users and add them to the "Seattle Staff" group (represented by the *$group* variable). Finally, validate the membership of the group:

```
$group = New-MsolGroup -DisplayName "Seattle Staff" -Description "Staff in Seattle, WA"
Get-MsolUser -City "Seattle" -State "WA" |
    ForEach-Object `
    {
        Add-MsolGroupMember -GroupObjectId $group.ObjectId `
            -GroupMemberObjectId $_.ObjectId
    }
Get-MsolGroupMember -GroupObjectId $group.ObjectId
```

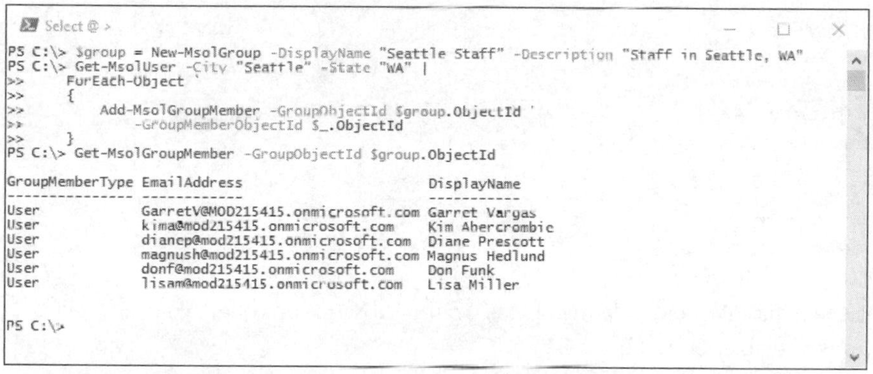

FIGURE 2-21 Add all users in Seattle, WA, to the "Seattle Staff" group.

Working with licenses

We'll do the following to demonstrate working with licenses:

- Get licensing information
- Manage licenses

GET LICENSING INFORMATION

For a user to have access to the full range of services, he must have an Office 365 license. The license determines which services the user has access to. Licenses are associated with a subscription. For example, you might have 25 licenses in an Office 365 Enterprise E5 subscription for your office workers and 50 licenses in an Exchange Online Kiosk subscription for basic email for your part-time retail staff.

To view the subscriptions available to you, use Get-MsolSubscription. (See Figure 2-22.) Note that each subscription has an SKU that uniquely describes it:

```
Get-MsolSubscription | Select-Object SkuPartNumber, TotalLicenses, Status, IsTrial
```

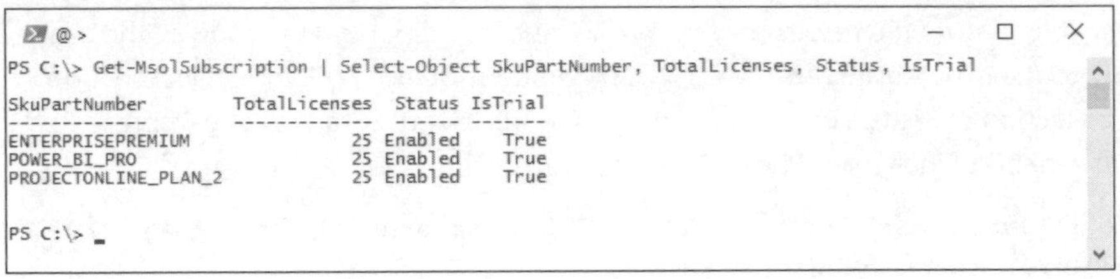

```
PS C:\> Get-MsolSubscription | Select-Object SkuPartNumber, TotalLicenses, Status, IsTrial

SkuPartNumber          TotalLicenses  Status   IsTrial
-------------          -------------  ------   -------
ENTERPRISEPREMIUM               25    Enabled     True
POWER_BI_PRO                    25    Enabled     True
PROJECTONLINE_PLAN_2            25    Enabled     True


PS C:\> _
```

FIGURE 2-22 Get-MsolSubscription

As you can see in Figure 2-22, the Office 365 tenant has 25 licenses of ENTERPRISEPREMIUM (Office 365 Enterprise E5) and 25 licenses of PROJECTONLINE_PLAN_2 (Project Online with Project for Office 365). To see how many of these licenses are assigned, use Get-AccountSku. As you can see in Figure 2-23, 19 licenses of Project Online and 23 of E5 have been assigned.

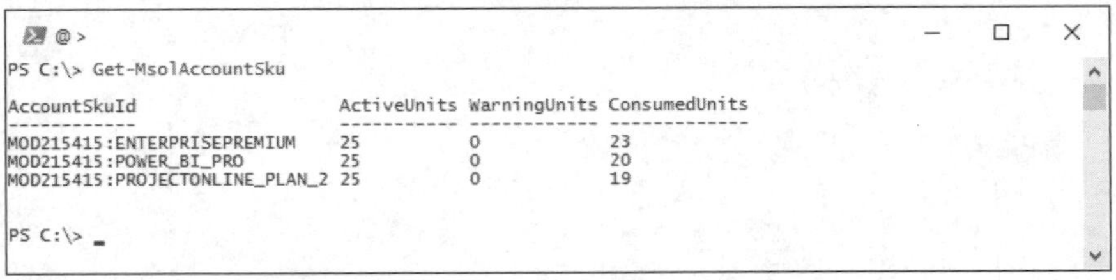

```
PS C:\> Get-MsolAccountSku

AccountSkuId                       ActiveUnits WarningUnits ConsumedUnits
------------                       ----------- ------------ -------------
MOD215415:ENTERPRISEPREMIUM        25          0            23
MOD215415:POWER_BI_PRO             25          0            20
MOD215415:PROJECTONLINE_PLAN_2     25          0            19


PS C:\> _
```

FIGURE 2-23 Get-MsolAccountSku

You can also see this information in the portal. On the Subscriptions page, you can view all the subscriptions available. (See Figure 2-24.)

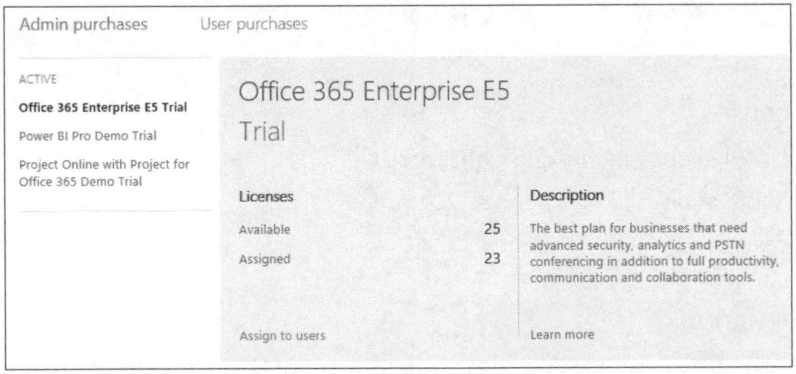

Admin purchases	User purchases	
ACTIVE	Office 365 Enterprise E5	
Office 365 Enterprise E5 Trial	Trial	
Power BI Pro Demo Trial		
Project Online with Project for Office 365 Demo Trial	**Licenses**	**Description**
	Available 25	The best plan for businesses that need advanced security, analytics and PSTN conferencing in addition to full productivity, communication and collaboration tools.
	Assigned 23	
	Assign to users	Learn more

FIGURE 2-24 Office 365 Enterprise E5 Trial licenses from the Office 365 Admin Center's Subscriptions page

The Licenses page, shown in Figure 2-25, tells you how many licenses have been assigned.

Home > Licenses

Name	Valid	Expired	Assigned
Office 365 Enterprise E5	25	0	23
Power BI Pro	25	0	20
Project Online with Project Pro for Office 365	25	0	19

FIGURE 2-25 Viewing assigned licenses on the Licenses page

MANAGE LICENSES

You use the Set-MsolUserLicense cmdlet to grant a license to a user or to remove one. To
assign licenses, use the -*AddLicenses* parameter along with a comma-delimited list of licenses
to add. Not surprisingly, the -*RemoveLicenses* parameter removes a license from a user. You
can use both at the same time, if you want. You need to use the specific license SKUs assigned
to your tenant. You get these from the *AccountSkuId* field in the Get-MsolAccountSku
results. For example, in Figure 2-23, you can see that the tenant has two license SKUs:
MOD215415:ENTERPRISEPREMIUM and MOD215415:PROJECTONLINE_PLAN_2.

To continue our example, we'll assign the five new users an Office 365 E5 license. (See Figure
2-26.) As you'll see, we won't be able to add E5 licenses to three users because only two are
available:

```
$newUsers | Set-MsolUserLicense -AddLicenses "MOD215415:ENTERPRISEPREMIUM"
```

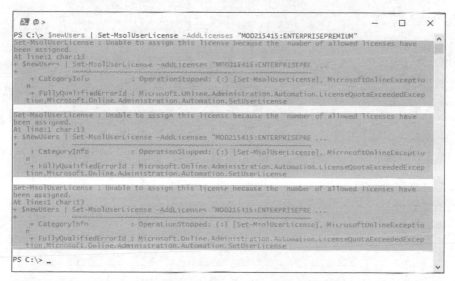

FIGURE 2-26 Set-MsolUserLicense fails because licenses are not available

To free up those licenses, we can arbitrarily remove licenses from the last five users. (This is just an example, after all.) Finally, we assigned the licenses once again—and this time it worked:

```
Get-MsolUser | Where-Object {$_.IsLicensed -eq $true} | Select-Object -Last 5 |
    Set-MsolUserLicense -RemoveLicenses "MOD215415:ENTERPRISEPREMIUM"
Get-Content -Path C:\Temp\NewUsers.csv | ConvertFrom-Csv |
    Set-MsolUserLicense -AddLicenses "MOD215415:ENTERPRISEPREMIUM"
```

Note that it does take a small amount of time for the Admin Center to catch up with what you did in PowerShell.

Next level

A peek under the hood

f you want a glimpse into what might be going on under the hood with Office 365, take a look at the results of the Get-MsolServicePrincipal cmdlet:

```
PS C:\> Get-MsolServicePrincipal | Select-Object DisplayName, ServicePrincipalNames | Sort-Object DisplayName

DisplayName                              ServicePrincipalNames
-----------                              ---------------------
Azure Media Service                      {803ee9ca-3f7f-4824-bd6e-0b99d720c35c, 803ee9ca-3f7f-4...
ComplianceCenter                         {80ccca67-54bd-44ab-8625-4b79c4dc7775, ComplianceCenter}
Device Registration Service              {urn:ms-drs:enterpriseregistration.windows.net, 01cb28...
IbizaPortal                              {c44b4083-3bb0-49c1-b47d-974e53cbdf3c, IbizaPortal}}
Microsoft Power BI Information Service    {0000001b-0000-0000-c000-000000000000/ssim.powerbi.mic...
Microsoft.Azure.ActiveDirectory          {https://graph.windows.net, 00000002-0000-0000-c000-00...
Microsoft.Azure.ActiveDirectoryUX        {0000000c-0000-0000-c000-000000000000/activedirectory....
Microsoft.Azure.AgregatorService         {https://ags.windows.net, 00000003-0000-0000-c000-0000...
Microsoft.Azure.GraphExplorer            {0000000f-0000-0000-c000-000000000000/graphexplorer.wi...
Microsoft.Azure.Portal                   {https://manage.windowsazure.com, 00000013-0000-0000-c...
Microsoft.Azure.RMS                      {https://api.aadrm.com/, 00000012-0000-0000-c000-0000...
Microsoft.Azure.Workflow                 {00000005-0000-0000-c000-000000000000/*.workflow.usgov...
Microsoft.DiscoveryService               {6f82282e-0070-4e78-bc23-e6320c5fa7de/api.office.com, ...
Microsoft.Exchange                       {00000002-0000-0ff1-ce00-000000000000/outlook.office36...
Microsoft.ExchangeOnlineProtection       {https://*.protection.outlook.com, https://*.dataservi...
Microsoft.ExtensibleRealUserMonitoring   {e3583ad2-c781-4224-9b91-ad15a8179ba0/na.myservice.com...
Microsoft.Intune                         {0000000a-0000-0000-c000-000000000000/manage-beta.micr...
Microsoft.Lync                           {00000004-0000-0ff1-ce00-000000000000/*.infra.lync.com...
Microsoft.Office365.ChangeManagement     {601d4e27-7bb3-4dee-8199-90d47d527e1c/changemgmt.admin...
Microsoft.Office365.Configure            {aa9ecb1e-fd53-4aaa-a8fe-7a54de2c1334/configure.office...
Microsoft.Office365Portal                {00000006-0000-0ff1-ce00-000000000000/portal.microsoft...
Microsoft.OfficeClientService            {https://office.microsoft.com, https://ols.officeapps...
Microsoft.OfficeModernCalendar           {https://eus2-hxcalendar.officeapps.live.com, https://...
Microsoft.OfficeWebAppsService           {67e3df25-268a-4324-a550-0de1c7f97287, Microsoft.Offic...
Microsoft.SellerDashboard                {0000000b-0000-0000-c000-000000000000/sellerdashboard....
Microsoft.SharePoint                     {00000003-0000-0ff1-ce00-000000000000/*.sharepoint.com...
Microsoft.SMIT                           {8fca0a66-c008-4564-a876-ab3ae0fd5cff/lowlatency.cloud...
Microsoft.SupportTicketSubmission        {595d87a1-277b-4c0a-aa7f-44f8a068eafc, Microsoft.Suppo...
Microsoft.YammerEnterprise               {00000005-0000-0ff1-ce00-000000000000/*.yammer.com, 00...
MicrosoftIntuneAPI                       {c161e42e-d4df-4a3d-9b42-e7a3c31f59d4, MicrosoftIntune...
MicrosoftIntuneServiceDiscovery          {9cb77803-d937-493e-9a3b-4b49de3f5a74, MicrosoftIntune...
MicrosoftOffice                          {8d3a7d3c-c034-4f19-a2ef-8412952a9671, MicrosoftOffice}
Office Personal Assistant at Work Service {28ec9756-deaf-48b2-84d5-a623b99af263}
OfficeManagePlatform                     {c5393580-f805-4401-95e8-94b7a6ef2fc2, OfficeManagePla...
Outlook Service for Exchange             {13d54852-ae25-4f0b-823a-b09eea89f431}
Outlook Service for OneDrive             {2728b157-fe96-4203-a49f-cc31c93a2ba3}
Power BI                                 {00000009-0000-0000-c000-000000000000/analysis.windows...
ProjectWorkManagement                    {09abbdfd-ed23-44ee-a2d9-a627aa1c90f3/tasks.office.com...
serviceAccount                           {c20fffa4-0c49-4817-8111-ee72e4c59ffa, serviceAccount}
Sway                                     {905fcf26-4eb7-48a0-9ff0-8dcc7194b5ba, Sway}
UnifiedApiConsumer                       {c177078f-a1a8-4e46-bdeb-8a26d937086f}
Windows Azure Service Management API     {https://management.core.windows.net/, 797f4846-ba00-4...

PS C:\>
```

In this context, a Service Principal is basically an application that has access to your Azure Active Directory tenant. You'll see Microsoft.Exchange, Microsoft.SharePoint, and Sway, for example. So what does this all signify?

Azure Active Directory is the base platform upon which everything is built by using applications that are added to it, including all the Office 365 core components. Exchange Online, Azure, Office Web Apps, SharePoint Online, Sway, Office ProPlus, and others are all separate services with which your Azure Active Directory tenant has a configured trust. Even the Admin Center and browser user interfaces are just applications added to the platform (Microsoft.Office365Portal).

Microsoft can continue to grow the scope of what it calls Office 365 by adding more service principals for new services. Plus, if you add your own applications to Azure Active Directory (outside the scope of this book), you'll see them listed alongside all of Microsoft's applications. As far as the platform is concerned, your applications are peers to, say, SharePoint Online and Exchange Online. So Office 365 is "simply" an amalgamation of lots of trusted individual applications laid on top of Azure Active Directory, including components you might think are core to and indistinguishable from the service (like the interface).

Work with SharePoint Online

To begin working with SharePoint Online, make sure the Microsoft.Online.SharePoint.Power-Shell module has been loaded:

```
Import-Module Microsoft.Online.SharePoint.PowerShell -DisableNameChecking
```

Additionally, you need to connect to SharePoint Online using the Connect-SPOService cmdlet. You need to supply the -Url parameter, which is the URL of the SharePoint Online Admin Center. For example, you run the following command to connect to SharePoint Online. If you do not provide credentials (as we did earlier), you will get a browser window that prompts you to sign in:

```
Connect-SPOService -Url "https://contoso-admin.sharepoint.com"
```

Unfortunately, at this time, the list of SharePoint Online cmdlets is quite small, especially when compared to what is available on-premises. We hope Microsoft continues to build out the cmdlets.

To get a list of the loaded cmdlets, run the following:

```
Get-Command -Module Microsoft.Online.SharePoint.PowerShell
```

We'll look at the following for examples of working with SharePoint Online PowerShell:

- Working with site collections
- Working with users and permissions

MORE INFO For an excellent resource for SharePoint Online PowerShell, including a description of the cmdlets, visit "Introduction to the SharePoint Online Management Shell" at *https://support.office.com/article/Introduction-to-the-SharePoint-Online-Management-Shell-c16941c3-19b4-4710-8056-34c034493429*.

Working with site collections

The following are some of the things you can do when you work with site collections:

- List site collections
- Create a site collection
- Delete a site collection
- Restore a deleted site collection

LIST SITE COLLECTIONS

As will be described later, the site collection is the top-most level of organization and security in SharePoint Online. You can create site collections under the /sites or /teams managed paths, and inside of a site collection you can create subsites. Technically, each My Site is its own site collection.

To get a list of all your SharePoint Online site collections, you use the Get-SPOSite cmdlet. (See Figure 2-27.) In the following example, we grab the *Url*, *Title*, and *Template*:

```
Get-SPOSite | Select-Object Url, Title, Template
```

```
PS C:\> Get-SPOSite | Select-Object Url, Title, Template

Url                                            Title                  Template
---                                            -----                  --------
https://mod215415.sharepoint.com/                                     EHS#1
https://mod215415.sharepoint.com/portals/hub                          POINTPUBLISHINGHUB#0
https://mod215415.sharepoint.com/search                               SRCHCEN#0
https://mod215415.sharepoint.com/sites/bicenter  BI                   BICenterSite#0
https://mod215415.sharepoint.com/sites/communities  Communities       COMMUNITYPORTAL#0
https://mod215415.sharepoint.com/sites/contoso   Home                 BLANKINTERNETCONTA...
https://mod215415.sharepoint.com/sites/contosobeta  Contoso Beta      STS#0
https://mod215415.sharepoint.com/sites/contosopartners Contoso Partner Portal BLANKINTERNETCONTA...
https://mod215415.sharepoint.com/sites/Dev       Developer Site       Dev#0
https://mod215415.sharepoint.com/sites/ediscovery  Legal Discovery Center EDISC#0
https://mod215415.sharepoint.com/sites/Equivio   Team Site            STS#0
https://mod215415.sharepoint.com/sites/pwa                            PWA#0
https://mod215415.sharepoint.com/sites/SMBverticals  SMB Verticals     STS#0
https://mod215415.sharepoint.com/sites/visiodemos  Visio Demos        STS#0
https://mod215415-my.sharepoint.com/                                  SPSMSITEHOST#0

PS C:\>
```

FIGURE 2-27 Get-SPOSite

CREATE A SITE COLLECTION

To create a new site collection via PowerShell, you use the New-SPOSite cmdlet. It requires the following parameters: *Url*, *Owner*, and *StorageQuota*. You need to provide the full URL (for example, *https://mod215415.sharepoint.com/sites/SeattleOffice*), and the owner needs to be an individual user already in Azure Active Directory. By default, the site collection is created with US English. You can specify another language when you create the site using the *-LocalId* parameter.

When you create a site, you need to specify the template to use. The template determines which features are pre-enabled in the site collection, and it does some basic configuration of the site collection for you. You can specify a template when you create a new site, although you don't have to. If you do not specify a template, you will be prompted for the template the first time you go to the site. To get a list of available templates and the template codes (which you need for New-SPOSite), use the Get-SPOWebTemplate cmdlet. The result is shown in Figure 2-28.

```
PS C:\> Get-SPOWebTemplate

Name                          Title                                     LocaleId CompatibilityLevel
----                          -----                                     -------- ------------------
STS#0                         Team Site                                 1033                     15
BLOG#0                        Blog                                      1033                     15
BDR#0                         Document Center                           1033                     15
DEV#0                         Developer Site                            1033                     15
OFFILE#1                      Records Center                            1033                     15
EHS#1                         Team Site - SharePoint Online configuration 1033                   15
BICenterSite#0                Business Intelligence Center              1033                     15
SRCHCEN#0                     Enterprise Search Center                  1033                     15
BLANKINTERNETCONTAINER#0      Publishing Portal                         1033                     15
ENTERWIKI#0                   Enterprise Wiki                           1033                     15
PROJECTSITE#0                 Project Site                              1033                     15
PRODUCTCATALOG#0              Product Catalog                           1033                     15
COMMUNITY#0                   Community Site                            1033                     15
COMMUNITYPORTAL#0             Community Portal                          1033                     15
SRCHCENTERLITE#0              Basic Search Center                       1033                     15
visprus#0                     Visio Process Repository                  1033                     15

PS C:\> _
```

FIGURE 2-28 Get-SPOWebTemplate

In our example, we'll create the Seattle office site. Because this is a place the staff will use to collaborate, we choose the standard Team Site template. Allie Bellew has responsibility for the site, so we make her the owner. We set the storage quota to 5 GB and set the time zone to Pacific Standard Time, which happens to be ID 13. (Do an online search for "SPRegionalSettings. TimeZones property".) To create the site collection, we run the following command:

```
New-SPOSite -Url "https://mod215415.sharepoint.com/sites/RedmondOffice" `
    -Owner "allieb@mod215415.onmicrosoft.com" -StorageQuota 5120 `
    -Title "Seattle Office Site" -Template "STS#0" -TimeZoneId 13
```

Note that it will take a couple of minutes for the command to complete. To skip the wait, add the *-NoWait* switch to the command.

> **MORE INFO** New-SPOSite requires the *StorageQuota* parameter. If, however, Site Collection Storage Management is set to Automatic, this parameter will be disregarded. It still is required, though, so you can input any value.

DELETE A SITE COLLECTION

If you look closely, you'll notice there was a mistake. It's the Seattle office, not Redmond. Thankfully, we haven't done anything with the site collection yet, so you can just delete it and create it again with the new URL. To do this, you use the Remove-SPOSite cmdlet:

```
Remove-SPOSite "https://mod215415.sharepoint.com/sites/RedmondOffice"
```

When a site collection is deleted, it moves into the site collection recycle bin. This way, you can undelete the site collection if needed. You'll be asked to confirm the deletion.

Note that the site collection needs to be fully created before it can be removed. If in the SharePoint Online Admin Center sites page there's a green spinning icon, the site collection is still being created.

RESTORE A DELETED SITE COLLECTION

What happens if you delete a site collection by accident? Fortunately, SharePoint Online provides a site collection recycle bin. You can access it by clicking Recycle Bin in the ribbon on the Site Collections page in the SharePoint Online Admin Center. The same information can be obtained in PowerShell by using the Get-SPODeletedSite cmdlet.

You can restore the site collection in the browser, but you also can use the Restore-SPODeletedSite cmdlet, as in this example:

```
Restore-SPODeletedSite "https://mod215415.sharepoint.com/sites/RedmondOffice"
```

You also can permanently delete a site collection by using the Remove-SPODeletedSite cmdlet.

Working with users and permissions

To demonstrate working with users and permissions, we'll do the following tasks:

- Get permissions
- Add or remove a user
- Make a user a site collection administrator
- Work with groups
- Work with external users

GET PERMISSIONS

You use Get-SPOUser to get a list of the users in a site collection. (See Figure 2-29.) For example, the following command retrieves the list of users in the newly created Seattle Office site collection:

```
Get-SPOUser -Site "https://mod215415.sharepoint.com/sites/SeattleOffice"
```

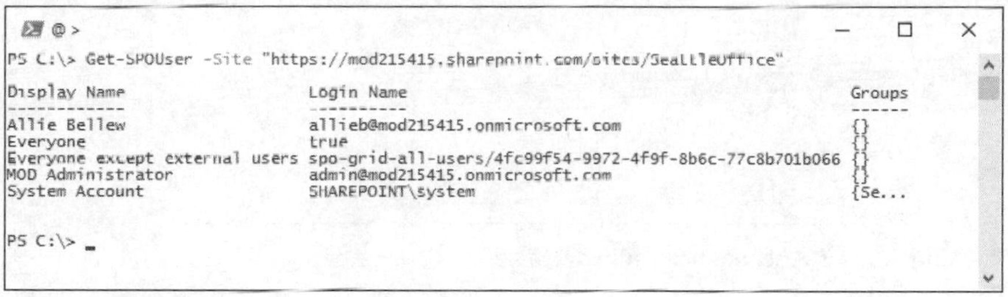

FIGURE 2-29 Get-SPOUser

You'll notice Allie Bellew and MOD Administrator in the list, and they're not currently members of any SharePoint groups. They're included in the list because they were made site collection administrators but not members of a group.

One of the more important pieces of information you get back from this cmdlet is Share-Point group membership. It tells you what SharePoint groups the user is a member of. (See Figure 2-30.) For example, here's a list of users and their memberships in another site collection:

```
Get-SPOUser https://mod215415.sharepoint.com/sites/Contoso |
    Select-Object DisplayName, Groups | Format-List
```

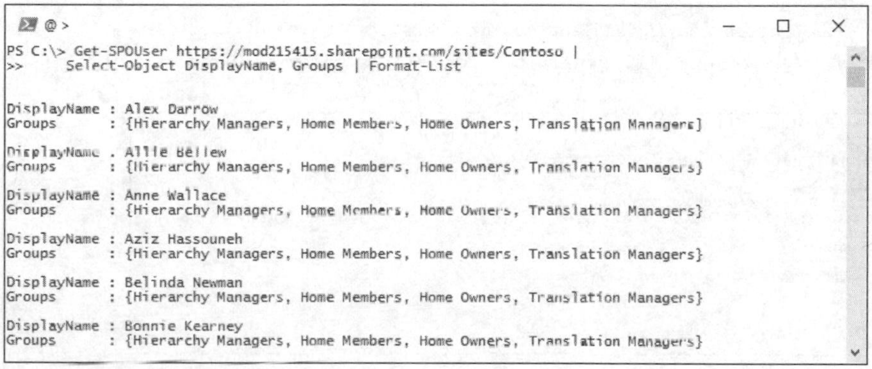

FIGURE 2-30 Get-SPOUser to display group membership

You can use the -Group parameter to retrieve group members. The following command gives you all users in the Contoso site's "Home Owners" SharePoint Group:

```
Get-SPOUser -Site "https://mod215415.sharepoint.com/sites/Contoso" `
    -Group "Home Owners" | Select DisplayName, IsSiteAdmin | Format-Table -AutoSize
```

Finally, you can get a specific user by using the -LoginName parameter. (See Figure 2-31.) This parameter is particularly useful if you're checking to see whether the user is already in a site:

```
If ( Get-SPOUser -Site "https://mod215415.sharepoint.com" `
    -LoginName "karif@mod215415.onmicrosoft.com" )
    { Write-Host "The user is in the site" }
```

```
PS C:\> If ( Get-SPOUser -Site "https://mod215415.sharepoint.com" `
>>     -LoginName "karif@mod215415.onmicrosoft.com" )
>>     { Write-Host "The user is in the site" }
The user is in the site
PS C:\>
```

FIGURE 2-31 Checking to see if a user has been added to a site

ADD OR REMOVE A USER

You use the Add-SPOUser cmdlet to grant a user access to the site collection. When you do, you need to place the user into a SharePoint group. For example, suppose you want to grant Magnus Hedlund access to the new Seattle Office site collection. You add him to the Seattle Office Site Members group (which was created by default). To do this, you first need to allow his account to sign in to Office 365. Because it takes a little time for this change to take effect, pause for 30 seconds before adding him to the site. (See Figure 2-32.)

```
Set-MsolUser -UserPrincipalName "magnush@mod215415.onmicrosoft.com" `
    -BlockCredential $false
Start-Sleep -Seconds 30
Add-SPOUser -Site "https://mod215415.sharepoint.com/sites/SeattleOffice" `
    -LoginName "magnush@mod215415.onmicrosoft.com" -Group "Seattle Office Site Members"
```

FIGURE 2-32 Add-SPOUser

If you then want to remove Magnus from the site, use Remove-SPOUser:

```
Remove-SPOUser -Site "https://mod215415.sharepoint.com/sites/SeattleOffice" `
    -LoginName "magnush@mod215415.onmicrosoft.com"
```

MAKE A USER A SITE COLLECTION ADMINISTRATOR

To make a user a site collection administrator, we use the Set-SPOUser cmdlet. The *-IsSiteCollection-Admin* parameter determines whether or not the user is a site collection administrator. Continuing with our scenario, we realize that Kari Furse should be the site collection administrator, not Allie. To correct this, we run the following commands:

```
Set-SPOUser -Site "https://mod215415.sharepoint.com/sites/SeattleOffice" `
    -LoginName "allieb@mod215415.onmicrosoft.com" -IsSiteCollectionAdmin $false
Set-SPOUser -Site "https://mod215415.sharepoint.com/sites/SeattleOffice" `
    -LoginName "karif@mod215415.onmicrosoft.com" -IsSiteCollectionAdmin $true
```

> **REAL WORLD**   There might be times when a user needs to be kicked out of SharePoint
> Online, OneDrive for Business, or both. This could happen if, for example, an employee has
> been let go or if a device has been lost. You normally disable the user to prevent unauthorized
> access. However, user sessions can continue for some time (such as with the OneDrive for
> Business sync client). To shut down these sessions, use the Revoke-SPOUserSession command,
> as shown in the following example:
>
> Revoke-SPOUserSession -User alexd@mod215415.onmicrosoft.com

WORK WITH GROUPS

To add or remove users from SharePoint groups, you continue to use Add-SPOUser and
Remove-SPOUser. For example, Anne Wallace is a member of the Home Owners and Home
Members groups in the Contoso site. If you want to remove her from the Home Owners group
while keeping her in the Home Members group, you simply need to run the following:

```
Remove-SPOUser -Site "https://mod215415.sharepoint.com/sites/Contoso" `
    -LoginName "annew@mod215415.onmicrosoft.com" -Group "Home Owners"
```

WORK WITH EXTERNAL USERS

The ability to share content with users outside of your organization is one of the great benefits
of SharePoint Online and OneDrive for Business. When you do this, the external user is able to
sign in with her own account (or anonymously, if it's shared that way) after accepting an email
invitation. After the invitation has been accepted, a special user is created in Azure Active
Directory. No user is created until the invitation is accepted.

Microsoft has given us a way to view the external users separately from internal users:
Get-SPOExternalUser. It operates a bit differently than the other cmdlets in that you need to
provide a *PageSize*. *PageSize* specifies the maximum number of users to return. If a value is not
specified, only one external user will be returned. The *-SiteUrl* parameter can be used to filter
the users to a specific site collection. If it's omitted, all external users are returned. For example,
the following command returns the first 10 external users in the tenant (see Figure 2-33 for the
results):

```
Get-SPOExternalUser -PageSize 10
```

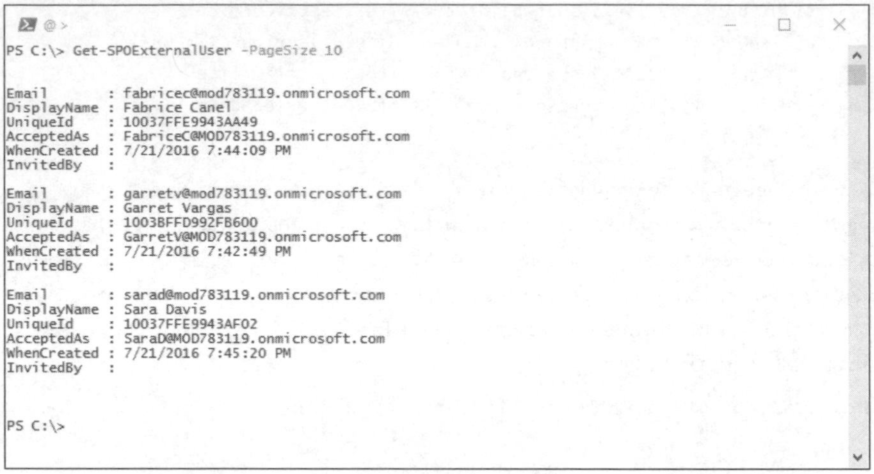

```
PS C:\> Get-SPOExternalUser -PageSize 10

Email       : fabricec@mod783119.onmicrosoft.com
DisplayName : Fabrice Canel
UniqueId    : 10037FFE9943AA49
AcceptedAs  : FabriceC@MOD783119.onmicrosoft.com
WhenCreated : 7/21/2016 7:44:09 PM
InvitedBy   :

Email       : garretv@mod783119.onmicrosoft.com
DisplayName : Garret Vargas
UniqueId    : 1003BFFD992FB600
AcceptedAs  : GarretV@MOD783119.onmicrosoft.com
WhenCreated : 7/21/2016 7:42:49 PM
InvitedBy   :

Email       : sarad@mod783119.onmicrosoft.com
DisplayName : Sara Davis
UniqueId    : 10037FFE9943AF02
AcceptedAs  : SaraD@MOD783119.onmicrosoft.com
WhenCreated : 7/21/2016 7:45:20 PM
InvitedBy   :


PS C:\>
```

FIGURE 2-33 Get-SPOExternalUser

If, for whatever reason, you need to revoke an external user's access, you use the Remove-SPO-ExternalUser cmdlet. When you use this cmdlet, the user is removed from the entire tenant, not just a single site. Because the cmdlet requires the external user's *UniqueID*, you need to first grab the external user object. The following command revokes access to Fabrice Canel (see Figure 2-34 for the results):

```
$user = Get-SPOExternalUser -Filter fabricec@MOD783119.onmicrosoft.com
Remove-SPOExternalUser -UniqueIDs @($user.UniqueId)
```

```
PS C:\> $user = Get-SPOExternalUser -Filter fabricec@MOD783119.onmicrosoft.com
PS C:\> Remove-SPOExternalUser -UniqueIDs @($user.UniqueId)

Confirm
Are you sure you want to perform this action?
Performing the operation "Remove external users." on target "UniqueIDs".
[Y] Yes  [A] Yes to All  [N] No  [L] No to All  [S] Suspend  [?] Help (default is "Y"): Y
Successfully removed the following external users
10037FFE9943AA49
PS C:\>
```

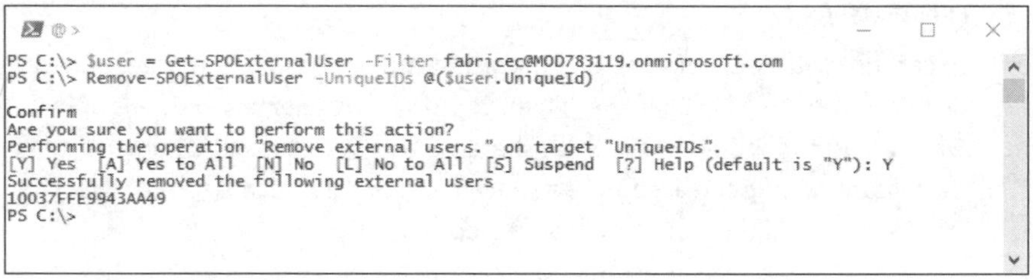

FIGURE 2-34 Remove-SPOExternalUser

Next level

Important knobs and subtle switches

Although the SharePoint Online Admin Center does a great job of making available most settings in the SharePoint Online tenant, some additional settings are available only via PowerShell. Some of these can be quite important to some users. To see what's available, use the Get-SPOTenant cmdlet:

```
PS C:\> Get-SPOTenant

StorageQuota                                  : 1074176
StorageQuotaAllocated                         : 15728640
ResourceQuota                                 : 11100
ResourceQuotaAllocated                        : 5100
OneDriveStorageQuota                          : 1048576
CompatibilityRange                            : 15,15
ExternalServicesEnabled                       : True
NoAccessRedirectUrl                           :
SharingCapability                             : ExternalUserAndGuestSharing
DisplayStartASiteOption                       : True
StartASiteFormUrl                             :
ShowEveryoneClaim                             : True
ShowAllUsersClaim                             : True
OfficeClientADALDisabled                      : False
LegacyAuthProtocolsEnabled                    : True
ShowEveryoneExceptExternalUsersClaim          : True
SearchResolveExactEmailOrUPN                  : False
RequireAcceptingAccountMatchInvitedAccount    : False
ProvisionSharedWithEveryoneFolder             : False
SignInAccelerationDomain                      :
EnableGuestSignInAcceleration                 : False
UsePersistentCookiesForExplorerView           : False
BccExternalSharingInvitations                 : False
BccExternalSharingInvitationsList             :
UserVoiceForFeedbackEnabled                   : True
RequireAnonymousLinksExpireInDays             : 0
SharingAllowedDomainList                      :
SharingBlockedDomainList                      :
SharingDomainRestrictionMode                  : None
OneDriveForGuestsEnabled                      : False
IPAddressEnforcement                          : False
IPAddressAllowList                            :
IPAddressWACTokenLifetime                     : 15
UseFindPeopleInPeoplePicker                   : False
OrphanedPersonalSitesRetentionPeriod          : 30


PS C:\>
```

As Microsoft rolls out new features, the list of options continues to grow. At the time of this writing, at least seven options have not yet been documented on TechNet. The Set-SPOTenant command is used to change these settings. Here are some of the more interesting options:

- *ShowEveryoneClaim, ShowAllUsersClaim, ShowEveryoneExceptExternalUsers Claim*   These three options control whether or not the large umbrella groups are displayed in People Pickers. You might want to disable these if you want to reduce the risk of users providing tenant-wide permissions to resources.

- *ProvisionSharedWithEveryoneFolder*   By default, when a user gets access to OneDrive for Business, there's a folder named "Shared with Everyone." You can prevent this folder from being created by default. If needed, you can use this setting as another way to prevent tenant-wide sharing.

- *BccExternalSharingInvitations* and *BccExternalSharingInvitationsList*   These two properties are used in conjunction with one another. If *BccExternalSharingInvitations* is set to *True*, the email addresses in *BccExternalSharingInvitationsList* are blind-copied (BCC'ed) on all sharing invitations. This can be a powerful way of monitoring external sharing (and intercepting invitations if needed).

- *SearchResolveExactEmailOrUPN*   If this setting is set to *False*, the search feature is disabled in People Pickers. Instead, the user needs to manually enter an email address or User Principal Name. This feature can be important in situations where users should not be able to see who else is in the user directory.

Work with the Security & Compliance Center

To begin working with Security & Compliance Center, make sure the session has been loaded:

```
$complianceSession = New-PSSession -ConfigurationName Microsoft.Exchange `
    -ConnectionUri "https://ps.compliance.protection.outlook.com/powershell-liveid/" `
    -Credential $credential -Authentication Basic -AllowRedirection
Import-PSSession $complianceSession
```

Remember, a lot of the Security & Compliance Center cmdlets overlap with Exchange Online. You can be work around this situation by using the technique shown earlier in the chapter (by adding a prefix).

To get a list of the loaded cmdlets, run the following command:

```
Get-Module | Where-Object {$_.Description -like "*compliance.protection.outlook.com*"} |
    Select-Object ExportedCommands -ExpandProperty ExportedCommands
```

> **MORE INFO**   You can find the "Office 365 Security & Compliance Center cmdlets" reference at *https://technet.microsoft.com/library/mt587093(v=exchg.160).aspx.*

As we discussed, PowerShell is most effective when you use it to automate repeated tasks or to do advanced configuration. At times, though, it can be just as effective to use another tool.

Although you absolutely can manage the Security & Compliance Center via PowerShell, most likely you will not need to. You'll likely be just as efficient and effective (if not more so) working in the browser. Because of this, we'll skip the PowerShell examples and encourage you to simply use the browser on this one. However, read through the list of cmdlets so that you know what is available. You never know when you're going to need them. For example, they could be important if you're managing a large tenant, you have to perform eDiscovery with lots of sites or users, or both. Those scripts, though, are outside the scope of a PowerShell 101 chapter.

## CHAPTER 3

Working with Azure Active Directory for Office 365

In this chapter, we talk about Microsoft Azure Active Directory (Azure AD) and identity in Microsoft Office 365. First, we discuss the features of Azure AD, compare it to the on-premises Active Directory (AD DS) you're familiar with, and review the various pricing tiers available. Next, we dive into the three identity scenarios: cloud-only, synchronized, and federated.

We then discuss synchronizing your on-premises Active Directory users with your tenant using Azure AD Connect (AD Connect) product. This step is important not only to provide your users with a better sign-in experience but also to enable various hybrid scenarios, which we discuss in a later chapter. Identity synchronization might be the most difficult step of the hybrid journey, but AD Connect is making it easier. Finally, we discuss deploying Active Directory Federation Services (AD FS) to enable the federated identity scenario and give your users single sign-on (SSO).

There is a tremendous amount to discuss on these topics; entire books can be written on them. Because we don't have the luxury of diving deeply into this subject, our focus will be on giving you what you need to understand the concepts and get started with these technologies. There are terrific resources online for diving deeper, and we're not going to insult your intelligence by pretending you can't find them. Instead, we want to equip you to approach these subjects holistically as a Cloud Pro and get your mind around what it takes to cloud-enable your company. Outside of networking, identity management is perhaps the most important and fundamental aspect of cloud computing.

Azure Active Directory

The core of Office 365 is Azure AD. To borrow a phrase from one of our favorite movies (*Star Wars*), Azure AD surrounds Office 365 and penetrates it. It binds the services together. Let's take a closer look.

What is Azure Active Directory?

Azure AD is a Microsoft Azure Platform as a Service (PaaS) offering that is included in every Office 365 tenant. Azure AD is a free Azure service, and any developer can take advantage of it as an identity store. You can access your Azure AD tenant by selecting Azure AD under the Admin Centers menu in the Office 365 Admin Center, as shown in Figure 3-1.

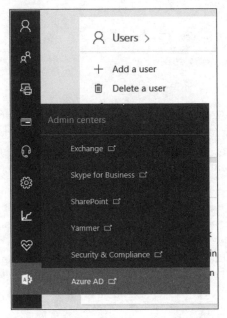

FIGURE 3-1 Accessing your Azure AD tenant

The first time you open Azure AD from the Admin Center, you are prompted to set up your Azure subscription. The subscription is free and only takes a few clicks for you to set it up. After a couple of minutes, the subscription will be ready and you can start exploring. At this point, there is nothing in the Azure subscription other than the single Azure AD directory, but you can add additional Azure services if you want. At the time of this writing, Azure AD is still managed through the old Azure portal. Scroll down in the left pane and select Active Directory. Your directory is shown in the right pane, as you can see in Figure 3-2. Click the cell with your tenant's name to start working with your directory.

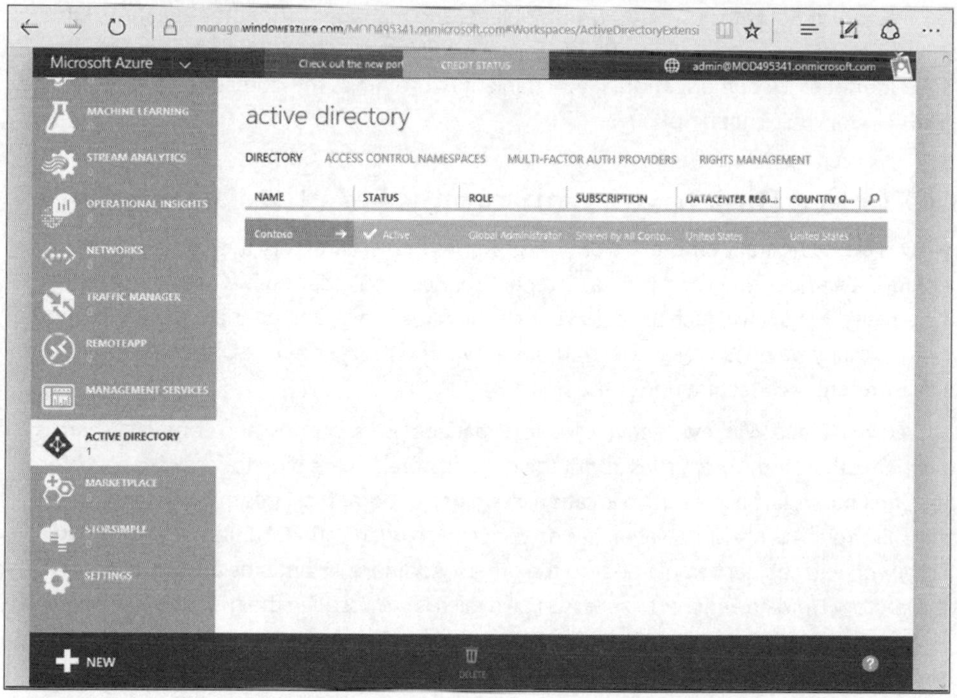

FIGURE 3-2 Accessing your tenant in the Azure portal

You can work with Users, Groups, Applications, and Domains, and you can perform advanced configuration, view the status of your on-premises Active Directory integration, and view reports. You also might want to work with your users and groups in this portal. That's certainly an option, and it is supported. However, chances are good that you'll need to do additional Office 365–related actions with your users and groups, such as assigning licenses, configuring services for the users (like setting up mailboxes), and assigning service-level admin roles (like SharePoint Administrator). Those activities need to be done through the Office 365 Admin Center, so it likely will be more efficient to simply work there. However, working in the Azure AD Admin Center is akin to managing via Microsoft Windows PowerShell, so feel free to use it in that way if it is an experience you prefer.

So what does Azure AD actually do, and why should you care? The various Microsoft cloud services require users to have an identity in order to interact with the service, just as your on-premises systems do. Resources and systems need to be secured from public access. On-premises, we have Active Directory or some other Lightweight Directory Access Protocol (LDAP) directory service for this. The on-premises systems trust the directory and rely on it to identify and manage the users. But what do you do in the cloud, when services are offered by external companies? Enter Azure AD.

Azure AD is the identity store of the Microsoft cloud. If you think of the various cloud services as traditional server applications in an on-premises domain, Azure AD is the Active Directory that these servers are hooked into for their identity needs. Like an on-premises

Active Directory, it holds the user and group objects and manages user authentication. Office 365 services (such as Microsoft SharePoint Online) act like server-based systems and use Azure AD identities for authorization. If you think of Azure AD as the domain controller for the Microsoft cloud, you're not far off.

Azure Active Directory vs. on-premises Active Directory

Azure AD is fundamentally different from on-premises Active Directory in that it was born in the cloud. It was designed and built as a tenant service. This means it has all the benefits cloud-native systems have, such as massive scale, high resiliency, and a tenanted service model. Although in many ways it's similar to a traditional Windows Server Active Directory, it has a radically different architecture under the hood.

Both Azure AD and Windows Active Directory manage users, groups, and contacts. There is a data schema that stores properties about the objects stored in the directories. Both have, for example, first name, last name, office location, manager, geographical information, and group membership. Your Azure AD, however, has no concept of organizational units (OUs). It's a flat hierarchy, with each object being a peer to the others. Additionally, until the advent of Azure Active Directory Domain Services (Azure AD DS) (which is discussed in the next section), there really wasn't the concept of a domain that is a boundary encapsulating objects. Instead, Azure AD uses the concept of *tenants*, wherein a company is able to securely manage a collection of objects that it owns. You can almost think of your tenant as a forest, but that's not quite accurate.

Until Azure AD DS (which is an add-on service), there was also no concept of machine objects in Azure AD. Machine objects are critical in Windows Active Directory because they establish membership within a domain and allow such things as Windows Authentication. The normal Azure AD services do not have machine objects; therefore, it's not possible for servers or virtual machines to be joined to Azure AD like an on-premises server would be joined to a local Active Directory instance. Microsoft has begun adding additional services to Azure AD and Office 365, changing the situation a bit. You can, for example, join Windows 10 devices to Azure AD. However, the devices are associated with users and managed through the Mobile Device Management service (Microsoft Intune), not directly joined to Azure AD.

Azure AD provides a number of additional, powerful services that are unavailable in Active Directory. For one, companies can register applications in Azure AD as service principals. These applications can then have permission (if approved) to the suite of Azure services, including users in Azure AD. These applications can be published to users and provide a kind of new distribution model. This is how core Office 365 services like Exchange Online and SharePoint Online work and gain access to Azure AD. But you can also use Azure AD for single sign-on (SSO) to a wide array of third-party cloud services, such as Salesforce. As shown in Figure 3-3, Salesforce has been added to the Azure AD tenant, allowing users to sign in to Salesforce from the Office 365 App Launcher using their Azure AD account.

As a Cloud Pro, you can hook up various Software as a Service (SaaS) applications with Azure AD and give your users a simple sign-on experience with just their one Azure AD account. This can help your users be more efficient and reduce the number of accounts and passwords they need to memorize. Adding these SaaS applications is simple and easy to do.

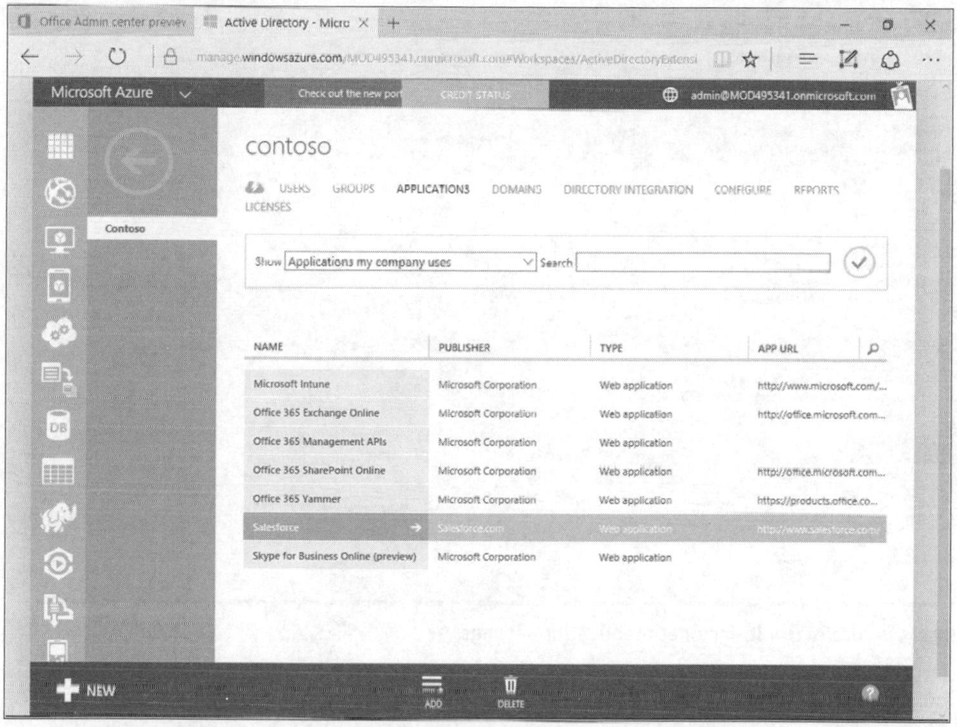

FIGURE 3-3 Salesforce as an application in Azure AD

Additionally, if you purchase Azure Premium, you get advanced features such as multi-factor authentication (MFA). With only a few clicks, you can greatly enhance the security of all systems using Azure AD by implementing MFA. This benefit applies to Exchange Online, SharePoint Online, Skype for Business, OneDrive for Business, Power BI, the administrator portals, and any third-party SaaS application you configured. MFA can even include on-premises applications you publish to Azure AD through the Azure AD Application Proxy (which will be discussed in Chapter 6, "Hybrid Office 365"). The Azure AD Application Proxy can securely publish to the internet that 10-year-old legacy, on-premises, web-based system that everyone is afraid to touch—and the Azure AD Application Proxy can do it without having to deploy Active Directory Federation Services or modifying the code. Figure 3-4 shows the options available in the Azure AD MFA configuration.

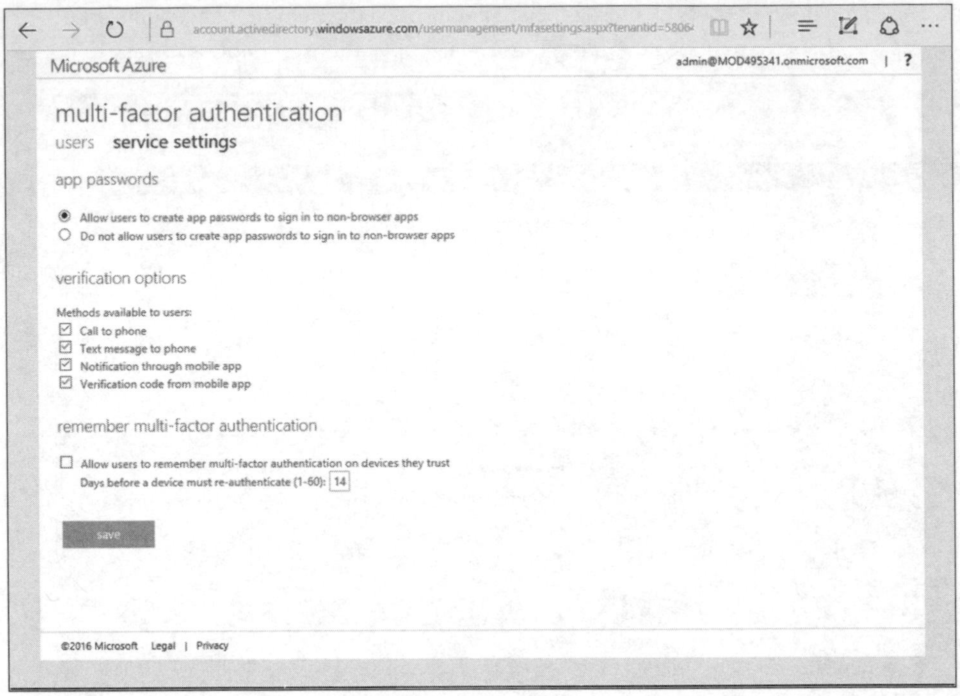

©2016 Microsoft   Legal | Privacy

FIGURE 3-4 Azure AD multi-factor authentication settings

Finally (and this list of services has not been exhaustive), Azure AD provides powerful capabilities around threat detection and reporting that is unavailable with on-premises Active Directory. The Azure AD service proactively watches for threats, both known and developing, and uses machine learning to determine whether or not your tenant (or individual users in your tenant) is under attack. If it sees that it is, it can take automatic actions to protect your tenant and your users.

Azure AD also provides you with useful reports that can help you manage your identities. (See Figure 3-5.) For example, there is a report that can identify sign-ins from multiple geographies, which might be an indication that an account has been hacked. Premium Azure AD subscribers receive additional reports, such as one that uses machine learning to determine irregular sign-in activities for individual users. All of this would be extremely difficult, if not impossible, for most companies to do through a traditional on-premises Active Directory instance.

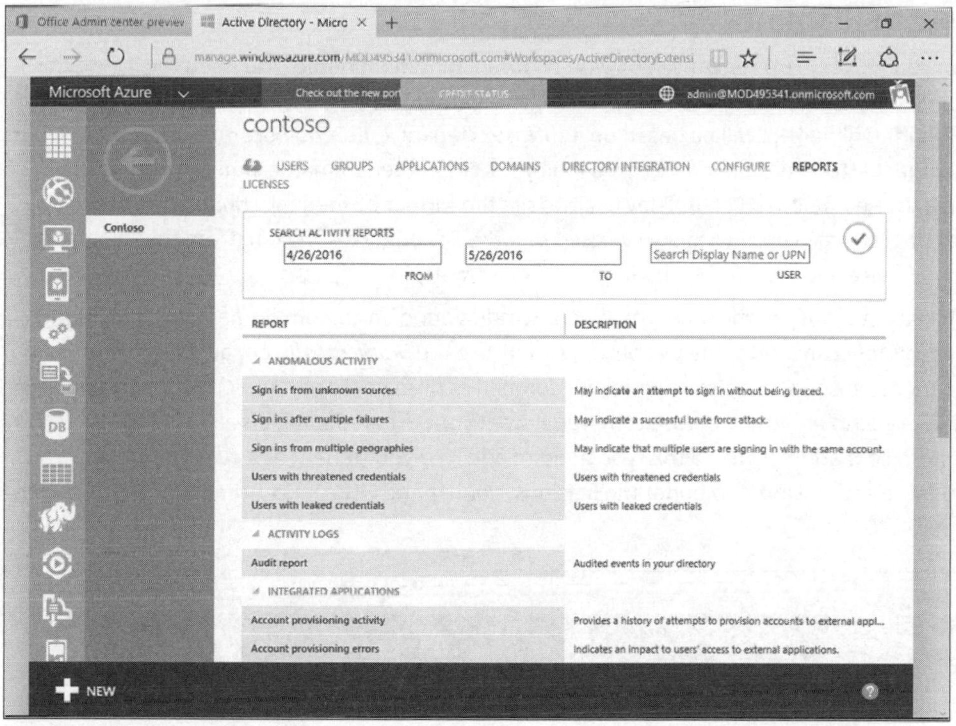

FIGURE 3-5 Azure AD reports

Azure Active Directory Domain Services

As we mentioned previously, when Azure AD first appeared, there was no concept of a computer object as there is in Active Directory. You were unable to join servers to Azure AD like you would with an on-premises Active Directory instance. In 2016, Microsoft added a new add-on service called *Azure Active Directory Domain Services (Azure AD DS)*. This subscription service enables Azure virtual machines (VMs) to join an Azure domain without needing to deploy a domain controller. This service is not used by Office 365, but it's good for you as a Cloud Pro to be aware of this capability in Azure AD.

When you sign up for Azure AD DS, Microsoft creates a domain that your Azure VMs can then join. Only Azure VMs can join the domain; it's not possible to join on-premises servers. Like Azure AD, it is a tenant service, so you do not have complete ownership of it. You cannot have domain administrator privileges, for example, and you're restricted in what you can do. However, it can be an excellent way to shift applications to Azure without having to configure and support a domain-controller infrastructure. Although you cannot set up a trust with your on-premises domains, you can use AD Connect to synchronize your domain to Azure AD. Once your domain is synced, you can then use your corporate credentials to access resources and services hosted in Azure VMs.

Custom domains

When you first sign up for Office 365, you choose your tenant name. You need to choose this well, because it will be the basis for some important things going forward. For example, your SharePoint Online URL will be based on it (*https://*<tenant>*.sharepoint.com*). You won't be able to change it after it has been set. This will be your default tenant name, and all users will be given a user name based on it. They're always in the format of <tenant>*.onmicrosoft.com*. In the examples we've used so far, we've used *mod495341.onmicrosoft.com* (from the Microsoft Demos service available to Microsoft partners and staff).

The vast majority of the time, you'll want to add your own custom domain name. Although you absolutely can (and some people do) simply use the *onmicrosoft.com* address, it will likely make more sense to associate it with your company's domain. For example, if your company is named Contoso and uses *contoso.com*, you'll want your users sending email using an *@contoso.com* address. To do this, you need to add it to your tenant as a custom domain. You do so by selecting Domains under the Settings menu in the Office 365 Admin Center, as shown in Figure 3-6.

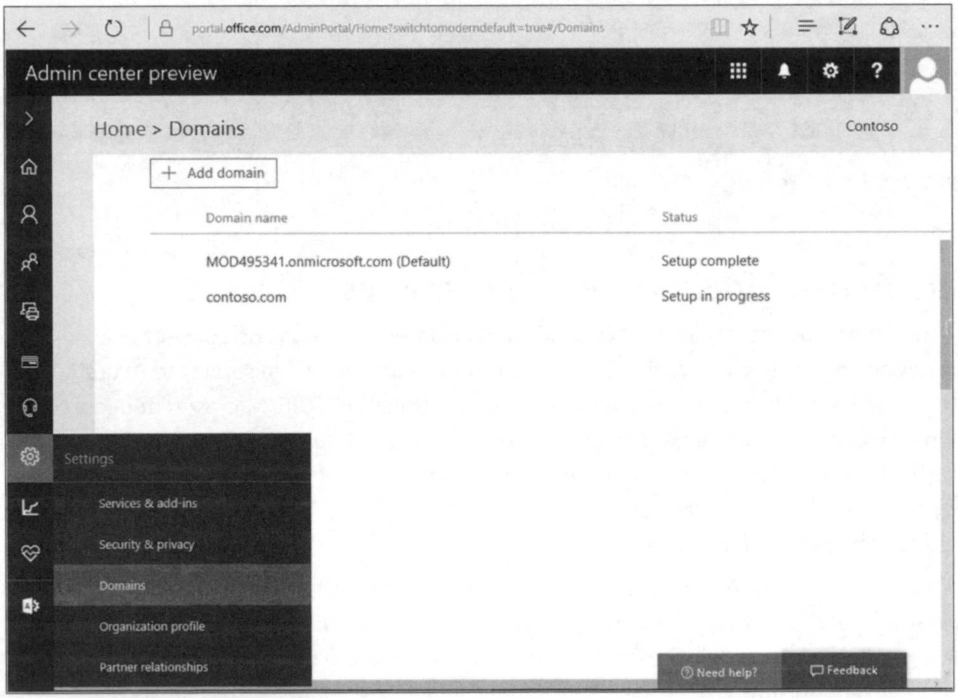

FIGURE 3-6 Accessing your Office 365 domains

To add a custom domain to Office 365, you must have ownership of it. You also have to verify that ownership. This means you must be able to add and modify DNS records for the domain at your domain registrar. The Add Domain Wizard in the Admin Center will tell you what you need to do to verify ownership.

In the following example, you'll see that we're adding *adatum.com* as a custom domain. To verify the domain, you need to create a TXT or MX record in your DNS. As shown in Figure 3-7, the wizard will tell you exactly what to add. (It will be different for each domain.) After you do this and give DNS a little time to propagate, click the Verify button.

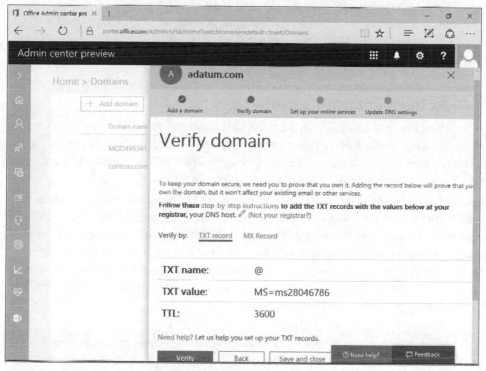

FIGURE 3-7 The Verify Domain page of the Add Domain Wizard

After Office 365 verifies the existence of the records in your registrar, it helps you set up the rest of the DNS records you need to support the various Office 365 services. If your domain is hosted with GoDaddy, Microsoft sets up the services automatically for you. If your domain is not hosted with GoDaddy, you can still choose to have Microsoft manage the DNS records. Don't do it, though, if you have a website registered under your DNS name.

We recommend that you choose the option to manually configure your DNS. If you choose this option, Microsoft gives you all the DNS records you need to add to support the Office 365 services. This includes records for email, Exchange Online, Skype for Business, and mobile device management (MDM). Once you get this list of records, add them to your DNS registrar to fully configure your custom domain for Office 365. Do not, however, change your MX record if you still need to keep your current email solution. You should wait to change the MX record until you're ready to migrate your email to Exchange Online.

Although adding a custom domain isn't necessary for most scenarios, it is required for implementing identity federation. This requirement exists because you must be able to add to the domain registrar a DNS record for the public endpoint of your AD FS proxy.

> **MORE INFO**   For more information about how to add a custom domain, see "Add your users and domains to Office 365" at *https://support.office.com/article/Add-your-users-and-domain-to-Office-365-6383f56d-3d09-4dcb-9b41-b5f5a5efd611*.

Azure Active Directory service tiers

There are three tiers available for Azure AD: Free, Basic, and Premium. The Free tier is exactly that: free. It is available in all Azure subscriptions, including Office 365. The Free tier will be sufficient for most users because it supports all the basic Office 365 workloads. The Basic and Premium tiers, though, add some powerful capabilities to your tenant.

One of these is the Azure AD Application Proxy (one of our favorites). You use this feature to install a little service on-premises through which you can securely publish your on-premises web-based applications (via Windows or Claims authentication)—all without opening an inbound port in the firewall. You can use all the features of Azure AD, such as MFA, with the published app. With Premium, you get the ability to do self-service password reset, change, and unblock, and have the updated password write back to your on-premises Active Directory. This alone can significantly reduce help-desk calls.

> **MORE INFO**   For more information on using Azure AD to securely access on-premises applications, see "How to provide secure remote access to on-premises applications" at *https://azure.microsoft.com/documentation/articles/active-directory-application-proxy-get-started*.

Figure 3-8 shows the current set of features available across the three tiers, as taken from *https://azure.microsoft.com/pricing/details/active-directory*. See that webpage for more details.

		FREE	BASIC	PREMIUM
Common Features	Directory Objects [1]	500,000 Object Limit	No Object Limit	No Object Limit
	User/Group Management (add/update/delete)/ User-based provisioning, Device registration	✓	✓	✓
	Single Sign-On (SSO)	10 apps per user[2] (pre-integrated SaaS and developer-integrated apps)	10 apps per user[2] (free tier + Application proxy apps)	No Limit (free, Basic tiers +Self-Service App Integration templates[3])
	Self-Service Password Change for cloud users	✓	✓	✓
	Connect (Sync engine that extends on-premises directories to Azure Active Directory)	✓	✓	✓
	Security/Usage Reports	3 Basic Reports	3 Basic Reports	Advanced Reports
Premium + Basic Features	Group-based access management/provisioning		✓	✓
	Self-Service Password Reset for cloud users		✓	✓
	Company Branding (Logon Pages/Access Panel customization)		✓	✓
	Application Proxy		✓	✓
	SLA		✓	✓
Premium Features	Self-Service Group and app Management/Self-Service application additions/ Dynamic Groups			✓
	Self-Service Password Reset/Change/Unlock with on-premises writeback			✓
	Multi-Factor Authentication (Cloud and On-premises (MFA Server))	...[2]	...[3]	✓
	Microsoft Identity Manager user CAL[4]			✓
	Cloud App Discovery			✓
	Connect Health			✓
	Automatic password rollover for group accounts			✓
Azure Active Directory Join – Windows 10 only features				
	Join a device to Azure AD, Desktop SSO, Microsoft Passport for Azure AD, Administrator Bitlocker recovery	✓	✓	✓
	MDM auto-enrolment, Self-Service Bitlocker recovery, Additional local administrators to Windows 10 devices via Azure AD Join			✓

FIGURE 3-8 Comparing Azure AD service tiers

At the time of this writing, the retail Basic license is $1 per user per month and the retail Premium license is $6 per user per month. If you own Enterprise Mobility Suite (EMS) licenses, you already have Azure AD Premium licenses. If not, you need to purchase a license for each user who will be using the extra features. If a user somehow receives a benefit from the feature, either directly or indirectly (such as being in a report), that user needs a license. Although you don't *necessarily* have to license every user, you likely will. Carefully consider what your users will be doing (or what will be done for or to them) when determining the number of licenses to purchase.

The Basic and Premium tiers are available through standard means: Microsoft Enterprise Agreement or Open Volume License. You can also purchase licenses through a Cloud Solution Provider partner. Perhaps the easiest way to purchase licenses, though, is to simply go through the Office 365 Admin Center. You'll find Basic and Premium licenses listed as "Microsoft Azure Active Directory Basic" and "Microsoft Azure Active Directory Premium." Previously, Azure AD Basic was not available for purchase online, but we're pleased that it is now an online option.

Identity scenarios

We talked about Azure AD and what it has to offer. Now, let's take the discussion a step back and talk about the broader subject of *identity*. It's a large and important subject, and it's one we'll only scratch the surface of. The topic is critical, though, to the rest of the chapter, and it's incredibly important to understand as a Cloud Pro. Although you're likely familiar with on-premises identities via Active Directory, and although you might have some experience with AD FS and Security Assertion Markup Language (SAML) identities, new identity models and single sign-on (SSO) will become very real, accessible, and needed in the cloud. Identity is what binds disparate cloud services together, and implementing it well can greatly improve the end-user experience.

Before we go further, it will be helpful to define "identity." An *identity* is an object that represents a user. It can also represent a device, application, or service that can act like a user. Typically, this object is registered and owned by a directory of some sort, but this doesn't have to be the case (such as with an anonymous user). An identity is usually associated with a name and a password to allow sign-in to digital systems. Identities are unique within their directories, and this uniqueness is usually ensured by a unique key (like a user principal name, GUID, or both). The directory is responsible for providing the means of authenticating the identity, and the digital system is responsible for associating the identity with a resource (authorization). In simplistic terms, just think of an identity as a user account.

Cloud-only identities

The first and simplest identity scenario in the cloud is *cloud-only identities*. This model resembles the one you're already familiar with on-premises. The concept applies to virtually any cloud service, but we'll narrow our focus to Azure AD. With cloud-only identities, users are given a user account in Azure AD. It is the directory of record for the identity. It has lots of properties related to it, such as the person's name, manager, email address, phone number, and other useful details. The difference, though, is that the identities exist only in the cloud.

When you sign up for Office 365 and create users, these are cloud-only identities. They are uniquely identified in Office 365 by the User Principal Name (UPN), which is used to sign in to Office 365. The default UPN is a <tenant>.onmicrosoft.com user name, but you can change it to your custom domain if you add one. Typically, the UPN will look like an email address (user-name@tenant.microsoft.com or username@contoso.com), but the UPN doesn't actually have to be the user's email address. It can be simpler and easier for users to work with if it is, though.

Any system that trusts Azure AD as an identity provider can use this identity to gain access. All of the Microsoft cloud trusts Azure AD, meaning you can use your Azure AD account to access any number of Microsoft cloud services. When you access SharePoint Online, for example, you do so using your Azure AD identity.

Again, in a cloud-only identity scenario, a user has an account only in the cloud. The user does not have an on-premises identity because that user might not be using Active Directory.

Synchronized identities

Most companies have an on-premises instance of Active Directory (or other directory). This Active Directory instance is usually the company's system of record for identities. When a company enables Office 365 for its users, it faces an identity dilemma. By default, Office 365 doesn't know anything about the company's on-premises implementation of Active Directory and doesn't allow users to sign in with their Active Directory account. Therefore, a company needs to create accounts in Office 365 for its users. As a result, users have two accounts to manage, including two passwords to memorize. The users will use their Active Directory account credentials on-premises and their Azure AD account in Office 365. This situation can be made even more confusing when the user signs in to both accounts using the same user name but then the passwords don't match.

Thankfully, this issue is not difficult to solve. You do so using *synchronized identities*. In this scenario, the on-premises Active Directory instance is still the master of identities, but a service runs to regularly push on-premises user data to Azure AD. All changes are made on-premises and the service, AD Connect, runs regularly to make sure Azure AD looks the same as the on-premises Active Directory. This synchronization process can include passwords. Technically, the passwords are not synchronized with Azure AD, just the password hashes. If you choose to include the password hash, your users will be able to sign in to both environments using what looks to them like the same credentials with the same password. Syncing the password hashes is not required, though, and you might have a policy that prohibits it. However, we highly recommend that password sync be implemented.

Note that this is not the same as single sign-on (SSO). It's frequently called *same sign-on*. With SSO, a single identity is used to access multiple systems. With same sign-on, although it might look like they're only using one identity, the user actually has two separate identities in two separate directories. The magic of synchronization, though, hides this reality from them. The drawbacks are that because there are two accounts, there technically can be additional maintenance and the potential for identity drift. Tools are available that can help you avoid these drawbacks. Unfortunately, we don't have the space in this book for a deep dive into the technical implications of same sign-on vs. SSO.

Federated identities

The next scenario involves *federated identities*. This is the single sign-on model you likely have heard much about. It is far and away the most complicated (and costly) model, but its coolness and utility is commensurate with that cost.

With federated identities, one directory trusts another one for authentication. More specifically, it trusts the tokens that the other one provides. We'll get to tokens in a moment. Although it's not an approach required in all federated identity scenarios, Office 365 layers the federated identity on top of synchronized identities. In its case, Office 365 has all the information about the user and is able to leverage that information to provide rich experiences when the user interacts with its various services.

The big difference between federated identities and synchronized identities with Office 365 is that Office 365 does not do the authentication. Instead, it relies on an external federated-identity provider to do the authentication. This provider most commonly is a customer's Active Directory Federation Service (AD FS), although third-party federation services are supported as well. Our focus is going to be on AD FS.

When an AD FS farm is deployed, it's connected to the on-premises Active Directory. When a user signs in to Office 365, instead of using the regular sign-in page, the user actually is redirected to the company's AD FS servers, where she then signs in. This user is signing in to the on-premises domain. The AD FS server then redirects the user back to Office 365, except this time it assigns a security token telling Office 365 that the user has successfully been authenticated. Because a trust has been established (technically, they both trust the same certificate that signs the token), Office 365 lets the user through to wherever she was trying to go. Office 365 has delegated the authentication to the on-premises Active Directory.

> **REAL WORLD**   Not everybody will be using AD FS with Office 365 for identity federation. At this time, Microsoft supports federation with 18 other federation providers in addition to AD FS. To see a list of list of these providers and a description of what support exists for clients, see the "Azure AD federation compatibility list" at *https://azure.microsoft.com/documentation/articles/active-directory-aadconnect-federation-compatibility*.

The security token that AD FS creates and sends to Office 365 is a short-lived cookie that is stored in the user's session. By default, the lifetime for an AD FS security token is 60 minutes long. This security token is actually an SAML token that makes certain claims about the user. A *claim* is a piece of information about the user, like the user's User Principal Name (UPN), name, and group membership. The receiving system takes a look at the token, verifies that it is signed by the correct certificate and, because it also trusts that certificate, allows the user into the system.

Think of the token as if it was a passport. To enter another country, you must provide proof of your identity. It must be in a specific format that countries will recognize as official. Before letting you into the country, the border official will ask you for your passport. The official checks to make sure it's valid and that you look like the picture on the passport. If everything checks out, the border official allows you into the country. If not, you're turned away and are unable to enter the country legally.

The process is depicted in Figure 3-9. In step 1, the border official stops you from reaching your destination. You've previously received your passport from your home government, as shown in step 2. In step 3, you present your password to the border official, who then lets you through.

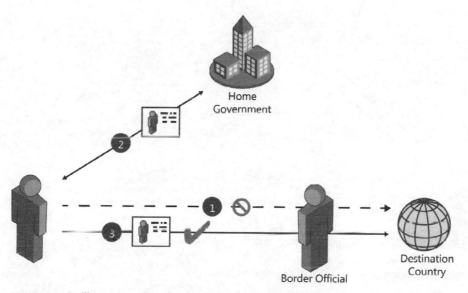

FIGURE 3-9 An illustration of border security requiring a passport

With identity federation and SAML claim-based authentication, the security token is like the passport. This is depicted in Figure 3-10.

The user asks to get a document in Office 365, just as a traveler asks to enter a country. Like the border official, Office 365 asks for proof of identity before it allows the transaction to occur (step 1). The user goes to AD FS to get the token (step 2), like the traveler in the previous illustration went to her government for a passport. AD FS authenticates the user against Active Directory (step 3). The user receives the token from AD FS (step 4), which is the equivalent to the passport, and presents it to Office 365 (step 5). Because Office 365 has been configured to trust the signature of the AD FS that issued it (just as the border official trusts the country that issued the passport), the security token is recognized as official. It then knows about the user based on the claims in the token, such as the user's name and UPN. Office 365 looks in Azure AD for the UPN (step 6), finds a match, associates the user's session with the Azure AD account, and gives the user access to the document (step 7).

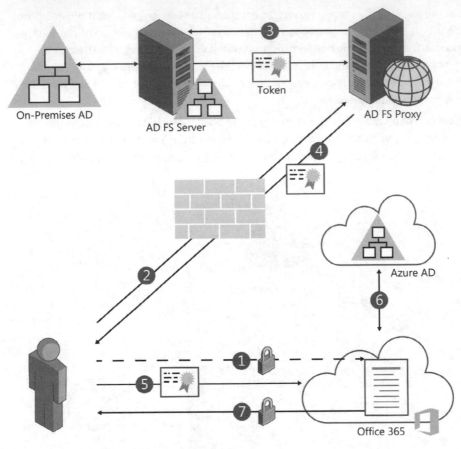

FIGURE 3-10 The federated-identity authorization process

So why bother? Why go through all that extra work, when you can just do identity sync? There are a number of good reasons to do the extra work, and Microsoft outlines some of them in the page "Determine which directory integration scenario to use" at *https://msdn.microsoft.com/library/azure/jj573649.aspx*. Table 3-1 is taken from that article.

TABLE 3-1 Decision matrix for password sync vs. single sign-on

I need to	Dirsync with Password sync	Dirsync with single sign-on
Sync new user, contact, and group accounts created in my on-premises Active Directory to the cloud automatically	Y	Y
Sync incremental updates made to existing accounts in my on-premises Active Directory to the cloud automatically	Y	Y
Set up my tenant for Office 365 hybrid scenarios	Y	Y
Enable my users to sign in and access cloud services using their on-premises password	Y	Y
Reduce password administration costs	Y	Y

I need to	Dirsync with Password sync	Dirsync with single sign-on
Control password policies from my on-premises Active Directory	Y	Y
Enable cloud-based multi-factor authentication solutions	Y	
Enable on-premises multi-factor authentication solutions		Y
Ensure user authentications occur in my on-premises Active Directory		Y
Implement single sign-on using corporate credentials		Y
Customize the user Sign-In page		Y
Limit access to cloud services based on the location, client type, or Exchange endpoint of the client		Y

Companies usually choose AD FS for four primary reasons:

- **Passwords are kept on-site**   Because users sign in to AD FS, which is on-site and controlled by the company, external systems don't need to have the users' passwords. Passwords stay within the firewall, which is considered safer. However, with Office 365 and Azure AD, the plain-text password itself is not actually synced, only the password hash.

- **AD FS can provide some additional authentication controls**   This approach might include an extra level of filtering, such as basing it on IP addresses. It can, for example, be used to prevent OneDrive for Business from syncing to noncorporate locations. It also can provide MFA, although Azure AD also can do it with Premium licenses.

- **AD FS can be a single-identity provider that can be used by many services, both on-premises services and services in the cloud**   Any system that is configured to trust AD FS identities can be accessed by a single log-on. With the token, the user potentially can sign in to hundreds of systems and services but only have to sign in once. This reason is often the primary one for choosing AD FS.

- **AD FS can be configured so that users don't have to sign in to Office 365 when they're using a domain-joined device**   Saving users from having to log on to Office 365 can reduce friction and increase productivity.

If you want to implement federated identities, you need to deploy at least one AD FS server and at least one AD FS Proxy server, although you'll likely want two of each to prevent a single point of failure. The AD FS Proxy will often live in your perimeter network because it will require inbound connectivity from the internet. If you already have an AD FS infrastructure in place, you can take advantage of this investment and use it with Office 365. If you do not, AD Connect can easily deploy everything you need through a simple interface. You also need to configure identity sync using AD Connect. Some companies who configure federation choose not to sync the password hashes. This will be especially true for companies with a policy requiring passwords to stay on-premises.

REAL WORLD If you don't have a policy to keep all passwords on-premises and are looking to implement federation, we highly recommend including the password hash when you
configure identity sync. Because federation introduces a dependency on the on-premises
AD FS system, if that system goes down, users will be unable to sign in to Office 365. If the
password hash is synced, you could turn off federation temporarily (or even permanently)
and there will be less of an impact on the users. Otherwise, you'll have to assign new passwords to all users if you decide to turn off federation. Including the password hash with your
sync is a good tool to have in your back pocket.

Identity sync with Azure Active Directory Connect

We mentioned Azure Active Directory Connect (AD Connect) multiple times, and now it's time
to start diving in. Our goal in this section is to equip you to understand the product so that you
can make the important design and configuration decisions needed for your organization. You
need to build it right the first time and then make sure it runs well.

MORE INFO For details on how to actually install and configure AD Connect, see "Set
up directory synchronization for Office 365," at *https://support.office.com/article/Set-up-
directory-synchronization-for-Office-365-1b3b5318-6977-42ed-b5c7-96fa74b08846*, and
"Custom installation of Azure AD Connect," at *https://azure.microsoft.com/documentation/
articles/active-directory-aadconnect-get-started-custom*.

Azure AD Connect overview

Azure AD Connect is the third generation of tools Microsoft has given us to sync identities
with Azure AD. The first one was simply called the Directory Synchronization tool, or DirSync.
Although that tool is still supported, DirSync is not released individually anymore. However,
because it had such a great impact, you'll still hear the synchronization process referred to as
"DirSync" even though AD Connect is being used. After DirSync, Microsoft released Azure AD
Sync, or AAD Sync. Although that's still supported, like DirSync, AAD Sync is no longer being
updated and will be retired. Both are being deprecated, and support ends on April 13, 2017.

In place of these two tools, Microsoft released AD Connect, which incorporates elements of
both and adds some significant capabilities. The most significant component AD Connect adds
is a wizard that can deploy, and integrate with, an AD FS farm for federated identities. Excellent.

AD Connect is a standalone service you install on a machine in your organization that will act
as the middleman between your on-premises Active Directory and Azure AD. It will regularly
read from Active Directory and synchronize users, groups, contacts, distribution lists, and other
items with Azure AD. If AD Connect is enabled and you have Azure AD Premium licenses, it can

synchronize passwords from Azure AD back to the on-premises Active Directory. AD Connect also can be used to deploy an AD FS farm to support federated identities. AD FS can be quite complicated to deploy, but AD Connect makes it simple through an easy-to-use wizard interface. Finally, it also provides a means to monitor the health of your sync and AD FS. AD Connect Health tracks usage and prevents critical issues from occurring. AD Connect Health is a Premium feature, though.

If you already have an AD FS farm deployed that you'd like to use, you can still use AD Connect. If it's a Windows 2012 R2 AD FS farm, you can integrate it with AD FS. If the farm is AD FS 2.0, you need to hook up the federation manually.

> **MORE INFO**   For an extremely good reference for AD Connect and an index of related material, see the following articles:
>
> - "Integrating your on-premises identities with Azure Active Directory" at *https:// azure.microsoft.com/documentation/articles/active-directory-aadconnect*
> - "Azure AD Connect sync: Understand and customize synchronization" at *https:// azure.microsoft.com/documentation/articles/active-directory-aadconnectsync- whatis*

Before you deploy AD Connect, you need to understand some important concepts and be aware of key decisions that need to be made. The default settings provided in the tool should be sufficient for most organizations. The tool even includes an Express Settings option that deploys a full sync of all the needed attributes for a single forest, including the password hashes. Before you choose this option, though, make sure you read through the design choices in the next section to ensure that it's a good option for you. If you have a more complicated environment, such as you do when you have multiple Active Directory forests or multiple Office 365 tenants, make sure you review the topology options to understand which are supported.

Design choices

When designing your AD Connect deployment, there are four primary factors to consider. The first factor is your *sourceAnchor*, which uniquely identifies each object. The second is the *userPrincipalName*, which is what a user will use to sign in. The third factor is deciding what to do if your on-premises Active Directory contains a nonroutable domain (like contoso.local). The final factor is related to considerations about the availability of the AD Connect service.

Choosing the right sourceAnchor

If you're familiar with the concepts of relational databases and lookup tables, then think of the sourceAnchor as the primary key for your sync. The sourceAnchor is a single attribute that will be *immutable* for the lifetime of the object, and it's used to uniquely identify an object in both

Active Directory and Azure AD. It's used by the sync to tie the two objects together and, as such, the sourceAnchor must never change.

By default, objectGUID is used, and it's perfect for most environments. However, if you have multiple Active Directory forests and you need to move objects between them, objectGUID is not going to be a good choice. Even if you have a single forest, if you think there's a good chance that your company will be merged with another in the future, you might want to consider another attribute as well. It's important that you choose an attribute that will not change. No, email is not a good option, because some people in the organization might change their names.

You need to be sure to get the sourceAnchor correct the first time you set up AD Connect because it cannot be changed. Make sure you record which attribute you use because you will need to select it again if it becomes necessary to redeploy AD Connect. Ensure that it's recorded as part of your disaster-recovery processes.

> **MORE INFO**   For a thorough treatment of the sourceAnchor, see Paul Williams' blog
> "Windows Azure Active Directory Connector part 3: immutable ID" at *https://blog.msresource*
> *.net/2014/03/10/windows-azure-active-directory-connector-part-3-immutable-id.*

Choosing the right User Principal Name

An early decision to make is how you want your users to sign in to Office 365. Do you want them to use the same login they use to sign in to their computer? Their email address? Do you want them to use AD FS and single sign-on? The answers to these questions dictate what the User Principal Name (UPN) should be in Azure AD.

The UPN is like the sourceAnchor in that it uniquely identifies a user. However, unlike the sourceAnchor, it doesn't have to be immutable and users will need to know it. The UPN is what the users will enter when they sign in, and it comes in the form of *[username]@[domain]*, such as *brian.smith@contoso.com* or *brian.smith@contoso.onmicrosoft.com*. Although it looks like an email address, it does not have to be. Regardless, the UPN must be based on a domain name that is internet-routable.

> **MORE INFO**   For more information about the sign-on options and their impact, see "Azure
> AD Connect User Sign on options" at *https://azure.microsoft.com/documentation/articles/*
> *active-directory-aadconnect-user-signin.*

Each user in your on-premises Active Directory implementation has a UPN. It is what your users use when they sign in to their work computers. By far, it is best if the UPN chosen for Azure AD matches the user's on-premises UPN. If for whatever reason this is not a good option (such as if the on-premises domain is not routable), you have the option of choosing something else instead of the UPN. This is known as an *alternate login ID*. You can set this up in the Azure AD Sign-In Configuration page, shown in Figure 3-11, by changing the value of the User Principal Name. Using an alternate login ID can let you choose something like the email address instead of the UPN.

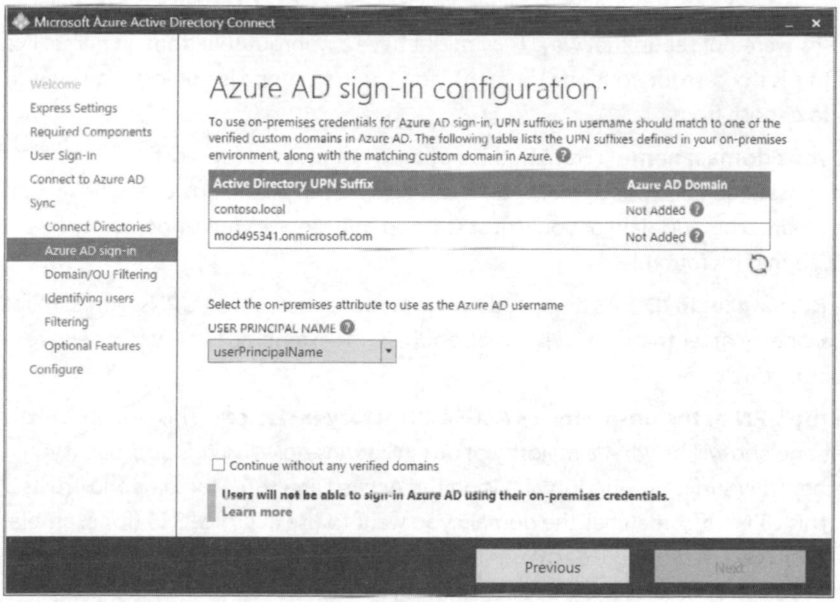

FIGURE 3-11 Azure AD Sign-In Configuration page in AD Connect

CAUTION Before you choose to use an alternate login ID, understand that it's not compatible with all Office 365 scenarios. The issues are primarily related to Exchange Online hybrid deployments. Also, the Azure AD Application Proxy (a feature available in the Basic and Premium tiers) requires the UPN from Active Directory, so don't select an alternate login ID if you expect to use this feature. Although Microsoft might solve the issues over time, it's by no means a certainty. We recommend you read the following resources if you're considering an alternate login ID:

- "Configuring Alternate Login ID" at *https://technet.microsoft.com/library/dn659436. aspx*
- Joe Palarchio's blog "Office 365 – The Limitations of Alternate Login ID" at *http:// blogs.perficient.com/microsoft/2015/02/office-365-the-limitations-of-alternate- login-id*

Dealing with a nonroutable domain

For users to sign in to Office 365, they must use a login ID that is associated with a domain registered and validated with Office 365. This ID can be either the default <tenant>.*onmicrosoft.com* domain or a custom domain (like *contoso.com*). For a lot of companies, their Active Directory domains were not set up that way. They might have a nonroutable domain name, like *contoso.local*. If this is the case for your environment, don't worry—hope is not lost. You have several options to choose from:

- **Change your domain name**   Frankly, this option is not realistic for most organizations. Changing your domain name can be a nightmare. If, however, you're about to create a new domain or you're just starting one, now is your opportunity to change it so that it's routable.

- **Use an alternate login ID**   As discussed earlier in the section about UPNs, you can opt to use a property other than the UPN (email address, for example). However, be aware of the risks if you do so.

- **Change the UPN of the on-premises Active Directory instance**   This option is likely your best one and will be what a majority of organizations do. With this approach, you add another UPN suffix to your domain using the Active Directory Domains and Trusts snap-in. This UPN suffix matches the domain you want to use in Office 365 (for example, *contoso.com*). Next, you update each user to use the new suffix. Although you can do it manually, you can update all users at once using the Windows PowerShell Set-ADUser cmdlet.

> **MORE INFO**   For more information about assigning a new UPN suffix, see "How to prepare a non-routable domain (such as .local domain) for directory synchronization" at *https://support.office.com/article/How-to-prepare-a-non-routable-domain-such-as-local-domain-for-directory-synchronization-e7968303-c234-46c4-b8b0-b5c93c6d57a7*.

- **Do nothing**   Technically, you do not have to address the issue at all. If not, users will just be synced using the *default @<tenant>.onmicrosoft.com*. Although the sync will work, expect that some Office 365 scenarios may not work as expected, such as SharePoint hybrid. You also will not be able to use single sign-on with AD FS.

You can change the UPN at a future time. However, doing so is complicated and will affect your users, so it's best to choose wisely up front.

Availability

As a Cloud Pro, you know that it's important that services remain available. It's imperative that you give your users no reason to balk at adopting cloud technologies. As such, we would be remiss if we did not touch on the topic of high availability for AD Connect.

Unfortunately, you don't have the options for high availability for AD Connect that you do with most of Microsoft's current server technology. You're limited to running only a single instance of the sync for a given tenant. There are, however, several ways to work around this limitation to maximize uptime:

- **Make SQL Server highly available**   By default, AD Connect will install and use SQL Server 2012 Express LocalDB to host its databases. However, you can use a full-featured remote SQL Server instance instead. You can then configure that server for high availability using standard means, such as SQL Server AlwaysOn Availability Groups or Failover Clustering.

- **Deploy a stand-by server in Staging Mode**   One of the options you have in the AD Connect Wizard is to place the server in Staging Mode. With it, the server can be fully set up for sync, except that the sync is not actually performed. As a result, a second or third AD Connect instance could be set up (such as at a disaster-recovery location) in Staging Mode and kept prepared for action. If the active instance is lost or needs to be taken offline, you simply run through the wizard on the second server to take it out of Staging Mode.

- **Take advantage of virtualization**   Most, if not all, modern virtualization providers have a way to move a virtual machine between hosts, either manually or automatically (such as if there is a physical hardware failure). By simply deploying AD Connect in a virtual machine on such a system, you have a means of moving the service to another host should there be an outage of the physical host.

- **Rebuild**   Deploying and configuring AD Connect is quite quick and simple. As long as the settings chosen have been documented (especially the sourceAnchor and UPN), it might be just as easy to redeploy onto a new server. Correctly setting the sourceAnchor allows the sync to reconnect to existing objects and pick up where the last one left off.

> **MORE INFO**   For more information about these availability strategies, see "Azure AD Connect sync: Operational tasks and consideration [sic]" at *https://azure.microsoft.com/documentation/articles/active-directory-aadconnectsync-operations*.

Topologies

Before you configure anything, you need to evaluate your Active Directory and Office 365 tenants to decide on a suitable topology. There are specific topologies Microsoft supports and some that are not supported. The general rule is you can have only one AD Connect instance per Office 365 tenant. We do not have the space to go into each topology in detail, but if anything below raises a red flag, make sure to review "Topologies for Azure AD Connect" at *https://azure.microsoft.com/documentation/articles/active-directory-aadconnect-topologies*.

Supported topologies

The following topologies are supported by Microsoft:

- **A single forest synchronizing through one AD Connect server to a single Azure AD directory**   This scenario is your simplest and most likely. Express Settings in the wizard supports this topology.

- **Multiple forests synchronizing through one AD Connect server to a single Azure AD directory**   Note that the AD Connect server does not need to be domain joined. It just needs to be able to communicate with the domain.

- **Multiple forests synchronizing to multiple Azure AD directories, each with their own AD Connect server.**

- **A single forest synchronizing with multiple Azure AD directories through multiple AD Connect servers**   In this topology, an object can exist in only one Azure AD directory, so careful filtering must be implemented in each AD Connect instance.

- **Any of the other topologies in this list with one AD Connect server and one or more staging servers**   Adding an AD Connect server in Staging Mode can provide increased availability for the service.

Unsupported topologies

The following topologies are not supported by Microsoft:

- **Single or multiple forests synchronizing through multiple AD Connect instances to the same Azure AD directory**   An Azure AD tenant can work with only one AD Connect instance.

- **One object synchronizing to multiple Azure AD directories**   An object can be synchronized to only one Azure AD directory at a time.

Prepare for sync

After you figure out the architecture of your sync, you need to prepare to implement it. You'll want to verify you can connect to Office 365 and run some scans. You also need to make sure your on-premises Active Directory objects are clean and ready to be synced.

Validate health and connectivity

Obviously, if you're unable to connect to Office 365, you won't be able to sync with it. Your Active Directory must also be healthy. The easiest way to do a simple validation of your environment is by running the health, readiness, and connectivity checks from the server that will host AD Connect. To run these checks, launch a wizard from the AD Connect server by either going to *https://portal.office.com/tools* or walking through the Directory Synchronization Wizard (which is launched from the Users page). The wizard will install the Microsoft Office 365 Support Assistant, which will perform the checks. It will tell you if there are any issues to resolve.

Chapter 1, "Getting started as an Office 365 Cloud Pro," discusses networking and connectivity, and it provides some additional information on validating and preparing connectivity. It might be a good idea to go back and review this material.

Clean up your Active Directory

If your environment is like most organizations, your Active Directory has been around for many years and has seen many changes. It has likely built up all kinds of cruft. There might be dark, dimly lit recesses of your Active Directory that haven't been reviewed in years. For the synchronization to work, you need to make sure your Active Directory is as clean as possible.

For many Office 365 projects, this cleanup is often the most time-consuming and difficult part. This cleanup includes making sure that each synchronized user has a unique email address in the *proxyAttribute* attribute, has a valid and unique User Principal Name, and ideally has correct demographic information (such as their name, department, title, and office information). You also want to ensure each user doesn't have any invalid characters in the synced attributes. If the domain is configured with a nonroutable name, now is the time to address that issue. All of this can be a daunting task.

> **MORE INFO**   For more information about what's involved in preparing the domain for sync, see "Prepare to provision users through directory synchronization to Office 365" at *https:// support.office.com/article/Prepare-to-provision-users-through-directory-synchronization-to-Office-365-01920974-9e6f-4331-a370-13aea4e82b3e.*

Thankfully, Microsoft provides you with a tool to make all of this easier: *IdFix*. This little tool scans your Active Directory and reports any problem it finds. (See Figure 3-12.) Beware—the first time you run it, the results can be quite overwhelming. IdFix makes the cleanup work easier by automatically suggesting fixes to the objects. You can even make the changes right there in the tool. Although you don't have to run IdFix before you sync, doing so will save you from repeatedly fixing failed syncs. Usually, the process is an iterative one in which you keep chipping away at the list of errors until none are found. When IdFix comes back clean, it's time to go ahead with the sync.

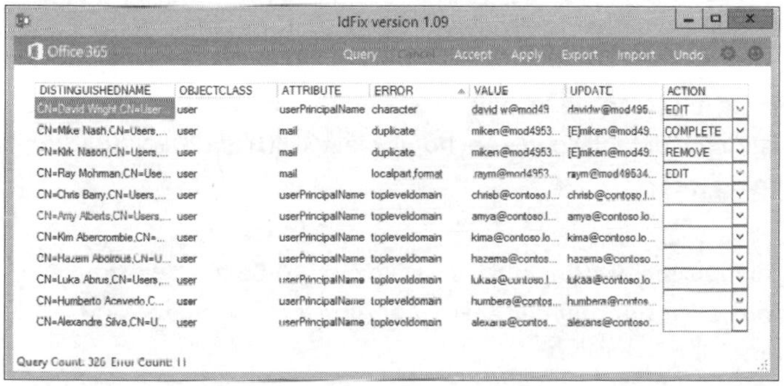

FIGURE 3-12 The IdFix tool

As you can see in Figure 3-12, the IdFix tool found 326 items in the directory and 11 errors. The vast majority of these errors are related to a nonroutable domain (*contoso.local*) being used in the *userPrincipalName* field. David Wright's UPN has a space, so we're accepting the edit the IdFix tool suggested. You also can see that two users have the same email address. We've told the tool to keep it for Mike but remove it for Kirk. Finally, Ray Mohman's email address begins with a period. We removed it and told IdFix that we edited the field.

> **MORE INFO**   For more information about IdFix, see "Install and run the Office 365 IdFix tool" at *https://support.office.com/article/Install-and-run-the-Office-365-IdFix-tool-f4bd2439-3e41-4169-99f6-3fabdfa326ac*.

Deploying AD Connect

After you resolve all the issues found in your Active Directory, decide on the sourceAnchor and UPN, and set up your custom domain setup (if needed), it's finally time to deploy AD Connect. Although you can install it on a domain controller, it would be best to install it on its own server. AD Connect is lightweight and doesn't require many resources. If you're looking to do a small deployment, the server can double-up as an AD FS server (although just make sure you size the machine appropriately). We highly recommend you deploy on Windows Server 2012 R2, especially if you want to use AD FS.

There are great resources online that will walk you through all the details. It's all wizard-driven, so it's actually quite simple. Again, see "Set up directory synchronization for Office 365," at *https://support.office.com/article/Set-up-directory-synchronization-for-Office-365-1b3b5318-6977-42ed-b5c7-96fa74b08846*, and "Custom installation of Azure AD Connect," at *https://azure.microsoft.com/en-us/documentation/articles/active-directory-aadconnect-get-started-custom*, for information on installing Azure AD Connect.

> **MORE INFO**   To download Azure AD Connect, go to *https://www.microsoft.com/download/details.aspx?id=47594*.

The first thing you need to decide is whether to do an express or custom install. You can choose Use Express Settings if you have a simple Active Directory deployment and are planning to use all the defaults. Use it if you have a single forest, you want to sync all users and all attributes, and you want to keep the default sourceAnchor (objectGUID) and UPN (*userPrincipalName*). It will set up everything for you.

> **MORE INFO**   For more information, see "Getting started with Azure AD Connect using express settings" at *https://azure.microsoft.com/documentation/articles/active-directory-aadconnect-get-started-express*.

However, if you're like us and you like to have a little more control, select Customize on the first page of the wizard. Even if you decide to keep all the defaults, it can be good to see what your options are. With a customized deployment you can do the following:

- Specify a custom installation location (such as on a data drive).

- Use an already-existing SQL Server instance (if you want high availability or greater control).

- Use an existing service account (which is not really recommended unless you're using a proxy that requires authentication or you're using an existing SQL Server instance).

- Define custom local sync groups (but it's unlikely you'll want to).

- Choose to deploy AD FS. If you do so, there will be another section of the wizard that will walk you through deploying AD FS, including specifying AD FS and AD FS Proxy servers. Deploying AD FS has never been easier.

- Add multiple Active Directory directories. (No domain trusts needed.)

- Specify the User Principal Name (either *userPrincipalName* or an alternate ID—but again, beware of doing so).

- Configure which Active Directory organizational units (OUs) to sync.

- Specify the sourceAnchor and, if users are in multiple domains, what identifies a user as unique.

- Specify a security group that contains the list of users to sync. This action is really meant only for pilot deployments, not for production.

- Specify which attributes to include in the sync. The wizard does so on a per-Office-365-application basis. If, for example, you know you're never going to use Skype for Business, you can avoid syncing the attributes it needs.

- If it's available with your licensing option, enable password or device writeback.

- If you chose AD FS as the sign-in method, specify whether or not to sync the password hashes (to act as a fallback in case AD FS isn't working or needed).

- If Exchange is deployed in the domain, specify whether or not to configure Exchange hybrid mailboxes or Office 365 Groups writeback.

- Choose additional attributes in the sync. A primary use case relates to user profiles in SharePoint Online. You can map Azure AD properties to user property fields (either existing or new ones) for use in such things as SharePoint customizations and SharePoint Audiencing. An example of this is an employee ID. Attributes can also be used for dynamic group membership.

- Place the server in or out of Staging Mode.

Note that you can run the wizard any time. You can use it to change settings, such as deploying AD FS, adding AD FS servers, switching the authentication method, adding attributes, and working with Staging Mode.

MORE INFO   For an excellent resource on installation using customized settings, see "Custom installation of Azure AD Connect" at *https://azure.microsoft.com/documentation/articles/active-directory-aadconnect-get-started-custom*.

Running a sync

In previous tools, the syncs were scheduled using Windows Task Scheduler or a separate Windows service. Beginning with version 1.1 of the tool, AD Connect includes a scheduler that can be customized, removing the need for external sync methods. By default, the sync runs every 30 minutes, but you can change this to the frequency you need. You cannot, however, schedule the sync to run more often than what Azure allows. This limit can be determined by running the Get-ADSyncScheduler cmdlet and reviewing the *AllowedSyncCycleInterval* property. The results of the cmdlet are shown in Figure 3-13.

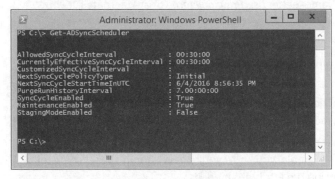

FIGURE 3-13 Results of Get-ADSyncScheduler

If for some reason you can't wait for the next sync (the time of which is displayed in the *NextSyncCycleStartInUTC* property) and you need to start a sync, you can do so by running the following PowerShell command:

```
Start-ADSyncSyncCycle -PolicyType Delta
```

This starts a delta sync, but if you need to do a full sync, change the *PolicyType* to *Initial*. You can also stop a sync by running the Stop-ADSyncSyncCycle cmdlet. It finishes its current connection and then stops.

MORE INFO   Learn more about the scheduler by visiting "Azure AD Connect sync: Scheduler" at *https://azure.microsoft.com/documentation/articles/active-directory-aadconnectsync-feature-scheduler*.

Configuring identity federation with Office 365

At this point, we've implemented identity sync using AD Connect, pushing our on-premises user information into Azure AD and Office 365. This might be sufficient for most companies, especially because it's free (or nearly so). As discussed previously, we have another identity option available: federated identities.

Again, federated identities give users a secure, single-sign-on experience by using a trusted external identity system that authenticates the user and issues a token that systems use to sign in the user. This is most commonly done with AD FS, which is deployed on-premises. In this section, we'll talk about how to configure identity federation with Office 365 using AD FS.

A brief intro to Active Directory Federation Services

We already talked a bit about AD FS, and we walked through an example scenario of a user needing a document in Office 365. With AD FS, you have one or more AD FS servers. These are the heart of the system, and they're what users log in to and what hands off the secure token. AD FS can be used to provide single sign-on to services (like Office 365) using SAML tokens or Windows Integrated authentication using Kerberos-constrained delegation. To do the latter, the AD FS server must be in the same domain as the service or in a domain with a trust.

When a user requests access to a system configured for AD FS, that system redirects the user to a page on the AD FS server. The user then enters his credentials and AD FS attempts to log the user into the domain. If the login is successful, AD FS creates a token signed by a trusted certificate, adds the token to the user's session, and redirects the user back to the system. At this point, the system sees that the session now has the token and, because it also trusts the same certificate that signed the token, grants access to the user. As long as the user has the token and the token hasn't expired, the user can then use that same token and sign on to other services that trust that same AD FS system. The user needs to sign in only once instead of once per system (hence, *single sign-on*). If the user is coming from a domain-joined machine and other settings are correct, that initial sign-on is done for the user automatically. He can go straight to Office 365, for example, without having to enter his credentials.

When using AD FS on-premises, you can generally stop with just the AD FS server. Actually, it's highly recommended that you deploy at least two (behind a load balancer) for redundancy. If, though, you want to use AD FS to authenticate users to systems from the internet, you need to go a step further. It's important to protect your AD FS servers as you would a domain controller, so you don't want to expose them directly to the internet. Instead, you deploy one or more AD FS Proxy servers in your perimeter network (also known as DMZ, for demilitarized zone). These servers protect the AD FS servers from direct access and channel appropriate requests to them. As with the AD FS servers, you'll probably want at least two for redundancy (also behind a load balancer).

This latter configuration with AD FS Proxy servers is what's recommended for use with Office 365. With it, you configure an entry in your public DNS that points users to the AD FS Proxy (or load-balanced endpoint).

In the example topology shown next, we use *fs.contoso.com* as the DNS name, and it points to the IP address on the load balancer, which is exposed in the perimeter firewall on port 443. The internal DNS also has an entry for *fs.contoso.com*, but because we want users to go directly to AD FS and not have to go out to the internet and back in through the proxies, we point the record directly to the load balancer in front of the AD FS servers. Both internal and public DNS records have the same name, *fs.contoso.com*, but they each point to a different IP address. This configuration is what's called *split-brained DNS*, and it's primarily used to optimize performance for internal users.

Figure 3-14 is an example of a typical, redundant AD FS topology we recommend.

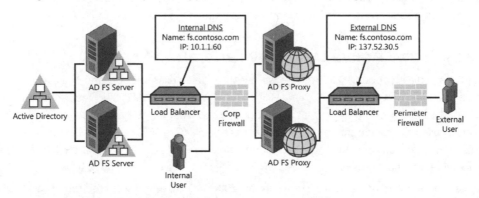

FIGURE 3-14 A typical AD FS topology

Deploying AD FS for Office 365

Unfortunately, once again, we do not have the space to go into detail about how to deploy AD FS for Office 365. If you are able to deploy AD FS on Windows Server 2012 R2 servers, you can use AD Connect to configure the servers. It will, however, still be up to you to provide any load-balancing and firewall configurations you might need. You'll also need an SSL certificate from a third-party provider (like VeriSign or DigiCert) that includes the DNS name of the AD FS Proxy endpoint (such as *fs.contoso.com*). The domain should be at the 2008 functional level or higher.

If you have access to Windows Server 2012 R2 servers for the deployment, AD Connect can deploy most of this infrastructure for you in a simple wizard. You need to have the PFX certificate ready for the wizard or already installed on the servers. Then you simply give it the name of the AD FS servers and proxies and tell it which custom domain to configure for federation. The wizard does the rest.

> **MORE INFO** For more details on how to do this, see the "Configuring federation with AD FS" section of "Custom installation of Azure AD Connect" at *https://azure.microsoft.com/ documentation/articles/active-directory-aadconnect-get-started-custom/#configuring-federation-with-ad-fs*.

MORE INFO   For more information about AD FS on Windows Server 2012 R2, see the "AD FS Design Guide in Windows Server 2012 R2" at *https://technet.microsoft.com/library/dn554245%28v=ws.11%29.aspx*.

If you already have an existing AD FS farm, don't worry—you can use it instead of deploying a new one. If you don't already have an extranet scenario with AD FS Proxies accessible from the internet, plan on adding this capability as part of the rollout. If the existing AD FS farm is running Windows Server 2012 R2, you can integrate it with AD Connect using the wizard. (Choose "Use an existing Windows Server 2012 R2 AD FS farm.") If, however, it's an AD FS 2.0 farm (Windows 2008 or 2008 R2), you won't be able to use AD Connect to configure federation. Instead, you must manually configure the federation from the AD FS server using PowerShell cmdlets.

MORE INFO   For more information about AD FS 2.0 on Windows 2008 or 2008 R2, see the "AD FS 2.0 Design Guide" at *https://technet.microsoft.com/library/dd807036(ws.10).aspx*.

Configuring Office 365 for federation

After the AD FS farm and its proxies have been fully configured, the last step is to configure Office 365 for federation. Nonfederated domains are called *managed* or *standard*. You can configure individual domains as either federated or managed. Both can exist in the same tenant side by side, and you can even have multiple domains each federated with different AD FS farms. The important thing, though, is that you verify the custom domain before you attempt to federate it. You will not be able to configure federation on a nonverified domain.

If you deployed AD FS using Windows Server 2012 R2, you can simply use AD Connect and select Federation With AD FS as the sign-in method. (See Figure 3-15.) The wizard will walk you through the rest and configure Azure AD for you.

FIGURE 3-15 The User Sign-In page of the AD Connect wizard

If you're using an AD FS 2.0 farm, you need to convert the domain manually via PowerShell. You can do this from an elevated PowerShell console either on the primary AD FS server or from another machine. Before doing so, make sure the Azure AD PowerShell module and the Microsoft Online Services Sign-In Assistant have been installed. If you're running the commands somewhere other than on the primary AD FS server, you first need to connect to the AD FS server by using the Set-MsolADFSContext cmdlet, giving it the name of the primary AD FS server. You will be prompted for administrator credentials. This command isn't needed if you're on the AD FS server:

```
Set-MsolADFSContext -Computer Win2008ADFS01.contoso.com
```

In the same PowerShell session, use the Convert-MsolDomainToFederated cmdlet to convert the domain. The *DomainName* parameter specifies the domain to be converted. If your Azure AD tenant needs to support federation with more than one domain, it's important to use the *SupportMultipleDomain* switch each time. If, for example, you need to federate two domains, use the *SupportMultipleDomain* switch with each of the Convert-MsolDomainToFederated commands:

```
Convert-MsolDomainToFederated -DomainName "contoso.com" -SupportMultipleDomain
Convert-MsolDomainToFederated -DomainName "adatum.com" -SupportMultipleDomain
```

Notice that the cmdlet doesn't have a parameter specifying the AD FS farm or its sign-in URL. This is because either we are on the AD FS server when we run it or we used the Set-MsolADFSContext cmdlet to connect to the AD FS server. The cmdlet reads the AD FS configuration and configures the relying party trusts for us. Pretty nice!

Once this is done, the domain should now be configured for federation with our AD FS farm. Test it out by attempting to sign in to Office 365 using a federated account. Either you should be able to sign directly into Office 365 using your currently signed-in credential or you should be redirected to your AD FS sign-in page. If after signing in you are successfully signed in to Office 365, you have successfully configured federation. Congratulations!

We recommend you consider doing one last optional thing: include the password hash in the sync. With AD FS, you do not need to sync the password hash. It's more secure. However, if you include the password hash, you have a contingency plan in case you need to temporarily disable (or fully remove) federation. Otherwise, you'll have to generate new passwords for all your users and distribute them. That certainly would not be a pleasant day. After your federation is complete, simply go back into the AD Connect Wizard, choose the Customize Synchronization Options task, and ensure that Password Synchronization is selected on the Optional Features page. With luck, you'll never need to use it, but it's good to have it as a backup if needed.

> **REAL WORLD** Most organizations would like to pilot a technology before they decide to adopt it. If you're just getting started with federation, implementing this strategy isn't a challenge. However, it's not simple to pilot federation if the domain is already being synced with Office 365. This is because the Convert-MsolDomainToFederated cmdlet converts all users in the domain to federated. You cannot convert just a subset of users.
>
> To pilot federation, you need to register a new, separate domain in Office 365 and go through the whole sync and AD FS process. Yes, this means provisioning a new certificate. From a high level, the process looks like this:
>
> 1. Register and verify the new domain.
>
> 2. Obtain a certificate for the new domain.
>
> 3. Remove the users' Office 365 licenses before making the switch to ensure the UPN change is synced (or use *Set-MsolDirSyncFeature -Feature SynchronizeUpnForManage-dUsers-Enable $True* to enable UPN changes while licensed).
>
> 4. In the local Active Directory, add the new domain as a UPN suffix and switch the pilot users to that suffix.
>
> 5. Configure AD FS for federation using that domain.
>
> 6. After the users have been synced with the pilot domain and AD FS has been configured, use Convert-MsolDomainToFederated to convert the pilot domain.
>
> After the pilot is complete, you need to undo all that work to bring the users back to their original UPNs. As you can see, this process involves a lot of work. If you haven't yet implemented directory sync and you're looking to deploy AD FS, we recommend that you do your federation proof of concept at the beginning, before all your users have been onboarded to Office 365.

Switching back to managed identities

After you convert to federated identities, you might find it necessary to switch the domain back to managed or standard. You might do this permanently if you no longer want to use federated identities, or you might need to do this temporarily if your AD FS infrastructure is offline.

The process to do it is simple, but the method you use to do it depends on whether or not the AD FS server is available. If you're doing it because of an AD FS failure, chances are that it won't be available. If you're going to make the switch, keep in mind that it can take up to two hours for it to take effect. Chances are, though, it won't take that long, but plan for it in your decisions and timing for the conversion. The more users you have, the longer it will take.

If your AD Connect is online and it was integrated with your Windows Server 2012 R2 AD FS farm, your easiest choice is to use the wizard to change the sign-in from Federation With AD FS to Password Sync. AD Connect should take care of it for you.

If your AD FS server is available, you can use the Convert-MsolDomainToStandard cmdlet. This is the preferred method. As mentioned earlier, either run it from the AD FS server or use Set-MsolADFSContext first to connect to the AD FS server. You need to supply the *PasswordFile* parameter and give it the path to a file that will be created (for example, C:\Temp\Passwords.txt).

If password sync is operational, the passwords will be overwritten and you won't need to care about this file. (It's still required, though.) However, if you aren't syncing your passwords, you need to distribute the passwords in this file to your users. You also need to use the correct *SkipUserConversion* parameter. If you're permanently moving away from federated identities, this value should be *$false*. A value of *$false* converts all the users to managed identities. If, however, this is a temporary conversion, make sure the value is *$true*.

The following command permanently converts the *contoso.com* domain from federated to managed:

```
Convert-MsolDomainToStandard -DomainName contoso.com -SkipUserConversion $false
-PasswordFile C:\Temp\Passwords.txt
```

If your AD FS server is not available, you can't use the Convert-MsolDomainToStandard cmdlet. Instead, you need to use Set-MsolDomainAuthentication. For example:

```
Set-MsolDomainAuthentication -DomainName contoso.com -Authentication Managed
```

When AD FS is available again, either switch the sign-in method in AD Connect or run Convert-MsolDomainToFederated:

```
Convert-MsolDomainToFederated -DomainName contoso.com
```

CHAPTER 4

SharePoint Online administration and configuration

Microsoft SharePoint Online contains three distinct management roles: Developer, Business Pro (Biz Pro), and Cloud Pro. Developers primarily create custom solutions in Microsoft Visual Studio, enhancing and extending the native platform. They solve problems with code. Biz Pros understand the business first; they're responsible for managing the content and processes. They often create lists, libraries, forms, and workflows that automate and modernize a single business process. Developers and Biz Pros are necessary for performing a successful SharePoint Online implementation.

This chapter, however, focuses on the role of the Cloud Pro. Cloud Pros are responsible for managing the platform, services, site collections, Microsoft Azure Active Directory (Azure AD), and hybrid features. Additionally, Cloud Pros usually are the professionals who make bulk changes and complex modifications via Microsoft Windows PowerShell.

This chapter begins with an overview of the SharePoint Online architecture, which serves as a foundation to learning the concepts in the rest of the chapter. Whether you're a new SharePoint professional or you've used it for many years, this chapter will help differentiate between SharePoint Server on-premises implementations and SharePoint Online. We also discuss update channels, configuration, and search management (from a Cloud Pro's perspective).

SharePoint Online architecture

SharePoint Online is similar to its cousin, SharePoint Server 2016 on-premises, but it differs from that version in many ways. Although there's much feature parity, there's also plenty of uniqueness. Why? Because the platforms serve two different purposes—one is built for multitenancy in the cloud, and the other is built for greater flexibility in a full-control server farm. Microsoft's vision is to keep much of the user experience the same between the two versions while leveraging the advantages of each. Note that an on-premises farm can be provisioned in Azure Infrastructure as a Service (Azure IaaS), so you can have a cloud implementation of SharePoint with full control and flexibility.

> **MORE INFO** Office 365 features are constantly evolving, thus affecting parts of the SharePoint Online architecture. For more information on the Office 365 Roadmap, see *http://fasttrack.microsoft.com/roadmap.*

The differences in SharePoint Online and SharePoint Server on-premises are constantly shifting and evolving, so be sure to validate your known platform differences before performing any new configuration or major project update. Table 4-1 lists major differences between the platforms as of the writing of this book.

TABLE 4-1 Differences between SharePoint Online and SharePoint Server on-premises

Native SharePoint Online	SharePoint Server on-premises
Video Portal	Configuration Database Access
Delve	Complete service application control
Power BI	Full trust code
Admin center	Web Application User Policies
Pay as you go	Farm servers administration
Mobile integration	Control over patching and updates
Rights management	Complete control over migration and upgrades
Data Loss Prevention (DLP)	Control over physical storage location
Maintenance-free patching and updates	

You'll quickly notice that challenges are often the flipside of this benefits/challenges coin. For example, you can't fully manage web applications in SharePoint Online, but the flipside of this is that you don't have the complexity, disaster recovery, or Continuity of Operations (CooP) challenges of managing web applications because Microsoft hosts the service for you. There are many examples of this, so before deciding against SharePoint Online features for control reasons, or changing the default behavior, make sure you aren't missing the positives of the service or breaking the very things that make SharePoint Online appealing.

SharePoint Online vs. SharePoint Server on-premises

As introduced in Table 4-1, several services exist only in SharePoint Online and not in its on-premises counterpart. Be aware that these services are constantly changing. As of the time this book was written, here are some key examples and descriptions:

- **Power BI**   This service can be leveraged with SharePoint Server on-premises, but it isn't as easily integrated. Power BI transforms your data into rich dashboards and visuals so that you can analyze and organize data. Although you'll find it much easier to start building Power BI solutions with data in SharePoint Online, Power BI integration with on-premises data sources is certainly possible and makes data easy to visualize. In SharePoint Online, you need only a license to immediately start using the service.

- **Delve**   This service connects all your cloud services via Office Graph. Development is under way to extend this capability to on-premises services, but it's limited as of this writing. With SharePoint Online, Delve becomes the home for your personal view of SharePoint Online, CRM, Exchange Online, Skype for Business, and more. The underlying smart-learning engine, Office Graph, stores and recalls recent documents, emails, attachments, people, projects, and work, as shown in Figure 4-1.

FIGURE 4-1 Delve provides rich analytics about your data and those connected to you

- **Video Portal**   This is a new feature that leverages Azure Media Services within SharePoint Online. Video Portal is a compelling feature of SharePoint Online that provides a multichannel, drag-and-drop, video service. It's easy to consume from SharePoint Online webpages. Apps for mobile devices are available that further enhance the user experience.

Some services can be integrated into an on-premises implementation, but doing that requires a significant amount of infrastructure and administration resources. In SharePoint

Online, the following items basically are turnkey solutions that take much less time and fewer resources to implement than the on-premises equivalents:

- **Data Loss Prevention (DLP)**   This service is available on-premises in SharePoint Server 2016 but requires additional configuration beyond what it takes in SharePoint Online. DLP provides a centralized console to report about and take action on high-risk data. Examples of such data are Social Security numbers, credit card numbers, and corporate intellectual property. Many templates come with the product, and you also can create your own, custom policy templates.

- **Information Rights Management (IRM)**   In SharePoint Online, rights management is based on Azure Rights Management. When using IRM on-premises, you must have an Active Directory Rights Management Server infrastructure built. That is not a simple proposition for most organizations. Even though the cloud and on-premises products are largely the same today, the future will bring many changes that will enhance Azure Rights Management well beyond the capabilities of its on-premises counterpart.

- **Mobile Device Management (MDM)**   In SharePoint Online, you leverage Microsoft's cloud version of Windows Intune. You can set access-control policies that ensure the protection of data on mobile devices. For example, you can limit email and Microsoft iOS applications from synchronizing on a device without a passcode or on one that is jail-broken. Many MDM features are included in the base Office 365 license. If you want to manage Windows tablets and desktop devices, you need to purchase additional licenses. However, doing so is much easier than building and managing an on-premises MDM solution.

- **Office Online Server**   This service is available to implement on-premises, but doing that takes a significant amount of computing power and the service can be difficult to configure and manage. Why does it use so much computer power? Because Office Online Server must completely render multiple applications like Word and PowerPoint. It's quickly becoming a mandatory package for Microsoft server products. When using SharePoint Online, Office Online Server is always on from the moment you create your tenant. It enables multi-user editing, tight integration with OneDrive for Business, and features that were once served by Excel Services.

> **MORE INFO**   For more information on compliance tools and configuration, see Chapter 8, "Managing governance, security, and compliance."

Last, there are many third-party products that have both SharePoint Online and SharePoint Server on-premises offerings but might provide different features. Why? Third-party products often vary because Microsoft has different levels of extensibility in platforms along with different feature availability in SharePoint Online versus SharePoint Server on-premises. As a result, many third-party vendors don't have identical cloud and on-premises products. When purchasing or migrating your third-party products, be sure to test your required features and ensure they're available in the Office 365 version. This is a learning point for the modern Cloud Pro—you must be vigilant in spotting the differences between cloud and on-premises platforms, including customizations and third-party products!

SharePoint Online architecture 101

SharePoint Online is similar to SharePoint Server on-premises at the core. It includes site collections (SPSites), subsites (SPWeb), and service applications that connect the SPSite silos across a tenant. The major difference is that you don't manage the servers, databases, power, HVAC, Internet Information Services (IIS) sites, or web applications.

In the early days, we used to have little control over service applications in SharePoint Online, and this was a barrier to entry for many organizations. But now we're getting increasing access to the management of SharePoint service applications, such as Search and the Managed Metadata Service (MMS), as the product evolves. Don't assume the platform limitations of yesterday will still exist tomorrow.

For a quick overview, Figure 4-2 shows only the SharePoint Online architecture in Office 365.

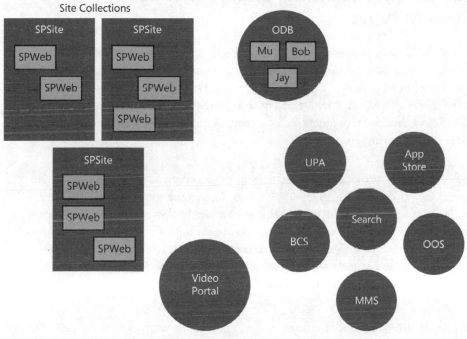

FIGURE 4-2 The SharePoint Online environment consists of many technologies under a single umbrella.

However, a big part of taking on the Cloud Pro role in Office 365 is understanding how all SharePoint sites, SharePoint service applications, and other Office 365 products interact.

As you can see in Figure 4-3, Office 365 has many moving parts. You don't need to know how to completely manage all Office 365 services, but you do need to understand what settings affect SharePoint Online. Many tenant-level settings will be discussed in the next section, which deals with configuring SharePoint Online.

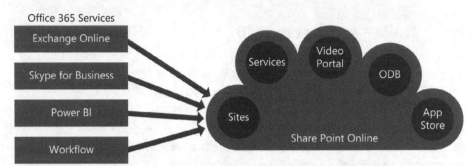

FIGURE 4-3 Office 365 services that interact and integrate with SharePoint Online.

Understanding licensing, update channels, and tenant types

Depending on licensing, update channels, and your tenant type, the organizational and end-user experience will vary greatly. Updates are important to how your organization evolves in its use of SharePoint Online, as well as to determining how you manage user expectations and promote user adoption of SharePoint Online. License types enable features such as Power BI, Project Online, Azure Rights Management, DLP, and MDM. New features are usually released in the Enterprise version first, with government versions coming after that.

> **NOTE** If you decide to not preview certain features, you might find that some dependent features stop working. A good example is Power BI. If you decline the preview in Power BI, users can no longer use Excel Services to view and edit workbooks that rely on Power BI. In that case, users can still use standard Excel Services features. This is an important change for many IT pros. Building and keeping a spreadsheet of features is important for a Cloud Pro. A good start is using classic Enterprise Architecture techniques, such as those found at *https://msdn.microsoft.com/library/bb466232.aspx.*

Government Office 365 versions usually require certification with government policies and might take months longer to release a feature than SharePoint updates for commercial tenants. Not all features are available in all regions; check with your Microsoft sales representative for available features. Government Office 365 data centers are hosted within a nation's borders and have specialized security, both technical controls and physical controls, and new features take time to test and validate. Further, there are multiple government tenant types, depending on country, location, and need. This book is aimed at the commercial and education tenant types. If you're a Cloud Pro for a government tenant, you need to build and update a spreadsheet with your available features, release dates, and feature-governance decisions by executive stakeholders.

REAL WORLD   Releasing features into a production tenant is a possible usability and security risk. Cloud Pros don't generally assume risk; you define risk. It's your job to define what the pros and cons are of features and to let the executive stakeholders make the final decision on when they are released and the breadth of their general availability to users. Be aware of this, however; you cannot refuse releases into the tenant—you can only delay feature releases for testing purposes by opting out of First Release in your production tenant.

As an example, the following URL describes update channels and the availability for Office 365 ProPlus: *https://technet.microsoft.com/library/mt455210.aspx*. The Message Center displays all planned releases, updates, fixes, and issues relevant to your specific tenant. Detailed plans are included as well. You can get to the Message Center by going to *http://go.microsoft.com/fwlink/p/?LinkID=402336*. As it is with every page in SharePoint Online, you must first be authenticated and have the appropriate privileges before viewing content. Next, if you're making production-level decisions for your tenant, be sure you're viewing your production tenant or that you're in an identically configured test tenant.

NOTE   The tenant you use for software development and testing should be licensed identically to your production environment.

Configuring SharePoint Online

When you first create a new Office 365 tenant, SharePoint Online is not provisioned, as you can see in Figure 4-4. It might take some time for Office 365 services to appear. Your users will not be able to access services, nor will your administrators be able to administrate services until you assign them roles, which is a process that's also described in Figure 4-4.

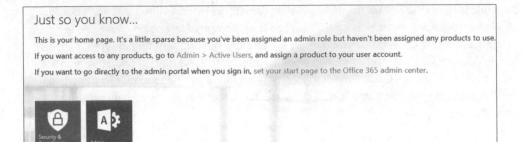

Just so you know...

This is your home page. It's a little sparse because you've been assigned an admin role but haven't been assigned any products to use.

If you want access to any products, go to Admin > Active Users, and assign a product to your user account.

If you want to go directly to the admin portal when you sign in, set your start page to the Office 365 admin center.

FIGURE 4-4 SharePoint Online is not provisioned when the tenant is created.

Provisioning SharePoint Online

For on-premises SharePoint versions, discussing the provisioning process took several chapters. For SharePoint Online, it's much simpler. First, you need to provision a new Office 365 tenant. The details for doing this can change over time, so the best place to start your tenant provisioning is at *https://products.office.com*. After you create a tenant, you select Admin from the app launcher. Many in the industry call the app launcher the *waffle*. Figure 4-5 shows an example of a tenant during the provisioning sequence.

> **MORE INFO** For more information on provisioning SharePoint Online, see *Microsoft SharePoint Online for Office 365: Administering and configuring for the cloud* by Bill English (Microsoft Press, 2015).

FIGURE 4-5 When creating a new tenant, it might take several minutes for services to be provisioned.

When you enter the Admin Center on a new tenant, you might not immediately see services at the bottom left, where the product-specific Admin Centers are listed; either those services are still provisioning or you have not purchased a license for that product.

Configuring

The first noticeable difference in managing SharePoint Online is the graphical administrative interface. In an on-premises installation, you often use Central Administration. When using Central Administration, you can directly manage the configuration database and other service databases. However, in Office 365 you are a tenant in a shared (yet, controlled) space. Thus, you have a focused view of configuration settings.

SharePoint Online is similar to living in a high-rise apartment. You have shared infrastructure such as plumbing, parking, air conditioning, fire suppression, stairways, and elevators. Yet, you still have your own place and can do most anything you want within your space. However, there are rules you have to follow because some changes affect all tenants. In SharePoint Online, you are a tenant and have control over your "apartment." You even have some control over your utilities, such as the User Profile Service Application and Search.

> **NOTE** This chapter assumes you're using the advanced Admin Center experience found at SharePoint Admin Center, Settings, Admin Center Experience.

While we were writing this book, Microsoft released a second-generation administrative interface that makes configuring things in SharePoint Online more intuitive. Figure 4-6 shows an example of the new, advanced administrative interface. It makes navigation easier, and it's also easier to use on touch devices.

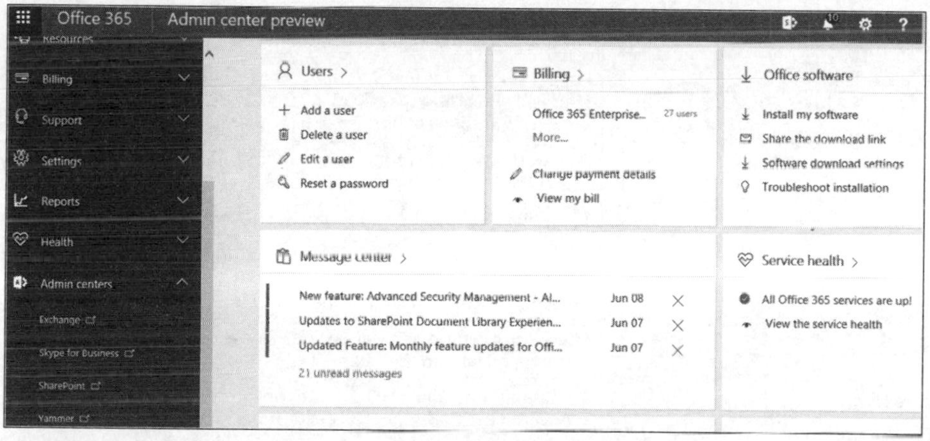

FIGURE 4-6 The new Administrative UI makes it easier to find information and to use on touch devices.

When you first browse to your Office 365 tenant (*https://portal.office.com*), you'll be taken to the tenant Admin Center. At the bottom of the left navigation menu, as shown in Figure 4-6, you'll see a menu item named Admin Centers. Upon expanding that menu item, you'll see several product-specific Admin Centers, which vary depending on your licensing. The Admin Center shown in Figure 4-6 is the tenant Admin Center. Most of this chapter will be spent in the SharePoint Admin Center.

> **NOTE** Some settings in the tenant Admin Center affect the configuration of SharePoint Online, such as External Sharing. Using that example, if External Sharing is not enabled in the tenant, you cannot configure External Sharing in the SharePoint Online Admin Center.

Upon entering the SharePoint Admin Center, you'll see several configuration menus as described in Table 4-2.

TABLE 4-2 SharePoint Admin Center configuration options

Configuration Option	Description
Site Collections	The default page when entering SharePoint Admin Center. You can manage site collections from the Site Collection tab (which looks like a Ribbon UI). Managing site collections is covered in multiple sections later in this chapter.
InfoPath	For basic management of InfoPath browser forms.
User Profiles	For detailed management of user profiles, My Sites (OneDrive for Business), profile properties, user property mappings, and links published to client applications. This section is covered in Chapter 7, "Social capabilities, Office Groups, and apps."
BCS (Business Connectivity Services)	Outside the scope of this book, this service is commonly used to connect to data sources external to SharePoint Online, whether they are part of SharePoint Server on-premises or other online services.
Term Store (Managed Metadata Service)	The management interface for your noun taxonomy, which is covered in greater detail later in this chapter.
Records Management	For managing the location of your Records Management centers.
Search	For access to the significant search capabilities of SharePoint Online. This setting takes you into an extensive search and indexing configuration section. Search is covered later in this chapter.
Secure Store	A shared utility for storing and mapping credentials. It's primarily used with BCS.
Apps	For managing installed apps and the governance of your app installation policy.
Sharing	For managing the sharing of content outside of your Azure AD. This topic is covered later in the chapter.
Settings	SharePoint Online general settings. These settings are covered in more detail later in this chapter.
Configure Hybrid	For configuring SharePoint Server on-premises hybrid. This topic is covered in Chapter 6, "Hybrid Office 365."

These options are likely to change over time, but they provide you with a starting place to learn how to configure SharePoint Online. Note that Office 365 Groups, Yammer, and External Sharing all have configuration options elsewhere in the tenant, yet they integrate with SharePoint Online. Likewise, components such as Azure Active Directory can be managed externally and separately from SharePoint Online, thus providing greater control and features than those surfaced in SharePoint Online. Other prime examples of this are Azure Rights Management and the Compliance Center.

Configuration checklist

There are many items you need to deliberately configure in SharePoint Online. Many of these settings have a default that can be easily overlooked and possibly be incorrect for your requirements.

If you go to Tenant Admin, SharePoint Admin Center, and click the Settings tab, you'll find a largely disconnected configuration page reminiscent of the Farm Settings in on-premises SharePoint Server. As features and products get added and evolve, this page will continually change—welcome to a new world! Prominent features and products get their own tab and, therefore, are not included here. Table 4-3 shows the options on the Settings page at the time this book was written.

TABLE 4-3 SharePoint Admin Center Settings page

Item	Options
Show or Hide Options (OneDrive for Business and Sites)	Show and Hide
Site Collection Storage Management	Automatic and Manual
UI experience (ODB, SharePoint List and Libraries, Admin Center)	Classic Experience and New Experience (Note: several options offer this choice. This will continually change as new features are updated within the platform.)
OneDrive Sync button	Hide and Show (Note: This changes the OneDrive for Business sync button and does not affect OneDrive Personal.)
Admin Center Experience	Simple and Advanced (Note: If you're reading this book, you should use the Advanced options.)
Office Graph	Allow Access and Don't Allow Access
Enterprise Social Service	Use Yammer.com and Use SharePoint NewsFeed
Streaming Video Service	Enable or Disable video through Azure media services and Enable The Video Portal. (Note: Most users will want to enable this compelling feature of SharePoint Online. This feature is described in more detail later in this chapter.)

Item	Options
Global Experience Version Settings	Allow Creation Of Old Version Site Collections (SPSites), Allow Creation Of Both Old and New Versions, or Prevent Creation Of Old Version Site Collections. Old Version Site Collections refers to a past release of SharePoint Online that changed the UI and branding.
Information Rights Management (Azure Rights Management)	Use The IRM Service Specified For Your Configuration or Do Not Use IRM For This Tenant. (Important: To use IRM in SharePoint Online, you must have first configured it in Tenant Administration, Settings, Services & Add-ins, Microsoft Azure Rights Management.)
Start a Site	Show or Hide A Link For Users To Create Team Sites. (Note: "Sites" refers to "SPWebs" and not SPSites.)
Custom Script	Allow or Prevent Users From Running Scripts On Personal Sites (OneDrive for Business) and Self-created Sites. (Note: This option is an example of where configuration options can be found in multiple locations. This option is for ODB but is found in SharePoint Online settings.)
Preview Features	Enable or Disable Preview Features (Note: Preview features have limited support and likely do not meet all Office 365 service requirements. Do not use preview features for business-critical processes.)
Connected Services	As services are introduced into Office 365, this section will contain options for blocking those services.
Access apps	Enable or Disable Office Access Services Apps

This book is not intended to show you how to configure every setting in SharePoint Online—it's about how to change your way of thinking to that of a Cloud Pro. TechNet contains rich information about many items discussed in this chapter. The following section discusses cloud-specific changes and provides examples of those changes in SharePoint technologies.

Site Collection administration

This section discusses the configuration of both site collections and subsites. Because of the common confusion with these terms, we'll mostly use the object-model terms *SPSite* (when referring to a site collection) and SPWeb (when referring to a subsite). Those are the terms SharePoint developers understand, and using them disambiguates architectural conversations. However, Microsoft uses the terms *site collection* and *site* interchangeably throughout the product.

Table 4-4 shows the correlation between UI names and object-model names. The terms can be confusing, but they're a must-know for Cloud Pros and they readily identify the object type. Many things, such as features, can be set in either place, but one is set on the SPSite container and another on the SPWeb within the container.

TABLE 4-4 User interface to object-model name correlation

User Interface	Object Model
Site Collection	SPSite
Site	SPWeb
Root Web	SPWeb
Root Site	SPWeb
Subsite	SPWeb
Subweb	SPWeb

Also, note that the root web is the SPWeb at the root of the SPSite. All other subsites are also SPWebs, called *subwebs*, under that root SPWeb. Many IT professionals also refer to the root web as the *root site*; they are one and the same. Much of the site collection configuration is the same as SharePoint Server on-premises inside the SPSite container, so most of those actions are omitted in this Cloud Pro book.

Figure 4-7 shows an example of an SPSite architecture.

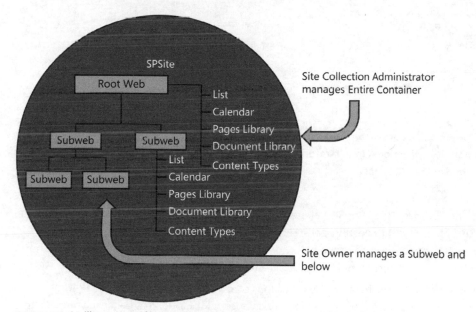

FIGURE 4-7 An illustration of how the site collection is a structured, hierarchal group of SPWebs.

As seen in Figure 4-7, all sites are in the hierarchy beneath the root web. Permissions, content types, columns, branding, and other items, depending on license and configuration, are inherited from this root web. However, this fact does not equate to a site owner in the root web also being a site collection administrator. The site owner of the root web cannot manage site collection settings (SPSite settings), but can only site settings (SPWeb settings).

A site collection administrator manages the entire container and everything within it. A site owner manages an SPWeb and subwebs of that hierarchy. Figure 4-8 shows the common differences in the roles of Site Collection Administrator and Site Owner, as seen in a Site Collection site settings menu. The items in the Settings menu differs based on your license type and provisioned features. To see the different roles, authenticate to SharePoint Online as a site collection administrator and then browse to Settings, Site Settings. In Figure 4-8, "Site Administration" equates to a Site Owner role.

Site Administration	Site Collection Administration
Regional settings	Recycle bin
Language settings	Search Result Sources
Site libraries and lists	Search Result Types
User alerts	Search Query Rules
RSS	Search Schema
Sites and workspaces	Search Settings
Workflow settings	Search Configuration Import
Site Closure and Deletion	Search Configuration Export
Site output cache	Site collection features
Term store management	Site hierarchy
Popularity Trends	Search engine optimization settings
Content and structure	Site collection navigation
Manage catalog connections	Site collection audit settings
Content and structure logs	Audit log reports
Site variation settings	Portal site connection
Translation Status	Content Type Policy Templates
	Storage Metrics

FIGURE 4-8 Site Owner vs. Site Collection Administrator

NOTE If you do not see the Site Collection Administration group as shown in Figure 4-8, you lack Site Collection Administrator permissions or are in a subweb. Site collections are managed at the root web.

Lists and libraries are part of SPWebs, and SPWebs are contained in SPSites. It's reminiscent of the Russian matryoshka nesting dolls. However, although SPSites do have features and settings that control and change the behavior of SPWebs contained within them, they do not directly host lists and document libraries. Lists and libraries are always in SPWebs.

Beneath the root web, there can be thousands of SPWebs, with thousands of SPWebs beneath them. This is an important architectural concept for Cloud Pros because you need to keep this in mind when authoring PowerShell scripts, managing permissions, and providing information-architecture guidance.

One of the more important permissions-administration facts to know is that SPWeb inheritance begins at the root web, and not at the SPSite level. By default, all subwebs inherit permissions from the root web. What is not obvious is that site collection administrators are effectively site owners in all SPWebs. Site collection administrators will not show up as users in the SPWeb until they have accessed the site for the first time. This nuance is a challenge for many new Office 365 Cloud Pros. At first glance, the permissions model seems quite easy to understand. Please do not mistake it for a simple folder-share-type permission structure—it's not. Likewise, when adding Active Directory groups to SharePoint groups, users will not show up as individual users until they access the site for the first time. This is why the auditing capability is important to understand. This feature is described in more detail in Chapter 8.

You can change inheritance at the SPWeb level, also referred to as *breaking inheritance*, and site owners can do this without the approval of the site collection administrator. As a SharePoint Online Cloud Pro, the following are permissions challenges to be aware of:

- When finding an object with broken permissions, you cannot easily find the SPWeb, library, or list where permissions were broken.

- It's difficult to identify whether a user has access via an Active Directory group or directly assigned permissions.

- It's not easy to identify unauthorized policy changes by a site owner, such as content types, features, site columns, and SPWeb-level permissions management.

Site Collection user permissions

Site collection users are managed in much the same way as they are in SharePoint Server on-premises. Site groups are still used to manage groups of users with similar privileges. Security trimming prevents users from being presented with links to content they don't have access to. There are two ways to control access to objects in SharePoint Online:

- Permissions can be specified for a group, and then users can be given those permissions by being added to the group. Permissions Inheritance then applies the group permissions to the objects in the site.

- Objects can have their own permissions collections, which can be managed independently. For example, the permissions for a list can be managed independently of the permissions for the site in which it is contained. This allows for more granular management of objects. At its most granular level, this is called *item-level permissions*.

Site collection administrators and site owners

Site collection administrators are initially assigned when a site collection is created. There must always be at least one site collection administrator, and this account cannot be an Active Directory group. For reasons such as dealing with unused site confirmations and enabling administration in the event that the administrator leaves, it's always best to define at least two site collection administrators. Site collection administrators can be managed from the Site Collection Administrator tab in the SharePoint Admin Center. Highlight the site collection you want to modify, select the Owners option in the ribbon, and select Manage Administrators. Note that the Owners option is for an SPSite, not an SPWeb, as is usual with the term "owner." Site Collection administrators also can be set by selecting Site Collection Administrators in Site Settings in the root web.

People and groups

Groups are collections of individual users that are given the same permissions on a particular site. SharePoint Online sites are created with three basic security groups by default:

- **Owners**   Full control
- **Members**   Can contribute to existing lists and libraries
- **Visitors**   Read only

Create a custom site group

To create a custom site group, follow these steps:

1. From the site where you want to create a new group, click the Site Actions menu and choose Site Settings.
2. In the Users And Permissions section of the Site Settings page, click the Site Permissions link.
3. On the Site Permissions page, on the management Ribbon, choose Create Group.
4. On the Create Group page, in the Name And About Me Description section, type a name for the group and (optionally) a description of the purpose for the group.
5. In the Owner section, specify the group owner.
6. In the Group Settings section, specify who can view and edit group membership.
7. In the Membership Requests section, specify whether to allow requests to join or leave the group.
8. Also specify whether to auto-accept requests.

> **IMPORTANT**   If you specify that requests should be auto-accepted, users will be automatically added to the group and granted the permissions specified for the group.

9. Optionally, if requests are allowed, specify an email address where requests should be sent.
10. Click Create to create the new group.

View group permissions

Sometimes you need to determine what permissions a specific group has across the entire site collection. This can be achieved in the following way:

1. From the Site Actions menu, choose Site Permissions.
2. Click the name of the group for which you want to view permissions.
3. Click the Settings drop-down menu, and choose View Group Permissions.

4. Review the permissions of the group for various sites in the site collection. The View Group Permissions dialog box is shown in Figure 4-9.

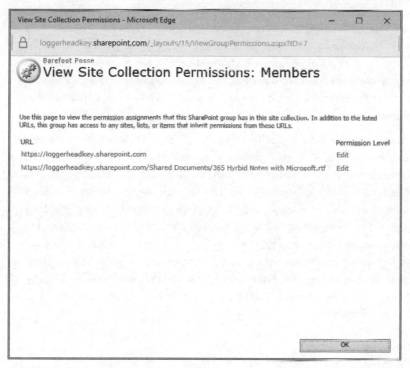

FIGURE 4-9 Viewing group permissions

Dynamic groups

I f you're an administrator of SharePoint Online sites, there are several ways you can manage who has access to your sites. A common way to do this is to use the built-in SharePoint groups and add users that need to have access to the appropriate groups. And while that is a good way to manage access, this becomes cumbersome when the number of members is high and there are lots of changes to the user population. A better alternative would be to use a dynamic group in Azure Active Directory and assign that group to provide access to the SharePoint Online sites. A *dynamic group* is a group where the membership is automated through a rule that you can configure for that group. An example of a rule is "All users where department equals Marketing."

Following this example, Azure Active Directory calculates which users need to be members of your group and will update the group members list accordingly. So if new users join and have their department attribute set to "Marketing," they will automatically become members of the group, and when the attribute is changed to some other value they are removed from the group. If you then use this group to assign the appropriate access in SharePoint Online, users who qualify through your rule will automatically be granted access.

Setting up a dynamic group is easy: create a new group in Azure Active Directory and enable the membership rule. You can use a simple drop-down dialog box to select attributes for the rule, or you can use a full text editor to configure more complex rules with multiple clauses. And because the dynamic rules can reference almost any user attribute in the directory (including custom attributes and multivalued attributes), almost any rule you need can be constructed with little effort.

There are several advantages to this approach over the traditional, manual access management. First of all, there is an important security aspect: you can now guarantee that only users who comply with your rule will have access, and there is a single point of administration for this rule, which makes the access control transparent and easy to manage. Second, it can save you a ton of work, as you no longer need to figure out and manually enter who needs to get access. Third, this approach also ensures that access rights for users who no longer need access are withdrawn automatically, something that is often not an integral part of existing access-control processes. And finally, this all happens in a timely fashion. Usually, access-right updates in SharePoint Online happen within a few minutes after a user's attributes are updated.

Rob de Jong
Microsoft Sr. Product Manager

PowerShell for configuring SharePoint Online

Every Cloud Pro must know PowerShell. In organizations with large data centers, many IT Pros already know a great deal of PowerShell. Because so much of our lives as Cloud Pros involves managing systems in someone else's data center, you need a quick and easy way to make large and complex changes. Although using the UI is fine for one-off, easy changes, nothing is better than PowerShell for managing sites when the required commands are available. Chapter 2, "PowerShell 101 for Cloud Pros," covered PowerShell basics, so in this section we'll cover only what you need to know for managing sites and services in SharePoint Online.

> **TIP** A *premise* is a previous statement, proposition, or assertion. *Premises* is a house or building together with its land. When referring to *on-premises*, remember the "s." It will save you some Cloud Pro embarrassment. Many Cloud Pros use the lingo *on-prem* for *on-premises*.

If you have been using PowerShell for SharePoint Server on-premises, adapting to SharePoint Online will be straightforward. There are some differences, mainly around what you can and can't access through the object model. If you're new to PowerShell, the TechNet guide to SharePoint Online at *https://technet.microsoft.com/library/fp161364(v=office.15).aspx* is a must read. If you have been writing PowerShell on-premises, be aware there are many differences. Be careful: many commands at *https://technet.microsoft.com/library/ff678226(v=office.15).aspx* will not work in SharePoint Online. It's easy to do a quick Bing search and accidentally end up using the wrong examples! Remember that all SharePoint Online cmdlets will include "SPO" in their names.

> **TIP** Author all PowerShell commands in an editor. If a mistake occurs, it will be easier to understand what mistake was made if you have a complete record of the script that was executed. Also, building a commonly used PowerShell script library is useful for each tenant you administer.

Example PowerShell script to enhance DLP

First, there is a little known option when writing PowerShell to use a backtick "`". A backtick is PowerShell's escape character and allows us to wrap a line of script. Please know that has been used throughout this book, and several times in this chapter. When writing scripts found in this chapter, be sure to look for `, as that is a line of script that wraps.

Next is an example PowerShell script to enhance DLP. As an example of using PowerShell for an administrative task, consider the following scenario. Data Loss Prevention (DLP) is a quickly growing part of organizational governance and security. SharePoint Online DLP relies heavily on search. Using metadata and content found during the search process, the DLP engine can enforce rules and allow you to create rich reports on content. However, sites and libraries can be excluded from search results. If an object isn't in the search index, it will be excluded from DLP. To see if this is the case for a given document library, go to Library Settings, Advanced Settings, Search. Here, a library can be removed from search results, as shown in Figure 4-10. This is the *NoCrawl* switch.

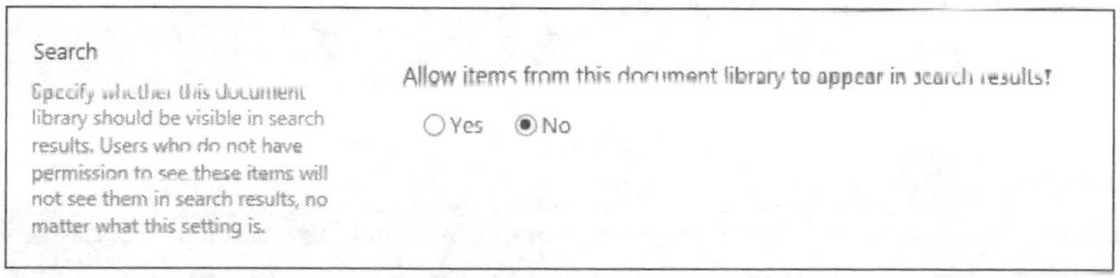

Search

Specify whether this document library should be visible in search results. Users who do not have permission to see these items will not see them in search results, no matter what this setting is.

Allow items from this document library to appear in search results?

○ Yes ● No

FIGURE 4-10 Specifying whether this document library should be visible in search results.

To find where objects have been set to *NoCrawl*, the following PowerShell example will meet the need. The code has been heavily commented to describe what it's doing. You run it for each site or site collection:

Find "No Crawl" Property in a SharePoint Online Site Collection

```
# Purpose: This script will inspect all sites (SPWebs) beneath the specified URL and
# generate a CSV file containing the NoCrawl properties for the SPWebs and their lists
# and libraries.
#       Usage: get-spoNoCrawlCSV.ps1 -spoUrl <url> -userName <string> -password <string>
#       Or:  get-spoNoCrawlCSV.ps1 -spoUrl <url> -userName <string> -password <string>
#                -csvFileName <path/name.csv>
# If a file name for the CSV is not specified a file named SPONoCrawlInfo.csv will be
# written to the current directory. #>
param(
   [Parameter(Mandatory=$true)] [string]$spoUrl,
   [Parameter(Mandatory=$true)] [string]$userName,
   [Parameter(Mandatory=$false)] [string]$csvFileName = "SPONoCrawlInfo.csv")
# This function will establish a connection with SharePoint online by creating a
# Client Context. The URL is the URL of the site collection or site the script will
# operate in context of. The user name and password are for the account that will
# execute the connection and create the client context.
# NOTE: All operations executed using this client context will execute as account used
# to create the connection.
function Get-ClientContext ($url, $userName, $password) {
   $context = New-Object Microsoft.SharePoint.Client.ClientContext($url)
   $cred = New-Object Microsoft.SharePoint.Client.SharePointOnlineCredentials($userName,`
              $password)
   $context.Credentials = $cred
   return $context
}
# This function returns an SPWeb object using the Client Script Object Model.
# The function will create its own client context using a URL, username, and password.
# While that makes the function very portable, it would be better to pass a client
# context object that was created elsewhere that could be reused.
function Get-ClientWeb($url, $userName, $password) {
   # Will get a new client context.
   $context = Get-ClientContext $url $userName $password
   # Creates an framework for an SPWeb. Not filled until ExecuteQuery is called.
   $web = $context.Web
   $context.Load($web)    # Queues loading the base properties when ExecuteWeb is called
   $context.Load($web.Webs) # Queues loading  the SPWeb's child SPWeb (subsites)
   $context.Load($web.Lists) # Queues loading  the SPWeb's lists
   $context.ExecuteQuery()   # Retrieves the data specified by $context.Load() commands
   $context.Dispose()        # Cleans up the $context variable
   return $web    # Returns the $web object retrieved from SharePoint Online.
}
```

```
# This function retrieves all of the lists and libraries for a site (SPWeb) using
# the Client Side Object Model
function Get-ClientLists($url, $userName, $password) {
    # Will get a new client context
    $context = Get-ClientContext $url $userName $password
    # Creates an empty framework for collection of lists and libraries
    $lists = $context.Web.Lists
    # Queues retrieving the list and library data from SharePoint Online
    $context.Load($lists)
    $context.ExecuteQuery()      # Retrieves the date queued using the load command
    $context.Dispose()           # Cleans up the $context variable
    return $lists                # Returns the list and library data
}
# This function creates a little PowerShell custom object with the $title of
# Sites (SPWebs), the URL Sites (SPWebs), the value of the NoCrawl property, the
# title of Lists or Libraries (where appropriate), and the type of item "SITE"
# or "LIST". NOTE: Libraries are not called out separately from lists.
function Get-WebInfoObject($title, $url, $noCrawl, $listTitle, $type) {
    # This codes uses a hash to quickly create custom objects.
    # Custom objects, along with arrays, are great for generating CSV files.
    # Each property will become a column.
    # For more info see: https://technet.microsoft.com/en-us/magazine/hh750381.aspx
    $result = New-Object -TypeName PSObject -Property @{
        "Site Title"= $title
        "List Name"= $listTitle
        "Site URL"= $url
        "No Crawl"= $noCrawl
        "Type"= $type
    }
    return $result               # Return the custom object.
}
# This function will process through the SPWeb with the specified parentWebUrl and
# all sub-SPWebs inspecting the SPWebs (site) and their lists' and libraries'
# NoCrawl property. The NoCrawl property will cause sites, lists, and libraries to
# be ignored by search, which could have negative effects on search-dependent
# functionality such as eDiscovery.
function Get-SubWebs($parentWebUrl, $userName, $password) {
    # This is used to generate clean output using String.Format
    $listMask="  {0,-7}   {1}"
    # Will get a new client context
    $parentWeb = Get-ClientWeb $parentWebUrl $userName $password
    # Write-Host output lets users see progress as script runs
    Write-Host " WebTitle: " $parentWeb.Title
    Write-Host " NoCrawl:  " -NoNewline
    if($parentWeb.NoCrawl) {
        # If NoCrawl, display in Yellow
```

```
            Write-Host $parentWeb.NoCrawl.ToString() -ForegroundColor Yellow
        }
        else {
            # If not NoCrawl, output using standard forecolor
            Write-Host $parentWeb.NoCrawl.ToString()
        }
        # Write the URL of the SPWeb (site) being processed
        Write-Host "   WebURL: " $parentWeb.Url
        # $info is a little object that contains the data that will be written to a CSV
        $info=Get-WebInfoObject $parentWeb.Title $parentWeb.Url $parentWeb.NoCrawl "" "Site"
        # Add the info about the site to the ArrayList that will generate our CSV
        $array.Add($info) | Write-Verbose
        # Fetch the SPWeb's lists and libraries
        $lists = Get-ClientLists $parentWeb.Url $userName $password
        Write-Host ""
        # Label user output
        Write-Host ([System.String]::Format($listMask, "NoCrawl", "Title"))
        Write-Host "   ---------------"
        # Process each list and library
        foreach($l in $lists) {
            $linfo = Get-WebInfoObject $parentWeb.Title $parentWeb.Url $l.NoCrawl `
                        $l.Title "List"
            if($l.NoCrawl){
                Write-Host ([System.String]::Format($listMask, $l.NoCrawl, $l.Title)) `
                        -ForegroundColor Yellow
            }
            else {
                Write-Host ([System.String]::Format($listMask, $l.NoCrawl, $l.Title))
            }
            # Add the info about the site that will be used in our CSV
            $array.Add($linfo) | Write-Verbose
        }
        Write-Host " "
        # Call this same function on all of the Site's (SPWeb's) child sites (SPWebs)
        foreach($w in $parentWeb.Webs) {
            Get-SubWebs $w.Url $userName $password
        }
    }
}
# The DLLs referenced below are required for the Client Side Object Model code to work.
# Install SharePoint Online Client SDK to get these DLLs
[System.Reflection.Assembly]::LoadWithPartialName('Microsoft.SharePoint.Client')
[System.Reflection.Assembly]::LoadWithPartialName('Microsoft.SharePoint.Client.Runtime')
Write-Host " "
# Prompt the user for their password, and store the value in encrypted form
$password = Read-Host -AsSecureString -Prompt "Enter Password:"
Write-Host "`nConnecting to $spoUrl... " -NoNewline
```

```
# A quick text query to test credentials
try {
    $context = Get-ClientContext $spoUrl $userName $password
    $context.ExecuteQuery()   # Does not do much. Success means we have connection to SPO
}
Catch{
    Write-Host "`nCould not connect SharePoint Online.`nThe most likely reason is an
improper user name or password." -ForegroundColor Red
    Write-Host "More detailed information has been written to the verbose output.`nYou
can rerun this command with -VERBOSE to see more information." -ForegroundColor Yellow
    Write-Verbose "`n`n"
    Write-Verbose $_.Exception
    Write-Host ""
    Exit
}
finally{
    $context.Dispose()       # Makes sure we clean up our client context no matter what
}
Write-Host "  Done.`n"
# The array list will be used to build our CSV file
$array = New-Object System.Collections.ArrayList
# Initiate the actual work to be done by the script
Get-SubWebs $spoUrl $userName $password
# The number of items added to the ArrayList is the number of objects processed
$count = $array.Count
Write-Host "`nProcessed $count objects."
# Creates CSV -Force overwrites existing files. -NoTypeInformation required for
# correct column names
$array | Export-Csv -Path $csvFileName -NoTypeInformation -Force
# All done. The `n adds an extra carriage return.
Write-Host "`n  Execution completed.`n"
```

Primer on SharePoint Online and the Client Side Object Model

For managing SharePoint Online, Microsoft provided the SharePoint Online Management
Shell, which is similar in intent to the SharePoint Management Shell you have with on-premises
installations of SharePoint. Both the online and on-premises management shells extend a
typical PowerShell console with a specialized set of commands for managing SharePoint.
Because the SharePoint Online Management Shell is a standard PowerShell console (except
with the addition of a specialized module), any PowerShell console can have the Management
Shell's command set added to it by executing the following command. Note that you will get a
warning message, but it executes correctly. You can add the -*DisableNameChecking* parameter
and suppress the annoying message.

```
Import-Module Microsoft.Online.SharePoint.PowerShell
```

TIP   Adding the command *Import-Module Microsoft.Online.SharePoint.PowerShell* to your SharePoint Online management scripts will allow them to be run from any PowerShell console or a script editor such as Microsoft's Integrated Script Editor. Be sure to install the *Microsoft.Online.SharePoint.PowerShell* module. Additionally, adding the *–Disable NameChecking* parameter will suppress a common error message due to non-standard verb usage.

Although the SharePoint Online Management console provides a great deal of functionality for interacting with SharePoint Online via PowerShell, it does have some limitations. One of the first challenges typically encountered is the lack of commands for dealing with SPWebs.

Inspecting or modifying all the sites (SPWebs) in a site collection (SPSite) is a common usage scenario for Cloud Pros, and this cannot be done directly with the SharePoint Online Management Shell. However, it can be done with a combination of PowerShell and the Client-Side Object Model (CSOM). CSOM is classically known as a developer tool, but Cloud Pros are quickly adopting developer tools to make their job easier and reduce human error through automation.

TIP   Over time, the feature set included in the SharePoint Online Management Shell will change and grow. In fact, by the time this book is published there might be additional SPWeb commands. To list all commands available for *Microsoft.Online.SharePoint .PowerShell*, execute the following commands:

```
Import-Module Microsoft.Online.SharePoint.PowerShell
Get-Command -Module Microsoft.Online.SharePoint.PowerShell | Select Name
```

CLIENT-SIDE OBJECT MODEL

The SharePoint CSOM was created to provide application programming interfaces (APIs) that provide access to SharePoint resources without requiring code to be executed on the SharePoint servers themselves. Although CSOM was created prior to SharePoint Online, the disconnected nature of its APIs makes it a perfect fit for interacting with SharePoint Online. The CSOM does not directly provide a PowerShell implementation—it provides APIs for JavaScript and .NET. Fortunately, PowerShell is able to use .NET classes and can use the CSOM .NET classes just like it can with other .NET assemblies. To make use of CSOM within PowerShell, you need to load the required assemblies. The assemblies can be loaded using the following commands:

```
[System.Reflection.Assembly]::LoadWithPartialName('Microsoft.SharePoint.Client')
[System.Reflection.Assembly]::LoadWithPartialName('Microsoft.SharePoint.Client.Runtime')
```

NOTE The .NET CSOM assemblies do not require you to install the SharePoint Online Management Shell. Instead, the necessary assemblies can be obtained with the SharePoint Online Client SDK, which can be downloaded from *https://www.microsoft.com/download /details.aspx?id=42038*.

You will follow some high-level patterns when using CSOM with PowerShell. At the most fundamental level, every PowerShell script using CSOM must implement three stages: making a connection, testing a connection, and accessing objects.

MAKING A CONNECTION

First, to make a connection, you create a *client context*. To create a client context with SharePoint Online, you need three pieces of information: the URL of the site to connect to, the user name of the user to connect as, and the password of the user making the connection. To create a client context, you execute the following commands:

```
$context = New-Object Microsoft.SharePoint.Client.ClientContext($url)
$cred = New-Object Microsoft.SharePoint.Client.SharePointOnlineCredentials($userName, `
        $securePassword)
$context.Credentials = $cred
```

There are few things to note about the process of making the connection and creating the client context. The first is that the password cannot be sent as clear text and must be encrypted (or stored in a secure string). This can be done with the following command:

```
$password = ConvertTo-SecureString -AsPlainText "the password" -Force
```

It's bad practice to store passwords in a script or type them into the console as plain text. Therefore, in the examples used in this book, passwords are always typed in by the user as a secure string. Handling passwords as secure strings lessens the chances of the password being compromised. To prompt the user to enter a password and store it as a secure string, execute the following command:

```
$password = Read-Host -AsSecureString -Prompt "Enter Password:"
```

TESTING A CONNECTION

Having made a connection and created a client-context object, it's a good idea to test it to make sure it's functional. The easiest and most reliable manner found for testing a connection is to execute a query as if you were actually performing an operation. Because this test query might fail (such as from a mistyped password), you want to make sure you handle a failure gracefully. To test a client-context connection, execute the following commands:

```
try {
        $context = New-Object Microsoft.SharePoint.Client.ClientContext($url)
        $cred = New-Object `
```

```
Microsoft.SharePoint.Client.SharePointOnlineCredentials($userName, $password)
        $context.Credentials = $cred
        $context.ExecuteQuery()
}
catch {
        Write-Host "Something went wrong. Please try again."
        exit
}
finally{
        $context.Dispose()
}
```

The *$context.ExecuteQuery* command will be used later to actually interact with SharePoint Online. For now, it's sufficient to know that if it succeeds you have a functional client context and, by extension, a connection to SharePoint Online. The *Try/Catch* block is used to handle any error. If something goes wrong in the *Try* section, commands in the *Catch* section are executed, displaying a message and terminating the script. If all goes as intended in the *Try* section, the *Catch* block is skipped.

When creating a client-context object, you need to properly clean it up after use. The *Finally* section runs last no matter what, with success or failure. In the *Finally* block, you call *$context. Dispose*. This terminates the client-context object and releases any resources it was using. Because you need to properly clean up after creating a client context and because it takes time to create one, it's a good idea to create a client-context object and use it repeatedly. In this chapter, there is an example script to find SharePoint sites and lists that have a property that keeps them from being crawled by search. This script repeatedly creates and disposes of client-context objects. It demonstrates the added lines of code and extra effort required to create and re-create multiple client-context objects. A proven scripting pattern is to create a given context once and then dispose of it within a *Finally* block at the end of script execution.

> **TIP** You should create a given client-context object only once and pass the context within your scripts. Doing so saves lines of code, helps your code execute more efficiently, and makes it easier to clean up after.

ACCESSING OBJECTS

The disconnected nature of the Client-Side Object Model necessitates some differences in how it interacts with SharePoint resources. In an on-premises SharePoint implementation, you can retrieve a site (SPWeb) object with the following command:

```
$web = Get-SPWeb <url>
```

To retrieve the same object using CSOM, you execute the following commands:

```
function Get-ClientWeb($url, $userName, $password){
```

```
$context = New-Object Microsoft.SharePoint.Client.ClientContext($url)
$cred = New-Object Microsoft.SharePoint.Client.SharePointOnlineCredentials
($userName, $password)
$context.Credentials = $cred
$web = $context.Web
$context.Load($web)
$context.ExecuteQuery()
$context.Dispose()
return $web
}
```

Understanding the code to retrieve an SPWeb is fundamental to using CSOM and PowerShell to interact with SharePoint Online. Here is how the process works.

First, note that because you must establish a connection with a remote system, not only is a URL required, but also a user name and password. With the URL, user name, and password, you can create a connection to SharePoint Online by establishing a client context:

```
function Get-ClientWeb($url, $userName, $password)
```

> **TIP** In practical use, it would be better to create a client context and pass the context instead of passing the URL, password, and user name.

Next, note that you have a line that seems similar to using Get-SPWeb:

```
$web = $context.Web
```

If you're new to using CSOM statements, they can be a bit confusing. If you inspect the *$web* variable created in the preceding code example, you'll find it seemingly has all the properties and methods expected for an SPWeb. There is only one catch: none of them have values yet!

To see an example of creating an empty object with CSOM, execute the following:

```
$context = New-Object Microsoft.SharePoint.Client.ClientContext($url)
$cred = New-Object `
    Microsoft.SharePoint.Client.SharePointOnlineCredentials($userName, $password)
$context.Credentials = $cred
$web = $context.Web
$web | Get-Member | Format-Table Name
Write-Host "This is an empty web title:" -NoNewLine
Write-Host $web.Title
```

The object created with *$web = $context.Web* is like a skeleton. It has all the right places for all the right parts of an SPWeb, but it has not been fleshed out. Two more commands are required to actually get a complete SPWeb object:

```
$context.Load($web)
$context.ExecuteQuery()
```

The *Context.Load* command instructs the Client-Side Object Model to load the values for the *$web variable*. Multiple *Context.Load* instances can be executed simultaneously, as in this example:

```
$context.Load($web)
$context.Load($web.Webs)
$context.Load($web.Lists)
```

This provides a way to retrieve multiple objects without making multiple roundtrips to SharePoint Online. This approach is considerably more time efficient. Because you can make more than one call to load information using the client context, you must have a way to know when it's required to load the data. Because the information for most SharePoint Online objects reside in SQL, it's natural to name the command to actually execute loading data, such as *ExecuteQuery*. With *Context.Load*, you specify which object or objects should be retrieved; with *Context.ExecuteQuery*, you actually initiate the retrieval.

> **TIP** It's easy to accidently forget to add *Context.ExecuteQuery*, particularly when you're first using CSOM. To catch such accidents, remember that retrieving information from a remote SharePoint Online tenant will take time. If there isn't a delay in the process of retrieving the data, you might not be attempting to load it all! Always look for code that runs too quickly and doesn't work.

Administrators and owners

First and foremost, you need to define who the SharePoint Online administrators and Site collection administrators will be. Remember, Site Owner roles are at a lower level and, while they're important, they aren't as critical as SharePoint Online administrators and Site collection administrators. Giving people elevated platform access should be intentional, and they need to be trained on the underpinnings and features of the platform.

The following are some prime examples of settings that should be restricted to trusted administrators:

- SharePoint Online User Purchases are valuable for power users to provision functionality without getting in the way. But these purchases might be contrary to your enterprise architecture and governance plans. As Cloud Pros, we must understand this is the modern world—we cannot manage every feature that is needed and provisioned by our power users. Our job is to manage, align, and monitor—not restrict. We need to investigate and integrate, but not block progress. We should ensure it's within our security, governance, and application boundaries. But to succeed, we must trust our organizational visionaries to move forward with minimal input from IT. User Purchases are managed through SharePoint Admin Center, Apps. To leverage apps, you must create an app catalog, configure store settings, and set app permissions. For more information, see *https://support.office.com/article/Configure-settings-for-the-SharePoint-Store-6B806FB8-9295-441D-B954-07009021DC48*.

- Tenant-wide settings like Records Management should be thoughtfully enabled and carefully managed. We use a single tenant-wide example here, because if we wrote about all available tenant settings you'd be reading a large novel! Additionally, the constant evolution of the cloud will make some tenant-wide settings text outdated quickly. As Cloud Pros, we must learn the patterns and practices of configuring and managing services, and then we should apply that logic to new services and options. Using Records Management as an example, we can modify the Edit Control Block (ECB) for all users. The ECB is constantly evolving, so caution should be used if you use custom code to edit the ECB. The best practice is to modify the ECB only through the options Microsoft gives you. Figure 4-11 shows an example of an ECB within SharePoint Online.

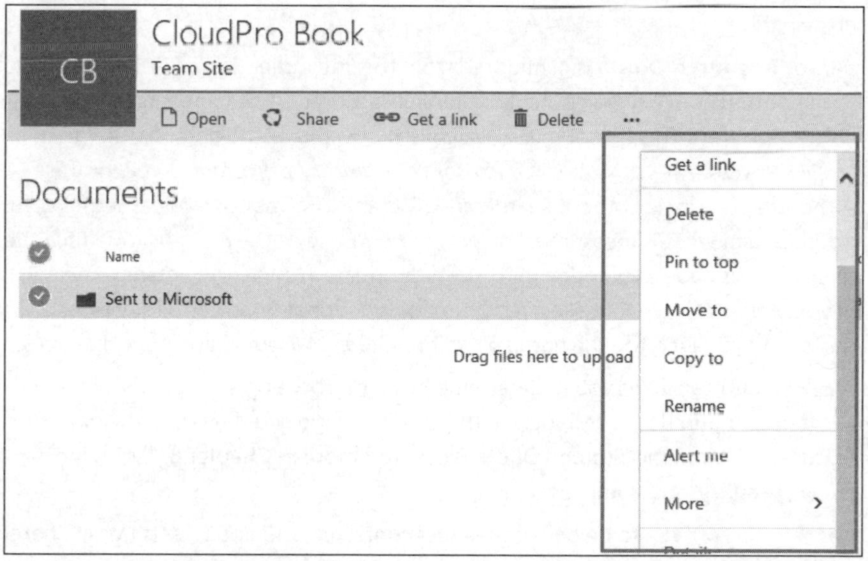

FIGURE 4-11 The ECB in SharePoint Online

A common records-management requirement is that official records must be sent to a secure repository. Creating a SharePoint Online Records Center and then configuring the Records Center Sent To connection enables you to meet the requirement. This feature is one of many such enterprise features added to enhance the user experience. To configure Records Center Send To Connections, browse to SharePoint Admin Center, Records Management and then configure the following options:

- **Display name** is what the users will see in the ECB.
- **Send to URL** is the URL of the Records Center that has the Content Organizer feature installed and configured.
- **Send-to action** defines whether you will copy the file to the Records Center, move it, or move it and leave a link in the original location. There are no best practices for this—it completely depends on your organizational governance.
- **Explanation** will be shown in your audit logs.

- **Service Applications** allow you to provide centralized services to sites, but because they affect all sites, you need to exercise caution when deciding who is allowed to manage them.

> **NOTE** Not all service applications have delegated control. We recommend that you do not let the lack of technical controls alter your governance policy.

- **Office 365 service applications** include BCS, Search, User Profile Application, MMS, Secure Store, and others, depending on your licensing and the evolution of the platform. MMS is managed differently than other service apps and is covered in the next section.
- **Server Resource Quota** is configured from the Site Collection's Administration tab. In the ribbon, you'll see an option for Server Resource Quota appear after you select a site collection. There's not much available that explains the details, other than an MSDN resource at *https://msdn.microsoft.com/library/office/gg615462(v=office.14).aspx*. Although the article is about SharePoint 2010, the information about metrics gives you a good idea of what is measured. The primary purpose of the quota is to reduce the effect of erroneous code and dodgy third-party products. However, if you have heavy usage in your tenant, you might see a reduction of functionality on certain features and web parts until you increase the quota or wait until the 24-hour usage period expires.
- **Storage Quota** allows you to determine how you carve up your SharePoint Online allotted and purchased storage. On the Settings page, you have the ability to turn this feature to Automatic. Storage Quota is covered more in Chapter 8, "Managing governance, security, and compliance."
- **Sharing** has proven to be one of the most contested and critical settings in SharePoint Online. Sharing controls how documents are shared with people outside of your Azure Active Directory. Most organizations (all, from the authors' experience) have SPSites that sharing is not enabled for. There is middle ground, however. External sharing doesn't have to be enabled on every site collection. You can also choose to enable external sharing with only a selected number of other email domains. Before allowing sharing with the entire world, verify that sharing with only specific tenants won't solve your problem.
- **Hybrid Settings** should be guarded and periodically audited. You'll encounter significant problems if an inexperienced professional incorrectly modifies these settings. The two largest impacts would be missing or duplicate OneDrive for Business locations and disappearing team sites from the app launcher.

Site collection life cycle

Before creating lots of SPSites, you need to understand when to create them and how you will manage them. The two big advantages SPSites have over SPWebs are storage and security boundaries. However, because an SPSite is a security boundary, creating many SPSites will result in additional administrative challenges. Many objects inherit from the parent SPWeb, but SPSites cannot inherit from another SPSite. Thus, although one SPSite might appear to inherit from another SPSite, it cannot.

> **NOTE** The health of your site collection throughout its life cycle is important. Microsoft added a Health Check page for your convenience. Run a health check by going to Site Settings, clicking Site Collection Health Checks, and clicking the Start Checks button. You will then be sent to a results page. The page displays conflicting content types, parent-absent content types, customized files, missing galleries, missing site templates, and supported language-pack references.

The first challenge to creating many SPSites is the lack of navigation inheritance. By default, SharePoint navigation is dynamically built on SPWebs and pages libraries within a single SPSite. When you create multiple SPSites, you're forced to manage each individual SPSite navigation structure. Second, branding is inherited throughout the SPWeb structure. So creating multiple SPSites necessitates managing multiple branding scenarios. Third, workflows are contained within an SPSite boundary, so you might find it challenging to modernize processes across multiple SPSites without a third-party product. Features, display templates, search settings—anything that inherits through out an SPWeb structure—will become increasingly challenging as you increase the quantity of SPSites in the tenant.

Figure 4-12 shows an example of the Site Collections Administration tab. To select one or many site collections, select the check box to the left of the URL heading. The Ribbon will appear and show you options for that site collection.

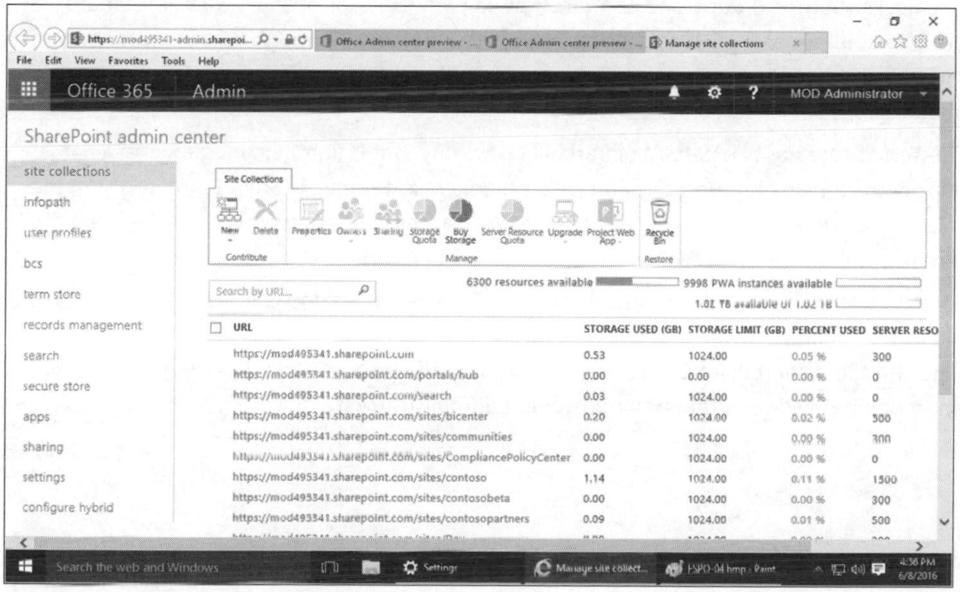

FIGURE 4-12 Site Collections Administration tab

Managed Metadata Service

The Managed Metadata Service (MMS) hosts two distinct services: the Content Type Syndication Hub and the Term Store.

First, the Content Type Syndication Hub is created as its own site collection. In the root web of the Content Type Syndication Hub, you can create content types for any enterprise content management need, also known as *enterprise content types*. The majority of enterprise content types you see in the real world are for data-retention policies, compliance, and document templates. You cannot leverage subwebs for enterprise content types, only the root web. MMS serves the content types in the root web to your entire tenant by publishing them to the other site collections. Caution should be used when modifying content types in the Content Type Syndication Hub; although you can modify hundreds or thousands of documents in a single action as a positive action, you can also easily and accidentally modify hundreds or thousands of documents in a single, negative action!

> **NOTE** We recommend enabling the Publishing infrastructure features so that you can syndicate publishing content types such as page layouts.

The second service in the MMS is the Term Store. The Term Store is the central repository for the hierarchical representation of terms that can be used through syndication to classify (or tag) data stored within your tenant. SPSites subscribe to the Term Store and consume terms. The subscription of terms can be used for data classification, retention, retrieval, and consumption. The Term Store provides a vehicle for the management of these terms and their hierarchical structure, groups, and relationships. In early editions of SharePoint, metadata was applied via columns at the SPSite, SPWeb, list, or library levels. Although you still can apply metadata via columns, you also can manage your metadata in a proper noun taxonomy via the Term Store.

The Term Store has two parts: a hierarchal taxonomy that is tightly managed, and a flat taxonomy to store ad-hoc user tagging (also called a *folksonomy*). In SharePoint, terms in the latter portion are referred to as *enterprise keywords*. In this chapter, we focus on the hierarchal taxonomy.

You can set governance at several levels in the Term Store. As you can see in Figure 4-13, the Term Store administrator can manage all items. The Term Store Administrator role is automatically granted to a SharePoint Online administrator. At the next level down, Groups, you can begin to delegate administration to non-tenant administrators.

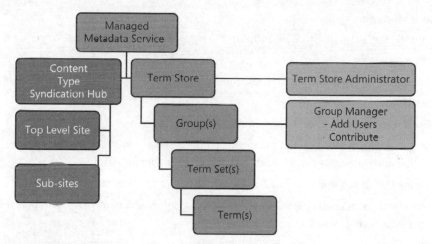

Term Store Roles

- **Contributor (Site member)**
- Create, rename, copy, reuse, move, and delete term sets.
- Modify a term set's description, owner, contact, stakeholders, submission. policy, and determine whether the term set is available for tagging.
- Create, rename, copy, reuse, merge, deprecate, move, and delete terms.
- Modify a term's description, labels, default label, and whether the term is available for tagging.

- **Group manager (ECM Administrator)**
- Perform all actions of the contributor role.
- Import a term set.
- Assign or remove users from the contributor role.

- **Term store administrator (ECM Administrator)**
- Can perform all actions of the group manager role.
- Create and delete Term Set Groups.
- Assign or remove users from the group manager role.
- Change the working languages for the term store.

FIGURE 4-13 The Content Type Syndication Hub and Term Store are served by MMS.

As a quick reference, the following rights are associated with Term Store roles:

- **Term Store Administrator**

  - Can perform all actions of the Group Manager role

  - Can create and delete term set groups

  - Can assign or remove users from the Group Manager role

  - Can change the working languages for the Term Store

- **Group Manager**
  - Performs all actions of the Contributor role
  - Imports a term set
  - Assigns or removes users from the Contributor role
- **Contributor**
  - Creates, renames, copies, reuses, moves, and deletes term sets
  - Modifies a term set's description, owner, contact, stakeholders, and submission policy, and determines whether the term set is available for tagging
  - Creates, renames, copies, reuses, merges, deprecates, moves, and deletes terms
  - Modifies a term's description, labels, and default label, and determines whether the term is available for tagging

Terms can be defined at the enterprise Term Store level, or they can be defined at the Site collection level. Each Site collection has its own term group that is automatically created and is available only within that Site collection. Term groups are often used for taxonomy-based Site collection navigation (called *managed navigation*), and they can be useful for giving Site collection administrators a means of defining a taxonomy in isolation from other Site collections.

A taxonomy is more than a way of organizing terms to classify and tag data. One of the most important aspects of managed terms, with respect to taxonomy, is the ability to arrange them into a cascading hierarchy. This arrangement provides a self-describing term set with which to associate navigation, search, sort, and filter, and with which to apply policy. Because of this, you can copy terms and reuse terms. The following options are available to manage your taxonomy:

- To copy a term or term set, highlight the term or term set name and select the Copy Term [<Set>] option from the drop-down menu. The term or term set is duplicated at the same level as its source. The name of the new term or term set is prepended with "Copy of."

- To copy a term with all its child terms, highlight the term and select Copy Term With Children from the drop-down menu. This duplicates all child terms to the new term. Remember to rename the new term copy after duplication.

- To reuse the original term or term set elsewhere without actually duplicating the terms (as you do with a copy), you can use the Reuse Term [<Set>] functionality.

- To merge terms, highlight the term, select Merge Term from the drop-down menu, and then select the term you want to merge into. Doing this removes the term that is being merged, but all content that has been tagged with this term still references the legacy term. The term being merged is added as another label on the destination term.

> *TIP*   After terms are merged, the other label cannot be deleted.

- To deprecate a term, highlight the term and select Deprecate Term from the drop-down menu. Doing this discontinues the use of the term and removes it from availability for tagging. This procedure does not remove all references to the term, and the term can still be used for search and backward compatibility.

- To move a term or term set, highlight the term or term set and select Move Term [<Set>] from the drop-down menu. Select the new parent for the term or term set for the term being moved, or select the new group for the term set being moved.

Search settings

Unlike its on-premises counterpart, SharePoint Online search is functional and returns search results when SharePoint Online is provisioned. By default, all your SharePoint Online and One-Drive for Business content is crawled and findable in the out-of-the-box search center.

Immediate crawl

Unfortunately, SharePoint Online does not provide a method to schedule a crawl of your content. Instead, it's continually crawling on a schedule managed by Microsoft.

> **NOTE** Our experience is that the fastest an immediate crawl will occur is in about 15 minutes. It's possible, though, that it will take several hours.

However, you can request that the crawler re-index a site or a list or library as soon as it can. The ability to request exists at both the SPWeb and list and library levels. To request a re-index of an SPWeb, go to Site Settings, Search And Offline Availability and click the Re-index Site button. Likewise, to re-index only a single list or library, go to List Settings, Advanced Settings and click the Re-index List button.

Search schema

The collection of Crawled and Managed Properties is collectively known as the *Search Schema*.

SharePoint Online search does more than crawl content and create an index. As content is indexed, relevant information is extracted and stored for use when running search queries. Content and metadata that are processed when content is crawled are called, unsurprisingly, *crawled properties*. Examples of crawled properties are creation date, author, and the URL for the content. Search processes a large number of crawled properties by default. To make use of crawled properties in search, you need to map them to managed properties. Managed properties are added to the index as additional metadata about content and can be used to enhance search. Although managed properties can be created manually, SharePoint Online automatically creates managed properties for all site columns. By extension, content types, which are composed of one or more site columns, will therefore automatically have managed properties created for all the content type's site columns.

Managed properties have one or more crawled properties mapped to them. If multiple crawled properties are mapped to a managed property, there are two possible methods to execute the mapping.

First, you can have all matching crawled properties be included in the managed property. For example, a managed property can be created for U.S. postal codes that's mapped to a nine-digit postal code crawled property and a five-digit postal code crawled property. A search using that managed property can use either postal code. A second option is to just map the first non-empty crawled property in the list. For example, let's say the nine-digit code property was listed before the five-digit code property in the crawled property mappings. If both properties have data, only the nine-digit code is returned because it was the first nonempty crawled property. If you had only the five-digit property, it would be returned. If there was a third crawled property mapped as well and it had a value, it wouldn't be available in the query because the search stopped with the five-digit crawled property (because it wasn't empty).

Managed properties contain a number of core options that affect how they can be used within search, and these core options need to be considered before you create new managed properties. Table 4-5 summarizes the core options.

TABLE 4-5 Core options for managed properties

Option	Description
Searchable	Adds the property to the index as if it were content on a page or in a document.
Queryable	Allows the managed property to be used in queries by referencing its name—for example, Path:http://msn.com
Retrievable	Includes the content managed property in search results.
Allow multiple values	If an item has multiple values for the managed property, all of them will be included.
Refinable	Allows the managed property to be used as a refiner.
Sortable	Allows the property to be used to sort search result sets.

Query suggestions

Query suggestions provide suggested terms and autocomplete words or phrases for users as they begin typing search queries. As an example, when a user begins typing "Sha", query suggestions might suggest "SharePoint" as a possible query term. Query terms that have been used four or more times for successful queries will be added to the Query Suggestions list automatically. You also can add terms manually to improve the search user experience. When manually creating query suggestions, remember that providing too many suggestions can be confusing.

NOTE There might be a delay as the change propagates before query suggestions become active.

Usage reports

To understand how search is working and to better optimize SharePoint Online, Office 365 provides a number of search usage reports. Usage reports are Microsoft Excel spreadsheets that can be downloaded and that provide metrics and graphs related to current search utilization. The information the reports provide include the number of queries, top queries, abandoned queries, no-result queries, and query rule usage.

NOTE For more information about result sources and query rules, see Chapter 6.

## CHAPTER 5

Managing the client: OneDrive for Business, Office ProPlus, and Mobile Device Management for Office 365

A discussion about Office 365 would not be complete without talking about its impact to the client. By "client," we mean any device that's using Office 365 services, whether it's a laptop, iPad, Android phone, or Microsoft Surface. As a Cloud Pro, you need to keep the entirety of the user experience in mind, not just the cloud services. A Cloud Pro's responsibilities span both the cloud and the local environment. If a user is unable to have a positive experience on her device, whether it's in a browser or a mobile app, it won't matter how great everything is plumbed or which features are available.

In this chapter, we discuss the ways Microsoft Office 365 affects the client. Microsoft has added some powerful capabilities for clients in the platform. We talk about the available clients, OneDrive for Business, and Office ProPlus. If the client is the doorway through which your users enter the cloud, it's also the way data leaves. So we talk about options (namely, Mobile Device Management for Office 365) to help you make sure the device is secured.

Office 365 and the client

A user can touch Office 365 in a wide variety of ways. Most commonly, users work in the browser. However, Microsoft made a major effort to produce high-quality mobile apps. It will continue to do so as more and more users consume Office 365 from their mobile devices. It's not just a matter of users actively interacting with Office 365, though. Mobile

Device Management (MDM) works behind the scenes to protect the device, and the OneDrive for Business sync client runs in the background to keep folders synced with SharePoint Online or OneDrive for Business.

Supportability

On the "System Requirements for Office" page (*https://products.office.com/office-system-requirements*), Microsoft lists the client requirements for using Office 365. Table 5-1 summarizes the current supported mobile devices and browsers.

> **TIP** The Office 365 client requirements will change over time. Make sure to review them before starting any major update to the clients, such as a new version of a browser.

TABLE 5-1 Mobile device and browser supportability

Mobile Devices	Supported
iOS	8.0 and later (Office for iPad Pro requires 9.0)
Android	4.4 (KitKat) and later
Windows Mobile	Windows 10 for Office Mobile apps
Browsers	**Supported**
Microsoft Edge	Only the newest version is supported. See Knowledge Base article 3083635 for known issues.
Internet Explorer	Internet Explorer 10 and 11. Experiences are diminished and Yammer is unusable on Internet Explorer 8 and 9. Office Online is unusable on Internet Explorer 8.
Safari	Current version
Chrome	Current version
Firefox	Current version

Interacting with Office 365 on the client

There are many ways to access and interact with Office 365 from the client. The following are nonbrowser tools that are currently available:

- **The Microsoft Office suite**   The whole Office suite has been designed with Office 365 in mind. Office 2016 has added further depth, such as providing in-application support for Office 365 Groups.

- **Office 365 Admin app**   The Office 365 Admin app provides administrators quick and easy access to manage the tenant, such as working with users and licenses. It and the Office 365 Admin Center will continue to have a more unified experience as time goes on.

- **Email clients**   Nearly any email client, whether it's mobile or desktop, can be configured to sync email with Exchange Online.

- **Mobile applications**   Microsoft has produced many mobile apps that connect with Office 365. There are too many to list. Nearly every service in Office 365 has an app, and Microsoft continues to build more and more features into the Office mobile apps.

> **TIP**   You can use the Office mobile apps to work with Office files stored in your Dropbox. For more information, see "Office and DropBox frequently asked questions" at *https://support.office.com/article/Office-and-DropBox-frequently-asked-questions-88931030-47f9-4134-bc52-a8863bb0169f.*

- **Skype for Business desktop and mobile clients**   The Skype for Business clients enable the full range of features. The browser-based client is primarily used for interacting with meetings.
- **OneDrive for Business sync client**   The OneDrive for Business sync client manages the synchronization of OneDrive for Business and SharePoint Online libraries on a desktop. On mobile devices, the Microsoft OneDrive app is used to manage both business and personal OneDrive accounts.
- **Power BI Desktop**   The Power BI Desktop application provides full-featured, rich capabilities for authoring reports and data visualizations.
- **PowerShell**   As discussed at length in Chapter 2, "PowerShell 101 for Cloud Pros," and again in Chapter 4, "SharePoint Online administration and configuration," Windows PowerShell on the client can be used not only to configure the services but also to work with their data.

Working with SharePoint Online from Windows Explorer

Did you know you can actually work with SharePoint Online and OneDrive for Business sites, lists, and libraries using Windows Explorer? You absolutely can, and it can be a powerful way to use the services. However, you need to be cautious when doing so.

Because nearly everything in a site can be exposed in Windows Explorer, it's extremely easy to do the wrong thing and cause serious damage. If the wrong item is deleted or renamed, you might cripple or destroy the site (perhaps irrevocably). Therefore, we don't recommend teaching everybody to use this method of access. This information is probably better to keep for administrator use or for use by those who can be trusted. Consider establishing a "You broke it, you bought it" support policy when distributing knowledge about this technique.

You can access a library or site in Windows Explorer in three ways. For these methods to work, the site URL (or just "*.sharepoint.com") needs to be added to the Trusted Sites zone in Internet Options. You can accomplish that by following these steps:

1. In Internet Explorer (because this doesn't work in other browsers), browse to the library you want to open in Windows Explorer. If you're using the traditional interface, open the ribbon, go to the Library tab, and click Open With Explorer. If you're using the "new" document library experience, expand the View Options drop-down menu at the top right side of the page and click View in File Explorer.

2. Map the site or library as a local drive. To do this, open File Explorer and right-click This PC in the left pane. Click Map Network Drive. Select a drive letter and paste the site or library URL into the Folder text box.

3. Open a site or library directly via the UNC path. Take the URL to the library or site, remove the "https:", change all "/" characters to "\", and add "@ssl" after "sharepoint. com." For example, "https://contoso.sharepoint.com/sites/sales/Shared%20Documents" becomes "\\contoso.sharepoint.com@ssl\sites\teams\Shared%20Documents". Paste the result into File Explorer's address bar or anywhere else UNC paths are used.

   Again, be careful with this method because it can really damage a site. If used well, however, it can be an excellent way to work with multiple files and folders at the same time. It can be especially helpful when reorganizing the content in a site.

Networking

The network, both the local area network (LAN) and the wide area network (WAN), is critically important to the client. They are the legs on which the whole user experience walks. As such, you'll find it's well worth taking the time to make sure the network is in top shape and that the WAN is configured optimally for Office 365. A lot of factors come into play, such as proxies and NAT, and sometimes you simply have to deal with a slow network. We talked somewhat about preparing the network back in Chapter 1, "Getting started as an Office 365 Cloud Pro," so make sure you take a look. As a Cloud Pro, you must form a good relationship with the networking team (if there is one), because members of that team can have a huge impact on the user experience.

There are many topics that can be discussed relating to Office 365 and the network, but we don't have the space here to cover them all. Thankfully, Microsoft has us covered and has published many great resources on the subject:

- "Client connectivity" at *https://support.office.com/article/Client-connectivity-4232abcf-4ae5-43aa-bfa1-9a078a99c78b*.

- "Best practices for using Office 365 on a slow network" at *https://support.office.com/article/Best-practices-for-using-Office-365-on-a-slow-network-fd16c8d2-4799-4c39-8fd7-045f06640166*.

- "Network and migration planning for Office 365" at *https://support.office.com/article/Network-and-migration-planning-for-Office-365-f5ee6c33-bcd7-4b0b-b0f8-dc1d9fb8d132*.

- "Plan for network devices that connect to Office 365 services" at *https://support.office. com/article/Plan-for-network devices-that-connect-to-Office-365-services-073433ca- 3511-4db9-b173-7a2edca57691.*

- "Routing with ExpressRoute for Office 365" at *https://support.office.com/article/Routing- with-ExpressRoute-for-Office-365-e1da26c6-2d39-4379-af6f-4da213218408.*

- "NAT support with Office 365" (for very large customers) at *https://support.office.com/ article/NAT-support-with-Office-365-170e96ea-d65d-4e51-acac-1de56abe39b9.*

- "Top 10 Tips for Optimising & Troubleshooting your Office 365 Network Connectivity" at *https://blogs.technet.microsoft.com/onthewire/2014/06/18/top-10-tips-for-optimising- troubleshooting-your-office-365-network-connectivity.*

Managing OneDrive for Business

OneDrive for Business is not unique to Office 365. It has been available for on-premises systems through SharePoint Server since the 2013 release. However, OneDrive for Business has two things that aren't available in an on-premises format that are incredibly valuable: massive free storage and easy external sharing. As such, OneDrive for Business can be a primary moti- vation to get users into Office 365 beyond just email.

What is OneDrive for Business?

OneDrive for Business can be a little confusing. Not only does it share a name with Microsoft's consumer product, but the name is also used by people to refer to two different things.

People frequently confuse the OneDrive for Business sync client with OneDrive for Business itself. OneDrive for Business is actually the name of a specific folder and interface in a user's My Site. (We'll say more about that in a moment.) The sync client is used to make available on the local machine the files and folders that are on OneDrive for Business so that they can be used offline. Changes made to the items locally will be automatically synced back up to OneDrive for Business when the connection is available. It can be used to sync SharePoint Online and SharePoint on-premises libraries, as well.

As stated in "Overview of OneDrive for Business in SharePoint Server 2013" (which you can find at *https://technet.microsoft.com/library/dn167720.aspx*): "OneDrive for Business is the default document library in a user's My Sites in SharePoint Server 2013 or SharePoint Online." However, it's a bit more than that in Office 365. Microsoft incorporated a special user experi- ence that brings the interface closer in line with the commercial OneDrive, and it heavily domi- nates, if not hides, the My Sites features. The interface has become so successful that Microsoft has been rolling it out to libraries in SharePoint Online to provide a unified user experience. Increasing emphasis is being placed on OneDrive for Business, so it will be important to know about it.

MORE INFO For resources related to managing OneDrive for Business, go to "OneDrive for Business in Office 365 – Admin Help" at *https://support.office.com/article/OneDrive-for-Business-in-Office-365-Admin-Help-3e21f8f0-e0a1-43be-aa3e-8c0236bf11bb.*

OneDrive for Business architecture

Again, OneDrive for Business really isn't much more than a folder in a My Site with a fancy ASPX page plus an icon in the App Launcher. To help you understand better how to manage it, we'll take a look at OneDrive for Business under the covers.

SharePoint Server 2003 introduced the world to My Sites. A My Site is a special SharePoint site collection that's created for each user in a location called a My Site Host (which itself is a special site collection). The idea is to provide a place where users can put their personal documents and maybe create some lists they might need. It was also envisioned as a place where people would go to work with their user profile, find others with similar interests, and take part in early enterprise social networking. Users generally start out using their My Site only to hold documents, primarily because only a minimum number of features are enabled by default. However, there's nothing stopping the user from enabling any of the site or site-collection features, building a fully featured SharePoint Online site collection, and inviting people to collaborate. Users are site-collection administrators in their My Sites, so they can do whatever they like with it.

TIP Users might be tempted to move their collaborative business process into their My Site as a result of the lack of constraints. However, you should strongly discourage this, and you should attempt to eliminate such usage if identified. My Sites do not have the same level of oversight and control as SharePoint Online sites, and they're deleted automatically after the user's account is deleted. As a result, there are tremendous risks to any business process running in a user's My Site.

In SharePoint Online, the *https://<tenant>-my.sharepoint.com* site collection is the My Site Host. It doesn't do much more than act as a container for My Sites and hold profile pictures. All the My Sites are located under this URL, under the "/personal" managed path. A managed path is just a way that site collections can be organized in a SharePoint URL. The My Sites themselves are independent site collections with URLs based on the user's name. Again, My Sites are full-featured site collections for which the user is the site-collection administrator.

Inside the My Site Root Web (which you can read more about in the "Site collection administration" section of Chapter 4) is the Files folder. This, along with the onedrive.aspx page, is considered the user's OneDrive for Business. However, users can also have additional content in their My Site, including additional lists, libraries, and even subsites.

Figure 5-1 demonstrates the My Site structure. You can see that all three users have OneDrive for Business. David Ahs has the default configuration: just OneDrive for Business. Toni Poe also has a subsite, and that subsite has a document library. Shu Ito does not have a subsite but does have a library and a list.

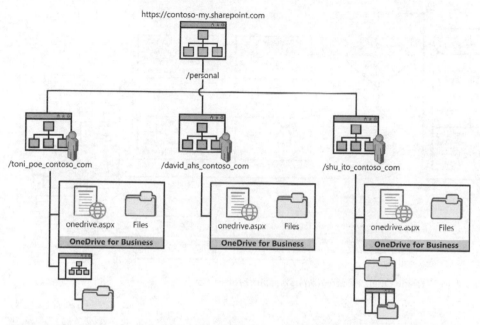

FIGURE 5-1 My Site site hierarchy in SharePoint Online

> **TIP** The My Site Host, *https://<tenant>-my.sharepoint.com*, contains all the profile pictures (along with different-sized thumbnails of each) in a document library called User Photos. Access them by going to *https://<tenant>-my.sharepoint.com/User%20Photos* and opening the Profile Pictures folder.

What happens to OneDrive for Business when a user is deleted?

A user's My Site is closely connected to the user and her profile. When a user is deleted in Azure AD, ownership of the My Site is given to the user's manager (if one exists) and is scheduled for automatic deletion 30 days later. The retention period can be changed (extended up to 10 years) by using the *OrphanedPersonalSitesRetentionPeriod* parameter of the Set-SPOTenant cmdlet. If there is no manager set in the user's profile, the Secondary Owner (if specified) is given ownership instead. Any content in the My Site that needs to be retained must be copied elsewhere by the new owner before the My Site is deleted. Upon deletion 30 days later, the

My Site goes into the normal site-collection recycle bin, where it's permanently deleted after another 30 days. After the My Site is placed in the recycle bin, it can be restored only by using PowerShell (specifically, the Restore-SPODeletedSite cmdlet). Figure 5-2 shows the full flow of the My Site and OneDrive for Business cleanup process.

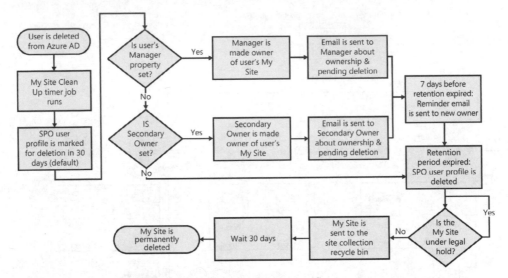

FIGURE 5-2 My Site and OneDrive for Business cleanup process flow

> **TIP** Make sure to set the Secondary Owner to an account with an email address that somebody actually watches. This could be an actual user, a shared mailbox, and so on. Also, it is recommended that you set a service account as the My Site Secondary Admin as early as possible. When a My Site is created (and only when it is created), this account will be added as a site collection administrator. Doing so can provide administrators a way to work with My Sites and OneDrive for Business should they need to. Secondary Owners and My Site Secondary Admins are configured by going to the SPO Admin Center, User Profiles, Setup My Sites.

What about OneDrive?

OneDrive and OneDrive for Business sound like they could be the same thing. After all, they both have "OneDrive" in their name. However, they are two completely separate cloud services offered by Microsoft.

OneDrive for Business is available only through an Office 365 subscription. It's a paid-for service, and it's hosted in SharePoint Online. OneDrive, on the other hand, is a free, personal, cloud-storage service based in Microsoft Live. It's the Microsoft competitor to services like Apple's iCloud, Google Drive, and DropBox. Currently, even though they have similar interfaces and features and can use the same sync client, the two services do not have anything in common.

A tale of two clients

You might remember that OneDrive for Business used to be called SkyDrive Pro. It was based on an old product created by Ray Ozzie at Groove Networks. Microsoft purchased Groove Networks in 2005, and the product was later included in Office and SharePoint 2007 as Microsoft Office Groove. With the SharePoint 2010 release, the product was renamed to Microsoft SharePoint Workspace. Despite the multiple renames of the product, the original groove.exe application (with updates, of course) still persists to this day as the OneDrive for Business sync client.

In September 2015, Microsoft announced the next generation of the sync client that would overcome some limitations of the classic groove.exe client and provide a more reliable sync. This new client, currently known as the Next-Generation Sync Client, was released in December 2015, and it's included in Windows 10 and Office 2016. You know you're running the next-gen sync client if you see the onedrive.exe process running. This new, long-awaited client adds important new capabilities, provides a better sync, and syncs both OneDrive and OneDrive for Business.

At the time of this writing, the next-gen sync client is not yet at feature parity with the groove.exe client. For example, it currently cannot sync SharePoint libraries or on-premises OneDrive for Business. The classic sync client, groove.exe, is still needed for this purpose. Thankfully, the two can run side by side.

> **TIP** When both the old (groove.exe) and next-gen (onedrive.exe) sync clients are installed and running on a machine, multiple OneDrive icons will appear in the taskbar. You can tell which one is which in two ways. First, when you hover over the icon, the groove.exe client displays "OneDrive for Business" rather than starting with "OneDrive – ." Second, if you right-click the icon and you see a Settings or Manage Storage option, it's the next-gen sync client.

To get the classic OneDrive for Business sync client, go to Knowledge Base article 2903984 at *https://support.microsoft.com/kb/2903984*. From there, you can download the 32-bit or 64-bit installers for your language, as well as obtain the free license key (3V9N8-W93CC-FQPB8-Y9WVF-TVGJ3).

To get the next-gen OneDrive for Business sync client, download it from *http://go.microsoft.com/fwlink/p/?LinkId=248256*. Again, you should already have it if you have Office 2016 or Windows 10. If you're already using OneDrive personal, you can simply add your Office 365 account through the OneDrive sync settings. For more information on this topic, see "Get started with the OneDrive for Business Next Generation Sync Client in Windows" at *https://support.office.com/article/Get-started-with-the-OneDrive-for-Business-Next-Generation Sync-Client-in Windows-615391c4-2bd3-4aae-a42a-858262e42a49*.

Next Level

Enterprise OneDrive for Business Next-Gen Sync Client Deployment

Microsoft provides guidance for deploying the OneDrive for Business next-gen sync client in an enterprise. For more on how to do this, see the following resources:

- "Plan to deploy the OneDrive for Business Next Generation Sync Client in an enterprise environment" at *https://support.office.com/article/Plan-to-deploy-the-OneDrive-for-Business-Next-Generation-Sync-Client-in-an-enterprise-environment-6af6d757-0a73-4fe8-99bd-14c56a333fa3*.

- "Deploying the OneDrive for Business Next Generation Sync Client in an enterprise environment" at *https://support.office.com/article/Deploying-the-OneDrive-for-Business-Next-Generation-Sync-Client-in-an-enterprise-environment-3f3a511c-30c6-404a-98bf-76f95c519668*.

Managing OneDrive for Business

Unfortunately, it's not a simple task to manage OneDrive for Business. There's not much you can do from a browser. However, because we're Cloud Pros, that shouldn't be a problem! There are three primary aspects for managing OneDrive for Business: configuring a My Site secondary administrator, PowerShell, and Group Policy.

> **TIP** Want more information on how OneDrive for Business is being used in your organization? Office 365 includes a report that does just that. Go to Admin Center, Reports, and select OneDrive Usage. See "Office 365 Reports in the Admin Center Preview - OneDrive for Business usage" for more information at *https://support.office.com/article/Office-365-Reports-in-the-Admin-Center-Preview-OneDrive-for-Business-usage-0de3b312-c4e8-4e4b-a02d-32b2f726a680*.

My Site Secondary Administrator

By default, only the user has administrative access to his OneDrive for Business and My Site. Because the My Sites are not visible in the Site Collections page in the SharePoint Online Admin Center, you might find it challenging to set the site-collection administrator. You have to use PowerShell to do so. However, there's a way to avoid this. You can make a user or a security group a site-collection administrator on every My Site that gets created. This role is called the My Site Secondary Admin. Only one user or group can be set in this way. The Secondary Admin will be added to the My Site's site collection administrators when the My Site is first created. Updating it will not affect already-created My Sites, so it's a good idea to set the Secondary Admin as soon as possible.

To set the My Site Secondary Administrator, go to the SharePoint Online Admin Center, go to User Profiles, Setup My Sites. Make sure to select the Enable My Site Secondary Admin check box. Figure 5-3 shows a group named "SharePoint Online Administrators" defined as the My Site Secondary Admin.

My Site Secondary Admin

Add a secondary admin for all My Sites.

You can add a user or security group as a second admin to users' My Sites. Typically, the user who the site is being created for is the only site admin. When you enable a secondary admin, the user or security group selected will always be a site admin on all new My Sites.

☑ Enable My Site secondary admin

Secondary admin:
SharePoint Online Administrators

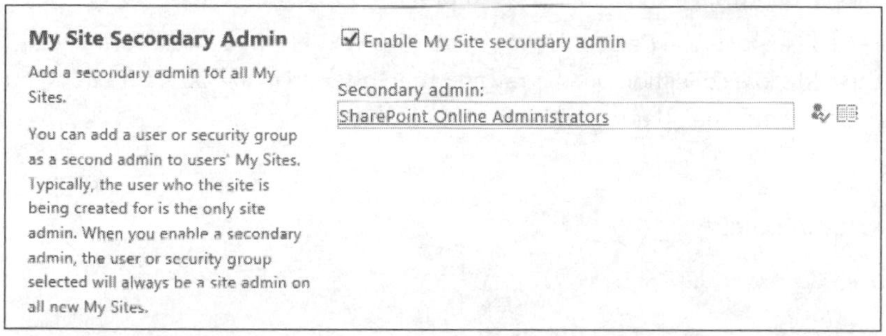

FIGURE 5-3 My Site Secondary Admin

> **TIP** When setting a My Site Secondary Administrator, use a service or user account with a safe or understandable name. OneDrive for Business is a user's personal storage, and users might believe that it's sacred space that only they can access. If they share an item in their OneDrive for Business or look at permissions, they'll see the Secondary Administrator and potentially feel a violation of privacy. If the Secondary Administrator is an account not tied to an individual and has a name that uses words that make a user feel safe (like "administrator" or "audit"), it's more likely that its presence will not be controversial for the users.

PowerShell

As with pretty much all things in Office 365, you can use PowerShell to interact with OneDrive for Business. After you get access to the My Site, you can work with it like any other SPO site collection. However, it can be a little tricky.

One thing you'll likely need to do is grant an account site collection administrator privileges. You can't do this through the SPO Admin Center; instead, you must complete this task using PowerShell. You use the Set-SPOUser cmdlet with the *IsSiteCollectionAdmin* parameter. For example, to grant the admin account site-collection administrator access to David Ahs' My Site (and thus his OneDrive for Business), you use the following command after connecting to the SPO service:

```
Set-SPOUser -Site https://contoso-my.sharepoint.com/personal/david_ahs_contoso_com
    -LoginName admin@contoso.com -IsSiteCollectionAdmin:$true
```

This approach is great for individual My Sites, but what if you need to process *all* the My Sites? For example, what if you want to add an account as site-collection administrator to each My Site (such as for auditing)? To do this, you need to take advantage of SPO's user-profile web service. The location of each user's My Site is stored in the *PersonalSpace* property of the user's profile. The URLs are generally predictable and thus can be guessed somewhat easily. If you want a reliable URL, though, you need what's in that *PersonalSpace* property. The process and PowerShell code to do this can be found in the article "How to display a list of OneDrive for Business site collections" at *https://technet.microsoft.com/library/dn911464.aspx*.

The code in the article exports the *PersonalSpace* values to a text file, but it can be easily modified to store the URLs in a collection or an array and then be used in a loop. To do this, you first need to add the following line up top somewhere:

```
$mySiteUrls = @()
```

Then remove the following line:

```
$Url | Out-File $LogFile -Append -Force
```

And replace it with this one:

```
$mySiteUrls += $AdminURI.Replace("-admin", "-my") + $Url.TrimEnd("/")
```

You do this to store the results in a variable called *$mySiteUrls*. You're creating a full URL while you're at it, and you're removing the final "/" because the Get-SPOSite cmdlet won't like it (if you need to use it in the future). At the end of the script, you have all the My Site URLs in the *$mySiteUrls* variable. You can then loop through them, output them, or do whatever you need.

In the following example, you append some code to the prior script so that you can add an account as a site-collection administrator to all the My Sites:

```
$cred = New-Object System.Management.Automation.PSCredential `
        -ArgumentList $AdminAccount, $sstr
Connect-SPOService -Url $AdminURI -Credential $cred
ForEach($mySiteUrl in $mySiteUrls){
    Set-SPOUser -Site $mySiteUrl -LoginName "admin@contoso.com" `
        -IsSiteCollectionAdmin:$true
}
```

Group Policy

If your clients are in a domain, you can use Group Policy to configure OneDrive for Business even further. The policies affect sync only through the next-gen client (onedrive.exe), though. The following are examples of controls you can set through group policies:

- Enable or disable coauthoring and sharing of Office files in Office 2013 or Office 2016
- Delay updating the client until the second release wave (which is several weeks after the first release wave)
- Set the default location of a user's OneDrive folder (such as to place it on an encrypted disk)
- Prevent users from changing the location of their OneDrive folder

- Prevent users from syncing personal (consumer) OneDrive accounts
- Prevent users from using personal OneDrive's capability to fetch files from the PC

To use these policies, you first must download the OneDrive Deployment Package and copy the OneDrive.admx and OneDrive.adml files to your group policy store. The package can be downloaded from *http://go.microsoft.com/fwlink/p/?LinkId=717805*.

For more information, see "Administrative settings for the OneDrive for Business Next Generation Sync Client" at *https://support.office.com/article/Administrative-settings-for-the-One-Drive-for-Business-Next-Generation-Sync-Client-0ecb2cf5-8882-42b3-a6e9-be6bda30899c*.

> **TIP** You don't want to encourage users to sync libraries to their desktops? If so, you can hide the sync button at the top of a SharePoint Online library. Do so in the SharePoint Online Admin Center by going to Settings and choosing the Hide The Button option in the One-Drive Sync Button section.

Restricting OneDrive for Business sync to safe domains

Many companies are concerned about the potential for data leakage through OneDrive for Business sync. After all, the sync process is all about copying files out of SharePoint Online and OneDrive for Business. To help alleviate this concern, Microsoft provides administrators with the ability to restrict which domains a machine must be in to allow a sync.

By default, a user can sync any file to any machine as long as she is connected via her sync client. However, you can disable users from syncing on non-domain-joined machines or restrict sync to only machines joined to specific domains. For example, you can ensure that content in the Contoso tenant is synced only to machines joined to the Contoso domain. You also can determine whether or not to allow Macs to sync, and you can block certain file types from getting synced. Note, though, that these settings do not affect mobile OneDrive clients. These settings also only block files from downloading; new items or updates to items will still be uploaded. The configuration applies to both the groove.exe and onenote.exe sync clients.

To configure domain restrictions, use the Set-SPOTenantSyncClientRestriction cmdlet with the *DomainGuids* parameter. You give it a comma-delimited list of the domain GUIDs the machine can be in and still sync. For help obtaining a domain's GUID, see "How to enumerate a domain GUID in an Active Directory forest" at *https://technet.microsoft.com/library/dn938435.aspx*.

To block sync with Mac clients, use the *BlockMacSync* parameter. Exclude one or more file extensions by using the *ExcludeFileExtensions* parameter, and block the old groove.exe client by using the *GrooveBlockOption* parameter. For example, the following commands allow downloads in a OneDrive for Business sync client only if the machine is joined to the Contoso domain. However, in it, you do want to allow Macs to sync, because many of your users use them. This code also blocks Excel files and certificates from being downloaded:

```
Set-SPOTenantSyncClientRestriction -Enable `
        -DomainGuids "786548DD-877B-4760-A749-6B1EFBC1190A" -BlockMacSync:$false
Set-SPOTenantSyncClientRestriction -ExcludedFileExtensions "xlsx;pfx;cer"
```

For more information, see the description of the Set-SPOTenantSyncClientRestriction cmdlet here: *https://technet.microsoft.com/library/dn917455.aspx*.

> **TIP** The Office 365 Security and Compliance Center enables you to search the audit log. As discussed in Chapter 8, "Managing governance, security, and compliance," you can use the Audit Log Search page to specify events to filter on. There are six activities related to sync. For more information, including a description of each of the activities, see the "Synchronization activities" section of "Search the audit log in the Office 365 Security & Compliance Center" at *https://support.office.com/article/Search-the-audit-log-in-the-Office-365-Security-Compliance-Center-0d4d0f35-390b-4518-800e-0c7ec95e946c#syncactivities*.

Managing Office ProPlus

Microsoft Office was initially released in 1990. Not many pieces of software have Office's level of success, nor have many been so vibrantly maintained for so long. Office has been one of Microsoft's greatest successes year after year, and it's sure to have a long life ahead.

Traditionally, Microsoft Office was available only for purchase and installation like most any other software. You would purchase it on some kind of media and run a setup program to install it on your machine. The license would be yours to keep forever. Although you absolutely can still do this with Office, Microsoft gives us a new option in Office 365: Office ProPlus. Office ProPlus provides a subscription to an always-current version of Office on the desktop. As long as a user has a license in Office 365 that includes Office ProPlus, that user has a license for Office on his desktop. Additionally, a license unlocks premium features in the Office mobile apps.

> **TIP** Did you know that an Office ProPlus license allows you to install Office on as many as five PCs or Macs, five tablets, and five phones? It doesn't matter if they're owned by your company or are in your home. You can see and manage which machines Office ProPlus is installed on by going to your account in Office 365 (*https://portal.office.com/account/*) and viewing the Install Status page. From here, you can deactivate an install on a machine, as well as get a link to install Office ProPlus.

Office ProPlus includes the following Office desktop applications: Word, Excel, PowerPoint, Outlook, OneNote, Publisher, Access, and Skype for Business. If you need Project Pro or Visio Pro, subscriptions are also available at an extra monthly cost. The current version of the Office desktop applications will be available for installation, as well as the previous versions. Because they're installed on the local computer, the Office applications will work when the machine is disconnected from the internet (unlike Office Online). However, the user is required to connect to the internet at least once every 30 days.

The following Office 365 subscriptions include Office ProPlus:

- Office 365 ProPlus
- Office 365 Business, Business Premium
- Office 365 Enterprise E3, Government E3
- Office 365 Enterprise E4, Government E4
- Office 365 Enterprise E5, Education E5
- Office 365 Nonprofit Business Premium, Nonprofit E3, Nonprofit E5
- Office 365 Home, Personal

> **MORE INFO**   Built into OneDrive, OneDrive for Business, and SharePoint Online is Office Online, also known as Office Web Applications. Office Online includes online versions of Word, Excel, OneNote, and PowerPoint that enable you to view, edit, and create Office documents directly in the browser. These online versions can really improve productivity, and they're available for free across all Office 365 subscriptions. Although they're close in functionality to the full Office applications, they have not yet reached full feature parity (although they're improving all the time). For a comparison of features across Office Online and the desktop applications, see the "Office Online Service Description" at *https://technet. microsoft.com/library/jj819306.aspx.*

Deploying Office ProPlus

One of the most significant differences between traditional Office and Office ProPlus is the way that Office ProPlus is deployed. Instead of your traditional, MSI-based installation that uses something like a DVD or an ISO image and is an offline process, Office ProPlus uses something called *Click-to-Run*. With Click-to-Run, the installation is streamed to the computer, and the Office applications are ready in as soon as two minutes (even though they're not fully down-loaded yet). Click-to-Run is based on Microsoft's Application Virtualization (App-V), and a package encapsulates everything needed to run Office, including updates. Thus, the Office ProPlus installation is self-contained, enabling multiple versions of Office to be on the same machine at the same time if needed.

One of the great features of Office ProPlus is that it automatically and invisibly downloads and applies the latest version of Office, making it an evergreen service. The product is deliv-ered in blocks as needed. Even better, after Office ProPlus is fully downloaded and installed, it's usable offline like any other version of Office. There's no need for internet connectivity to use Office except for the requirement to connect at least once a month.

IMPORTANT You cannot install both the Click-to-Run and MSI installations of the same Office suite on the same machine. For example, you cannot have both Office ProPlus and the MSI version of Visio Pro 2016 or Project Pro 2016 (such as if you were to use MSDN or volume licensing). For example, to use Visio, you must install its Click-to-Run equivalent, Visio Pro for Office 365. You also can use App-V or the Office Deployment Tool to create a Click-to-Run deployment of Visio Pro, Project Pro, or both. (You can learn how at *https://technet.microsoft.com/library/mt703272.aspx.*) This detail is important to keep in mind when planning to deploy Office ProPlus.

There are two ways Office ProPlus can be installed: as self-service deployments or IT-managed deployments.

Self-service deployment

Users are able to install Office ProPlus themselves by going to their Software page in Office 365 at *https://portal.office.com/OLS/MySoftware.aspx.* The page is available from their account page or in their Office 365 Settings. Once on the Software page, the user can select which version he wants to download. You cannot control whether or not the user selects 32-bit or 64-bit, so make sure to give your users good instructions (including the fact that you can't install both on the same machine).

NOTE Office ProPlus licensing permits the user to install it on up to five computers. However, it's up to the user to manage those licenses. You, as an administrator, do not have any visibility into where they are installed, nor can you deactivate an installation on one of the machines. If the user gets the message that he has used all his activations, he must go into his account (at *https://portal.office.com/account/*) and deactivate a machine.

You can configure what applications are available to the user in a self-service deployment. To do so, in the Office 365 Admin Center, go to Settings, Services & Add-Ins, Software Download Settings. On this page, and as shown in Figure 5-4, you can select which Office versions you want to enable (2016 or 2013 for the PC, or 2016 or 2011 for the Mac). If you want to disable self-service Office ProPlus installations, simply disable all versions on the page.

If a version of Office is enabled, you can choose whether or not to include related software. For the 2016 version, you can enable or disable the following: Office (includes Skype for Business), Skype for Business (standalone), Visio (if they're licensed), InfoPath 2013, SharePoint Designer 2013. The 2013 version is similar, except it doesn't include InfoPath. For the Mac versions, you have the following options: Office and Lync for Mac 2011 (OS X 10.6 or higher).

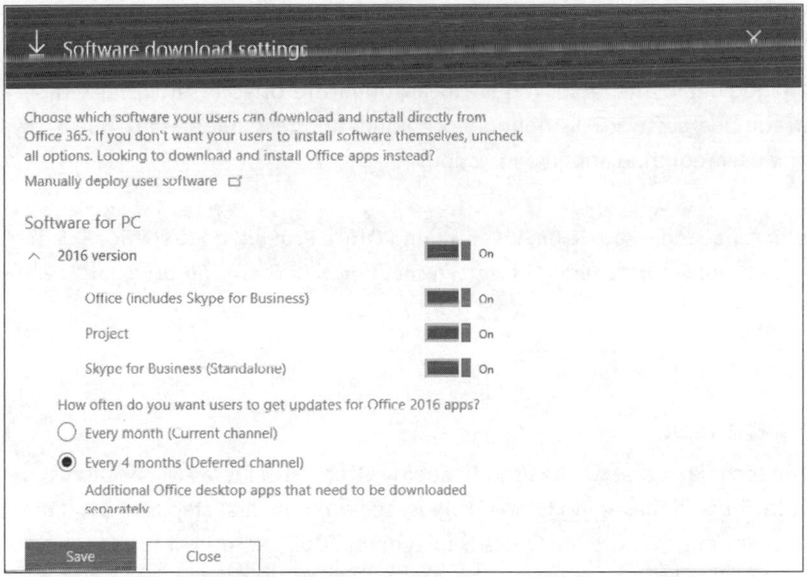

FIGURE 5-4 Office ProPlus download settings

One critical requirement might take the self-service option off the table for you: the user must be an administrator on the machine. There's simply no way around this requirement. For a user to install Office ProPlus herself from the site, she must be a local administrator.

IT-managed deployment

You might find that more control over the Office ProPlus deployments is needed. Self-service deployments might not always be desired. Here are some reasons why this might be the case:

- Users do not have local administrator rights.
- The company or users do not wish to take part in the rapid pace of change in Office and instead the company wants to release changes less frequently.
- Bandwidth is limited or costly, so local network distributions are needed.
- The complete Office suite is not desired for all users, or some users need specific versions of Office.
- Some users cannot be trusted or relied upon for self-service deployments. Some users simply might not be able to do it.

Regardless of the reason, self-service deployments of Office ProPlus might not be an option. Thankfully, that's not a problem because Microsoft provides tools to enable central ized IT-managed deployments. With this model, administrators download and package Office ProPlus to the local network and then push it to the users. The networked location becomes the source for the Office ProPlus Click-to-Run package, not Microsoft.com. Traditional software distribution tools and techniques can then be used to install the package. Additionally, you can configure Office ProPlus to retrieve its updates from a network location instead of the cloud. This flexibility gives you the ability to control the pace of Office change in the organization.

Note that IT-managed deployments still require local administrator access to install Office ProPlus. However, traditional software distribution techniques and technologies provide a way to do this without the user requiring admin permissions.

> **TIP** For a fantastic, one-stop resource for administering Office ProPlus, go to "Office 365 ProPlus – Deployment Guide for Admins" at *https://technet.microsoft.com/library/gg715562. aspx*.

THE OFFICE DEPLOYMENT TOOL

After deciding on the technique that will be used to deploy Office ProPlus (as will be discussed in the "Tools for deploying and managing Office ProPlus" section), the first step is to build the Click-to-Run package. For this, you use the Office Deployment Tool. For more information on how to use the tool, as well as links to download the 2013 or 2016 versions of the tool, go to *https://technet.microsoft.com/library/jj219422.aspx*. You use the tool to do three things:

- Download the Office installation media
- Install, configure, or remove Office ProPlus based on a configuration
- Convert the Click-to-Run package into an App-V package

You do each of these by running the Office Deployment Tool in three different modes: */download*, */configure*, and */packager*. It's all done from the command line. At the core of the process is a configuration XML file. Although a separate XML file can be used for each step or mode (because each mode has its own set of required elements), most likely you'll use one file for all modes.

THE CONFIGURATION XML

You can go to *https://technet.microsoft.com/library/jj219426.aspx* to see a complete reference work on the Click-to-Run configuration file used by the Office Deployment Tool.

The XML configuration file defines everything needed to download, configure, and deploy the Click-to-Run package. For example, it specifies one or more products to download, which edition (32-bit or 64-bit) to use, the language or languages to include, and the path to the package. There is one *<Add>* element, and it's used to define the media location and the edition (32-bit or 64-bit). You can also choose to specify the Office version number to download and which update channel to use. (See the "Change management" section later in this chapter for more information.)

Inside the *<Add>* element are one or more *<Product>* elements. You have one for each product you want to download and include in the package. The available IDs are *O365ProPlusRetail*, *VisioProRetail*, *ProjectProRetail*, and *SPDRetail* (for SharePoint Designer). Inside the *<Product>* element you have the languages to include.

Inside the *<Product>* element, you can also have one or more *<ExcludeApp>* elements to remove specific products from the package. This is your way of customizing what's deployed to the users (something that isn't possible in self-service deployments). For example, you can remove Access or Skype for Business. See the preceding link for the complete list of IDs available.

The *<Updates>* element is very important, because it configures updates for the package. You can disable updates if you like. If updates are enabled, you can specify the path to them. This path can reference a place on the local computer, a file share, or a URL. If the *UpdatePath* attribute is empty, the Microsoft Click-to-Run CDN is used. The *TargetVersion* attribute can be used to install a specific version. (You leave it empty for the most recent version.) If needed, a deadline can be set to force the update (with multiple notifications to the user in advance). Finally, when you're using Office 2016, the *Channel* attribute can specify the update channel to use.

Some important options also can be configured using the *<Property>* element. Use an *AUTOACTIVATE* value of "1" to automatically activate the product, and use a *SharedComputer Licensing* value of "1" if shared computer activation is needed. This value is used when multiple users share the same computer, such as in Remote Desktop Services deployments. In this case, though, each user still needs to activate his or her license. These licenses need to be renewed every couple of days, so the machine will require continual access to the internet. A machine with shared computer activation enabled does not count toward a user's five activations.

You can also fine-tune the experience, such as hiding the interface that normally is shown when Office ProPlus is installed and pre-accepting the EULA (although this requires running the installation under the user's account). You can specify a location to write logs to, which is useful for monitoring deployments.

Finally, you can also use the configuration file to remove products or languages from a machine using the *<Remove>* element. Use *<Remove All="TRUE" />* to remove everything previously deployed.

The following is a comprehensive example of a configuration XML file. In it, we create a 32-bit package in the \\SHARES01\OfficeProPlus\Current share. The package contains all of Office, plus SharePoint Designer. However, we remove Access. We want to include English and Spanish versions of the product, but we want to remove any French versions. We're going to enable updates, but they're going to be pulled from the cloud. We want to give our users new features as soon as they're ready, so we'll set them to the Current update channel. We're going to hide the installation interface for our users, but we can't auto-accept the EULA because the installation won't run under their user contexts. We'll go ahead and write logs to \\SHARES01 \OfficeProPlus\Current_Log, and we'll attempt to auto-activate the licenses. We aren't deploying to shared computers, so we'll disable shared computer activation:

```
<Configuration>
    <Add SourcePath="\\SHARES01\OfficeProPlus\Current" OfficeClientEdition="32">
        <Product ID="O365ProPlusRetail" >
            <ExcludeApp ID="Access" />
            <Language ID="en-us" />
```

```
                <Language ID="es-es" />
        </Product>
        <Product ID="SPDRetail" >
            <Language ID="en-us" />
            <Language ID="es-es" />
        </Product>
    </Add>
    <Display Level="None" />
    <Logging Level="Standard" Path="\\SHARES01\OfficeProPlus\Current_Log" />
    <Property Name="AUTOACTIVATE" Value="1" />
    <Property Name="SharedComputerLicensing" Value="0" />
    <Remove>
        <Product ID="O365ProPlusRetail" >
            <Language ID="fr-fr" />
        </Product>
        <Product ID="SPDRetail" >
            <Language ID="fr-fr" />
        </Product>
    </Remove>
    <Updates Enabled="TRUE" UpdatePath="" Channel="Current" />
</Configuration>
```

> **TIP** You can create as many configuration XML files as you want. For example, you can
> create one standard configuration for most users and another that is a kiosk configuration
> for computers that multiple users share. Group Policy or a deployment tool can then use
> rules to determine which configuration file to use when deploying Office ProPlus.

OFFICE DEPLOYMENT TOOL NEXT STEPS

After the configuration XML file has been prepared and saved to a location (such as
\\SHARES01\OfficeProPlus\Configs\CurrentConfiguration.xml), you can download the media
and use it for installing Office ProPlus. To make life a little simpler, we copy the Office Deployment Tool's setup.exe file to \\SHARES01\OfficeProPlus\ODT\. We'll use it when installing Office
on the clients.

To build the Click-to-Run packages, use the Office Deployment Tool's setup.exe with the
/download switch and the full path to the configuration file. The time it takes to download
depends on what you enabled in the configuration file:

```
\\SHARES01\OfficeProPlus\ODT\setup.exe /download
\\SHARES01\OfficeProPlus\Configs\CurrentConfiguration.xml
```

When it comes time to actually install or configure Office ProPlus on a client, you do the
same thing, except you use the */configure* switch instead:

```
\\SHARES01\OfficeProPlus\ODT\setup.exe /configure
\\SHARES01\OfficeProPlus\Configs\CurrentConfiguration.xml
```

This command can then be run via any method desired (as long as it has administrative access).

TOOLS FOR DEPLOYING AND MANAGING OFFICE PROPLUS

Normally, IT-managed deployments are used in conjunction with Group Policy. Not only can the group policies fine-tune the Office ProPlus deployments and the user experience, but they can automatically install Office ProPlus. First, though, you need to download the Office 2013 or Office 2016 Administrative Template files to use Group Policy to manage the Office deployments:

- Office 2013 Administrative Template files (ADMX/ADML) and Office Customization Tool, located at *https://www.microsoft.com/download/details.aspx?id=35554/*
- Office 2016 Administrative Template files (ADMX/ADML) and Office Customization Tool located at *https://www.microsoft.com/download/details.aspx?id=49030/*

With the Administrative Templates in place, you can create group policies that can configure, among other things, the Office ProPlus update settings. They provide the same settings as those available through the Office Deployment Tool, plus the ability to hide update notifications and the option to enable or disable updates.

To use Group Policy to deploy Office ProPlus, you create a Group Policy with a computer startup script:

1. First, you need to create a batch file (.bat or .cmd) or PowerShell script (.ps1) that contains the */configure* command as shown earlier.
2. Save the batch file to an accessible location (for example, \\SHARES01\OfficeProPlus\ Scripts) or in the Group Policy Object.
3. Next, create or modify a Group Policy. Go to Computer Configuration, Policies, Windows Settings, Scripts (Startup/Shutdown), and double-click Logon to view the startup script.
4. Finally, click the Add button and enter the path to the batch file (for example, \\SHARES01\OfficeProPlus\Scripts\Configure_Current.bat).

After you save and deploy this policy, the batch file runs as an administrator when the user logs in and automatically configures Office ProPlus.

> **TIP** For an excellent example of how to manage Office ProPlus updates using a test group, see the TechNet blog article "Managing Updates for Office 365 ProPlus – Part 2" at *https://blogs.technet.microsoft.com/office_resource_kit/2014/01/28/managing-updates-for-office-365-proplus-part-2*.

You also can use enterprise software deployment tools like Microsoft System Center Configuration Manager (SCCM) and Intune. See "Deploy Office 365 ProPlus by using System Center Configuration Manager" at *https://technet.microsoft.com/library/dn708063.aspx* for instructions on how to use SCCM for the deployment. Note you need to adjust the configuration XML file to remove the *SourcePath* attribute from the *<Add>* element.

> **MORE INFO**   See the following resources to learn about additional Office ProPlus deployment options:
>
> - "Deploy Office 365 ProPlus by using Remote Desktop Services" at *https://technet. microsoft.com/library/dn782858.aspx/*
> - "Deploy Office 365 ProPlus as part of an operating-system image" at *https://tech- net.microsoft.com/library/dn314789.aspx/*

Managing change in Office 365

Office 365 and Office ProPlus are evergreen services. As discussed in Chapter 1, this means that they're ever-growing, ever-building, and ever-changing. Features are continually being released, and that's generally a good thing. It might be a large part of why you're in the cloud, and it's why a lot of companies are choosing Office ProPlus. Isn't it nice to not have to worry about an upgrade project for the next Office release, another upgrade project for the next Exchange release, and yet another upgrade project for the next SharePoint release? As a Cloud Pro, breaking the cycle of upgrade project after upgrade project enables you to focus on delivering new services to your business or unlocking further capabilities in your current services.

This is great, but it's not quite 100 percent realistic. Change is risky, and unmanaged change is especially so. Because it's Microsoft's responsibility to manage and deal with the services and their impact on customers, you can feel pretty well assured that the changes will be well tested and low risk. The continual drip of smaller changes helps to make them less disruptive. However, it's still change, and we don't live in a perfect world with perfect systems and perfect users. As such, you still need to be mindful of changes as they roll out and have a plan for them. Sure, you can point to Microsoft if the company breaks something, but you better be sure you have a well-thought-out story to tell management about what you did on your side. A service-level agreement (SLA) is no replacement for due diligence, especially when the negative impact is functional and as intended and not from faulty code or an outage.

As a result, we strongly recommend you take some time to think through (and document) an Office ProPlus and Office 365 change-management plan. The plan answers the questions that need to be asked related to changes in the products. How do you need updates to be managed? How are changes to be deployed? How often do you want them? What kind of testing is needed? Should some users get them before others? What is the rollback plan in case an issue is too disruptive? In short, *define the risks related to change in Office ProPlus and Office 365, and then come up with a plan to mitigate those risks.*

Once again, Microsoft provides some resources to help you develop this plan. We highly recommend you review the excellent guide "Change management for Office 365 clients" at *https://technet.microsoft.com/library/mt584223.aspx*. This awesome guide walks through Microsoft's new Servicing Model for client updates, describing the release options and update channels, the client release cadence, the types of changes, how to manage updates, and what your role and Microsoft's role are in managing all this. If you're managing Office ProPlus for your clients, it's well worth your time to read it.

How Office ProPlus updates are released

Microsoft has a carefully orchestrated manner in which it releases updates to the service and to Office ProPlus in particular. It's important to understand how they're released so that you can choose the correct update cadence for your users.

Office 365 release validation

Before going into the details around how Office ProPlus updates are released, let's take a moment to look at how Microsoft manages releases to Office 365 as a whole.

Microsoft is one of the largest and primary users of Office and Office 365. As such, it is just as important to them as it is to you that changes are reliable and well tested. Not only does Microsoft use the products, but the company also must support them for the entire world as part of their Software as a Service (SaaS) offering. Microsoft has a lot on the line with any given update, so products go through rigorous testing before they even reach a customer. In fact, Microsoft itself is the first customer to receive any updates—so they better be solid!

This quality-assurance process is managed by rounds of testing and validation called *rings*. Each ring defines a larger and larger audience who receives, tests, and validates the updates. The product teams listen to feedback from users in each ring and incorporate any needed fixes before the product is moved to the next ring. It starts with Ring 0, which comprises the feature teams who are building and testing the product. Next is Ring 1, which includes the whole Office 365 team. Ring 2 includes all of Microsoft, so the updates better be pretty solid by this point. Ring 3 is the first time that customers see updates, since it includes individuals in First Release or one of the Insider programs. The final ring is Ring 4, which is the worldwide release.

Again, the updates are validated at each ring, and feedback is received and incorporated into the product. This means the updates are well validated by the time they reach full, worldwide release.

> **NOTE** You can configure either the entire Office 365 tenant or a subset of users to be part of First Release. You generally should set your tenant to Standard Release, although some organizations (like those who might be more technology-focused) might want to see releases as soon as they hit Ring 3. This setting is controlled in the Office 365 Admin Center by going to Settings, Organizational Profile, Release Preferences. Choose from Standard Release, First Release for Everyone, or First Release for Selected Users.

Figure 5-5 depicts the rings of validation for Office 365. It also shows how the Office ProPlus update channels fit in.

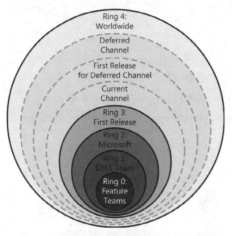

FIGURE 5-5 Office 365 validation rings with update channels

Update Channels

When using Office ProPlus, users no longer receive a long list of patches or updates that they need to install through Windows Update. Instead, they receive regular, monthly updates that are deployed silently in the background. Organizations can control how often their users receive these updates. This is done through opting into *update channels*. Although you can manually control which users get which specific versions through IT-managed deployments, you'll likely not want to take on this burden but instead choose an update channel. An update channel defines the cadence by which Office ProPlus updates will be released. There are three primary channels: Current, Deferred, and First Release for Deferred.

In the Current channel, updates occur monthly, with new features getting deployed as soon as they're widely available. This channel is great if you always want your users to have the latest and greatest. As such, it might also be a little riskier. Again, though, it might result in less disruption to users because they receive smaller updates more frequently.

The Deferred channel, on the other hand, receives updates only every four months. The pace of change is therefore much slower. The updates might be a little more solid, though, because they've had more time to be tested. However, there's a higher risk of disruption because there are more change at each release. The Deferred channel is the default for Office ProPlus.

Microsoft also provides two channels that can help test updates before they are released. The first is the First Release for the Deferred Channel. It enables testing of updates in the Deferred channel before they are released to that channel. Deferred channel updates are released four months early, enabling organizations to have an extra four months of testing. If your company uses the Deferred channel, it's a good idea to have a selection of users in the First Release for the Deferred Channel in order to provide testing and identify potential impacts.

There also is First Release for the Current Channel. It's the equivalent of the Office Insider build. Users in this channel get early access to new features. It's the riskiest build because the updates have not been as widely tested as in the other channels, but it gets you updates as quickly as possible. If you have users in the Current channel, consider also having users in the First Release for the Current Channel to provide testing.

> **MORE INFO** For details on the updates included in the three primary channels, see "Office 365 client update channel releases" at *https://technet.microsoft.com/office/mt465751*. Table 5-2, taken from *https://technet.microsoft.com/library/mt455210.aspx*, summarizes the three primary update channels.

TABLE 5-2 Update channels

Update channel	Primary purpose	How often updated with new features	Default update channel for the following products
Current Channel	Provide users with the newest features of Office as soon as they're available.	Monthly	Visio Pro for Office 365 Project for Office 365 Office 365 Business, which is the version of Office that comes with some Office 365 plans, such as Business Premium.
Deferred Channel	Provide users with new features of Office only a few times a year.	Every four months	Office 365 ProPlus
First Release for Deferred Channel	Provide pilot users and application compatibility testers the opportunity to test the next Deferred channel.	Every four months	None

MORE INFO   For the list of version and build numbers for Office ProPlus, Visio Pro for Office 365, and Project Pro for Office 365, see "Version and build numbers of Update channel releases for Office 365 clients" at *https://technet.microsoft.com/library/mt592918.aspx/*.

Configuring update channels for users

There are multiple ways to configure which update channels your users are in. Which one you use depends on your Office ProPlus deployment strategy. Remember that Office ProPlus defaults to the Deferred channel, so no changes are needed if this is what you want.

- **Software Download Settings in the Office 365 Admin Center**   If users are installing Office ProPlus themselves from the Office 365 portal, select the channel in the Software Download Settings in the Office 365 Admin Center. As you saw in Figure 5-4, you can select from the Current and Deferred channels.

- **Office Deployment Tool**   If you're using the Office Deployment Tool for IT-managed deployments, specify the update channel in the *Channel* attribute of the *<Add>* or *<Updates>* elements. You can choose any of the four: *Current*, *Deferred*, *FirstReleaseDeferred*, or *FirstReleaseCurrent*.

- **Group Policy**   After you install the Office 2016 Administrative Templates (it's not available in the Office 2013 templates), you can set the channel in a group policy by editing the "Update Channel" setting under Computer Configuration\Policies\Administrative Templates\Microsoft Office 2013 (Machine)\Updates. Just enter the name of the channel as you would for the Office Deployment Tool.

Remember that multiple configuration files and group policies can be created, each with their own settings and each targeting their own users.

TIP   We recommend you identify some individuals or groups to receive updates earlier than the rest of the company. Provide a mechanism by which they can easily provide feedback, such as a Yammer group, and then regularly encourage them to use it. Ideally, enlist some individuals in the business units who are heavy users of Office 365 to solicit feedback through real-world testing. Your technology champions might be excellent candidates for First Release.

Protecting your data through Mobile Device Management for Office 365

To this point, we've been discussing applications on the client that users actively interact with. They provide a clear benefit because they increase productivity and enable users to get their work done. However, there's more to the client story with Office 365, and that's mobile device management (MDM). No, it's not likely to be something that will excite your users. It's possible that some might even resent it. However, it can be very important to the company because it can protect against data loss on mobile devices. Not many people love dealing with security on their systems, but the loss of secrets can heavily damage a company or even lead to it going out of business.

What is mobile device management?

MDM is a general concept concerned with—surprise, surprise—managing mobile devices. More and more work is being done on mobile devices. Traditionally, this was not the case. Users came to their place of business, sat down in front of a company-owned and company managed computer, and did their work from 9 to 5. Information was largely contained within a reasonably secured network.

Nowadays, there's the expectation that users should be able to get their work done at any time, from anywhere, and from nearly any device. This work can include email, working on documents, collaborating with coworkers, viewing one's calendar, and so on. The work device can be a mobile device like a phone or a tablet, a company-provided laptop, a PC at home, or an employee-owned laptop as part of a Bring Your Own Device (BYOD) policy. The company's data is not necessarily contained strictly within its walls anymore. It's actually quite possible that a lot of company data is distributed across devices in people's pockets.

This reality poses a real security challenge for companies. What happens if that device is lost or stolen? Is there data on that device that can be accessed by someone else (maybe even someone with harmful intent)? How well protected is that device? If someone turns it on, can that person get direct access to the company systems? These questions might be answerable if the company managed the devices, but that's rare nowadays. Most office workers use personal devices that might or might not have been "on-boarded." This can be quite frightening to most organizations, but many feel like there's not much they can do about it. Quite often, the risk is simply part of the cost of doing business these days.

However, companies can do something to protect themselves and their data: deploy a mobile device management system. An MDM system provides tools companies can use to control who and what has access to data from mobile devices. It enables them to ensure some baseline of protection for both on-boarded (company-managed) and non-on-boarded (personal) devices. This policy usually includes enforcing things like using a PIN, requiring encryption, or deploying a secured browser. Organizations also can provide a way to remotely wipe the device (or a part of the device) if it's stolen or otherwise compromised. An MDM system can be the next-best thing to a company directly managing a mobile device, and such a system is highly recommended for a distributed workforce that needs to bring sensitive company data down to their devices.

Options for mobile device management

A good number of vendors supply MDM solutions. These solutions include VMware AirWatch, MobileIron, Citrix's XenMobile, IBM's MaaS360, and Sophos Mobile Control. Microsoft also provides an MDM product called Microsoft Intune. It provides a full range of MDM capabilities as well as mobile application management (MAM). It can be purchased as a separate subscription service, or it can be acquired as part of the Microsoft Enterprise Mobility Suite. Much of Intune's functionality is included for free in Office 365 in something that's called Mobile Device Management for Office 365 (or more casually, Intune Lite). This functionality will be the focus for the rest of the chapter.

> **MORE INFO** VMware's AirWatch is a popular option for MDM. If your company uses AirWatch, be sure to read VMWare's "AirWatch Support for Office 365 Whitepaper" at *http://www.air-watch.com/resources/white-papers/#airwatch-support-for-office-365-whitepaper*.

Mobile Device Management for Office 365

Mobile Device Management for Office 365 (or MDM for O365) is built into Office 365 as part of all subscriptions (except those operated by 21Vianet). That basically makes it free. Again, it's kind of a light version of Microsoft Intune, and it provides both MDM and MAM abilities. In fact, the MAM abilities it provides with mobile applications are unique to the product.

One of MDM for O365's most compelling features is its ability to perform a selective remote wipe of the device. Remote wipes are a standard feature of MDM, and it's included in Exchange ActiveSync. Typically, they reset a phone back to factory settings and destroy all data on the device. This is pretty drastic, especially for personal devices, which might include personal photos and videos. Instead, when a selective wipe is issued, only the company's Office 365 data in some of Microsoft's key mobile apps is destroyed. Although we expect more apps will be added to the list, the apps affected include the Outlook and OneDrive for Business mobile apps. The apps are not removed, but the data in them is.

From a high level, MDM for O365 works by defining policies for mobile devices. These policies can range from requiring a PIN to blocking rooted jailbroken devices. The company can create as many policies as it needs to. The policies are then assigned to one or more security groups. You can create, for example, one MDM policy that's applied only to sales staff and another that's applied to users dealing with corporate secrets. The latter might be far more restrictive than the former, because there's much greater risk to the company if those users' devices were compromised. Additionally, policies can be created that only report violations instead of blocking access. See "Defining MDM policies" for more information about the policy options.

After a policy has been applied to one or more groups, members of those groups will be prompted to enroll their device when they attempt to use an app with Office 365 data. This usage includes email clients that are set up to sync using Exchange ActiveSync as well as the

Office apps. As part of the enrollment, an app called "Company Portal" is installed on Android or iOS devices. When group members enroll, if their device is not compliant with the policy, they are shown what is needed to bring the device into compliance.

The Company Portal app can assist in implementing some of the changes needed. An email message is also sent to the user explaining why the device was blocked and providing assistance in resolving the situation. The device is blocked from accessing Office 365 data via apps as long as it's out of compliance. Note, though, that this blocking affects only app access. The user still can access Office 365 via the browser. Once the device is enrolled and fully compliant with the MDM policy, the user then can access Office 365 data through the apps. To see what the experience is like for mobile device users, go to "Enroll your mobile device in Office 365" at *https://support.office.com/article/Enroll-your-mobile-device-in-Office-365-c8ac722d-dcaf-4135-8345-3e6327f5d3c5*.

> **IMPORTANT** If users are currently syncing company email to their devices and an MDM policy is implemented, the email will stop synchronizing until the user enrolls her device and the device becomes compliant. Therefore, you first must clearly communicate the impending policy rollout and be ready to support any employee who needs help.
>
> Not all devices support MDM for O365, like BlackBerry devices and older versions of iOS and Android. For these devices, you can choose to block Exchange ActiveSync email. These settings are in the Organization-Wide Device Access Settings (shown in Figure 5-6) on the Device Security Policies page in the Security & Compliance Center.

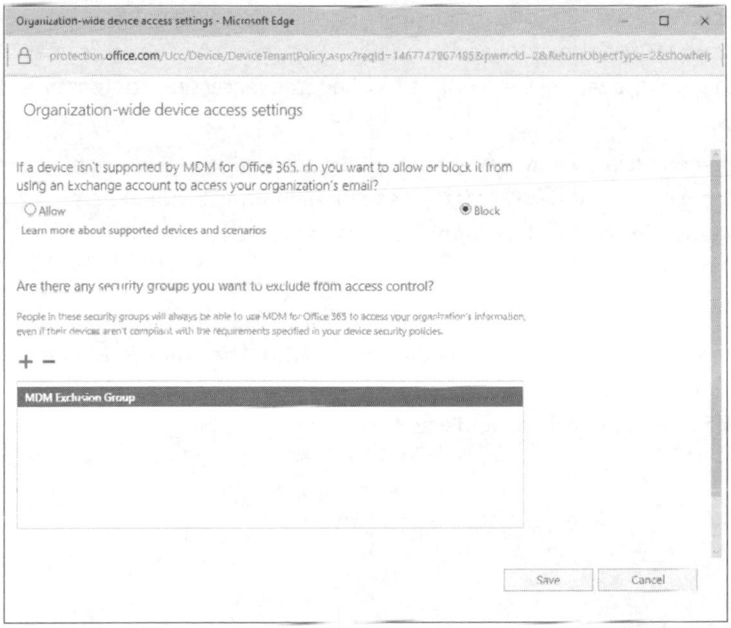

FIGURE 5-6 Organization-wide device access settings

Additionally, you can exclude users from the device security policies. You do this by adding one or more security groups under the heading "Are there any security groups you want to exclude from access control?" in the Organization-Wide Device Access Settings page (also shown in Figure 5-6). Most frequently, this option is used to provide short-term exemption to users who need to sync data but who, for whatever reason, are unable to enroll their device.

For a full description of the capabilities of MDM for O365, including the devices supported, the list of access-controlled apps, and the available policy settings, go to "Capabilities of built-in Mobile Device Management for Office 365" at *https://support.office.com/article/Capabilities-of-built-in-Mobile-Device-Management-for-Office-365-a1da44e5-7475-4992-be91-9ccec25905b0.*

SUPPORTED DEVICES

MDM for O365 currently supports the following devices:

- Android 4 or later versions
- iOS 7.1 or later versions
- Windows Phone 8.1+
- Windows 8.1
- Windows 8.1 RT
- Windows 10
- Windows 10 Mobile

For Windows 8.1 and Windows 8.1 RT, only Exchange Active Sync can be used to secure the devices. For Windows 10 and Windows 10 Mobile, you must first join the device to Microsoft Azure Active Directory (Azure AD). Windows 8.1 and Windows 10 devices can have additional settings to help manage them. However, they will not be blocked from accessing content in Office 365.

For devices not in the preceding list, we recommend you take advantage of Exchange ActiveSync device mailbox policies and device access rules to provide some protection. You can also disable Exchange ActiveSync email for all unsupported devices as well.

ACCESS-CONTROLLED APPS

Only certain kinds of apps require users to enroll their device for MDM. These are considered access-controlled apps, and they are what will be blocked if a user does not enroll. Table 5-3 contains a list of the current access-controlled mobile apps.

TABLE 5-3 Access-controlled mobile apps

App	Windows Phone 8.1+	IOS 7.1+	Android 4+
3rd-party Exchange ActiveSync (14.1+) app	X	X	X
Exchange Mail	X		
Mail		X	
Email			X
Outlook		X	X
OneDrive		X	X
Word		X	X
Excel		X	X
PowerPoint		X	X
Office Mobile			X (phone only)

Microsoft Intune

When MDM for O365 was first released, it was identified as a light version of Microsoft Intune, leading some people to call it "Intune Lite." Microsoft Intune can be purchased as a cloud-based subscription service, or it can be obtained as part of the Microsoft Enterprise Mobility Suite (EMS). If you obtain Intune, you can still use MDM for O365 as well.

One of the primary advantages Intune has over MDM for O365 is that, as a full-featured MDM product, it can manage PCs and Macs in addition to mobile devices. This is particularly useful for distributed workforces, because it doesn't require System Center Configuration Manager to be made available over the internet. Use it to push applications to PCs, ensure antivirus is enabled and running, or perform software updates. Additionally, you can use its MAM capabilities to control what's available through the mobile apps. For example, you can stop users from copying and pasting data out of the Office mobile apps.

For a comparison between the free and paid-for products, see "Choose between MDM for Office 365 and Microsoft Intune" at *https://support.office.com/article/Choose-between-MDM-for-Office-365-and-Microsoft-Intune-c93d9ab9-efb2-4349-9b93-30c30562ee22*.

Exchange ActiveSync

Included automatically in all Office 365 subscriptions is Exchange ActiveSync. Exchange Active-Sync is the primary method that most mobile email clients use to retrieve email, contacts, and calendars. It has been in use since the early days of Exchange and thus is supported by nearly every mobile device. Exchange ActiveSync provides much of the same protection and management as you get from MDM for O365. However, it can perform only a full wipe of a device, not a partial wipe. As such, it can be a good way of providing baseline security configurations for all devices, regardless of whether or not the device can (or the owner is willing to) enroll in MDM for O365.

Exchange ActiveSync policies are called *mobile device mailbox policies*. Multiple policies can be created, and one can be set as the default. Individual mailboxes (generally, users) can have different mobile device mailbox policies assigned. Figure 5-7 shows the options available in a mobile device mailbox policy when working in the browser. Additional options such as enabling or disabling Bluetooth or allowing the use of a storage card are available by using the New-MobileDeviceMailboxPolicy PowerShell cmdlet.

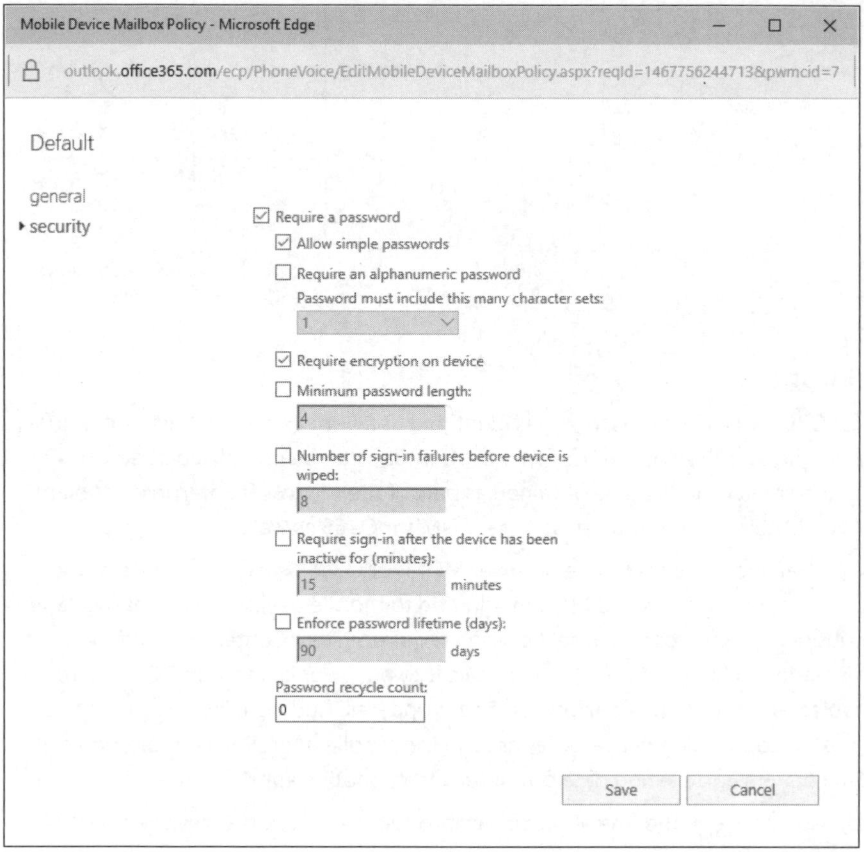

FIGURE 5-7 Exchange ActiveSync mobile device mailbox policy options

> **TIP** Device policies in MDM for O365 override Exchange ActiveSync device mailbox policies. Therefore, you can configure both in your tenant. We recommend doing this so that the device policies will act as the primary MDM policy, with Exchange ActiveSync acting as a secondary policy in case a device is not supported.

For more information, see "Exchange ActiveSync policies for managing devices in Office 365" at *https://technet.microsoft.com/library/dn792010.aspx*.

Configuring Mobile Device Management for Office 365

At this point, you should have a good idea as to why you should use MDM for O365. After all, it's free. Now, let's talk about how to actually implement it.

Preparing Mobile Device Management for Office 365

MDM for O365 is not enabled by default, so the first thing you need to do is activate it. To do this, click on Mobile Management in the Resources menu in the Office 365 Admin Center or go to *https://portal.office.com/EAdmin/Device/IntuneInventory.aspx*. If it has not yet been enabled, click on Let's Get Started at the bottom of the page (as shown in Figure 5-8).

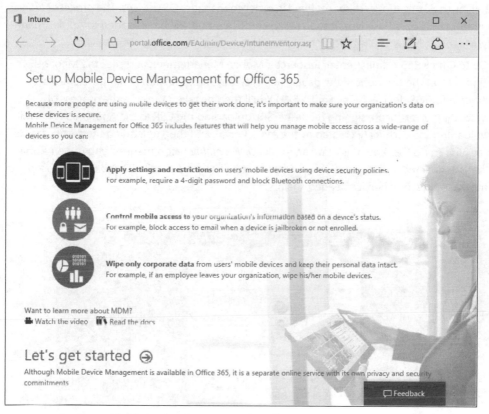

FIGURE 5-8 Setting up Mobile Device Management for Office 365

On the next page, you have the option of specifying the name of the default security policy Office 365 will prebuild for you. Feel free to change it to whatever you like. You can also choose whether or not to add your account to that policy. Once you're ready, click Start Setup

Next, a screen is displayed that keeps you updated on the status of the activation. Be patient—it can take some time for the process to complete. You can return to the page to see the latest status or, once the activation is complete, manage the service.

After the service has been activated, if you have a custom domain registered in Office 365, you need to make sure it's configured for MDM. The DNS records in Table 5-4 need to be added to your DNS host.

TABLE 5-4 DNS records for Mobile Device Management for Office 365

Host Name	Record Type	Address	TTL
EnterpriseEnrollment	CNAME	EnterpriseEnrollment-s.manage.microsoft.com	3600
EnterpriseRegistration	CNAME	EnterpriseRegistration.windows.net	3600

If you'll be managing iOS devices through the service, you also need to do some things to enable push notifications. This is required in order to manage iOS devices. The process involves generating an Apple Push Notification (APN) certificate that will be uploaded to Apple. Thankfully, Microsoft helps you with this.

Go to Office 365 Admin Center, Resources, Mobile Management, and click the Manage Settings link at the top right of the page. Then click the Set Up link for "Configure an APNs Certificate for iOS devices." (See Figure 5-9.) You'll then be taken through the process of downloading a certificate signing request (CSR), uploading the CSR to the Apple APNs Portal, downloading the certificate created by the APNs Portal, and then uploading the certificate to Office 365. To do this, you must have an Apple ID. We *highly* recommended you use an Apple ID that's associated with the company and not a specific user. Save the ID and the password somewhere safe for when it's needed again.

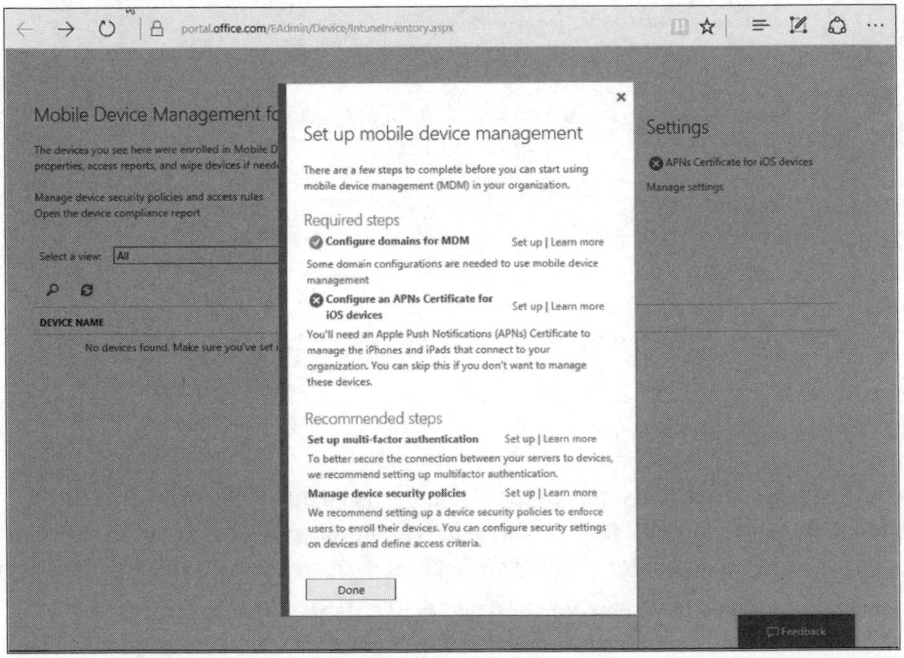

FIGURE 5-9 Setting up mobile device management

TIP The certificate generated by the APNs Portal expires after a year, so you'll need to renew it. If you have a centralized administrator calendar, set up an appointment for a couple of weeks in advance to remind yourself to renew the certificate. If there is no central place where tasks like these are tracked, at least send yourself and one or more other people a meeting request for the renewal.

The detailed instructions on how to configure your tenant for MDM are on the "Set up Mobile Device Management (MDM) in Office 365" page at *https://support.office.com/article/ Set-up-Mobile-Device-Management-MDM-in-Office-365-dd892318-bc44-4eb1-af00-9db-5430be3cd*.

Configuring MDM device policies

Now that MDM for O365 is ready, it's time to set up some device policies. You do this in the Security & Compliance center (*https://protection.office.com*) under Security Policies, Device Security Policies. On this page, you can see all the device policies and change the organization-wide settings. You can also come here for a link to see all the managed devices.

When you create a device policy, you are first given a wide selection of criteria you can require on the device to allow enrollment. If the device does not match all the selected criteria, it cannot be enrolled and therefore cannot sync data. Figure 5-10 shows the options available. Note that not all of them apply to all devices. See "Capabilities of built-in Mobile Device Management for Office 365" at *https://support.office.com/article/Capabilities-of-built-in-Mobile-Device-Management-for-Office-365-a1da44e5-7475-4992-be91-9ccec25905b0* to learn which requirements are supported for which device.

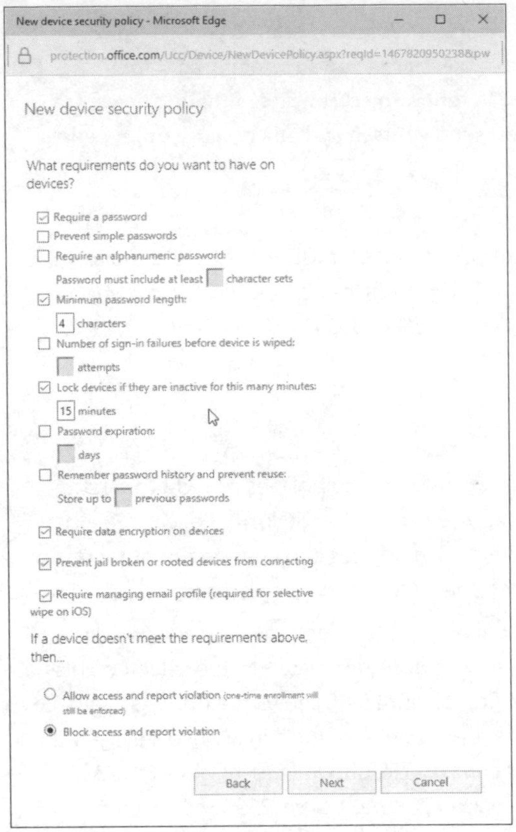

FIGURE 5-10 Available device policy requirements

The available settings are self-explanatory. The Require Managing Email Profile option could use a little more explanation, though. On iOS devices, you can create a custom email profile in the email app settings for email from Exchange Online. The problem, though, is that doing so will not allow the system to perform a wipe of the data. This setting forces the user to remove the custom email profile and instead use the company-managed profile.

> **TIP** Although it might be tempting to set a lot of requirements and really lock down the device through a policy, seriously consider the impact of doing so. If the policy is too onerous or invasive, chances are good that not all users will enroll. This will lead to decreased usage of the services and a reduction in Office 365's ROI, and it might drive people to use other less-secure or less-controlled solutions.

The If A Device Doesn't Meet The Requirements Above option at the bottom of the page is important. This is where you can determine whether or not to simply report whether a device is compliant or to outright block it. If the Allow Access And Report Violation option is selected, users still can sync their data after enrollment regardless of whether their device is compliant.

> **TIP** When creating new policies, it's highly recommended that they first be piloted by a subset of the users. Doing so can help determine whether the policy is appropriate by letting you receive feedback about its impact from the users. We recommend that you first configure the policy to only report on violations without blocking access. This starting point can help you judge how great the impact of the policy might be and thus help you prepare your users for when the policy is eventually fully enabled.

The next page is for optional configurations you can enforce on the device. See Figure 5-11 to see what's available through the browser. There are some additional configurations that are available only through PowerShell (New-MobileDeviceMailboxPolicy and Set-MobileDevice-MailboxPolicy). The vast majority of these are applicable only to iOS devices, such as Require Encrypted Backup and Require Password When Accessing Application Store. Very, very few of these are applicable to Android devices, though. Once again, see "Capabilities of built-in Mobile Device Management for Office 365" at *https://support.office.com/article/Capabilities-of-built-in-Mobile-Device-Management-for-Office-365-a1da44e5-7475-4992-be91-9ccec25905b0* to learn which options are supported for which device, as well as to see a list of the options that are available only through PowerShell.

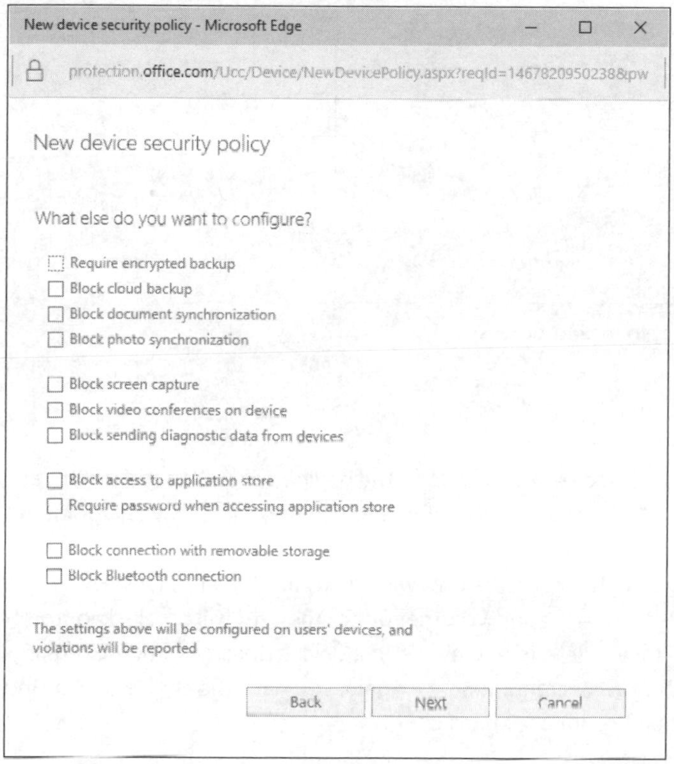

FIGURE 5-11 Additional options when creating a new device security policy

Your final option when configuring a device policy is whether or not you want to apply the policy. It won't be pushed out to users until Yes is selected for "Do you want to apply this policy now" and at least one security group has been added. The members of the security group or groups you add will receive the policy. In Figure 5-12, we opted to apply the policy to the Sales group.

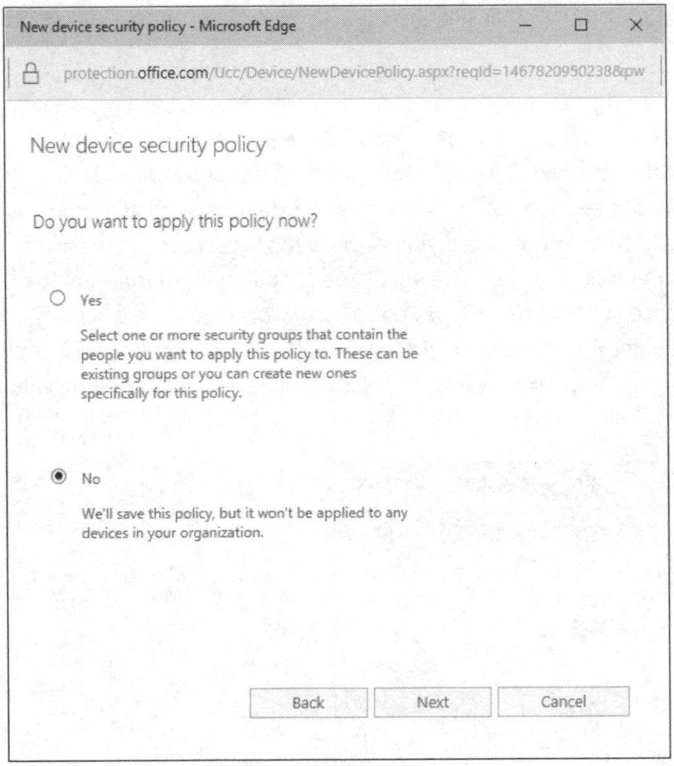

FIGURE 5-12 Applying a device policy to security groups

Publishing MDM policies

To publish an MDM policy, simply add a security group to the device policy. You can do this at creation time (as shown in Figure 5-12), or you can do it later by editing the policy and going to the Deployment page. For a policy to apply to a user's device, the user must be in a security group attached to a policy. Once this happens, the user will be required to enroll his device to access Office 365 data through the mobile apps. Whether or not the user will be blocked from enrollment based on his compliance is determined by the "If a device doesn't meet the requirements above, then..." setting in the access requirements. Again, you have the choice of allowing the device to connect if it is not compliant or of blocking it.

Managing devices through MDM

After device policies are configured and deployed, you have some capabilities to help you manage the devices. Much of this is done through the Mobile Device Management for Office 365 page (Office 365 Admin Center, Resources, Mobile Management). This page lists all the devices that have enrolled in MDM for O365. Here you can see the name of the device, who it's registered to, its operating system and operating system version, its status, its model, and the last time the device synced. To see which devices are blocked, switch the view to Blocked.

This is also where you can go to perform a full or selective wipe of a device. To do so, click on the device and select either Full Wipe or Selective Wipe. You'll be asked for confirmation before the wipe request is initiated.

> **TIP** It might be tempting to exempt VIPs from MDM policies. You also might face a lot of pressure to do so. However, we strongly recommend resisting these exemptions. Individuals like those in top management are the ones most likely to have sensitive information on their devices that could be very damaging if compromised. They also are more likely to be greater targets for theft. Instead, work directly with them or potentially enroll their devices for them.

Hybrid Office 365

M icrosoft is realistic when it comes to Office 365. The company knows that not everyone will, or is able to, migrate entirely to the cloud. There are many reasons why a company might choose to stay with on-premises systems, including security concerns, data-sovereignty requirements, the need for customizations in the product, or already-sunk costs. As such, Microsoft has committed to continuing to release on-premises software like SharePoint Server. Many Microsoft customers, however, use both Office 365 and on-premises software like SharePoint and SQL Server, and although some will migrate entirely to the cloud, most will continue to have a presence in both.

Companies who use both Office 365 and on-premises software like SharePoint have unique concerns. On their own, the Office 365 and on-premises systems are entirely separate. They are islands unto themselves and require their own administration. They don't use the same identities, and the data in one isn't visible to the other. However, this does not have to be the case. Instead, companies can use various techniques to build a bridge between the environments to share identities and surface data remotely. This bridge is what's generally described as a *hybrid* solution, and it's a major focus for Microsoft. Even though Microsoft might have once intended it to be a highway that moved people to the cloud, the company has come to realize that many customers won't or can't. Therefore, it has made hybrid a strategic priority.

Hybrid Office 365 is still rather new and in its early phases. In 2016, hybrid took some big steps forward with the release of the Cloud Search Service Application (Cloud SSA) and SharePoint Server 2016. Before then, its capabilities were more limited and a little awkward. The speed at which Microsoft is releasing new hybrid capabilities is getting faster. Although previously implementing hybrid solutions required careful, obscure work and might have felt to many IT pros as if they were using duct tape and bailing wire, hybrid is now being built into products and is becoming more robust. We have reached a point where deploying hybrid workloads is simply not that big of a deal anymore.

Hybrid Office 365 scenarios and considerations

Although hybrid Office 365 is not as large of a challenge to implement as it used to be, there's still plenty you need to consider as you plan a hybrid deployment. The challenges are more related to architecture, strategy, process, and user impact than about technology. In this section, we'll discuss some of these points so that you'll be able to think strategically about hybrid options and determine how they fit within your organization.

Overview of hybrid options

Before going too far, let's stop and take a quick look at the hybrid options currently available in Office 365. Although we'll briefly describe each, most will be explained in much greater detail later in this chapter. As you can see, most of it is based on SharePoint Server:

- **Outbound SharePoint hybrid search**   When a user performs a search in on-premises SharePoint Server, the user's query is also sent to SharePoint Online and its results are displayed in a block beside the on-premises search results.

- **Inbound SharePoint hybrid search**   This option is the same as outbound SharePoint hybrid search, except the user performs a search in SharePoint Online and the query is sent to the on-premises SharePoint farm. The on-premises results are displayed in a block beside the SharePoint Online results.

- **SharePoint Cloud Search Service Application (Cloud SSA)**   An on-premises SharePoint Server farm crawls content and sends the crawled metadata to Office 365 for inclusion in its search index. When a user performs a search, the query is executed in SharePoint Online, and results from both SharePoint Online and on-premises sources are displayed in a single set of relevant results.

- **Delve**   If the Cloud SSA has been deployed and on-premises content has been crawled, the on-premises content will be available in Delve.

- **Inbound hybrid Business Connectivity Services (BCS)**   BCS is a SharePoint technology that surfaces line-of-business (LOB) data in SharePoint as standard SharePoint lists. You can use hybrid BCS to surface and interact with on-premises data inside of SharePoint Online.

- **Hybrid OneDrive for Business**   When a user clicks on OneDrive in SharePoint Server, instead of going to her on-premises OneDrive for Business (ODB), she is sent to the one in SharePoint Online.

- **Hybrid SharePoint sites**   Hybrid SharePoint sites include the following features:

  - **Hybrid site following**   When a user follows a site in SharePoint Server or SharePoint Online, it's added to a single Followed Sites list instead of two separate lists.

  - **Hybrid extensible app launcher**   The extensible app launcher in Office 365 enables users to access their Office 365 services. The app launcher was recently added to SharePoint Server. The hybrid app launcher surfaces the same apps regardless of whether you're in the cloud or working with an on-premises system.

- **User profile redirection**   When this option is enabled in SharePoint Server and a user clicks on the profile of a cloud user or opens their own profile, the user is taken to the Office 365 profile instead of the on-premises profile.

- **Power BI, PowerApps, Flow, Logic Apps**   Deploying a free data gateway as part of an on-premises system enables LOB data to be presented as a data source in Power BI, PowerApps, Microsoft Flow, and Logic Apps.

- **Azure Active Directory (Azure AD)**   Several hybrid features are built in to Azure AD that can be used with on-premises implementations or with other clouds:

  - Profile synchronization using Azure AD Connect

  - Multi-factor authentication (MFA)

  - Password write-back

  - Single sign-on to other cloud services

  - Single sign-on to on-premises, claims-based systems like SharePoint Server

- **Azure AD Application Proxy**   You can use the Azure AD Application Proxy to publish on-premises browser-based applications to your users without going through a virtual private network (VPN) and, optionally, add Azure AD features like multi-factor authentication.

- **Hybrid Exchange**   A hybrid Microsoft Exchange deployment enables users to have a single email experience regardless of whether their mailbox is in the cloud or on-premises.

- **Hybrid Skype for Business**   A hybrid Microsoft Skype for Business deployment ties together on-premises and cloud Skype for Business services regardless of whether the user is cloud-only, on-premises, or federated.

- **Yammer**   When enabled in SharePoint Server, Yammer is added to the bar at the top of SharePoint pages.

- **Duet Enterprise Online**   An add-on feature, Duet Enterprise Online surfaces information from SAP applications in SharePoint Server and SharePoint Online.

- **Microsoft SharePoint Insights**   This feature is currently in preview, so little is known about it. According to *https://msdn.microsoft.com/library/mt622371*, "Microsoft SharePoint Insights aims at helping SharePoint administrators manage their infrastructure more efficiently. With SharePoint Insights, Office 365 reports are generated using your SharePoint 2016 on-premise [sic] diagnostic and usage logs."

Each of these options can be deployed independently, and you can use as many as you like.

Identity synchronization is foundational!

Nearly all the hybrid options just listed are dependent upon one thing: identity synchronization. Identity is really the one thing that binds together both Office 365 and on-premises systems. Without working, successful identity sync, just about all hybrid solutions would simply fail. The exception is the data gateway connecting to data sources other than SQL Server Analysis Services (which requires identity sync). Therefore, it's critical that you start any hybrid effort by making sure your identity sync is solid.

As you learned in Chapter 3, "Working with Azure Active Directory for Office 365," identity synchronization is primarily composed of three parts: Active Directory Domain Services (AD DS), Azure AD, and directory synchronization (Azure AD Connect). All users who will be using hybrid features must have an on-premises AD DS account that has been synchronized to Azure AD using a tool like Azure AD Connect. Active Directory Federation Services (AD FS) can be used as well, but it isn't required. If AD FS is not used, you need to include the users' password hashes in the identity sync.

> **IMPORTANT** A prerequisite for configuring identity synchronization is the cleanup of Active Directory user profile data, which can be a time-consuming exercise.

Additionally, for most SharePoint-based hybrid components to work (the exceptions being ODB and profile redirection), you need to configure identity federation on your on-premises farm. Microsoft Azure Access Control Service (ACS) is an Azure service that provides identity federation for Azure AD. It's effectively a gateway for external systems to provide authorization with Azure AD. Your on-premises SharePoint Server needs to have a server-to-server (S2S) trust established with Azure ACS to provide the identity federation needed for hybrid SharePoint. Once this trust is established, Azure ACS will act as a trust broker between SharePoint applications and Azure AD. You actually end up registering SharePoint Online as a high-trust app in SharePoint Server using Azure ACS as a trust broker. To do all of this, though, you need to ensure your farm is properly configured.

See Chapter 3 for more information on identity synchronization and Azure AD Connect.

Hybrid considerations

Although configuring hybrid is very technical, the operational and strategic implications are much less so. As you think through your hybrid strategy, make sure you consider the topics presented in the following sections.

Where should the workloads go?

One of the first things you need to consider when evaluating hybrid solutions is where your workloads should go. *Workload* can mean any category of work, either something broad like collaboration, intranet, social, or personal storage or something specific such as individual business processes or teams. Make a list of your workloads, and map them to your available or potential environments. The following topics should be considered when you evaluate which environment a workload should be deployed to:

- What are the workload's dependencies? It's possible that a critical dependency could dictate its location. For example, if there's a business process that's dependent on Microsoft PerformancePoint dashboards, the workload needs to stay on-premises.

- Don't split a workload across environments. You might be able to if the workload has clearly independent components or if it can be done in an automated manner, but we highly recommend against it.

- Consider how critical the workload is and how much control or governance you need over it. Which environment meets your requirements? On-premises implementations generally give you more control and so sometimes might be a better fit.

- Consider which features are available. Do they match what's required? Again, if you need PerformancePoint, SharePoint Online won't be an option. The same is true if you need a custom farm feature. To determine this, you need to have a solid understanding of the feature sets of both environments.

- Consider potential access patterns and bandwidth needs. Who will be using it? How? From where? If, for example, there's a large need to have access outside of the corporate network, SharePoint Online would be a good option. Additionally, if the solution requires the movement of large amounts of data, the cloud could be a better fit if the users are not on site. However, if the users are local, downloading the data from SharePoint Online could become a significant drain on bandwidth and increase latency.

- Consider the potential loss of connectivity, either outbound to the cloud or inbound. If it's a critical workload and the wide area network (WAN) is unstable, it might be best to keep it on the premises. We'll talk about this more in upcoming sections.

- Does there need to be interaction with external users? Is it an extranet scenario? If so, SharePoint Online and ODB have *significant* advantages over an on-premises solution.

- Consider the costs. Running an on-premises system can be costly. Moving a workload to Office 365 can potentially eliminate that system and thus the cost. Then again, if the costs have already been incurred and running the workload does not add any other costs, it might be cheaper to stay with that on-premises solution than to sustain a monthly subscription for your users. Also, cloud services usually represent an operational expense versus what is likely an on-premises capital expense. All of these considerations need to be taken into account, but be careful to perform a balanced analysis. It can be a challenge to calculate the full return on investment (ROI) of a cloud solution.

Not all workloads need to be deployed to the cloud all at once. Instead, build a one-year or two-year strategic plan that moves or implements workloads in a realistic and workable manner.

Generally speaking, we recommend favoring the cloud when considering a workload. Looking into the future, it's more likely that more workloads will be migrated to the cloud rather than be migrated from the cloud to on-premises. Deploying new workloads in the cloud can save potential future effort and cost, plus they can take advantage of the available cloud features.

Where's the data?

The location and accessibility of data are important to include in your analysis. The nature of hybrid means that you're connecting two remote systems. They are, by definition, separate from each other. As such, user behavior, user expectations, the network, and performance all can be a factor.

Hybrid has the potential of being confusing to users. This is especially true if the workloads are split between on-premises systems and the cloud. Users need to clearly understand where they need to go to do their work. Additionally, working across multiple environments can be confusing and overwhelming for some users. Many companies work hard to mask any differences between environments by making them both look and feel as similar as possible. This approach, however, can require significant effort. In general, keep the user in one location as much as possible. The data should follow the workload and be located with it. Doing so will greatly reduce confusion and the risk of lost productivity.

An additional strategy is to use the hybrid technologies to bring the data to the user in order to reduce the need to move between environments. Use technologies like search, BCS, and Power BI to surface remote data wherever the user is. Although doing so can result in additional work or cost, it should improve productivity. You can also take advantage of the Cloud SSA to merge Office 365 and on-premises data into a single relevant result set in a single location.

Temporary vs. permanent hybrid solutions

A hybrid solution can either be permanent or temporary. Microsoft's initial vision was that hybrid systems would be configured temporarily while companies migrated to the cloud. Microsoft has long since realized that it's going to be a permanent state for most companies.

Deploying hybrid solutions temporarily can certainly be the easiest approach. It doesn't require the same level of rigor and operational excellence that a permanent hybrid solution does. For example, many organizations will establish hybrid solutions temporarily with Exchange to migrate mailboxes to Exchange Online. After they've all been moved, the hybrid configuration will be torn down along with the Exchange deployment.

Chances are good you'll need hybrid for the long term. If so, understand that it will require some additional diligence and might require you to change some of your processes. You'll want to provide ongoing monitoring of the components (such as connectivity to Office 365 and the Azure AD Connect sync). Hybrid systems might require certificates, so you'll need to make sure they're maintained. A hybrid approach adds more complexities, especially when it comes to testing. Chances are you'll want a test environment. If so, that's going to require its own tenant and maintenance. (See the upcoming sections for more details about this.) Hybrid solutions also likely require more testing overall. You'll also want to truly understand all the moving parts in a hybrid implementation to understand which changes will break it. Hybrid can be rather fragile at times. Finally, you'll need to make sure to factor hybrid into your evaluation of support solutions, like monitoring or auditing.

What happens when connectivity is lost?

Chances are that you'll lose connectivity to Office 365 at some point. Even though loss of connectivity happens infrequently, you should be aware that significant portions of end-to-end internet connectivity are out of your hands. As you go forward, you should at least consider the impact of losing your connection to the internet and then, if possible, mitigate the risk.

For example, you can install redundant WAN connections in case a line fails. You can even go so far as to deploy WAN connections from two (or more) separate internet providers. Additionally, consider Azure ExpressRoute for Office 365 if a more reliable connection is required. Finally, if the workload is critical enough that it cannot tolerate a loss of connectivity, consider simply moving it to where the users are.

Regardless of which strategy you adopt, be aware of the possibility for disconnects and factor that possibility into your planning.

Building a hybrid test environment

We mentioned testing several times. Office 365 and hybrid implementations should be tested just like any other system. How do you know that a given script will work? What about updates? You can't uninstall a SharePoint Server cumulative update, so you can be assured of a very bad day if you deploy one to production that ends up breaking your hybrid solution. You won't know the impact of a change unless you test it first. This is fundamental to IT and is well understood.

Unfortunately, though, a lot of companies don't have a good strategy for testing Office 365 and hybrid solutions. Most forgo standing up test Office 365 tenants because it represents an additional, highly visible cost. As a result, most organizations end up testing directly in their production tenant. This practice is dangerous, especially when dealing with hybrid systems. However, the problem of setting up test hybrid environments is not easy to solve.

Because the financial challenge of paying for one or more Office365 tenants is clear, let's set it aside. Many companies have at least one SharePoint environment for testing patches or customizations. You might think testing is simply a matter of deploying hybrid systems to that farm as well, because hybrid connections to one tenant can be established with multiple on-premises farms. The problem for most organizations, however, comes when they have a separate test tenant.

The problem comes down to identity synchronization. Remember, identity sync is necessary in order to do hybrid. If your company is like most, you have only a single domain. Your test environments are probably in the same domain as production, although they're named differently and (hopefully) have their own service accounts. If end users need to do testing, they generally use their regular accounts when they log in to the test environment. Not only is this less burdensome for the users, but it makes environment refreshes much simpler. But there's a problem with this.

Recall from Chapter 3 that a domain object can be synchronized with only one Azure AD tenant. This limitation means you cannot sync the users of one domain to both production and test tenants. Unless you want to create separate users and use filtering to sync some users to one tenant and the rest to another, you're stuck with either not deploying identity sync to the test tenant or deploying a second domain. Creating a second domain, however, can be a significant challenge for a lot of companies, especially if they're small.

To really ensure your hybrid testing is representative of production, it becomes necessary to have a separate tenant with a separate domain with separate users and its own Azure AD Connect sync. This approach gives you the identity sync you need. This means your test SharePoint Server farm will be in that separate domain, which might mean rebuilding it if it's currently in your production domain. However, making this effort will enable you to truly test all aspects of hybrid systems in a production-like environment.

To be clear: You can still do some testing with a single tenant and a single domain. This is especially true if you're just using inbound and outbound query federation. (See upcoming sections for more information.) You can even do it with the Cloud SSA, although your capability to test it will be significantly limited. This is because there's a single cloud index, meaning any crawling in your test environment sends results to the same index as production. This behavior is dangerous because it confuses users to see test items in production search results, potentially leading them to work in the wrong place and thus lose work. The solution to this issue is to simply not crawl in test environments. As you can see, though, this is not a like-production test and therefore will limit what you can do to validate software updates or configuration changes.

Our recommendation is to take the time and incur the expense to build out a proper test environment with a separate domain and separate Office 365 tenant, especially if you expect your hybrid deployment to be permanent. Hybrid solutions are likely to become even more important in the future, so proper testing and validation will be a must and therefore a justifiable expense.

The problem of non-hybrid services

Not all services can be configured for hybrid systems. As you can tell by looking at the list of hybrid options shown earlier, currently they're primarily focused on SharePoint. Even in SharePoint, there are services that are not hybrid. You also might have only deployed a subset of the hybrid options in your system. As you consider your hybrid strategy, make sure you also think through the non-hybrid services.

Let's look at an easy SharePoint example: terms in the managed metadata service (MMS). Microsoft is currently working on a hybrid MMS solution, but we'll ignore that for now. Both SharePoint Online and SharePoint Server have their own, independent term stores. Each SharePoint instance uses its local term store for its terms and cannot use any from the remote location. Chances are extremely good you'll want both to have the same terms so that there's consistency across environments. At this point, if terms are created in one term store, somebody needs to create them in the other term store. This is an imperfect solution because the terms won't actually be the same. Underlying each term and term set is a GUID that will be different. This difference will be a problem if you ever choose to migrate SharePoint data from one environment to the other, because the GUIDs won't match.

> **TIP** One solution to the MMS hybrid issue is to write some code to push terms from one term store to another in a way that maintains the GUID. One of the authors of this book, Brian Laws, created a PowerShell solution to do this. If you're interested, see his blog entitled "Sync a Managed Metadata Term Group with SharePoint Online or On-Premises," which you can find at *http://summit7systems.com/sync-a-managed-metadata-term-group-with-sharepoint-online-or-on-premises.*

As you can see, non-hybrid services like MMS can be a real challenge. Although there's a potential solution to this specific problem, and Microsoft is preparing a hybrid term store solution, this will not be the case for all services. If the service exists in both locations, do you use only one? Both? If both, is one more authoritative than the other? How are changes in one reflected in the other? Should they be? If you decide that only one should be used, what do you do about the other one? How do you keep people from using it? These aren't easy questions to answer.

Let's take another example: user profiles. There aren't true hybrid SharePoint user profiles. User profiles are tied to a user's My Site. Therefore, a hybrid solution means having two user profiles and two My Sites. Companies normally choose to solve this problem by designating one service as the owner of the profiles. They then shut down the service in the other environment to prevent users from using it. For example, if Office 365 is the owner of user profiles, they disable as many My Site or profile-related features in the on-premises farm as possible. This approach effectively kills the on-premises SharePoint social features, but it's a trade-off companies often are willing to make.

As you plan your hybrid strategy, make sure you take into account the services that are not hybrid-ready. Doing so as early as possible can help you avoid confusion and extra work down the road.

SharePoint hybrid solutions

When most people think about hybrid implementations of Office 365, they usually think of hybrid solutions with Exchange or SharePoint. And when they think of hybrid solutions with SharePoint, they usually think about search. This is largely because SharePoint search was one of the earliest hybrid workloads. However, Microsoft has been continually growing the hybrid capabilities in Office 365 as a whole, as well as within SharePoint Online. SharePoint hybrid systems have gone past hybrid search, especially with the advent of SharePoint 2016.

Our focus is on the SharePoint hybrid options and architectures. We want to make sure you understand what moving parts you'll find in those systems so that you can speak intelligently about what's available. For the technical details, including how to deploy a hybrid SharePoint system, grab the free ebook from Microsoft Press: *Configuring Microsoft SharePoint Hybrid Capabilities* by Jeremy Taylor, Neil Hodgkinson, and Manas Biswas. The authors are among the most knowledgeable experts on the subject and will tell you everything you need to know. You can download a copy from *https://blogs.msdn.microsoft.com/microsoft_press/2016/07/06/free-ebook-configuring-microsoft-sharepoint-hybrid-capabilities*. We're relying on them to tell you the details of implementing a hybrid SharePoint solution. We simply don't have the space here.

Overview of hybrid capabilities in SharePoint

The SharePoint hybrid capabilities can be implemented in multiple ways depending on your requirements. Hybrid elements are focused primarily on SharePoint search, but they also include surfacing on-premises line-of-business (LOB) data using inbound Business Connectivity Services (BCS), hybrid OneDrive for Business and offline sync, user profile redirection, hybrid site following, and the extensible app launcher. Before going into specifics, we'll first talk about some important considerations.

Before you start implementing a SharePoint hybrid system, make sure you first understand your requirements. Why do you need it? Who's going to use it? What kind of experience does the user need? Where will users be working (on-premises, from outside the network, or both)? What data needs to be accessed? How does it need to be used once users have it? Also, review the hybrid considerations mentioned earlier to ensure you thought through as many of their potential effects as you can. Gathering your requirements and understanding your constraints will put you in a good position to choose and plan your hybrid SharePoint implementation. Not all options will make sense for your situation, so be sure to pick what's right for your company.

The problem of query federation

Before we get into the hybrid options, we need to review a key concept: *query federation*. This concept is critical to understanding the differences between classic hybrid search and the new hybrid search. With standard, traditional SharePoint Server search service applications (SSAs), the local SharePoint farm has its own index and query components. When you do a search, SharePoint issues a query to the SSA's query component, which then sends the query to the index component. The page eventually gets back the query results and displays them in a result block. This is the normal search experience that people are familiar with.

The SSA can also be configured to use a *remote result source*. A result source does several things, but the main purpose of a *remote* result source is to tell the SSA where another index is so that it can be sent queries as well. The remote index can be local on the network or it can be on the internet, like SharePoint Online or even Microsoft Bing. When the remote result source is used, the query component sends the query to that remote index and gets the result back, just like with the local index. Sending a query to a remote index and receiving a result back is called *query federation*.

But there's a problem. Usually, when someone configures hybrid search, that person does so because he wants the user to get results from both the local and remote indexes. This person doesn't necessarily care where the item is; he just wants it in the results. Unfortunately, the user experience with query federation is not quite ideal. You see, the remote results are retrieved via *query rules* that tell the query component to send the query to both indexes. The component does so, but it does it as two different queries with two different sets of results. Each index has its own complicated ways of determining the relevancy of the data to the user. It weighs all kinds of factors based on the data it has. The two indexes don't have access to the same data, nor do they necessarily have the same algorithms, so the meaning of "relevant" will be different with each. The query component, after it receives the results, has no way of knowing how relative a result from one index is compared to another result from the other index. Thus, the query component can't combine the results into the single, unified, interwoven set of results the user really wants. Instead, the two results must be displayed side by side. SharePoint gives you the option in a query rule of pinning the remote result block to the top of the primary search results or of letting the result block float within the primary results based on its perceived relevance. Either way, you only get the remote results in that block and not inter-woven with the primary results. This can be confusing or frustrating for users, and it can lead to remote results being missed. This is particularly problematic if the remote results are more accurate and actually contain what the user is looking for. It's not ideal.

All this being said, query federation is still excellent in many situations and might meet your needs perfectly. It isn't bad by any means. However, generally it means having two result blocks instead of one, and that might not be ideal for your users.

One-way, outbound, classic hybrid search

One-way, outbound, classic hybrid search is what people normally start with. It's considered the easiest search solution to deploy. In this scenario, query federation is configured in the on-premises SSA with SharePoint Online acting as the remote result source. Query rules are created in the on-premises SSA, which surfaces the SharePoint Online results in a result block within the on-premises results. Its architecture is described in Figure 6-1.

Nothing is needed for this configuration other than the basic requirements (which are dis-cussed more fully later): the S2S farm trust, the Azure ACS proxy, identity synchronization, and outbound internet connectivity. Result sources and query rules are created in the on-premises SSA.

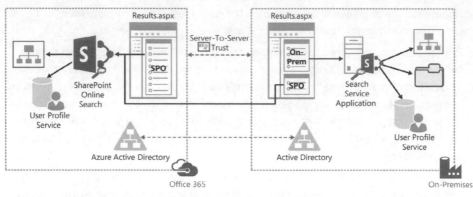

FIGURE 6-1 One-way, outbound, classic hybrid search architecture

One-way, inbound, classic hybrid search

One-way, inbound, classic hybrid search is rare. In this scenario, query federation is configured in SharePoint Online with the on-premises SSA acting as the remote result source. Query rules are created in SharePoint Online that surface the on-premises results in a result block within the SharePoint Online results. Its architecture is described in Figure 6-2.

Like outbound classic hybrid, inbound classic hybrid needs the same basic requirements: the S2S farm trust, the Azure ACS proxy, and identity synchronization. However, the result sources and query rules are created in SharePoint Online this time. The major requirement for an inbound hybrid solution is that the on-premises farm must be published to the internet via a reverse proxy using certificate-based pre-authentication. We recommend using the Microsoft Windows 2012 R2 Web Application Proxy. The certificate used to secure the reverse proxy's public endpoint must be from a public certification authority, like Verisign or DigiCert. The certificate used for the pre-authentication is stored in SharePoint Online's Secure Store Service in a *target application*.

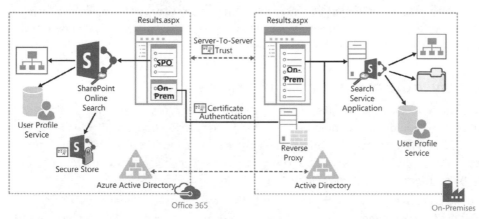

FIGURE 6-2 One-way, inbound, classic hybrid search architecture

Two-way classic hybrid search

Two-way classic hybrid search is a mix of both inbound and outbound classic search. In fact, you simply deploy both. Each environment will have result sources pointing to the remote service, as well as query rules. Searches in SharePoint Online will have an on-premises result block, and vice versa. Its architecture is described in Figure 6-3.

The requirements for deploying two-way classic hybrid search are everything from outbound hybrid search and everything from inbound hybrid search.

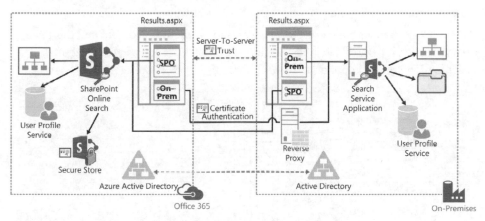

FIGURE 6-3 Two-way classic hybrid search architecture

Hybrid search via the Cloud SSA

In SharePoint Server 2016 and SharePoint Server 2013 with the August 2015 (or later) cumulative update is a new, improved method of doing hybrid search. Its impact is significant enough that Microsoft renamed the previous hybrid search techniques "classic!" This new method is called the Cloud Search Service Application, or Cloud SSA. If it's possible, the Cloud SSA should be your hybrid search solution going forward.

The Cloud SSA solves the query federation problem. Instead of having two distinct result sets, the Cloud SSA gives a single set of relevant results with both on-premises and SharePoint Online results interwoven. It does this because there's only a single index. The index is in SharePoint Online. The Cloud SSA is deployed in an on-premises system in effectively the same manner as a regular SSA. There is, however, one small switch that enables hybrid mode. You then run a Windows PowerShell script (provided by Microsoft at *https://www.microsoft.com /download/details.aspx?id=51490*) that hooks up the on-premises farm to the Office 365 tenant. This process is called *onboarding*

After all this is done, the Cloud SSA looks similar to a regular SSA, and it uses the same screens in Central Administration. The big differences, though, are in the crawling process (which we'll say more about in a moment) and the fact that the content processing, analytics, and index search components are idle and not used (even though they technically are still there). This happens because these three components have been offloaded to Office 365.

Normally, when an SSA crawls content, the crawler dumps the content into what's called the *content enrichment pipeline*. In simplistic terms, this pipeline is composed of the content processing and analytics search components. These items make sense of the content and determine how to make it relevant to users. The result of using the content enrichment pipeline is that the content's metadata is sent to the index, where it's then stored. Most of this process is dramatically different with the Cloud SSA. The crawler is the same, but instead of sending the content to the on-premises content enrichment pipeline, it parses the content and sends the parsed chunks to the Office 365 Search Content Service (SCS). The on-premises farm is now effectively done with its processing.

The SCS is an API responsible for receiving the parsed on-premises content (not the actual content) and getting it to the cloud index in SharePoint Online. As you can see in Figure 6-4, the SCS contains multiple components.

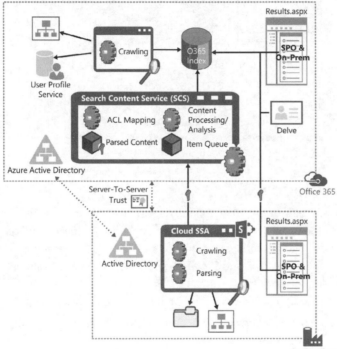

FIGURE 6-4 Hybrid search via the Cloud SSA architecture

First is the item queue, which receives the parsed content from the Cloud SSA. The parsed content is encrypted and stored in Azure Blob Storage. This allows Microsoft to rebuild the index if needed without having to recrawl all your data. The content then goes into content processing and analytics, followed by access control list (ACL) mapping. In this phase, the SCS maps the credentials that it sees on the content with identities in Azure AD. This order of events enables results to be correctly security-trimmed when a user does a search. Finally, the SCS sends all the metadata it collected to the SharePoint Online index and Office 365 Graph. Office 365 Graph is Microsoft's relationship-based *graph database* that powers functionality such as Microsoft Delve.

So what does all of this mean? In short, you crawl your stuff using your on-premises system and everything gets sent to the cloud index. Because both on-premises and SharePoint Online content are in the index together, your searches can thus bring back in a single block of results anything that's been crawled, regardless of its location. Additionally, because the on-premises results also get written to the Office Graph, you can use Delve to see on-premises results alongside your Office 365 results.

There are a number of implications from all of this:

- Because the index is in the cloud, you need to manage the search schema in the cloud as well. The *search schema* is the collection of crawled and managed properties. The on-premises search schema becomes irrelevant.

- Although you manage the search schema in the cloud, you still manage all aspects of crawling in the Cloud SSA. This includes configuring content sources and monitoring the crawls.

- Querying is primarily done in SharePoint Online. Microsoft generally wants the search experience to be in the SharePoint Online search center. In the on-premises system, because the index is remote (it's in the cloud), you actually need to deploy a remote result source pointing to SharePoint Online, just like with outbound classic hybrid. This is needed for any on-premises search-based solution, like content by search web parts (CSWP), and for the contextual search (the small search box at the top of a list or the small search box in the ribbon). You can still get search results in the on-premises SharePoint but you need to use remote result sources.

- Because queries go to SharePoint Online, all users who issue a search need to have a license that includes SharePoint Online. You will not be able to use the Cloud SSA for unlicensed or anonymous users.

- Because crawling is done in the on premises system and the parsed content is sent to the SCS, there will be increased utilization of your WAN. Make sure that you monitor your WAN or schedule crawling for times of low utilization.

> **TIP** If you have a geographically dispersed environment with data at each location (including if your SharePoint Server farm is hosted remotely, such as in Azure), it might be prohibitively slow to crawl each location remotely. Instead, you can deploy a small SharePoint Server farm at a subset of locations with not much more than a Cloud SSA configured to crawl the local resources. These search service farms would all be onboarded to the same Office 365 tenant and send their results to the same cloud index. Although it will come at a higher on-premises cost, distributing the workload across multiple farms can enable large-scale crawling while still giving the user a single search experience.

As with anything, there are some limitations when using the Cloud SSA. First, you can't deploy any custom entity extraction, custom security trimming, or custom content enrichment service, because the content processing is owned by the SCS. The Cloud SSA also doesn't support eDiscovery or cross-site publishing. If you need these items, you need to deploy a traditional SSA as well. There also are some limitations in the configurations you can make on managed properties, such as not being able to configure a managed property to be refinable. Additionally, because ACLs (permissions) are mapped in the SCS against Azure AD, you should have already synced all users who might potentially be granted access to something. Otherwise, the index might miss some permissions for some people. For a full list of the limitations, see "Plan cloud hybrid search for SharePoint" at *https://support.office.com/article /Plan-cloud-hybrid-search-for-SharePoint-33926857-302c-424f-ba78-03286cf5ac30?#BKMK_ what_experience*.

> **IMPORTANT** Crawling on-premises file shares can potentially reveal confidential information. Despite best intentions, most file shares degrade into a kind of information chaos. Users largely don't think much about permissions. When a file share is crawled, any file suddenly becomes easy to find.
>
> Although SharePoint security-trims results, files often become widely visible because permissions were wrong in the file share. Information is often buried many levels deep and quite frequently is protected from unauthorized access through obscurity. Search strips all this away and uses whatever permissions are actually on the items.
>
> Be prepared to respond quickly to concerns about incorrect data exposure. Either fix the permissions on the file and recrawl or remove the item from results using the search administration tools (at least temporarily until permissions can be fixed).

There are many benefits that can make up for some of these limitations. For one, you get the unified results from both the on-premises system and the cloud. The Cloud SSA also feeds into Delve, providing a richer and more accurate experience for users. The footprint of your search service in your SharePoint Server farm can potentially be dramatically reduced. Microsoft predicts that most companies will require only one instance of the search component services, because the main work has been offloaded. We recommend you deploy at least two instances to provide redundancy. These benefits can result in huge savings for companies with many search servers. The Cloud SSA also enables users in SharePoint Online to see on-premises items in the results without you having to deploy a reverse proxy. The Cloud SSA can also be tremendously helpful during migration projects, because searches return items regardless of which environment they're in.

The Cloud SSA can crawl anything that a regular SharePoint Server SSA can, including SharePoint 2007, 2010, 2013, and 2016 sites, file shares, websites, and LOB data through BCS. If you have a SharePoint 2010 farm, you can use service application publishing and configure the 2010 farm to subscribe to the Cloud SSA hosted in a SharePoint 2013 or 2016 farm.

IMPORTANT With a Cloud SSA, do not click the button to reset the search index! Doing so will lead to orphaned items in the cloud index. If you need to remove all on-premises results from the index, see "I can't remove all metadata for on-premises items from the Office 365 search index" in "Troubleshooting hybrid environments" at *https://technet.microsoft. com/library/dn518363.aspx#BKMK_RemoveAllOnPremItems*. In it, Microsoft provides the Windows PowerShell script **Delete-CloudHybridSearchContent.ps1** to clear the purged on-premises items from the cloud index. See the instructions for how to use it.

One-way inbound hybrid BCS

Business Connectivity Services (BCS), sometimes called the Business Data Connectivity (BDC) service, is a SharePoint service application you can use to surface LOB data in SharePoint like a regular list (among other capabilities). It's called an *external list,* and it behaves similarly to any other SharePoint list, except the data is external to the system. The LOB system could be a SQL Server instance, Oracle database, web service, or other such system.

SharePoint Online gives you an inbound hybrid BCS capability. Hybrid BCS lets you present data from an on-premises LOB system in SharePoint Online as an external list. BCS Online does this by sending the query through an on-premises instance of BCS hosted in SharePoint Server. This requires the on-premises SharePoint Server instance to be published to the internet via reverse proxy, just like with inbound hybrid search. It actually shares nearly all the same requirements as inbound search, including storing the pre-authentication certificate in the Secure Store Service.

BCS requires the creation of an *external content type* (ECT), which is used to create the external list. An ECT describes everything that's needed about the data, such as fields, data types, and actions, and how they map to the data source. It's easy to get started with BCS on-premises, because you can use a nice wizard in SharePoint Designer to connect directly to SQL Server, a web service, or an OData source. It creates an ECT for you. However, there's a major restriction with hybrid BCS: The ECT must connect to an OData source, and you can't use SharePoint Designer to set it all up for you. You must either use an existing web service presenting an OData stream or develop a custom one. Once such a web service exists, you must use Microsoft Visual Studio (or a third-party product) to create the ECT pointing to the web service. The ECT is created as a BDC model file (.bdcm) that you extract from your Visual Studio project, make tenant-ready, and then upload to both BCS Online and BCS on-premises.

Additionally, you need to create a connection in BCS Online that defines the URL of the OData web service, the URL of the reverse proxy's public endpoint, and the Secure Store Service target application holding the pre-authentication certificate, and you must specify the manner in which to authenticate with the OData stream. The credentials used to access the resource are stored securely in an on-premises Secure Store Service target application, the name of which you specify in the connection settings.

Let's take a moment and review the hybrid BCS flow, as depicted in Figure 6-5. An external list is created in SharePoint Online based on a BDC model that has been uploaded to BCS Online. BCS Online retrieves the pre-authentication certificate from SharePoint Online's Secure Store Service and makes a request to the on-premises BCS through the reverse proxy. If the user is authorized, the on-premises BCS retrieves from its Secure Store Service the credentials needed to access the OData web service. It then calls the web service, which in turn queries the back-end system. That data is returned back through the same channels and is displayed in the SharePoint Online external list.

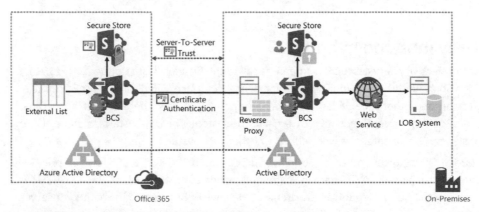

FIGURE 6-5 One-way inbound hybrid BCS architecture

Additional hybrid options

Other aspects of SharePoint can be configured for hybrid. One is hybrid site following. *Following* is related to SharePoint social networking. With hybrid site following, when you follow a site in SharePoint or SharePoint Online, a single list of sites is updated and visible both in the on-premises system and in SharePoint Online. Otherwise, the user would have two lists of sites that he follows (one per environment). Note, though, that this applies only to followed sites, not followed documents.

Another hybrid feature is hybrid profiles. An on-premises SharePoint user has a user profile both in the on-premises system and in SharePoint Online. This can be confusing for users. With hybrid profiles, the on-premises farm is configured so that users get sent to their SharePoint Online profile instead of to their on-premises profile when they click About Me in the upper-right corner of a SharePoint page.

Office 365 introduced the *extensible app launcher* (called the "waffle" by some). It's the icon at the top of the screen that makes available the user's applications in Office 365 (such as Outlook, Delve, and Sway). The app launcher has been added to SharePoint Server 2016 and will be added to SharePoint Server 2013. An Office 365 global admin can add additional applications to the list that the user can then pin to her app launcher. With the hybrid app launcher, a user in the on-premises system will be able to see the same apps in the SharePoint Server app launcher as he does in Office 365. To enable the hybrid app launcher in SharePoint 2013, install the July 2016 public update or a subsequent update.

As we described in the "Managing OneDrive for Business" section of Chapter 5, both on-premises SharePoint Server and SharePoint Online have their own OneDrive for Business (ODB). As with the user profiles, this arrangement can be confusing to users. To help avoid problems, your on-premises SharePoint Server instance can be configured so that users are sent to ODB in SharePoint Online when they click OneDrive at the top of an on-premises page.

> **TIP** Hybrid sites (site following, user profiles, and the extensible app launcher) and hybrid ODB aren't an all-or-nothing deal. You can use SharePoint audiences (defined in the user profile service application) to specify precisely who should receive these hybrid features.

Prerequisites for SharePoint hybrid

Again, we're going to refer you to the free ebook from MS Press called *Configuring Microsoft SharePoint Hybrid Capabilities* at *https://blogs.msdn.microsoft.com/microsoft_press/2016/07/06/free-ebook-configuring-microsoft-sharepoint-hybrid-capabilities* to give you all the gory technical details of deploying and configuring SharePoint hybrid solutions. However, we want to talk a bit about the prerequisites needed to deploy hybrid solutions. It can help round out your understanding of the moving parts.

As discussed at the beginning of this chapter, much of Office 365 walks on the legs of identity synchronization. It is a critical, fundamental component in tying together your Office 365 tenant and your on-premises environment. Identity is your first and primary hybrid workload. It is critical for SharePoint hybrid as well. The technology relies on identity sync to rehydrate passed credentials, match ACLs, and other such actions.

The other main requirement for all SharePoint hybrid solutions (except ODB and profiles) is that a sever-to-server (S2S) trust be established between the on-premises farm and SharePoint Online. We talked about this at the beginning of the chapter.

Establishing the S2S trust and creating the Azure ACS proxy is done either by running a PowerShell script (which you can learn more about in the free ebook or at *https://technet.microsoft.com/library/dn197169.aspx*) or using the Hybrid Picker. The Hybrid Picker is a tool you launch by going to the SharePoint Online Admin Center, opening the Configure Hybrid page, and clicking either Hybrid OneDrive or Hybrid OneDrive And Sites Features. If you run the Hybrid Picker, make sure you do so from a SharePoint server, you're a global admin in Office 365, you're a member of the on-premises farm admin group, and you have full control of the user-profile service application. It downloads and runs a little tool that will do whatever is needed to configure the S2S, including downloading and installing needed clients.

The S2S process relies on certificates trusted by both farms in order to sign hybrid communications. Optionally, you can specify a certificate when you configure the S2S manually via

PowerShell. If, however, you use the Hybrid Picker, it will use whichever certificate is currently configured as your Secure Token Service (STS) signing certificate. By default, SharePoint uses a nonexpiring, self-signed certificate. If you're going to use your own self-signed certificate or a third-party certificate (either from a public or local domain certification authority), you need to replace the STS signing certificate as well.

If you're configuring any kind of inbound hybrid, you need a reverse proxy that supports certificate pre-authentication. See *https://technet.microsoft.com/library/dn607304.aspx* for more information, including the list of supported reverse proxies. We recommend using the Windows Server 2012 R2 Web Application Proxy. The published endpoint needs to be secured by a certificate issued by a public certification authority. You need a certificate for the pre-authentication, as well. This certificate will be loaded in the Secure Store Service in SharePoint Online. It can, however, be self-signed or issued by a local certificate authority.

Finally, to use the Cloud SSA, you must either use SharePoint Server 2016 or use SharePoint 2013 with the August 2015 (or newer) cumulative update (CU). The hybrid extensible application launcher requires at least the July 2016 public update if you're using SharePoint 2013.

> **TIP** In both the new hybrid search and inbound classic hybrid search, consider deploying an Office Web Applications (OWA) or Office Online Server (OOS) farm and publishing it securely through a reverse proxy. The normal behavior in SharePoint Online search results is that, when a user hovers the pointer over an Office document, a preview of the document appears in a panel on the page (called the *hover panel*). This will not work, however, with on-premises SharePoint results unless you also deploy an OWA or OOS farm and make it available to the internet (for users outside the network).

> **MORE INFO** For more information on how to do this, see "Display previews of on-premises cloud hybrid search results in Office 365" at *https://technet.microsoft.com/library /mt668456.aspx*.

Publishing on-premises applications through Azure AD

Chances are good that your company uses web-based applications that are hosted on your internal network. They might be custom-built or vendor-provided applications, like SharePoint Server. There's also a good chance that users will want to access them when they're away from the office. Traditionally, we gave them access to network resources by using a VPN of some kind, or we opened up some holes in the firewall so that the applications were visible from the internet. VPNs aren't a simple matter, because they require hardware, software, licenses, some kind of client to be deployed, user training, and so on. Plus, they can be difficult to use with a mobile phone. Opening up the firewall is risky, and the application could be compromised by a hacker. The application can be placed in a perimeter network or protected by a reverse proxy, but both approaches can be complicated and add cost. Although these strategies are great for keeping a network or IT professional gainfully employed, they all ultimately amount to additional costs to the company. Some companies simply will not attempt it and require that users be on the network to do their work.

Microsoft has given us another option through Azure AD: the Azure AD Application Proxy. In this section, we'll talk about what it is and how to use it to publish an on-premises web-based application—all without opening the firewall or deploying a VPN. As a Cloud Pro, technologies like the Azure AD Application Proxy can be an important tool for enabling users to work from anywhere on anything.

Application options in Azure AD

The Azure AD Application Proxy is actually one of two hybrid application options Microsoft gives you in Azure AD. We introduced them back in Chapter 3.

> **MORE INFO** For a wide variety of topics related to applications in Azure AD, see "Integrated Apps and Azure AD for Office 365 administrators" at *https://support.office.com/article /Integrated-Apps-and-Azure-AD-for-Office-365-administrators-cb2250e3-451e-416f- bf4e- 363549652c2a*.

Integrated applications

You can use Azure AD to provide single sign-on (SSO) to a wide variety of applications. These can be either third-party Software as a Service (SaaS) applications or applications a developer built that uses Azure AD for authentication using the OAuth 2.0, OpenID Connect, WS-Federation, or SAML 2.0 protocols. When an integrated application is registered in Azure AD, users can access them using their Azure AD credentials, thus providing SSO.

Microsoft made available a large gallery of SaaS applications. At the time of this writing, there are over 2,600 applications in the gallery, including Salesforce, Box, Google Apps, and Jive. You can easily add any number of these applications to your Azure AD tenant. After you add one to the tenant, you can assign users or groups to the application. The users can then see and access the application through their Azure AD Access Panel (*http://myapps.microsoft. com*). If the application requires a login and password, they will be prompted for it the first time they use the application. The credentials are stored securely in Azure AD. From that point forward, every time they launch the application from their Access Panel, they will be automatically signed in to the application.

> **MORE INFO** For more information on this topic, see "Integrate Azure Active Directory single sign-on with SaaS apps" at *https://azure.microsoft.com/documentation/articles /active-directory-sso-integrate-saas-apps*.

Additionally, with an Azure AD Premium license, you can use an *app integration template* to get SSO to nearly any other web-based application that isn't listed in the gallery. This can include any application that has a sign-in page requiring a user name and password or any application that uses the system for cross-domain identity management (SCIM) protocol. You can also use an app integration template to enable what is effectively a cloud-hosted AD FS service for any application that supports SAML 2.0 identity providers. With this, Azure AD acts as an identity provider, eliminating the need to deploy AD FS on-premises in many scenarios. Because it's Azure AD, you can also take advantage of the other benefits, such as multi-factor authentication (MFA).

> **MORE INFO** For more information on using app integration templates, see "Configuring single sign-on to applications that are not in the Azure Active Directory application gallery" at *https://azure.microsoft.com/documentation/articles/active-directory-saas-custom-apps*.

Azure AD Application Proxy

Another way to present applications to your users is through the Azure AD Application Proxy. With the Azure AD Application Proxy, you deploy a small application called the Azure AD Application Proxy Connector to an on-premises server. It uses Azure Service Bus to securely publish nearly any on-premises web-based application without the need to open the firewall or deploy a VPN. The proxy is published using Azure AD, which can also be used to authenticate users. You can take advantage of other Azure AD features, like MFA, auditing, and threat detection.

Access to the application is controlled through assigning users and groups to it in Azure AD. Like integrated applications, an application published using the proxy shows up in the user's Azure AD Access Panel (*http://myapps.microsoft.com*). However, users also can access the application directly through the default *https://<prefix>.msappproxy.net* URL that Microsoft provides.

The Azure AD Application Proxy works for the following kinds of applications:

- Browser-based applications that use Windows Authentication
- Browser-based applications that use forms-based authentication (user name and password)
- Custom-built web APIs
- Remote Desktop Gateway–hosted applications

To help understand how the proxy works, see Figure 6-6, in which a SharePoint Server web application has been published using the Azure AD Application Proxy. The process starts with a user opening a browser and making a call to the application via the Azure AD Application

Proxy (1). If the user is not already signed in, she is directed to Azure AD to do so (2). Azure AD gives the user a token that has the User Principal Name (UPN) and the Service Principal Name (SPN), and the user presents that token back to the Azure AD Application Proxy. The proxy then sends the token to the on-premises Azure AD Application Proxy Connector (3), which uses Kerberos-constrained delegation to get a Kerberos ticket from the on-premises Active Directory (4). The connector then sends the user and the ticket to SharePoint Server (5). SharePoint Server verifies the Kerberos ticket against Active Directory (6) and logs the user into SharePoint. The communications from SharePoint pass back through the connector (5) and the proxy (3).

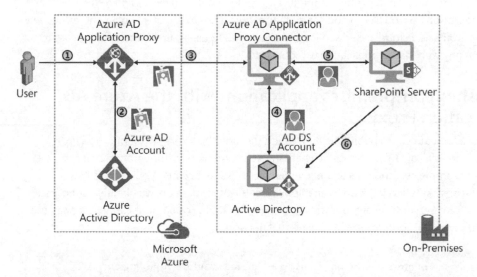

FIGURE 6-6 Azure AD Application Proxy flow

Again, all of this is done without opening a hole in the firewall or requiring a VPN. The proxy uses Azure Service Bus to do this. It does come at a small cost, though, because the need to pass through the Service Bus adds a little overhead. It's likely, though, that your users will never notice any difference. Also, because all outbound traffic needs to be encrypted, the CPU can potentially become a bottleneck. If you find this is the case, you can simply scale out by adding more servers that run the Azure AD Application Proxy Connector. They are stateless and require no load balancing, so doing so is simple. You'll want to monitor the connectors to ensure they're able to handle the load.

> **MORE INFO** For more information, see "All you want to know about Azure AD Application Proxy connectors" at *https://blogs.technet.microsoft.com/applicationproxyblog/2015/06/01/all-you-want-to-know-about-azure-ad-application-proxy-connectors*

Licensing requirements

Let's stop for a moment to talk about everybody's favorite subject: licensing. The application hybrid options are highly dependent on which Azure AD license you have.

Every Azure AD license allows for at least 10 integrated applications per user. In the free tier, this includes the SaaS applications in the gallery as well as developer-integrated applications you add. Although it's possible for more than 10 to be assigned to a user, only 10 will show in a user's Azure AD Access Panel. An Azure AD Basic license lets you deploy Azure AD Application Proxy applications and add them to the list as well. As you might expect, Azure AD Premium gives you everything. First, it removes the 10-application limit. You can assign to the user as many applications as you like. Second, it adds app integration templates. Again, this effectively gives you AD FS as a cloud-based service and allows you to use Azure AD to authenticate to just about any web-based application without code.

Publishing on-premises applications with the Azure AD Application Proxy

Let's take a look at how to publish an application through the Azure AD Application Proxy. The goal here is to give you a sense of what's involved and demonstrate how easy it can be. In this example, we publish a SharePoint Server 2013 site. Because you need to use Kerberos-constrained delegation to enable Windows Authentication, we already configured our SharePoint Server farm and our web application for Kerberos authentication. Let's say the site is *https://sp1301.contoso.com* on the internal network.

> **MORE INFO** For more information on using Integrated Windows Authentication and Kerberos with the Azure AD Application Proxy, see "Single sign-on with Application Proxy" at *https://azure.microsoft.com/documentation/articles/active-directory-application-proxy-sso-using-kcd*. For more information on publishing a SharePoint site using the proxy, see "Enable remote access to SharePoint with Azure AD App Proxy" at *https://blogs.technet. microsoft.com/applicationproxyblog/2016/04/06/enable-remote-access-to-sharepoint-2013-with-azure-ad-app-proxy*.

To get started, after you obtain your Azure AD Basic or Premium licenses, you need to enable the Azure AD Application Proxy. To do this, go to the classic Azure portal by browsing to *https://manage.windowsazure.com* or by clicking Azure AD in the Admin Centers menu in the Office 365 Admin Center. After opening your Azure AD directory, go to the Configure page. Select Enabled for the Enable Application Proxy Services For This Directory option (shown in Figure 6-7). Finally, click the Save button at the bottom of the page.

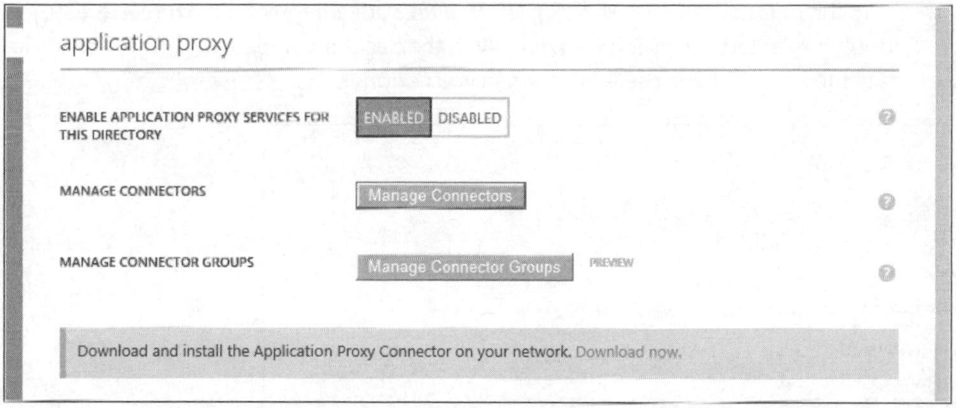

FIGURE 6-7 The Enable Application Proxy Services For This Directory option on the Configure page of the Azure AD Application Proxy

Next, you need to set up the Azure AD Application Proxy Connector. The connector is deployed to an on-premises Windows Server 2012 R2 machine. You can add as many connector servers as you like, and they're all presented to Azure AD as a pool of connectors. Although you can deploy the connector on the application servers, it really isn't recommended. The connectors are automatically load-balanced by Azure AD, even though no load-balancer hardware or software is used. They also automatically receive updates and configurations from Azure AD. They're pretty close to being a set-and-forget tool. Although domain membership isn't necessary, you need it here because you'll be doing Windows Authentication (via Kerberos constrained delegation).

To install the Azure AD Application Proxy Connector, sign in to the connector server and click the Download Now link in the Application Proxy section of the Configure page (which was shown earlier in Figure 6-7). Run the installer, and click through the wizard. You need to supply Azure AD global admin credentials to register the connector.

> **MORE INFO** For more information on installing and activating the Azure AD Application Proxy, including the outbound ports required, see "Enable Application Proxy in the Azure portal" at *https://azure.microsoft.com/documentation/articles/active-directory-application-proxy-enable.*

After the Azure AD Application Proxy Connector wizard is complete, you can create an Azure AD Application Proxy in Azure AD. Do this by going to the Applications page in Azure AD and clicking the Add button at the bottom of the page. Select Publish An Application That Will Be Accessible From Outside Your Network.

Next, as shown in Figure 6-8, name your application, specify the URL of the application (reachable from the connector server), and select your pre-authentication method. If you choose Azure Active Directory, the user first needs to be authenticated to Azure AD before being sent to the internal network. This step lets you take advantage of the Azure AD features. If Passthrough is selected, the user is sent directly to the back-end application, which needs to authenticate the user. Click the check mark when you're done.

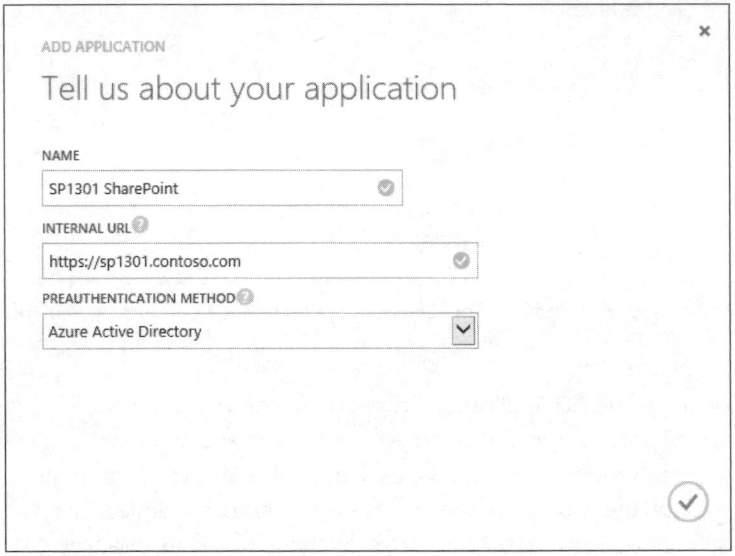

FIGURE 6-8 Azure AD Application Proxy Connector—Tell Us About Your Application page

After the initial creation of the application, you then go to its Configure page. Here, you configure the rest of the settings. Set the External URL value. This is the address that a user outside the network will use. You can either choose the default of "-<domain>.msapproxy. net" or a domain you've added. In this example, to decrease potential confusion and eliminate the need for an Alternative Access Mapping in SharePoint, change the External URL to be the same as the internal URL: *https://sp1301.contoso.com*. This requires that you configure your public DNS to use the CNAME Microsoft gives you on the page: "sp1301-contosocom. msapproxy.net". After you save this configuration, you need to come back and upload a certificate that covers the URL you selected.

> **MORE INFO** For more information on setting the External URL, see "Working with custom domains in Azure AD Application Proxy" at *https://azure.microsoft.com/documentation /articles/active-directory-application-proxy-custom-domains*.

Next, you need to configure the application's authentication to support Windows Authentication (as shown in Figure 6-9). To do this, select Integrated Windows Authentication from the Internal Authentication Method drop-down menu. You also need to enter the SPN you used to configure Kerberos for SharePoint. (In this case, it was *http/pm-vm-sp1301.contoso.com*.) Then select User Principal Name from the Delegated Login Identity drop down menu. Finally, SharePoint likes the original URL in its headers, so click No for Translate URL In Headers. After you configure all this, click Save at the bottom of the page.

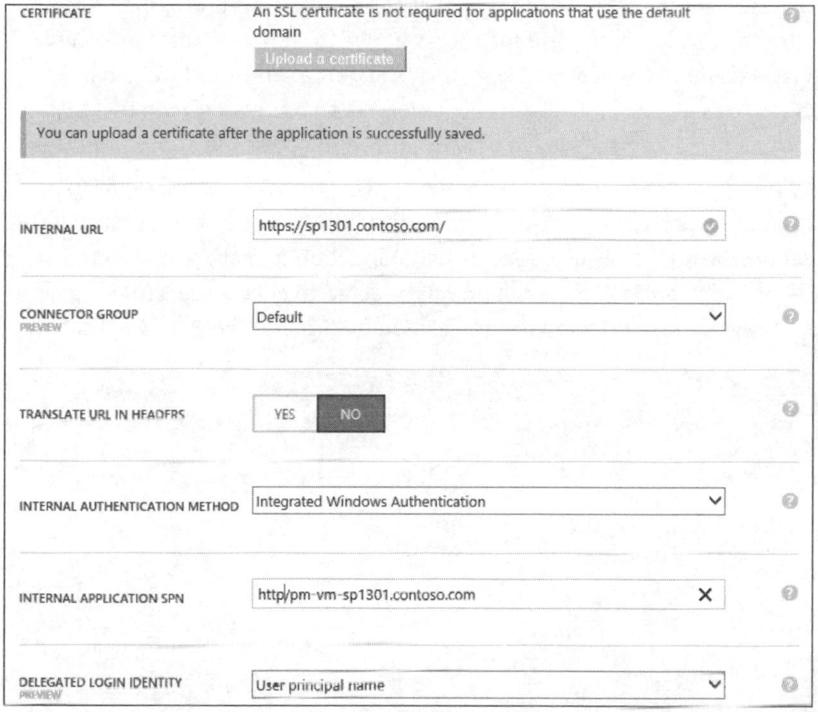

FIGURE 6-9 Configuring the Azure AD Application Proxy for Windows Authentication

If you set a custom external URL (like we did), you need to upload the certificate file (.PFX) that covers the URL. The certificate needs to have a private key, so make sure you know the password. You can also set a custom logo for the application. The final step is to assign users to the application. You do that within Azure AD the same as you would other applications.

> **TIP** When you use the Azure AD Application Proxy, you can take advantage of the other great features of Azure AD. If you have Azure AD Premium licenses, you can enable conditional access. This allows you to specify the following options for the app: require MFA, require MFA only when not at work, and block access entirely when not at work. These settings can be applied to all users or just groups of users. Not requiring MFA while at work can make a lot of sense and can eliminate some user frustration. You define "at work" in the MFA configuration page by defining ranges of IP address subnets.

MORE INFO For more information, see "Working with conditional access" at *https://azure. microsoft.com/documentation/articles/active-directory-application-proxy-conditional-access*.

When everything is ready, the users will be able to click on the application in their Access Panel or simply enter the URL in a browser. If the user is signed in with a Microsoft account or an organizational account that isn't in your directory, she gets a "Sorry, but we're having trouble signing you in" page. If she hasn't been assigned access, she gets a screen that says, "This corporate app can't be accessed. You are not authorized to access this application."

In this example, you grant Brad Sutton access to the application. As you can see in Figure 6-10, when Brad goes to his apps page (*https://myapps.microsoft.com*), he now sees the SP1301 SharePoint application. We previously uploaded a SharePoint logo to make it look a little nicer. If SP1301 SharePoint wasn't there, and if the option was selected to enable users to self-assign the app, Brad would have been able to add the application by clicking Get More Applications.

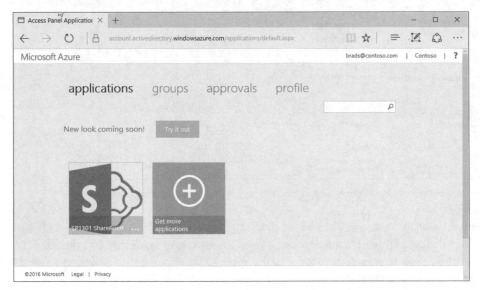

FIGURE 6-10 SP1301 SharePoint application in Brad Sutton's Access Panel

When Brad clicks on the SP1301 SharePoint application from anywhere on the internet, the SharePoint site opens up in a new tab (as shown in Figure 6-11) without prompting for credentials. Pretty easy!

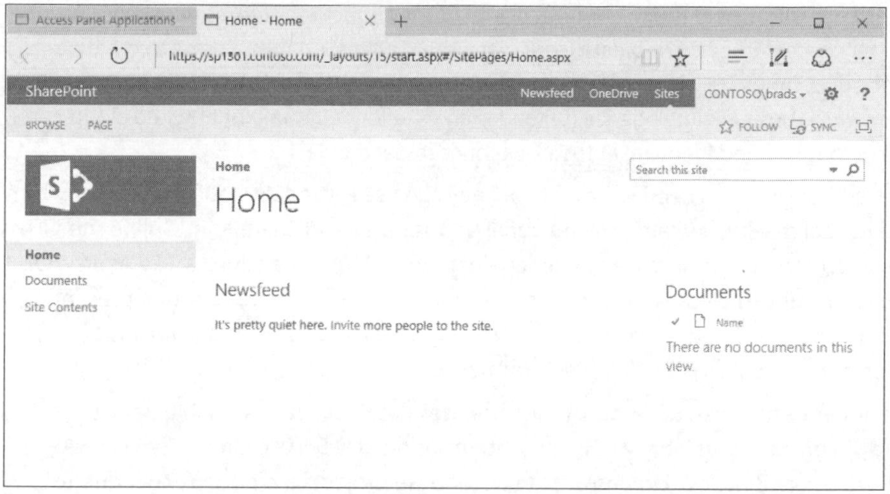

FIGURE 6-11 Successful logon to SharePoint Server through the Azure AD Application Proxy

> **TIP** Having problems with the Azure AD Application Proxy? If so, the troubleshooting tool might help. For more information on how to run it, see the Application Proxy blog post "Troubleshooting tool to validate connector networking prerequisites" at *https://blogs.technet.microsoft.com/applicationproxyblog/2015/09/03/troubleshooting-tool-to-validate-connector-networking-prerequisites*.

Surfacing on-premises data through Power BI

When you hear people talking about hybrid, they normally discuss SharePoint and OneDrive for Business. Maybe you'll hear about the Azure AD Application Proxy (although rarely). There's another important and powerful hybrid capability in Office 365 you'll almost never hear about: Power BI and the data gateway. This is a shame, because it's one of the most powerful ways to use on-premises data in the cloud.

As we talked about earlier, hybrid is about bridging the gap between on-premises data and the cloud to take advantage of the power and innovation of cloud technologies. A major reason why this is important is because traditional IT has had a hard time keeping up with the needs of its business partners. The speed of business is increasing. IT has struggled to keep pace and is often seen as a bottleneck or an impediment to innovation instead of the enabler it should be. As a result, users have turned to the new cloud services because of how easy it is for them to add new capabilities. The result often is a collection of disparate cloud services with few ties to each other, let alone to the traditional, on-premises, IT-run systems. Businesses are left with service and data sprawl.

All of this is why Power BI has become so powerful and important to business users. It simplifies the process of gathering data from disparate sources, enabling users to create powerful reports, innovate with the data, and find new patterns and opportunities. Power BI is about self-service business intelligence (BI) and is an excellent example of how the cloud can enable users to move and innovate at their own pace instead of IT's.

To do this, though, users need to have data. They can use Power BI to pull data directly from files on their local machines, OneDrive (personal or business), and SharePoint Online sites. They can use DirectQuery to perform live queries against some cloud data sources, like Azure SQL and Azure HDInsight. They can also connect to a wide range of *content packs* that present data in Power BI from other cloud services. (See *https://powerbi.microsoft.com/documentation /powerbi-content-packs-services* for more information.)

What's not as easy to get at, though, is on-premises data. The most valuable data is often locked away in on-premises legacy LOB applications using SQL Server, Oracle, Sybase, SAP, Teradata, and so on. Big, slow, expensive data warehouse projects are normally needed to bring that data to users. The resulting reports are usually static and don't allow for much innovation in analysis. They're usually accessible only from the network, too. Power BI, however, can change this by making those back-end data sources available in a curated form that users can then mash together to gain new insights. It does this via an *on-premises data gateway* (known by other services as a *data management gateway*).

In this section, we talk about this data gateway and how to surface your on-premises data in the Power BI service. Doing so can be a tremendous way for you to build political capital with your business partners and generate goodwill. If you have Power BI Pro licenses, a data gateway with published LOB data can be a huge win for a beleaguered IT department.

The on-premises data gateway

The concept of a data gateway, or a data-management gateway, is shared in several Microsoft cloud products. In fact, what is effectively the same gateway is wrapped in different interfaces by different services. It's used by Power BI, PowerApps, Microsoft Flow, and Azure Logic Apps. It used to be known as the *enterprise gateway*.

The on-premises data gateway is like the Azure AD Application Proxy Connector—it's a service that runs on the premises that connects to Office 365 via Azure Service Bus. Like the connector, it doesn't need any inbound ports, nor does it require a VPN. It's similar to the Power BI personal gateway, except the personal gateway is for on-premises data sources only. You actually use the same installer for both (*http://go.microsoft.com/fwlink/?LinkID=820925*).

> **MORE INFO** In this section, we approach the data gateway from a Power BI angle. However, it's similar to the data-management gateway used with Azure Data Factory. They actually are the same product, just different versions. As such, you might gain a deeper understanding of the gateway by looking at the Azure Data Factory documentation. If you're interested in learning more, see "Data Management Gateway" at *https://azure .microsoft.com/documentation/articles/data-factory-data-management-gateway*.

The on-premises data gateway can connect to many data sources. Some of them (identified in the following list) enable users to issue live queries to the data source through DirectQuery. All of them support either manual or scheduled refresh when using Power Query in a Microsoft Excel workbook located on a Power BI site:

Analysis Services Tabular (Live/DirectQuery)	SharePoint list (on-premises)
Analysis Services Multidimensional (Live/DirectQuery)	Web
SQL Server (Live/DirectQuery)	OData
SAP HANA (Live/DirectQuery)	IBM DB2
Oracle (Live/DirectQuery)	MySQL
Teradata (Live/DirectQuery)	Sybase
File	SAP BW
Folder	IBM Informix Database

For data sources other than SQL Server Analysis Services (SSAS), a single encrypted credential is stored for the data connection inside a gateway cloud service in Azure. All queries to the data source are made using this credential. With SSAS, your UPN that's stored in Azure AD is passed as the EffectiveUserName. This means, therefore, you need to have configured identity synchronization from your on-premises Active Directory to Azure AD. The SSAS server must also be joined to the same domain as the machine on which the on-premises data gateway is installed. You can, however, take advantage of the role-based and row-based security features in the product. Again, though, identity sync is required only if you're connecting to an SSAS data model.

Figure 6-12 describes at a high level the flow from Power BI to the on-premises data source. First, Power BI sends a query to a gateway cloud service in Azure (1). The gateway service retrieves encrypted credentials and places the credentials and the query in a service bus queue (2). The on-premises data gateway retrieves the credentials and query from the queue (3). The gateway then decrypts the credentials for use with the back-end system (4), which it then queries (5). When the query completes, the results are sent from the data source to the gateway (5), back through service bus (3), to the gateway service (2), and finally to Power BI (1).

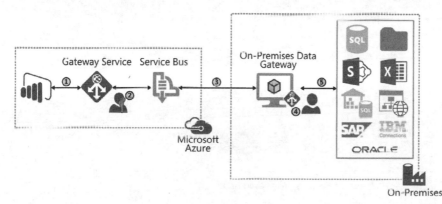

FIGURE 6-12 Flow from Power BI to on-premises data through the on-premises data gateway

To give you a sense of how to present on-premises data in Power BI, we'll walk through the process of deploying an on-premises data gateway to connect with a SQL Server database.

> **MORE INFO** For more information on the on-premises data gateway, including its requirements, the limitations for performing live queries against SQL Server Analysis Services, the outbound ports required, how to install and configure it, and links to additional resources, see "On-premises data gateway" at *https://powerbi.microsoft.com /documentation/powerbi-gateway-onprem*. For in-depth information about the data gateway, see "On-premises data gateway in-depth" at *https://powerbi.microsoft.com /documentation/powerbi-gateway-onprem-indepth*.

Deploying the on-premises data gateway

To deploy the on-premises data gateway, log in to a 64-bit machine that will host the gateway. Either download the gateway from *http://go.microsoft.com/fwlink/?LinkID=820925* or go to the Power BI site (*https://app.powerbi.com*), click the Download button at the top right of the screen, and click Data Gateway. Save the file and run it to kick off the install.

When prompted with the message Choose The Type of Gateway You Need (as shown in Figure 6-13), select On-Premises Data Gateway. Then click through the next couple of pages in the installation wizard.

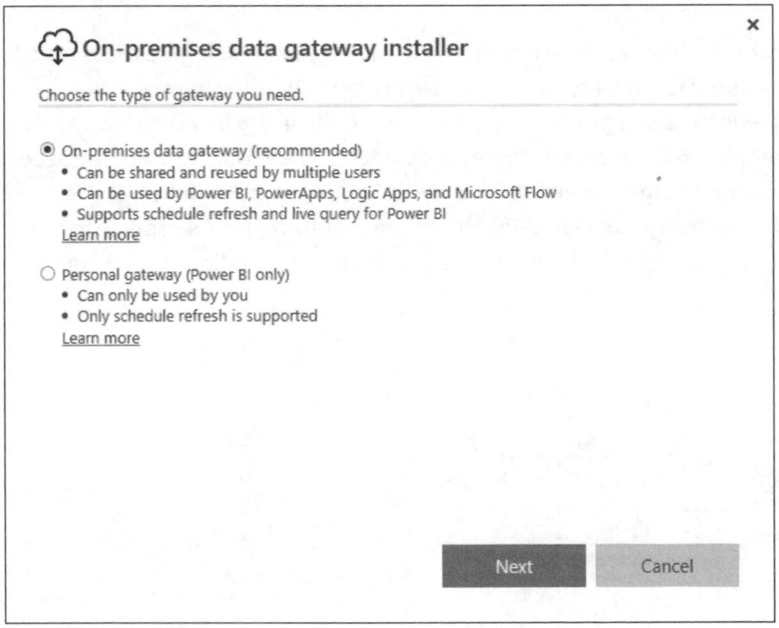

FIGURE 6-13 The Choose The Type Of Gateway You Need page

After the gateway installation finishes, you will be asked to sign in to register the gateway. (See Figure 6-14.) Pay attention to the login listed at the top of the page to make sure it's using the right one. Name your new gateway, and enter a recovery key. The recovery key is your password for restoring the gateway, so make sure you record it someplace safe and retrievable in case of disaster. After the gateway has been registered, you can then move on to registering a data source.

FIGURE 6-14 Registering the on-premises data gateway

Publishing data through the on-premises data gateway

Now that the on-premises data gateway has been registered, you can return to the Power BI site (*https://app.powerbi.com*) for the rest of the configuration. In the Ribbon, click Settings and then click Manage Gateway. Here you can view your gateways and provide some additional configuration, like assigning a department, description, and contact email, in addition to configuring additional administrators. It's also where you go to add a data source. You want to add the connection to the SQL Server database, so click + Add Data Source.

In this example, you connect to a database named AdventureWorksDW2014 on a SQL Server named PM-VM-SP1301. You connect using a SQL login named PowerBIReader (although you could select Windows as the authentication method and enter a domain login and password). You can see how the connection is configured in Figure 6-15. Click Add to complete the configuration. After it is added, you can go to the Users tab to select the users who are allowed to publish reports using the new data source.

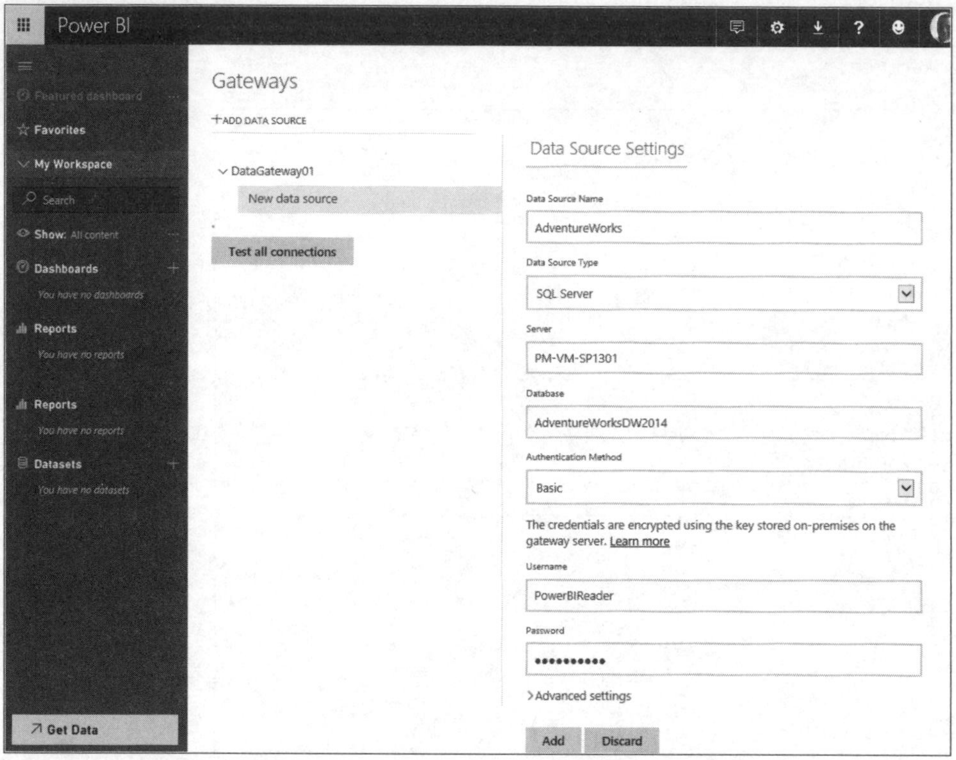

FIGURE 6-15 Adding a new SQL Server data source for an on-premises data gateway

You can then use the data source after it has been added. Anybody with permissions to the data source can use it to build a report. To do this, open up the Power BI Desktop application. If you don't already have it, download it by clicking the Power BI Desktop option under the Download menu on the Power BI Site. We use Power BI Desktop to build the data model that will be published to Power BI. Any reports that are built in it will also be published as reports in Power BI. At a minimum, you need to add whatever datasets you want made available in Power BI. The model you build will be listed in the Datasets section, enabling your users to build whatever reports they want from it. You can publish the datasets to your workspace or to an Office 365 Group for its members to consume.

After opening Power BI Desktop and signing in to your account, you have a blank model. In the External Data section of the ribbon, click Get Data. Choose SQL Server Database and click

Connect. In the SQL Server Database window (shown in Figure 6-16), you need to enter the name of the server and database exactly the same as you did in the data source you created. In this instance, type **PM-VM-SP1301** for the server and **AdventureWorksDW2014** for the database. Select DirectQuery as the access method to enable live data with the datasets and reports. Note that the SQL Server needs to be directly accessible from your machine at this time, so make sure you're on the same network.

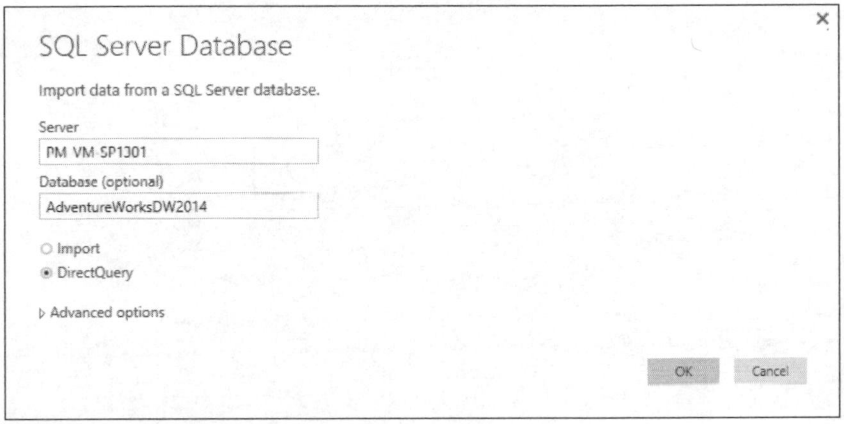

FIGURE 6-16 Adding a SQL Server database data source in Power BI Desktop

TIP If the data in the report or dashboard must always be available, if the query is complex and slow, or if the back-end data source is unable to handle the expected load from users frequently accessing the data in Power BI, select Import instead of DirectQuery. With DirectQuery, the query is sent to the live data source when the report or dashboard is opened by a user. If the data source or the on-premises data gateway is not online, the report or dashboard will fail to load. With Import, the data is imported into the data model and is always available in Power BI; queries do not go to the back-end data source. This gives you resiliency, and it protects the system from additional load. If Import is selected, the dataset can be scheduled for automatic refresh on the Power BI site. With a Power BI Pro license, a dataset can be scheduled for refresh up to eight times a day at a frequency of up to one hour.

MORE INFO For more information, see "Data refresh in Power BI" at *https://powerbi .microsoft.com/documentation/powerbi-refresh-data*.

If needed, you'll next be given the option to enter Windows or SQL Server credentials to access the database. The credentials you choose allow you to sign in and build the model, but the credentials specified in the on-premises data gateway configuration will be used after you publish the model. After signing in (if needed), you will be given a list of all the views and tables available in the database. Select whichever you need. In this example, we selected the tables related to internet sales. (See Figure 6-17.) Click Load to add them to your model.

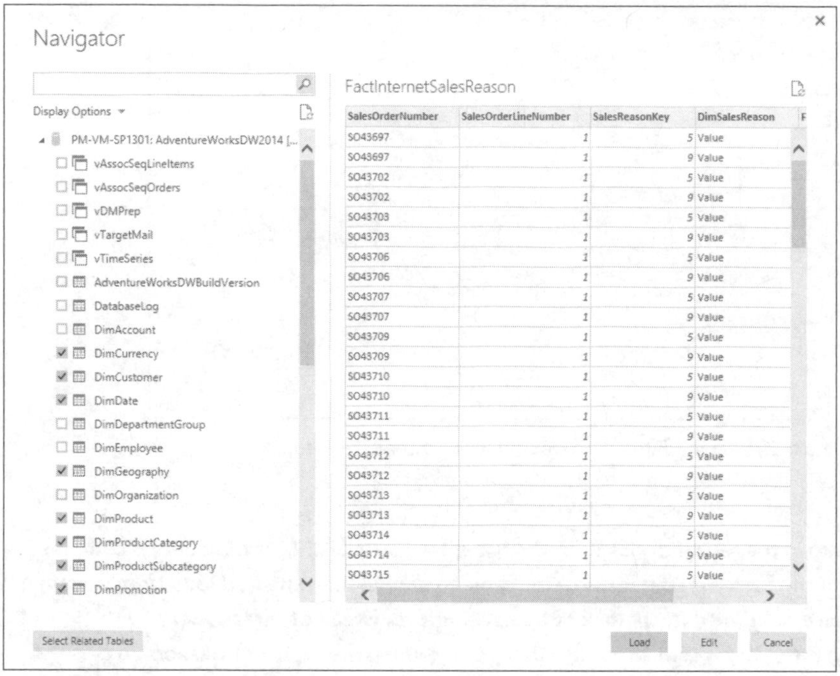

FIGURE 6-17 Add tables and views to the data model

After the tables have been added, you can configure any table relationships needed, edit queries, modify the table and columns, and create whichever reports you need. You don't have to create a report. If you publish the model without a report, the model you created will simply be made available as a dataset in Power BI. In this example, we created a simple geographic report to show the amount of sales per country. When you're ready, click Publish in the Ribbon. You'll need to save it, so give it a useful name. In our example, we'll call it FactInternetSales.

As you can see in Figure 6-18, you can select an Office 365 Group to publish the report to. You can also just save it to your workspace. Click Publish after you've made your choice.

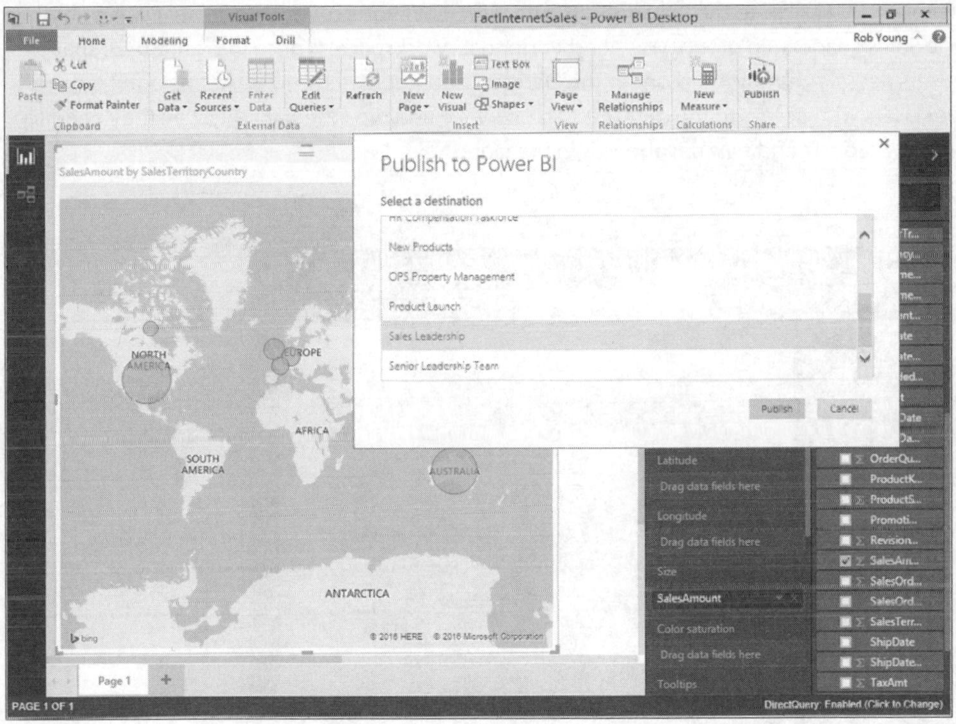

FIGURE 6-18 Select a destination when publishing to Power BI

Power BI Desktop then uploads the data model and reports to Power BI. You will receive confirmation when it's complete, as shown in Figure 6-19. If you look closely, you'll notice that it says, "The published report has been configured to use an enterprise gateway." Power BI recognized the fact that you used the same server and database names as our AdventureWorks connection and connected the data model to it. Excellent!

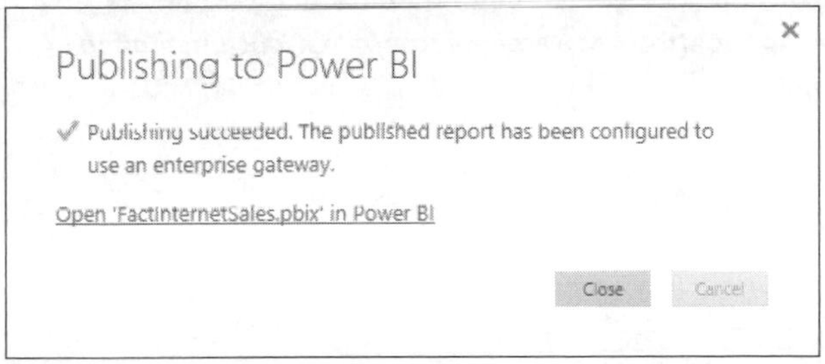

FIGURE 6-19 Data model published successfully and configured for an on-premises data gateway

Finally, you can go to the Power BI site and view what you created. Because it was published to the Sales Leadership group, you need to go to its workspace. Notice in Figure 6-20 that FactInternetSales is now listed under the Datasets and Reports sections. At this point, you're done! Users with access to the datasets can now slice and dice the data any way they need to build new reports and new dashboards in the cloud.

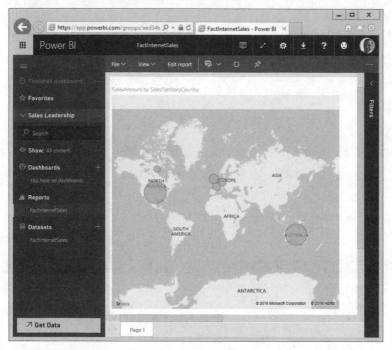

FIGURE 6-20 The report and dataset published in Power BI

> **MORE INFO** For more information on adding a SQL Server data source to Power BI, see "Manage your data source - SQL Server" at *https://powerbi.microsoft.com/documentation /powerbi-gateway-enterprise-manage-sql*.

## CHAPTER 7

Social capabilities, Office 365 Groups, and apps

I n today's modern world, you're able to collaborate and communicate in ways that once seemed to be only fantasy. The difference between fantasy and our reality is that communication and collaboration capabilities are developing at a rapid pace, which creates innovative new ways for people to work together.

Collaboration has shifted beyond just online meetings and instant messaging. It has become more content-centric and context-centric. Bringing social capabilities into the enterprise requires much more than just deploying technology. As a Cloud Pro, you need to understand the way in which people work and the *why*—the purpose of their work. As a Cloud Pro, you need to possess the skills to align technology with the *why*, *how*, and *what* challenges your organizations faces with regard to collaboration and, ultimately, innovation.

This chapter talks about the technologies and capabilities available to enable you, as a Cloud Pro, to drive your organization to be more agile and to adopt whatever it needs to become a truly modern-era business.

> **NOTE** Some social features that work for one organization might not work for another. Sharing lessons across organizations is important to do, but keep in mind that recipes for success are not "one size fits all" solutions.

When determining the best match for your organization's social-networking needs, it's best to take a people-centric view at first. That means considering the history of your organization and aligning social computing with those realities and current needs. Understand what your organization is collaborating on and then understand the ways in which it likes to collaborate. Here are a few topics to consider when doing this:

- **Content-Driven Socialization**   Occurs around a particular object that's specific to a particular topic. For example, the ability of your team to collaborate easily when creating new documents or procedures. These tasks often involve process-driven social needs and are characterized by needing to cross traditional departmental boundaries.

- **Context-Driven Socialization**   Happens fluidly and occurs often within the context of a particular aspect of your job. Contextual socialization often occurs in teams with a similar objective.

Socializing in the cloud world

After starting with *why*, you have to take one more step forward and understand the *how* of your collaborative needs. When you begin looking at this level, you truly blend your abilities directly with your organization's technological capabilities. More so than any other time in history, you now have the flexibility within a single platform to work with people. Office 365 social capabilities were built with two primary schools of collaborative thought in mind:

Structured collaboration   Refers to our need to collaborate in a specific context or relationship with others. This topic goes beyond just knowledge sharing. It envisions a collective group formed to move a specific aspect of the business forward—for example, Microsoft SharePoint sites.

Ad-hoc collaboration   An approach driven by our need to bridge context and content with just-in-time communications—for example, Microsoft Skype for Business.

Traditional social capabilities

When assessing the best ways to implement social capabilities within your organization, you not only have to understand the types of collaboration that exist, but also the context in which social collaboration occurs. The impact of "just deploying" a solution is broad and far reaching, so you must leverage an assessment method when putting social technologies in place. The need for an assessment methodology is part of a people-centric solution that accommodates the historical needs of your organization, the number of users, and the stakeholder requirements.

We recommend you start with four "buckets" for social capabilities and needs-based matching. Each bucket has its own unique profile, but they often have similar audiences. Here's a description of each category:

Enterprise   This approach provides a platform that enables bidirectional communication throughout the entire organization. This communication platform crosses traditional organizational boundaries and provides visibility throughout the entire organizational structure.

Role based With this approach, social capabilities are built or configured in such a way that promotes the ability for individuals with similar roles to work together and share lessons learned. A role-based approach provides a true knowledge-capture mechanism.

Project based As the name suggests, this approach deals with social capabilities that assist teams working on a specific project. Social capabilities here are similar to role-based ones, but they provide a mechanism to capture project-based intellectual property (IP).

Interest based This type of social collaboration is centered on core knowledge areas and interests.

> **TIP** The platform itself should provide the flexibility to align capabilities and social needs with organizational needs. Leverage the platform to provide a foundation, but use capabilities to enable social collaboration to capture knowledge and intellectual property in a way that can be archived, managed, and retained effectively.

Yammer

Yammer is one of the most powerful and dynamic social capabilities within Office 365. It's the primary social collaboration tool within Office 365. The difference between Yammer and the other social capabilities is that Yammer is truly designed for the enterprise social network. Its interface is familiar in appearance and functionality as the more commonly used consumer-centric social technologies such as LinkedIn and Facebook. Unlike other outward-facing social utilities, you must have an email address from your company's domain.

> **TIP** A less commonly used feature within Yammer is its capability to leverage external networks. External networks enable external users of your organization to collaborate with your organization. This type of interaction can be scary for your governance organization, but using external networks keeps valuable intellectual property within your cloud boundaries and off of public social networks.

A key concept with Office 365 and the tools within it is that the more you put into them, the more you get out of them. Although this sounds like a cliché, it's very important within Yammer and the machine-learning capabilities of Office 365. For instance, Yammer has the ability to surface likes, mentions, and notifications to keep you alert to changing information related to groups and conversations you're a part of. Additionally, Yammer is useful as a mechanism to further conversations by improving the inclusiveness of conversation. It does this by enabling conversations to be shared with specific groups or individuals, or enabling ad-hoc collaboration through chat-like instant messaging.

The Yammer difference

When and where to use Yammer vs. SharePoint Online's social capabilities was once a confusing decision to make. Some organizations continue to use SharePoint social capabilities, but their future is unknown. Microsoft's investment in this area is definitely focused on Yammer and not SharePoint. SharePoint social capabilities, by and large, do not provide enough structure for many enterprises. Yammer provides structured collaboration because it was once a market-leading, standalone platform, and it's tightly integrated with Office 365 and not just SharePoint Online.

However, to truly reap the benefits of a structured product you need a taxonomy. Many organizations struggle with Yammer's need for a taxonomy, and they often have only a folksonomy. Remember, the power and dynamic nature of the Yammer platform lies in its use of "tags." Tagging within Yammer involves much more than the traditional concept of defined metadata consistent with enterprise taxonomies. Yammer, with its tagging, fosters the growth of a folksonomy where the user base is defining the structure of what it uses to communicate.

Finally, when your organization feels it should choose which technology to use, be careful to not limit yourself and your capabilities. Consider using both technologies, because they're complementary. Just ensure you communicate which tool is best used in each of your business scenarios.

Yammer capabilities

When deploying Yammer, Cloud Pros need to understand its capabilities and the intersection of social scenarios and social technology capabilities. Table 7-1 describes particular social needs and the Yammer features that can fulfill those needs.

TABLE 7-1 Yammer feature summary

Social Need	Yammer Feature	Description
Collaboration with specific groups with a concentrated focus.	Groups	Work together with anyone across the company on projects, initiatives, and events. Groups provide open, flexible workspaces for team and communities by providing a central place for conversations, files, updates, and more.
Collaboration with people external to your organization, often as a part of specific business process.	External Collaboration	Add partners, customers, and vendors to group conversations for specific input. For ongoing collaboration, create dedicated external groups or external networks to foster deeper relationships and a sense of community
Search is core to being able to surface information specific to the context of a given social interaction.	Search	Search for experts, conversations, and files to cut down on duplicating work. Yammer uses Office Graph to deliver personalized search results based on your interests and interactions at the company.
There is a need to easily view information across multiple social threads.	Inbox and Notifications	Use your Inbox to view, prioritize, and manage what's most relevant to you in Yammer. Notifications and priority settings let you tackle the most important messages and announcements across your groups.

Social information aggrega-tion should be proactive and not reactive. Discovery feeds help make this a reality.	Discovery Feed	Discovery feeds keep you up to date on what's happening throughout your organization. Yammer surfaces people, information, and groups that might be relevant to you.
Social networking should be easy and fluid, which requires the interfaces to be familiar and friendly.	Office Integration	Your users can experience the familiar interface and rich capabilities of Office right in Yammer. They can preview, edit, and co-author documents using Office Online. Their work is automatically saved, and they can easily compare versions and finalize changes.

Keep in mind, that although the specific Yammer features named in Table 7-1 might morph and change over time, their use, purpose, and application within the organization are key knowledge areas that should be understood by Cloud Pros. Also, if your organization chooses to use Yammer, you need to understand that Yammer is not a covered service under the Office 365 Trust Center at this time. You need to read and agree to Yammer's updated privacy statement.

For an updated capability overview, reference *https://products.office.com/en-us/yammer/yammer-features*.

Updating social feeds

With Office 365, you can specify how to best leverage social capabilities in your organization. Two primary options are available: Yammer and SharePoint Newsfeed. Either of these features can be set as your default Enterprise Social Collaboration experience.

Social feed considerations

You must decide if you will use the SharePoint Newsfeed or Yammer. Keep in mind that SharePoint Online leverages the SharePoint Newsfeed by default. If you do nothing, you will be using the legacy feature, SharePoint Newsfeed. The primary difference between SharePoint Newsfeed and Yammer is the richness of social capabilities and features in the latter. Yammer can be integrated directly into your SharePoint sites and also launched directly from App Launcher. The primary benefit of App Launcher is that it provides the ability for users to actively navigate into Yammer across Office 365 applications rather than being dependent on a SharePoint deployment for social capabilities. The SharePoint Newsfeed makes sense only in the context of SharePoint Online—Yammer is more broadly applicable. Additionally, keep in mind that Yammer also is available as an app for Android and iOS devices. If mobile social capabilities are an important need, Yammer is the best fit.

Here are some major Yammer differentiators that might be important to you as your organization's Cloud Pro:

- Yammer can follow users as they move between Microsoft Office 365 products.
- Users can provide Yammer updates directly from Dynamics CRM or SharePoint.
- Yammer is engagement driven because people can respond in measurable ways.
- Users can create polls.
- Users can participate in polls.

- Users can ask a group a question.
- Administrators can provide full discussion visibility.

When you're considering whether to use Yammer or the SharePoint Newsfeed, it's best to consider the perspective of your users and account for their needs, and then compare those needs with the strengths of each application.

Like Yammer, the SharePoint Newsfeed enables users to post news and information to collaborate with their teams. At its core, the SharePoint Newsfeed summarizes all SharePoint interactions and activity for a user. A key aspect of the SharePoint Newsfeed is that it runs on any SharePoint platform—cloud based or on-premises. As such, you might consider using it, depending on your environment. The strength of the SharePoint Newsfeed can be summed up with its configuration. Configuring it is faster. In fact, it comes preconfigured and, as a part of the default functionality, with team sites.

Setting the default social collaboration

Specifying the Enterprise Social Collaboration setting when you've finally chosen whether to use Yammer or the SharePoint Newsfeed is not a complicated process. The following steps can help you adjust this setting:

1. In the App Launcher, select the Admin button.
2. In the admin center, in the menu on the left, select Admin Centers.
3. In the admin center, in the expanded menu, select SharePoint.
4. On the following screen, click Settings in the navigation pane on the left.
5. Depending on your screen resolution, you might need to scroll to the Enterprise Social Collaboration setting and select the appropriate setting for your desired feature.
6. After making your selection, scroll to the bottom of the page and click the OK button.

Yammer add-ins

The Yammer application life cycle continues to add new features and capabilities. Yammer, with Microsoft Azure Active Directory, can provide a common sign-in experience for your users. In fact, users can even sign in to your custom applications with Yammer by clicking the Sign In With Yammer button.

As of this writing, there are some interesting facts to note about Yammer:

- Yammer has over 10 million users.
- 300,000 enterprise organizations use Yammer.
- Users have access to Yammer's global App Directory, a different App store than what is available with Office 365.
- Integrations can be performed using Authentication, Open Graph, Embed and REST API.

Yammer has the ability to authenticate users with Yammer's internal authentication, as well as with Azure Active Directory. It also has numerous APIs currently available through SDKs for use in your environment. The availability of the SDKs and feature sets are continually being updated. However, in lieu of an in-depth analysis of each, we recommend evaluating whether the currently available SDKs listed next are of interest to your organization:

- JavaScript
- Ruby
- Python
- iOS
- Windows Phone 8
- .NET

If you want additional details on development SDKs and APIs, reference *https://developer.yammer.com/v1.0/docs/js-sdk*.

Office 365 Groups

One of the newer features added to Office 365 is Office 365 Groups. Office 365 Groups is a powerful feature that enables teams of people to work more dynamically with one another. Think of Office 365 Groups as everything that you wanted out of shared calendars, public folders, shared mailboxes, and those infamous distribution groups rolled up into a single capability. The primary benefit is that your teams now have truly agile flexibility within a managed environment that reduces the risk of important information being buried or stored in disparate information silos.

Office 365 Groups are a great example of how Microsoft combined ad-hoc collaborative features with a structured environment. Office 365 Groups are intended to be specific for teams of people working on a common effort that can either be short term or long term. The key features of Office 365 Groups are the following:

- Shared email inbox
- Shared Microsoft OneDrive for Business location
- Shared conversation threads
- Shared Microsoft OneNote

Office 365 Groups work to contain all this information within a single point of access. Microsoft calls this a *cross-suite service*. You can see the first iteration of the cross-suite service with the first deployment of Office 365 Groups across Microsoft Outlook, SharePoint, OneNote, Skype for Business, Power BI, and Dynamics CRM. You can see with this first deployment how the technologies were woven together to support cross-organizational collaborative scenarios. As these collaborative capacities mature, you'll see Office 365 Groups further develop dynamic, short-term, ad-hoc collaborative capacities like those you see with Delve, Planner, and Yammer.

TIP With the Microsoft acquisition of LinkedIn, keep in mind how Office 365 Groups evolve and possibly absorb LinkedIn capabilities. These new capabilities will be important for social-governance groups or individuals in your organization to be familiar with to ensure that potential intellectual property is not being shared outside of necessary groups.

For more information on Office 365 Groups, reference *http://groups.outlook.com.*

Mobile parity

Our modern world operates, and will continue to operate, with fixed and mobile computing environments. The modern cloud is enabling organizations to quickly shift to a device-agnostic platform. Recognizing this emerging reality is critical because working groups are no longer limited by traditional barriers. Office 365 Groups works toward facilitating active collaboration regardless of location or device through its mobile app, responsive browser design, and support of multiple end-user platforms.

The Outlook Groups mobile app for Windows Phone, iOS, and Android provides users the opportunity to work without barriers. Group collaboration rarely ceases when a team member is away and, as such, the app supports the collaborative workloads needed by team members. Here are four key areas of interest:

- Continue conversations when away from the laptop or desktop via mobile apps.
- View files and manipulate content from mobile devices and tablets.
- @mention team members and co-workers anytime, anywhere.
- Discover related groups without being wired to the corporate network.

Office 365 Groups configuration and management

There are four distinctive ways to create an Office 365 Group. Office 365 Groups are powerful, but you can also expect them to grow in usage because of how accessible they are. Organizations work differently, so to ease the adoption of Office 365 in your organization, you have the ability to create groups in the following ways:

- OneDrive for Business
- Office 365 Administration
- Microsoft Outlook 2016
- Outlook.com

Information workers are continually being driven for better efficiency and effectiveness in their ability to process and use information. A constant blocker for many information workers is their inability to quickly access information during an activity or task as it's needed. We call this the *point of need*. With Office 365 groups, information is surfaced within the relevant interface you are working in, such as Outlook Web Access, Outlook 2016, or SharePoint Online. Point of need is an important concept for information workers and in today's digital business environments. You need to enable your information workers to quickly and effectively collaborate within the specific context of their organizational roles and responsibilities. By leveraging Office 365 Groups, you can address the needs of users by addressing point-of-need access, thus helping to drive the adoption of technologies in an organization.

> **TIP** Office 365 Groups can be enabled for creation by anyone with access to your Office 365 environment.

Configuring Office 365 Groups

As mentioned, there are several options available when trying to create a new Office 365 Group. As an administrator you have the ability to configure and set up Office 365 Groups from the Office 365 admin center. Follow these steps to create your Office 365 Groups:

1. Navigate to the admin center by left-clicking the App Launcher (shown in Figure 7-1) and selecting Admin.

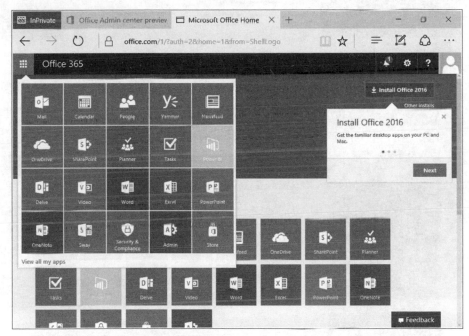

FIGURE 7-1 Office 365 App Launcher

2. After navigating to the admin center, click Groups. You'll see the admin center Groups page, as shown in Figure 7-2.

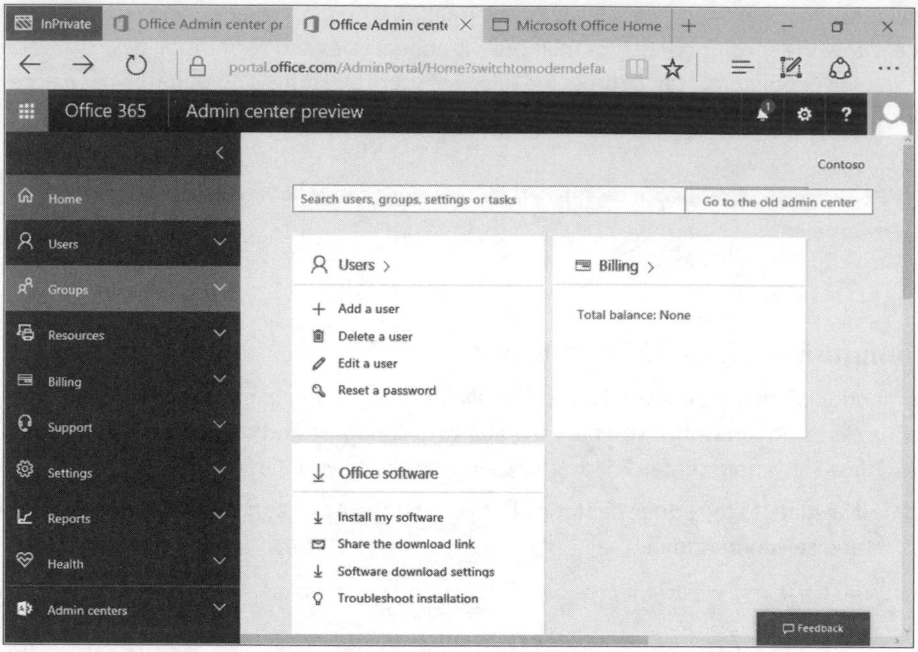

FIGURE 7-2 Admin center Groups home page

3. Click Add A Group, or click + Office 365 Group at the bottom of the page. (See Figure 7-3.)

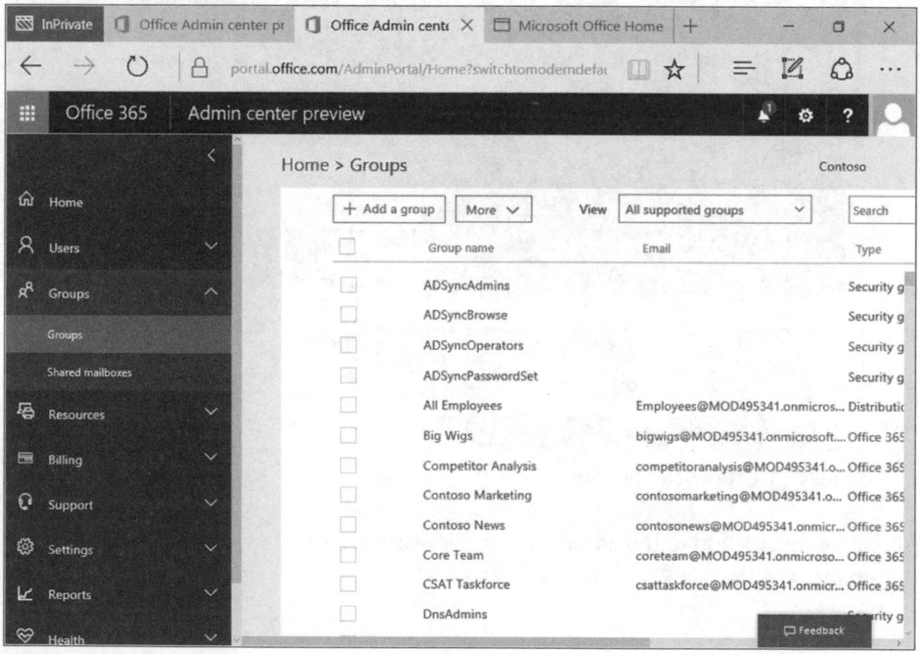

FIGURE 7-3 Groups settings page for adding a group

When the New Group dialog box appears, complete the necessary information as specified in Figure 7-4.

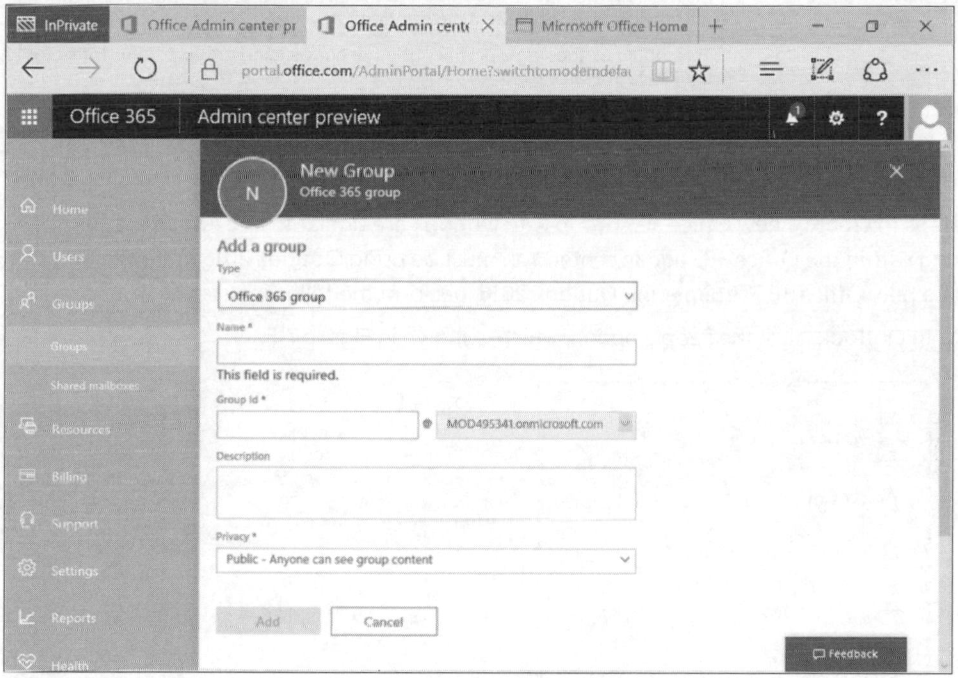

FIGURE 7-4 New Group dialog box

Table 7-2 summarizes the configuration options for Office 365 Groups.

TABLE 7-2 Office 365 Groups configuration options

Configuration Option	Description
Type	Specify whether the group being created is an Office 365 Group, distribution list, mail-enabled security group, or security group. Select Office 365 Group.
Name	The unique name that will be visible to everyone when viewing and searching for Office 365 Groups. Spaces are allowed in the name field.
Group ID	The unique Identifier needed to associate related content to this particular group. The Group ID defaults to the value of the Name Field. A unique Group ID needs to be created to ensure there's not a conflict with an email distribution list. Spaces are not allowed in Group IDs. Also, don't forget that you have the ability to set a naming policy or convention via Microsoft Windows PowerShell.
Description	Add descriptive text regarding the purpose and usefulness of the Office 365 group.
Privacy	The group-level permission is applied to the group. There are two options: **Public** Anyone can see group content. **Private** Only members can see group content.
Language	The welcome email will be in this language, as will the footer items in other group emails. You can't change the language setting after the group has been created.

Configuration Option	Description
Send copies of group conversations to group members' inboxes	This setting toggles between On and Off. Set it to On if users want to see messages in their inbox in addition to the Office 365 Groups interface. In this way, the group is similar to a distribution list.
Owner	This should be the single primary point of contact and group administrator for the Office 365 Group.

Creating Office 365 Groups with Outlook

The steps to create a new Office 365 Group with Outlook are similar to and just as easy as working within the Office 365 admin center. You must be using Outlook 2016 or newer. To create a new Office 365 Group using Outlook 2016, perform the following steps:

1. In Outlook, click the People option, which is shown in Figure 7-5.

FIGURE 7-5 Outlook People option

2. In the New section of the ribbon, click Group as shown in Figure 7-6.

FIGURE 7-6 Outlook ribbon Group button

3. In the Create Group dialog box (shown in Figure 7-7), provide a name for the group, select the privacy settings, and specify whether members will receive group conversations in their inbox.

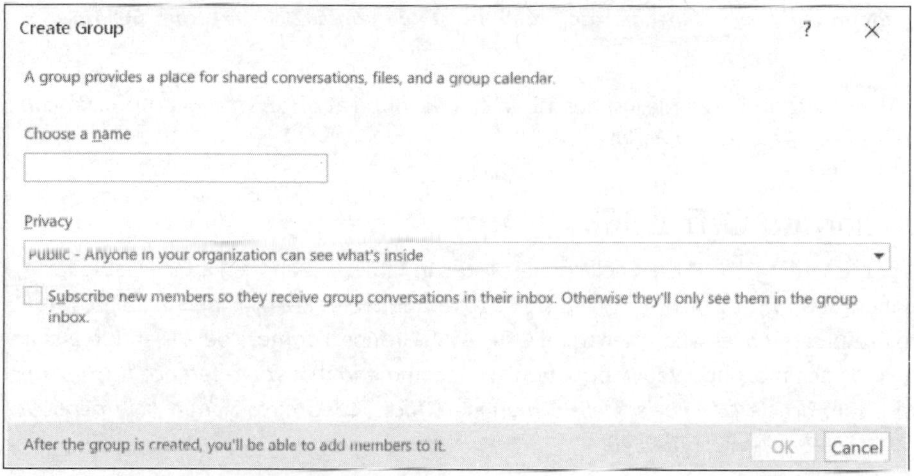

FIGURE 7-7 Create Group dialog box

4. After the group is created, provide a description, and add group members in the next dialog box.

Updating the privacy type

There might be times when you need to change the privacy type for an Office 365 Group. There are two options for doing this: one is to access the setting through the admin center and the other is to access it through Microsoft Exchange Online PowerShell. See Chapter 2, "PowerShell 101 for Cloud Pros," for instructions on how to get started with Exchange Online PowerShell.

If you need to change the privacy group settings from public to private, the following script can be used:

```
Set-UnifiedGroup -Identity "Legal Department" -AccessType Private
```

In the preceding script, replace "Legal Department" with the name of the Office 365 Group you want to change. If you need to change the privacy type from private to public, you need to replace the word *Private* in the preceding cmdlet with *Public*.

There might be times when the primary email address needs to be changed or you need to enable the group to receive email from senders external to your organization. If you need to change the primary email address associated with the group and want to enable the group to receive email from external senders, the following script can be used:

```
Set-UnifiedGroup -Identity "Marketing Department" `
    -PrimarySmtpAddress marketing@contoso.com -RequireSenderAuthenticationEnabled $false
```

TIP To run the preceding cmdlet, you need to ensure you have the correct permissions and that your permissions have access to all parameters being accessed by the cmdlet. If you have difficulty with this requirement or need to check permissions needed for Exchange cmdlets, reference *https://technet.microsoft.com/en-us/library/mt432940(v=exchg.160).aspx.*

The scripts and example just described can be found at *https://technet.microsoft.com/en-us/ library/mt238274(v=exchg.160).aspx.*

Managing Office 365 Groups

As of this writing, the PowerShell cmdlets listed in Tables 7-3 and 7-4 are available for configuration with Office 365 Groups. The following tables are provided by Microsoft and are useful references when managing Office 365 Groups. For more details and to ensure you have the most updated information, we recommend that you reference *https://support. office.com/article/Use-PowerShell-to-manage-Office-365-Groups-Admin-help-aeb669aa-1770-4537-9de2-a82ac11b0540.*

TABLE 7-3 Office 365 Groups cmdlets

Cmdlet name	Description
Get-UnifiedGroup	Use this cmdlet to look up existing Office 365 Groups, and to view properties of the group object.
Set-UnifiedGroup	Update the properties of a specific Office 365 Group.
New-UnifiedGroup	Create a new Office 365 Group. This cmdlet provides a minimal set of parameters. To set values for extended properties, use Set-UnifiedGroup after creating the new group.
Remove-UnifiedGroup	Delete an existing Office 365 Group.
Get-UnifiedGroupLinks	Retrieve membership and owner information for an Office 365 Group.
Add-UnifiedGroupLinks	Add members and owners to an existing Office 365 Group.
Remove-UnifiedGroupLinks	Remove owners and members from an existing Office 365 Group.

TABLE 7-4 Office 365 Groups photo cmdlets

Cmdlet name	Description
Get-UserPhoto	Used to view information about the user photo associated with an account. User photos are stored in Active Directory.
Set-UserPhoto	Used to associate a user photo with an account. User photos are stored in Active Directory.
Remove-UserPhoto	Remove the photo for an Office 365 Group.

Sending group email

Email continues to be the leading workflow tool of choice in business today. Email, in some regards, is embedded in our mode of operation as a business culture. This culture is changing and needs to be supported by technologies that bridge the gap between users who mostly work in legacy applications, such as email, and those who work in modern systems, such as Yammer.

For example, you want to bring together those who depend on email for collaboration with those who mostly use Yammer. You want to enable your organization to have the flexibility to operate as needed within Office 365, and sending emails as a group is an essential function. If you have users who need to change who they're "sending as," from within Yammer, this is the capability you're looking for. For example, Human Resources might want emails to be sent from a single group email address. This allows for replies to be sent directly to the group and provides a level of traceability, accountability, and the ability for teams of people to work with incoming requests.

To enable the ability to perform sending email from a group email address, you need to update the mailbox policy. This mailbox policy change needs to occur through Windows PowerShell. There are a total of four steps needed to make updates to the mailbox policy. The first two steps specify the information needed, as follows:

1. First, set the value of *groupAlias* to Human Resources:

   ```
   $groupAlias = "HumanResources"
   ```

2. Next, specify the user alias as HRGroup :

   ```
   $userAlias = "HRGroup"
   ```

3. Now that you have set the group and user aliases, you need to use these variables to commit the changes to the system using the Get-Recipient cmdlet:

   ```
   $groupsRecipientDetails = Get-Recipient -RecipientTypeDetails groupmailbox `
       -Identity $groupAlias
   ```

4. In addition to specifying the mailbox, you must also ensure that users can send as the group you are specifying by assigning the needed permissions:

   ```
   Add-RecipientPermission -Identity $groupsRecipientDetails.Name `
       -Trustee $userAlias  AccessRights SendAs
   ```

After these cmdlets are executed in this order, users will be able to add the group to the From Address in both Outlook and Office 365.

Group site quotas

Office 365 Groups cross many different functionalities throughout Office 365. One of the first considerations you must make is to assess the likelihood that use of Office 365 Groups will proliferate throughout your organization. Making it relatively easy for users to create groups increases the likelihood of both adoption and usage.

IMPORTANT When using Office 365 Groups, you'll notice that the Files location is actually located within the <tenant>.sharepoint.com URL structure. This is an indication that the group site quota will be associated with your SharePoint storage quota. We encourage you to evaluate your Office 365 license details to make the best decision for you and your organization.

As you evaluate the adoption and usage, you must manage the risk and concern for storage consumption of your tenant and budget accordingly. If there is a risk for using too much storage, consider setting and managing quotas for your Office 365 Groups. To set quotas for group sites, you need to use the Get-SPOSite cmdlet. Again, this PowerShell cmdlet must be executed within Windows PowerShell.

1. You need to get the details of the specific group site you're working with by using the following command:

```
Get-SPOSite -Identity https://<tenant>.sharepoint.com/sites/<groupname> `
            -detailed |fl
```

2. *Before* executing this step, ensure that your site collect storage management is set to Manual and is not using pooled storage. Then set the quota for the specific site with the following cmdlet:

```
Set-SPOSite -Identity https://<tenant>.sharepoint.com/sites/<groupname> `
            -StorageQuota 3000 `
            -StorageQuotaWarningLevel 2000
```

3. Do not assume the change was made; instead, you should run a final check. To run this final check, you simply run the Get-SPOSite cmdlet you ran as a part of step 1.

Diving into Delve

Machine learning is rapidly changing the modern workplace by moving beyond just a digital transformation and into intelligent organizational adaptation. Microsoft's foray into machine learning began with a project named Oslo, which has since morphed into what we now know as Delve. Delve provides the ability for users to have information proactively brought to them. The main difference with this type of information aggregation goes beyond just searching for and rolling up data. Instead, the proactive information aggregation is based on the user's interests, activities, or related documents. There are three key elements to Delve:

- The user experience (the Delve application).
- The intelligent platform (Office 365 Graph).
- Essentially, instead of users having to search for information, Delve presents that information to them proactively.

Office 365 Graph

Foundational to Delve is its reliance on Microsoft Office Graph technology. The Office Graph technology is equivalent to a digital neural network. Like your body's nervous system, the Office Graph technology acts as the brain by looking for specific signals across the Office 365 platform. These signals result in active links across the entire Office 365 application that exhibit some form of commonality that you or your users find useful. Essentially, Office 365 Graph is intelligently linking content, activities, and people to one another to provide a useful and informational perspective.

For more information on Office 365, visit *https://graph.microsoft.com*.

Delve

Delve is the actual application that sits on top of the Microsoft Office Graph technology. It's driven by three primary characteristics:

- Your information sources
- Cards
- Boards

Delve interface

At first glance, you'll notice that Delve has two primary information panels, as shown in Figure 7-8. The left panel focuses on your personal information sources and is organized by user-specific information, your co-worker network reflecting the people you follow and most often work with, and the ability to filter and group related information using *boards*. Boards are the tiles within Delve that surface information from content sources such as Microsoft Office.

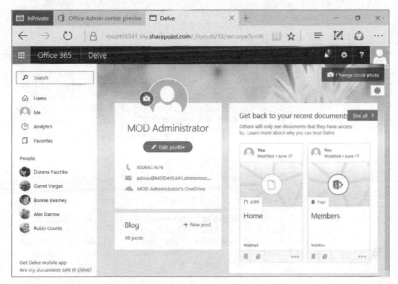

FIGURE 7-8 Main Delve user page

Delve users

It's not unheard of for users to both appreciate and worry about the power of Delve and Office 365 Graph. To help mitigate these concerns, you should have factual information and answers to some commonly asked questions.

> **IMPORTANT** Delve respects the permissions of each file and does not move documents. Delve surfaces the information using *cards*, which are visual pointers back to the original information source. People can see only what they have permissions for.

Table 7-5, provided by Microsoft, is a great overview of how to answer common user questions about Delve. Your ability to clearly answer user questions will help drive adoption and lower the overall concerns of your user base. To find an updated version of the table, you can reference *https://support.office.com/article/Are-my-documents-safe-in-Office-Delve-f5f409a2-37ed-4452-8f61-681e5e1836f3*.

TABLE 7-5 Addressing Delve user concerns

Question	Answer
Who can see my documents?	Only users who have permission to view or edit documents can see documents.
Who can see email attachments?	Only the contacts who are a part of the email discussion will see the attachment within Delve.
Can I share documents with others with Delve?	Yes, you have the ability to copy a link or email a link directly from the Delve card for the specific document. The options can be found in the ellipsis menu control for the specific card in the bottom-right of the card.
How can I keep a document private?	To keep a document private, a user needs to store the document in OneDrive for Business and ensure that the option to not share it is enabled. Site collection administrators can control this setting at the list or library level. See the "Hide documents from Delve" section in this chapter.
Where does Delve look for documents?	Delve looks inside of SharePoint Online and Office 365 for documents.
I see that a private document has been viewed 5 times. How is that possible?	This is an indication that the document has been opened by you five times. A private document should have a padlock displayed; if it does not, other users have access to view or perhaps even edit this document.
Can other people see what I am viewing?	Yes and no. If they have similar permissions, they can see what you're viewing. However, remember that the order of the cards being shown in Delve is different for each user.
Can users turn Delve off?	The application cannot be turned off by the users, but the users can turn off the feature for Delve to discover their documents.
How do I know if I'm looking at an email or a document?	If you're looking at a document, you see three options at the bottom of the card: the favorite icon, the boards icon, and the ellipsis used for the Delve card's Quick Launch. An email has only a chained link shown at the bottom-left corner of the card.

Your Delve Analytics

As shown in the earlier section, "Delve interface," you can see there are four navigation options at first:

- **Home**   This link is the default navigation option to take you back to your original Delve page.

- **Me**   This link provides a summary view of all information related specifically to your documents, your contacts, and your organization, and it provides you with the ability to adjust and edit your user profile.

- **Analytics**   One of the most powerful and useful tools within Office 365. It provides immediate insight into how you work. Take a look at Table 7-6 to get an idea of the insights provided by Delve Analytics. These are evolving at a rapid pace and new option appearing monthly.

- **Favorites**   This link takes you to a central launching point for all things favored such as Delve boards and documents.

Delve Analytics is powerful and can drastically influence how an organization works by providing unparalleled visibility into activities. Delve Analytics, at the time of this writing, focuses on five areas for analysis:

- **Your time**   A breakdown of how your workweek is spent

- **Network**   Who you do and do not collaborate regularly with

- **Meetings**   How many meetings you or other people scheduled for you

- **Email**   How much time you spend on email and email habits

- **Focus hours**   Time spent focused on specific activities

> **TIP**   Delve has default goals set for each of the analyzed areas listed, with the exception of Network. These goals are editable, and you're encouraged to specifically tailor them to meet the expectations of your organization. If you're unsure about your specific goals, use the default goals and adjust from there. The time settings and workweek hours are customizable as well.

TABLE 7-6 Delve Analytics definitions

Delve Analytics	Definition
Meeting hours	How many hours you have spent in a week in meetings.
Email hours	Comparative analysis of how much time you spent on email versus the company average. This time is also broken down by how much time is spent writing emails and reading emails.
Focus hours	Focus hours is defined by the amount of time you have available between meetings. Focus hours are defined by two consecutive hours without meetings.

Delve Analytics	Definition
After hours	The quantity of time spent after business hours with work-related activity such as email.
Key Contacts – Hours/week	Co-workers, ranked in order of the amount of time spent with a key contact.
Key Contacts – Your read %	The percentage of email you have read from that was received from a specific person.
Key Contacts – Your response time	The average time it takes for you to respond to an email written by a key contact.
Losing touch	This shows the people you have communicated with the least, and provides the last date you connected with that persons. You also have the ability to send an email or schedule a meeting with that person directly from this section as well.
You and your manager	A summary view of how much time was spent collaborating with your manager, broken down by email, hours in meetings, response time, and how quickly your manager responds to you.
Meeting hours	A comparative breakdown of the hours spent in meetings, compared to the company average. In addition, it also breaks down how many meetings you scheduled versus those that were scheduled by others.
Meeting habits	An insightful breakdown of your meetings by how often you're multitasking during meetings, how many meetings are after hours, recurring meetings, meetings that are longer than average, and the quantity of meetings that were conflicting.
Email habits	Again, more insightful information to show you how much of the email you send is read by others, and how much of your email is sent to a group versus individuals. This also provides insights into how much of your received email is read by you when sent to you or CC, versus that of which is sent to a group.

NOTE What users see in Delve is different for each user. The interface will be the same, but the information being shown will be different and viewed in a different logical order that's specific to that user.

Configuring and administering Delve

Before moving further into the configuration of Delve, you should always check your licensing for Delve availability. Remember, you do not want to communicate features and abilities to users who might not have a license for this feature set. At the time of this writing, Delve is offered with E1, E3, E5, Office 365 Business Premium, Office 365 Business Essentials, Office 365 Education E5, and Office 365 Nonprofit E5. Users must have a SharePoint Online license to use Delve.

Delve is often ready to go and set up by default. You'll immediately know that Delve is ready to roll by its availability in the Office 365 App Launcher. Because Delve is preconfigured, the presumptive choice as a Cloud Pro is whether or not your organization is ready for Delve. If the answer is no, you need to administratively remove Delve from the Office 365 App Launcher. To do this, follow these steps:

1. In the top left portion of your web browser, click the Office 365 App Launcher. The App Launcher menu is displayed, as shown in Figure 7-9.

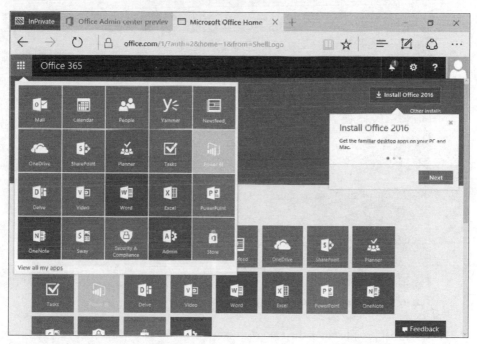

FIGURE 7-9 Office 365 App Launcher menu

TIP Always keep in mind that a majority of the responsibility for the configuration of Delve features rests upon that of the end users.

2. Once the App Launcher appears, click Admin.

3. In the admin center, in the left menu, click Admin Centers to display the page shown in Figure 7-10.

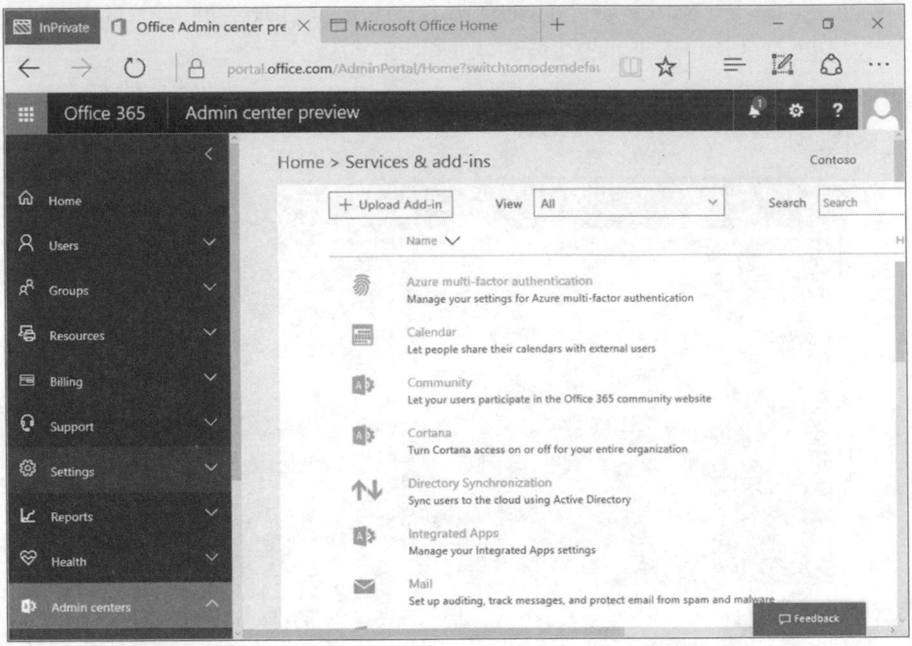

FIGURE 7-10 Admin center menu in the left pane

4. Click SharePoint. You're then redirected to the SharePoint admin center. (See Figure 7-11.)

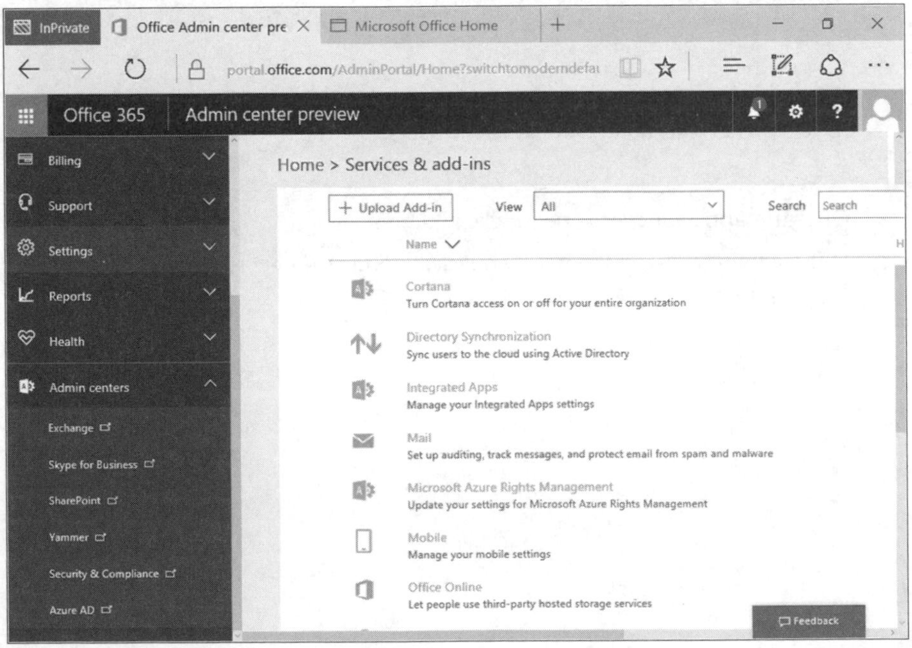

FIGURE 7-11 Admin center menu expanded

5. In the SharePoint admin center, click Settings in the left pane, which is shown in Figure 7-12.

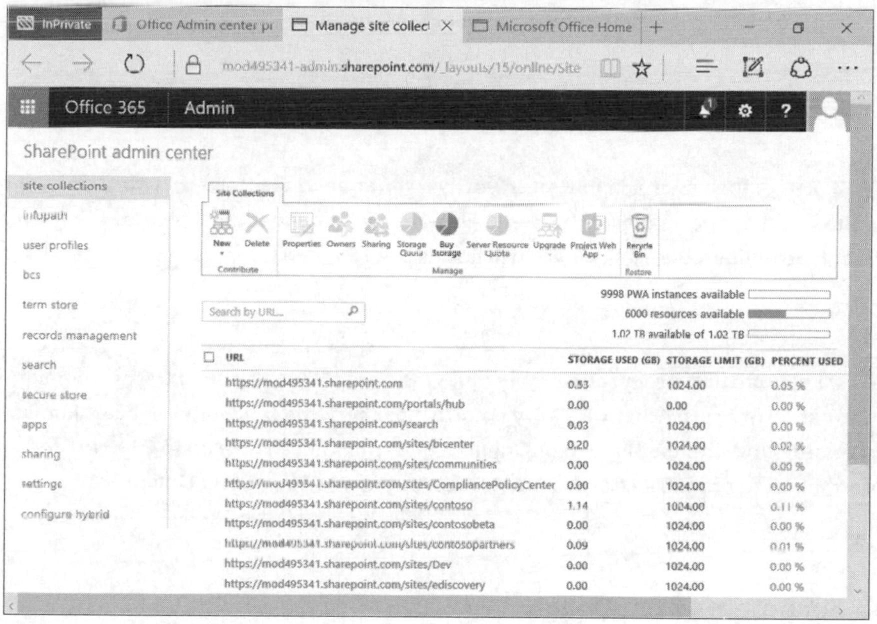

FIGURE 7-12 SharePoint admin center

6. On the Settings page, locate the Office Graph settings and click the Don't Allow Access To The Office Graph option button, which is shown in Figure 7-13.

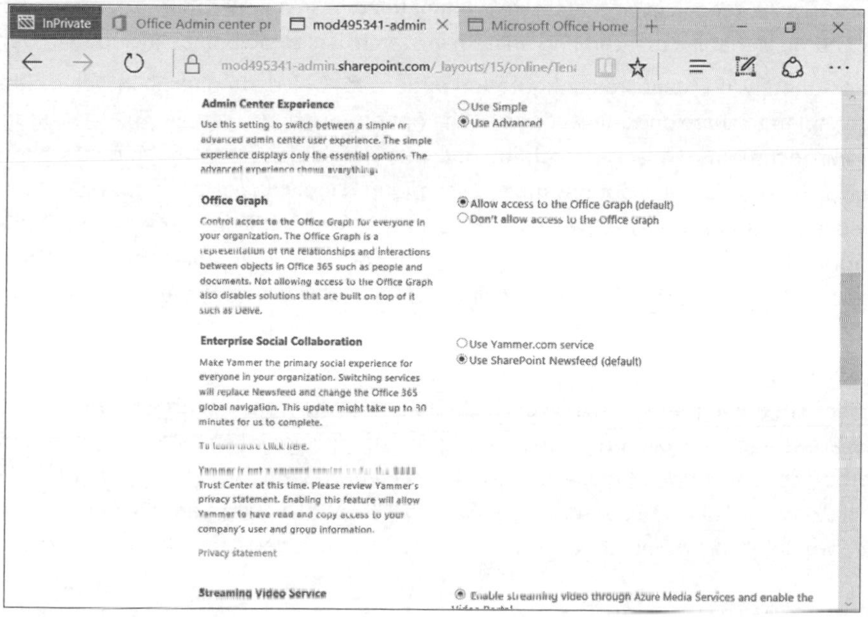

FIGURE 7-13 Office Graph Settings

NOTE By selecting this option, you disable all applications that are using Office 365 Graph, including custom applications your team has built.

7. Scroll to the bottom of the page, and click OK.

NOTE Remember, as an administrator, you will continue to see Delve on your App Launcher, but it should not be visible for the users. Also, keep in mind that the Office 365 Graph Index will still be built. However, the index will not be used by search to return search results.

TIP If users are incorrectly seeing colleagues inside of Delve, you need to ensure that the information in Azure Active Directory is correct or check the sync status and last known successful sync with the SharePoint Online user profiles. It can take up to 24 hours for information to propagate from Azure Active Directory to SharePoint Online.

Hide documents from Delve

Each organization has its own unique requirements—Delve is no exception. There are scenarios where you do not want documents to show up at all within Delve. An example of this scenario is employees, partners, or even competitors accidentally seeing or presuming information based on documents they might see when you visit your Delve in a screen-sharing scenario. Always keep in mind that Delve is ultimately a search application. Therefore, a good rule of thumb is that if a user can find an item in search, it is eligible to be included in Delve.

Unfortunately, the standard configuration options for Delve often result in Delve either being enabled to share documents or not—the options are pretty simple. The sharing option allows for documents that a user is adding or creating inside of Office 365 to be discovered. These Document Discovery options must be configured individually by each user. A user can mark documents as private in One Drive for Business, but this still does not prevent items from appearing on that user's Delve page. The other option is to disable Office 365 Graph as specified in the previous section, but this disables Delve and any applications dependent on Office 365 Graph from working correctly.

However, Microsoft has given us the ability to hide documents selectively. To do this, you must perform the following steps on *each* library or list where the documents you want to be hidden are stored. The following steps and important note are taken directly from *https:// support.office.com/article/Manage-the-search-schema-in-SharePoint-Online-d4fab46d-ba41-4c03-9d4c-32b5b33198b6?ui=en-US&rs=en-US&ad=US*. These are the best steps available, so we didn't see the need to rewrite them. They're included here for your convenience.

TIP To help make this option available for everyone, you can create this site column in the Content Type Hub. By doing this, you can ensure that the column is available for everyone and that users can add the column to the list from available site columns.

Log in as the site collection administrator for the site collection where the intended hidden documents are located. Then follow these steps:

1. Navigate to the site where the list or library resides.
2. Navigate to the list or library where the documents are located.
3. In the ribbon, click List (if it's a list) or left-click Library (if it's a library).
4. In the ribbon, click Create Column in the Manage Views group.
5. For the column name, type **HideFromDelve**.
6. Next, select the column type and then select the Yes/No check box.

IMPORTANT At the bottom of the Create Column form, change the Default Value to No. If you leave the default set to Yes, all new documents or items added to this list or library will not be included by Delve.

7. Follow the steps listed next as appropriate for your version of SharePoint:
   a. **SharePoint 2016 or SharePoint Online**   Clear the Add To All Content Types check box.
   b. **SharePoint 2013**   Clear the Add to default view check box.
8. Click OK.

After you complete these steps, users simply need to update the properties for a particular document or list item and ensure that the HideFromDelve check box is selected.

End-user Delve configuration

The end-user configuration options are simple. As of this writing, three configuration options are available to end users. These three options and their functions are listed in Table 7-7.

NOTE In Table 7-7 the descriptions for each configuration option are written to match the current specifications of Office 365 Delve configurations.

TABLE 7-7 Delve configuration options

Configuration Option	Description	Option
Profile Settings	Edit your user profile information that's seen by others in your organization. NOTE There is some information that can be updated only by administrators of the directory. These options typically are grayed out, or un-configurable.	About Me Picture Ask Me About Mobile Phone Fax Home Phone Office Location Assistant Past Projects Skills Schools Birthday Interests
Documents In Delve	Show documents on your profile page. You can also see documents that you have access to on other people's profile pages. If you turn this off, others still can find your documents in Office 365 if they have access to them. They just won't show up in Delve.	On/Off
Delve Analytics	Shows you statistics from Delve Analytics about how you spend your time at work. Your Delve Analytics dashboard is not shared with anyone else, but your data will be used in de-identified aggregated form to provide statistics and benchmarks to people in your organization.	On/Off

Office 365 Video Portal

The digital transformation of organizations is shifting beyond just active and passive collaboration and is rapidly moving to the creation and consumption of content through multiple channels. The use of video as both a communication and training medium is increasing in importance.

Every day, you can see people spending time consuming videos online. The ubiquitous nature of video consumption is yet another leading indicator that traditional consumer applications are rapidly advancing with their own purpose within organizations. Traditional video-sharing and streaming technologies were expensive, required lots of storage, and were implementation projects in their own right. The Microsoft Video Portal satisfies the broad needs of many organizations. With this capability comes yet another Cloud Pro knowledge area you must tackle.

The Office 365 Video Portal is accessed using App Launcher in Office 365. Not all Office 365 License Types offer the Video Portal feature. As of this writing, the following licenses come with the Video Portal capability:

- E1 and higher commercial licenses
- All academic license types
- Nonprofit E5 licenses

The Office Video Portal is made up of the components shown in Figure 7-14.

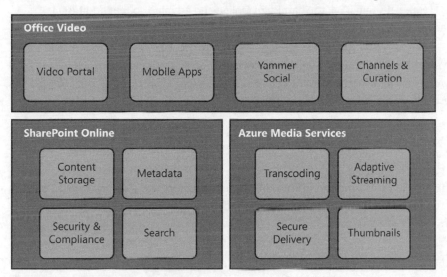

FIGURE 7-14 Video Portal components

To help you understand the architecture and components involved in Office 365 Video Portal, we'll walk through what happens when a video is uploaded. By walking through the production flow of publishing a video, you'll be able to understand the processes and how the architectural aspects fit together.

Users upload the Video Portal using the Office 365 Interface file. This file is first placed into SharePoint Online. This file's storage does count against the storage quota for that team sites quota.

> **TIP** Always check for your Office 365 SLA and current license allocations before making storage or license decisions.

After the file is uploaded, it's transferred to Azure Media Services for transcoding for different resolutions. Microsoft refers to this as *adaptive smooth streaming*, which was designed to enhance the user experience. This experience is driven by the ability and processing power of the consumer's device. This generally means that videos will be sent at a higher video resolution to a desktop, PC, or tablet than to a mobile device. Also, the user experience changes between mobile device types. For example, there is a Video app for iOS, but you must rely on in-browser streaming on an Android device.

Adaptive streaming also enables the streaming service to adapt based on device or network latency issues. For example, if the service detects an issue with bandwidth, the resolution is lowered to continue the viewing experience. This adjustment occurs throughout the full playback, and adjustments are made, on average, once every two seconds.

After transcoding is completed, Azure Media Services creates the thumbnail. After the thumbnail is created, it's sent back to SharePoint Online and enabled so that additional metadata can be added to the video.

> **IMPORTANT** Security is embedded by design throughout the life cycle of the video from upload to the transfer to Azure Media Services to streaming. This process includes encryption at rest and encryption in transit.

Video file formats

Table 7-8, taken from *https://support.office.com/article/Video-formats-that-work-in-Office-365-Video-dd1af01c-fd8e-4640-b17b-93ee02b9b817*, highlights the many video file formats supported by Office 365 Video.

TABLE 7-8 Accepted Office 365 Video Portal video file formats

Video file format	Video file extension
3GPP, 3GPP2	.3gp, .3g2, .3gp2
Advanced Systems Format (ASF)	.asf
Advanced Video Coding High Definition (AVCHD) [MPEG-2 Transport Stream]	.mts, .m2ts
Audio-Video Interleaved (AVI)	.avi
Digital camcorder MPEG-2 (MOD)	.mod
DVD transport stream (TS) file	.ts
DVD video object (VOB) file	.vob
Expression Encoder Screen Capture Codec file	.xesc
MP4	.mp4
MPEG-1 System Stream	.mpeg, .mpg
MPEG-2 video file	.m2v
Smooth Streaming File Format (PIFF 1.3)	.ismv
Windows Media Video (WMV)	.wmv

For an updated list, reference *https://support.office.com/article/Video-formats-that-work-in-Office-365-Video-dd1af01c-fd8e-4640-b17b-93ee02b9b817*.

Configuring the Office 365 Video Portal

The configuration of the Video Portal can be handled by an administrator by using the Video Portal settings page. You can find the Portal Setting option on the Video Portal home page that's accessed by clicking Video from the App Launcher menu.

Table 7-9 highlights the current the configuration options for the Video Portal.

TABLE 7-9 Office 365 Video Portal configuration settings

Configuration Setting	Description
Permissions	**Video Admins** These users can manage the home page and change permissions. **Channel Admins** These users can create channels.
Spotlight	Spotlight videos enable you to select a Spotlight video tile to show on the Office 365 Video Portal home page. You can select up to three Spotlight channels, each of which appears on the Video Portal home page.
Links to guidelines	This option creates hyperlinks to your organization's guidelines, and then the Video Portal automatically adds buttons for those links to the Office 365 Video Portal navigation bar.

When you upload videos to the Video Portal, they're uploaded to a particular *channel*. Channels are useful for grouping videos of similar content with one another. Channels can be created and managed only by someone designated as a Channel Admin. Channels also enable the channel administrators to specify who can view and share video content. Table 7-10 highlights the currently existing Video Portal channel settings.

TABLE 7-10 Office 365 Video Portal channel settings

Configuration Setting	Description
General	Allows you to change the channel name and the channel color.
Permissions	**Owners** These people can manage videos and change channel settings. **Editors** These people can add, change, or remove videos for this channel. **Viewers** These people can view videos.
Show Download Link For Videos	Enabling this option will show the URL for a video.
Spotlight	Select a Spotlight tile to choose videos to show on the channel page.
Yammer	Enables Yammer conversations to occur for this channel. This setting can be toggled on and off.

> **TIP** If you want to easily see how much storage space your video channel is consuming, you can find that information on the first page of the Channel Settings page.

Video Portal management

Videos continue to make up some of the most important assets that companies are producing today. The ability for everyone to become a videographer is a powerful skill to increase an organization's adaptability and communication methods when it reaches out to its constituency. However, with this skill comes the need for Cloud Pros to have continued visibility into and management of the consumption of online tenancy storage.

To find the storage consumption of the Office 365 Video Portal, you need three things:

- SharePoint Online Management Shell

- SharePoint Online Client Tools
- Get-AllVideoChannelStorage.ps1 script

The SharePoint Online Management Shell and Online Client tools should already be on your server. You'll need to download the third item from this webpage: *https://gallery.technet. microsoft.com/scriptcenter/How-To-Check-Channel-ac2a9b34*.

To find the storage consumption of the Video Portal, do the following:

1. First, launch the SharePoint Online Management Shell.
2. Next, change your directory to where you downloaded the script, such as E:\scripts.
3. Then, execute the script by typing **./Get-AllVideoChannelStorage.ps1** and pressing Enter.
4. Next, input your SPO Admin URL when prompted. It should be similar to *https://conto-so-admin.sharepoint.com*.
5. Next, input your SPO Portal URL when prompted. It should be similar to *https://contoso. sharepoint.com*.
6. Last, you'll receive a prompt for your user name and password. Enter credentials that have tenant administrator privileges. Your final output will contain a list of all your Office 365 Video Channels and each channel's storage detail.

Disabling the Video Portal

If you want to disable the Video Portal, you need to do the following:

1. Navigate to the SharePoint admin center.
2. Click Settings in the left navigation pane.
3. Locate the Streaming Video Service setting, and then select the option button labeled Disable Streaming Video Through Azure Media Services And Disable The Video Portal.
4. Scroll to the bottom of the page and click OK.

Know your roadmap

Social features, like most features, are continually and rapidly evolving. The social needs of an organization have an evolutionary path of their own, and it's important to keep that in mind. With that being said, a key point that must be made (and ultimately taken to heart) is that, as a Cloud Pro, you *must* continually keep yourself updated and informed about the Office 365 Roadmap. It's important for organizations to align and integrate technology roadmaps as a part of their strategy. The most common mistakes occur when governance and design decisions are made without organizations realizing the potential short-term or long-term impact. Many organizations discover many features and capabilities have been planned that can influence system integration plans or that they have planned other technology investments that could be avoided.

For more information, take a look at the Office 365 Roadmap at *https://fasttrack.microsoft. com/roadmap*.

## CHAPTER 8

Managing governance, security, and compliance

S ecurity is paramount as organizations make the transition from doing business in controlled, on-premises environments to Microsoft Office 365 and other cloud services. All but the largest and most highly secure data centers are as secure as Microsoft's. There are over 2,000 full-time security professionals working on Microsoft's cloud. The data centers are bulletproof, quite literally, and Microsoft has spent billions on solutions for fault tolerance such as power, HVAC, redundant network paths, and big data pipes.

> **MORE INFO**   For updated information on Microsoft's commitments to security and compliance, see *https://products.office.com/en-US/business/office-365-trust-center-welcome*.

This chapter is not about convincing you that Microsoft keeps your data safe—there's plenty of that material on Microsoft.com. Instead, this chapter is about learning how to keep your tenant as secure as possible with the technical controls you have at your disposal. For most readers of this book, this is completely new content. The Security & Compliance center is a new addition to Microsoft's tool set. Therefore, we take a little deeper dive into configuration than we have in other places in this book. We still discuss tips, but the goal of this chapter is to both introduce you to the configuration while giving you the knowledge to enforce compliance for your organization within Microsoft SharePoint Online, Exchange Online, and OneDrive for Business.

> **NOTE**   Site collection (SPSite)–scoped security is covered in Chapter 4 "SharePoint Online administration and configuration. For additional information on security with SPSites, see *https://support.office.com/article/Manage-site-collections-and-global-settings-in-the-SharePoint-admin-center-abacd1bb-295d-4235-afdd-15f5e4cc2e6c/*.

There's no perfect security (or compliance), and it's unlikely there ever will be. We can spend countless hours securing data and transmission mechanisms, but remember that most security incidents are caused by the end user, not the administrator. We can have a super-secure implementation, but if a user leaves her password under the keyboard, it then takes a single night worker only minutes to infiltrate your valuable cloud containers.

> **TIP** End-user security policies should be short. Anything longer than a dozen bullet points is likely to be completely overlooked by users. Decide on what is most important, and focus your training, governance planning, and compliance enforcement on that.

Microsoft works off of four core tenets when it comes to your data: built-in security, privacy by design, continuous compliance, and transparent operations. These principles come together to provide the supporting structure for a robust, rapidly evolving set of tools and reports. These give you a great deal of visibility into what is being done in your Office 365 environment and who is doing it.

> **MORE INFO** For more information on how Microsoft controls access to, and manages, your data, you can visit the Office 365 Trust Center at *https://products.office.com/business/office-365-trust-center-welcome*.

At first glance, the governance, security, and compliance features might seem to be in many places and disconnected. In reality, they're a cohesive set of features, but they're rooted in multiple product sets. Over time, and perhaps by the time you read this text, these features will come together as a comprehensive toolset to assist you with tenant security and compliance. In this chapter, we look at how these tools provide a framework for your SharePoint Online security posture. You'll see how they can help your organization easily establish and maintain compliance with many of today's most common security standards (such as HIPAA, FISMA, ISO 27001, EU, and others), permissions, alerts, security policies, data management, search and investigation, and reports.

> **TIP** It's highly recommended that administrators have two accounts: one account for administering Office 365 and one for ordinary work and collaboration. This recommendation does not apply to delegated roles unless specified by standards and regulations.

Service assurance

The Service Assurance page of the Security & Compliance center provides a set of documents, reports, and audited controls that are intended to allay concerns your organization might have regarding not only the security of your data but the privacy of that data as well. This information is tailored to your organization based on the choices you make on the Settings page of the Service Assurance Center.

> **TIP** Like many admin centers in Office 365, the rendered pages reflect the configuration choices you make. If you don't see the option you're looking for, be sure you enabled the feature in question and you have the correct security assigned to your account. A common mistake is that administrators are logged in with their unprivileged account and not their tenant administrator account.

Notice that you cannot access any pages of the Service Assurance Center until you configure the Region and Industry settings for the application, as shown in Figure 8-1. The Region drop-down menu contains choices that correspond to the regions where Office 365 is available. The multiple-choice Industry drop-down menu provides a list of common industries found around the world. Based on your selection, you receive content that is most relevant to you. This setting can be changed at any time.

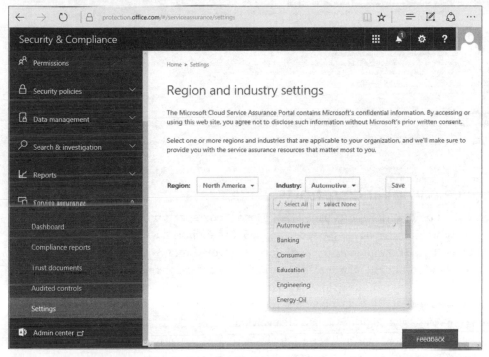

FIGURE 8-1 Service Assurance region and Industry settings

After you configure your region and industry, you can continue to the Service Assurance dashboard. (See Figure 8-2.) The dashboard provides an overview of the Service Assurance service itself, what's new, a link to add users to the Service Assurance User role, and, finally, an onboarding guide for providing nonadministrative users access to Service Assurance resources. Read these areas carefully, because misconfiguring your dashboard might provide unwanted access to secure data.

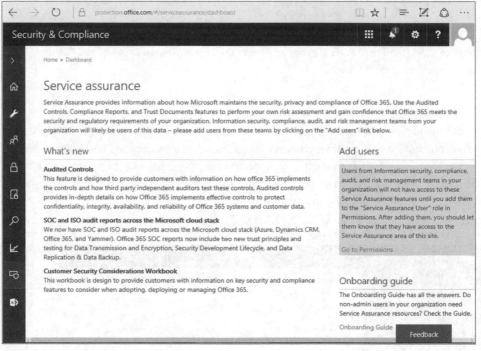

FIGURE 8-2 Service Assurance dashboard

Service compliance reports

The Service Compliance Reports page offers a long list of reports provided by independent third-party auditors that have assessed Office 365. The auditors have determined what you need to see, based on your industry, and convey how you comply with the common industry regulatory and security standards associated with your organization. These reports are grouped together by type. Keep in mind that these reports will be constantly evolving—so if your screenshot doesn't exactly match the text in this chapter, that's OK. It's another reminder of how our roles as cloud professionals are evolving.

- **GRC assessment reports** These are your governance risk and compliance summary reports.

- **ISO reports** These are your International Standards Organization Reports for ISO 27001 and 27018.

- **SOC/SSAE 16 reports** These are your Service Organization Controls (SOC) and SSAE 16, which is an enhancement to those controls.

Trust documents

Microsoft regularly publishes documents regarding how your information and data is managed and accessed in Office 365. These reports aren't just marketing content—they're directly related to your selected region and industry. Additionally, these reports are useful to explain to stakeholders the security controls, both technical and procedural, that apply to your tenant. Because these reports vary based on your industry and region, we will not cover them all here. Again, remember these reports are constantly changing as Microsoft enhances security and as the compliance requirements from various countries and industries are changing. The reports are divided into two sections:

- **FAQ and White Papers** These are informational documents focused on how data is managed within Office 365. This is an excellent resource for documentation on the features and functionality of your Office 365 tenant.

- **Risk Management Reports** In this section, Microsoft publishes annual security assessments related to Office 365, GRC (Governance, Risk and Compliance) policies, penetration testing results, and descriptions of the current risk-management life cycle.

Audited controls

If you're like us, you probably don't know the details of all industry regulations and standards around the globe. In fact, this hasn't been a focus of many IT Pros in the past. However, as we move data into the cloud, there's a greater need to ensure we are complying with regulations. The Audited Controls page provides you the ability to see the specific results of controls that are audited as a part of a specific set of security or regulatory standards. You can either download these results in .xlsx format or view them directly in the browser by clicking the title of the standard or regulation in the browser window. At a minimum, this page gives you easy access to information that will help you answer stakeholder questions about what controls are in place to meet a specific regulation or standard. Brian and Ben are tech guys and not compliance gurus, so we really appreciate the automation and detail put in place by Microsoft!

Upon entering the Audited Controls page, you are taken to a list view of the audited controls for the specific standard or regulation based on your industry and region. Click the down arrow on the right side of the screenshot to expand the selection you want to view, as shown in Figure 8-3. Alternatively, you can select the standard or regulation and choose Download at the top of the screen. By downloading controls, you can view and manipulate the content in Microsoft Excel. For large sets of controls, Excel is usually the best option because it can handle content of that size.

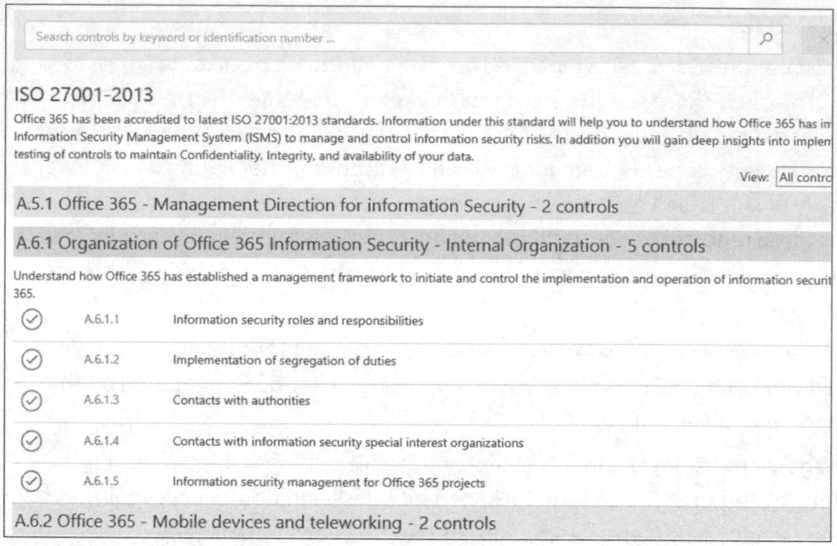

FIGURE 8-3 Expanded selection in the audited controls report for the ISO 27001-2013 standard

To view more information about a specific item in the list, you can click it to bring up a dialog window with the details around the control as shown in Figure 8-4.

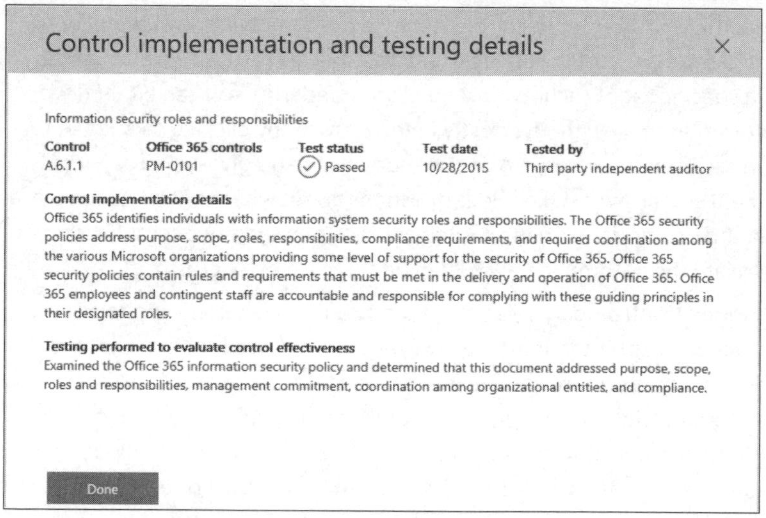

FIGURE 8-4 Control details in ISO 27001 – 2013 report

Permissions

Office 365 provides you the ability to control access for many underlying processes at a very granular level. Through a combination of members, roles, and role groups, Office 365 allows you to delegate compliance management access to users so that they have the ability to perform tasks in the Compliance Center. It's common for organizations to have different names for these roles than what Microsoft has named them in the user interface. Be sure to align your governance-plan roles with the Microsoft-defined roles. Microsoft includes the following roles:

- eDiscovery administrator
- Data Loss Prevention (DLP) administrator
- Auditing and Alerting administrator
- Compliance Reporting and Trust administrator

Each of these administrator roles is defined by permissions granted to users. It's important to understand the relationship between members, roles, and role groups in this instance:

- **Role groups** exist at the top of the structure of the security framework and can contain multiple roles. These multiple roles combine to control permissions for accessing features in the Compliance Center. For example, a member of the Compliance Administrator role group would have the ability to manage settings for device management, data loss prevention, and reports.

- **Roles** are the communications facilitators between the members they contain and the role groups they are members of. Roles grant a user the ability to perform an identified set of tasks that are associated with his role group. Think of roles as the permission being assigned.

- **Members** are the users who have been added to a role group. Members perform the tasks that are associated with the primary function of the role group. A user must be a member of at least one role group before she will have access to the Compliance Center.

Office 365 provides a number of default roles and role groups that will address most common situations. Instead of changing the default role groups, we recommend creating custom role groups that better reflect the needs of your organization. You do not have the ability to create custom roles, but you can add available roles from a predefined list of roles along with their associated permissions to your custom role group.

> **TIP** Instead of creating a new role group from scratch and then adding the appropriate roles, it's easier to decide which role group most closely resembles your desired end state and copy that role group as a baseline. Once that baseline is created, simply make your changes to the copy.

If you're new to Office 365, the user interface might be a little confusing. To show you how most of the modern administrative interface works, here's an example of how to create a new role group based on a copy of an existing group:

1. From the Permissions page of the Security & Compliance center, select the role group you want to copy and then click the Copy icon as shown.

A new tab opens in your browser. This tab is where you give your new role group a name and description. You then set up the roles it contains by clicking the Add (+) or Subtract (–) icon:

2. Clicking the Add icon opens another new tab in your browser. Here is where you can select from a list of predefined roles, each of which has a set of defined permissions that will be displayed in the description pane to the right of the screen. You make your selection by clicking once, and then next clicking the Add button at the bottom of the screen or by double-clicking your selection:

Display name ▲

Audit Logs

Case Management

Compliance Search

Export

Hold

Organization Configuration

Preview

Retention Management

Review

Role Management

Search And Purge

Lets people turn on and configure auditing for their Office 365 organization. This role also lets people view the organization's audit reports, and then export these reports to a file.

1 selected of 15 total

add ->

Save   Cancel

3. Now that you defined the roles for the custom role group, you can add the users who can perform the tasks associated with the role. To do that, you click the Add icon just below the Members label.

Roles

\+ −

Name ▲

Case Management

Compliance Search

Hold

Organization Configuration

Retention Management

Add

\+ −

Display name ▲   Email address

4. In the new Windows that opens, you see a list of all your users. You can select your user from the list by scrolling or searching for her name. As you add members to the role group, their names and email addresses appear in the display.

> **NOTE** Not all permissions related to the Security & Compliance center can be configured in the Permissions section of the Security & Compliance center dashboard. Some settings must be configured in the Exchange Administration Center. For more information on the Exchange Administration Center, see *https://technet.microsoft.com/library/jj200743(v=exchg.150).aspx*.

Alerts

Office 365 gives you the ability to create and configure alerts based on two criteria: the activity and associated user. With improved process options on the menu, you can monitor the daily operations of an Office 365 instance and create alert notifications on over 120 user and administrator activities. By default, there are no alerts created. This is certainly an area that needs to be covered during your tenant requirements gathering and design phases. However, this feature is new and still limited in functionality. As the add-on service Advanced Security Management evolves, you can expect additional free functionality to trickle down. If you need better alerting than what is offered for free, consider upgrading to the advanced alerts service.

> **NOTE** Alerts from this administrative location do not replace the alerts within SharePoint Online SPSites, nor is it meant to. These alerts are for overall compliance policy and risk mitigation, and they're usually configured by someone other than SharePoint Online site owners.

Working with basic alert management

With licenses below E5, currently defined at *https://products.office.com/en-us/business/office-365-enterprise-e5-business-software*, and tenants without advanced alert management licensed, you have only basic alert management. Creating a new alert requires that you provide a name for the alert, a description, one or more activities to search on, and one or more users (no groups). If one of the users listed performs any of the activities being monitored, an email is sent to the person identified on the "Send this alert to . . ." line. Be careful to not select a generic alert or you will likely be flooded with emails. There are exceptions to this, though. A good example is automating the alert email to integrate with another monitoring solution. To be notified when any user in your organization executes a monitored action, leave the "Users:" line blank. This is useful for items such as DNS monitoring, anonymous external sharing, and user account deletion.

After you create a security alert, any time an alert is sent it's recorded in the View Security Alerts page. The list view of security alerts includes information on the type of alert, the level of risk, details of the alert, the date the action occurred, and the action taken that caused the alert to be sent.

Manage advanced alerts

Microsoft offers Advanced Security Management as a part of the Office 365 Enterprise E5 subscription plan or as an add-on subscription to other plans. The Advanced Security Management Center gives you the ability to create policies that alert you to activities identified as anomalous or suspicious. Policies are based either on automatic algorithms that detect suspicious activities or on activity policies you create that defines activities or behavior as atypical for your organization.

NOTE Advanced Security Management for Office 365 is a separate online service that is powered by the Microsoft Cloud App Security service. It's integrated with the Security & Compliance admin center for convenience. This practice of integrating multiple services in a single UI is common throughout the Office 365 platform with both administrative and user pages.

After you add the service to your subscription, you can access it by clicking on the Manage Advanced Alerts link in the quick launch area. On the home page of the service, as shown in Figure 8-5, you have the option to turn on Advanced Security Management for your entire Office 365 tenant. If you do not see Manage Advanced Alerts, you either don't have the correct license or have not activated the service.

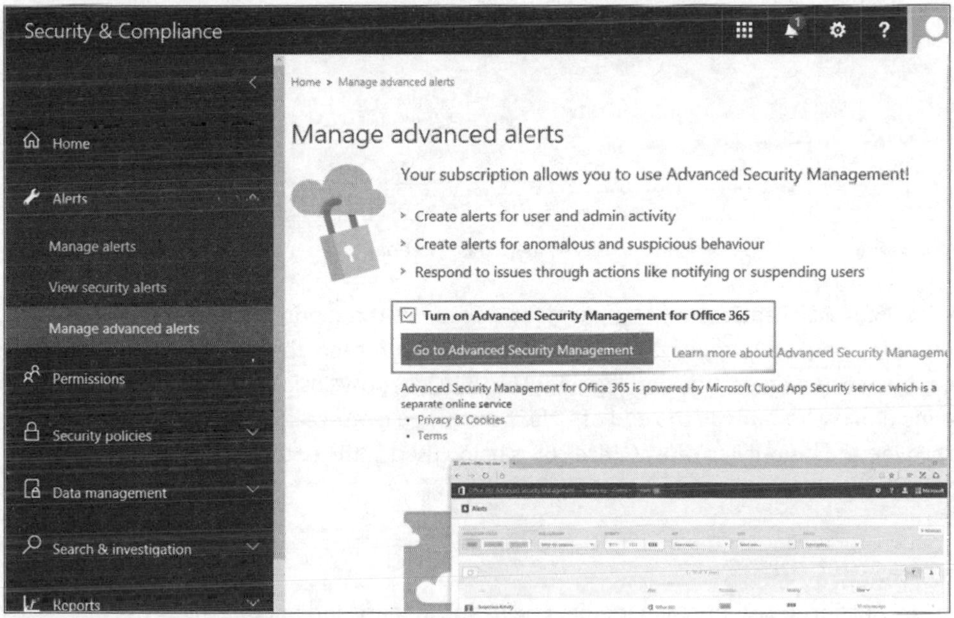

FIGURE 8-5 Activating Advanced Security Management for your entire tenant

After you activate the service, you can access the Advanced Security Management page by clicking the Go To Advanced Security Management button from the Manage Advanced Alerts page. You are taken to a new URL, one that is the administrative console for all of Office 365 Advanced Security Management. It's worth repeating that enabling this screen enables the feature for the entire tenant: Exchange, OneDrive for Business, and other applications you're licensed for.

Upon entering your tenant's Advanced Security Management console, you're taken directly to the Policies page, as seen in Figure 8-6. From here, you can see the granular options available for security alerting. Take some time and go through the configuration options for creating new policies. We recommend not creating alerts in the beginning, but instead get a good idea of the plethora of options available. When creating an action (such as suspending a user), be sure to test the policy as an alert only, without action. This prevents configuration errors from suspending active accounts. We recommend that you be especially careful when creating actionable policies on critical accounts.

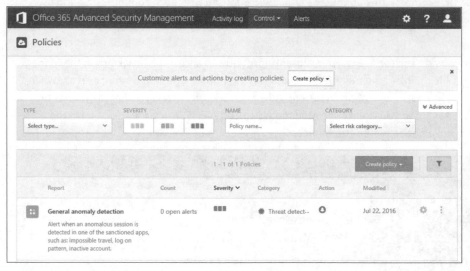

FIGURE 8-6 The Office 365 Advanced Security Management webpage

Office 365 Advanced Security Management is driven by three primary features: threat detection, logging, and insights. At the time this book was written, the primary focus of development was on detection and logging. The third category, insights, is planned to include reporting and dashboards by the end of 2016. These three features combined give you greater control over, and insight into, how Office 365 is being used in the enterprise and who is doing what with the platform (both users and administrators).

Threat detection

Office 365 Advanced Security Management helps you identify and mitigate high-risk or abnormal usage and security incidents through the use of policies. The anomaly detection feature scans all identified user activities and evaluates the risk level associated with those activities. This is done by comparing the activity against more than 70 indicators. Those indicators are grouped into six categories:

- **Logon Failures** Considers the anomalous patterns of logon failures and can be applied to either all monitored activity or a selected activity. It's likely that a properly configured Microsoft Azure Active Directory (Azure AD) is also monitoring this event. This rule can provide additional insurance and will also monitor connections not associated with your Azure AD.

- **Admin Activity** Considers anomalous patterns associated with administrative activities and can be applied to either all monitored activity or a selected activity. We usually configure this, if only minimally.

- **Inactive Accounts**   Examines the last time a user was active in Office 365 and can be applied to either all monitored activities or selected activities. Unused accounts might present a risk to your security.

- **Location**   Examines activity originating from new, infrequent, and suspicious locations and can be applied to either all monitored activities or selected activities.

- **Impossible Travel**   Examines concurrent activity from remote locations and can be applied to all monitored activities or selected activities. This is a particularly useful option, because many security breaches originate from other countries.

- **Device And User Agent**   Examines activity from new or untrusted devices and can be applied to all monitored activities or selected activities.

To detect threats that might be affecting the platform, Office 365 uses two types of policies to scan and filter user activity and behavior. The first type of policy we will look at is activity policies.

Activity policies

There are multiple locations where you can create a new policy for tracking user and administrator activities. For example, the front page of the Office 365 Advanced Security Management page has two links that can be used to create a new policy. In the following example, you create a new anomaly policy directly from the Policies page:

1. Start by finding the Control link in the header of the Security Management Center, and click for the drop-down menu. This is usually a different color than the rest of the screen and is easily overlooked.

2. Next, you must decide if you want to use a template or create a custom policy. After you pick one, give your policy a name and description and then choose a level from the Policy Severity and Category menus to assign the appropriate values to the new policy.

3. From the Policy Severity drop-down menu, select Low, Medium, or High.

4. Next, select the Category for your policy. The choices are Threat Detection, Privileged Accounts, Compliance, Sharing Control, Access Control, and Configuration Control.

5. Next, select the activities to filter on. This can be a simple, single activity filter or a complex filter with multiple activities. You have the option of Equals or Does Not Equal when selecting an activity to filter. There are currently 20 filter types, much like filter groups, that you can filter against. Depending on the filter type selected, you'll have different activity options available. This list will continue to grow, but examples of filter types are Administrative Activity, Device Type, and IP Address Tag. This is a first-class platform feature and, therefore, you'll find a substantial number of activity types under each filter type.

6. When you have the filters configured for the new policy, you can set up how email alerts are handled when a triggered activity is detected. The three configuration options are Alerting Threshold, Alert Configuration, and the option to save these alert settings as the default for your organization. Within each of these options, you can define a daily alert limit (with the default being five).

7. If you feel the policy you're creating is critical enough, you can configure it so that any user who violates the policy will immediately have their account suspended.

Anomaly detection policy

Anomaly detection policies use built-in, Microsoft-created algorithms to detect suspicious behavior. Little is disclosed about how exactly these algorithms work, but we do know machine-learning works in tandem with precoded logic under the hood. The type of anomalies detected include normal user behavior, industry trends in high risk activity, and predefined risks such as users adding known, risky content to data. There is data on the product that Microsoft acquired to seed this service, but making assumptions from those old product specifications would be risky.

> **MORE INFO** For more information on creating anomaly detection policies, see "Create anomaly detection policies in Advanced Security Management" at *https://support.office.com/article/Create-anomaly-detection-policies-in-Advanced-Security-Management-88935b4e-dcb1-47f1-8aca-1bf8fb069db6*.

One main difference in anomaly detection and activity detection is that anomaly detection can take several days before you see the full benefit. The heuristic machine learning takes time, so you might not see the full benefit until the service learns your users' normal behavior.

Multiple pages link to a new anomaly detection policy, but for this example we'll use the Policies home page. Be sure you create a new Anomaly Detection Policy and not an Activity Detection Policy, as shown in Figure 8-8. It's a small thing, but it's easily overlooked because an Activity Policy is the default. At the time this book was written, the new Anomaly Detection Policy page defaulted to the bottom of the configuration page, instead of the top. Be sure you scroll up before deciding the page isn't working correctly. The steps are included here in case you haven't licensed the product yet and want to be familiar with the options:

1. Start by finding the Control menu in the header of the Advanced Security Management home page. Click Control to display the drop-down menu, as shown in Figure 8-7.

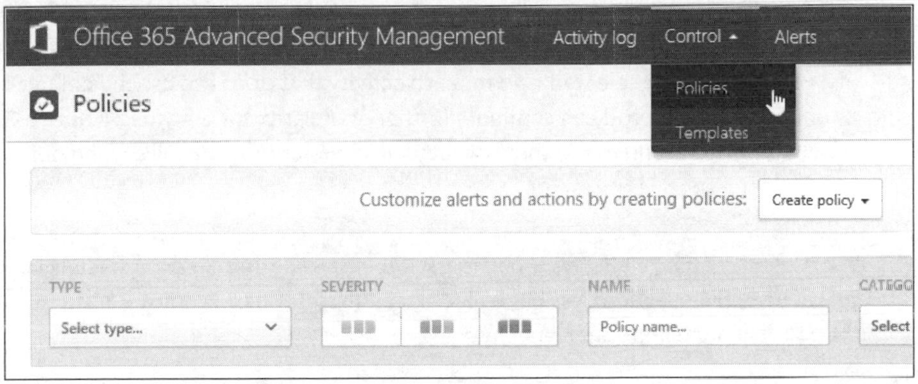

FIGURE 8-7 Select the Control menu from the top of the page

2. Next, you will next be taken to the Policies home page, where you can see any existing policies or create a new one. To create a new policy, click the drop-down menu as shown in Figure 8-8 to bring up the options for which type of policy you want to create. In this example, select Anomaly Detection Policy.

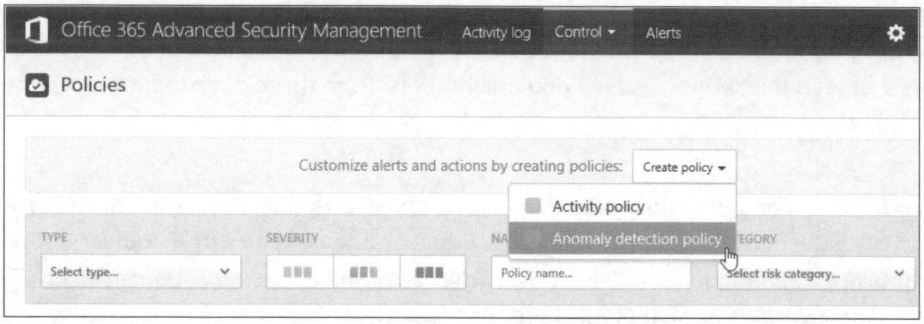

FIGURE 8-8 Double-check you're using the Anomaly Detection Policy

3. On the Create Anomaly Detection Policy page, either start with an existing template for a baseline or choose to create a new policy from scratch. You must give the policy a name, and it's strongly recommended you provide a description of the policy.

4. Next, assign a policy severity level and category. The default categories are Threat Detection, Privileged Accounts, Compliance, Sharing Control, Access Control, and Configuration Control.

5. Next, select the activity filters that are used for alert triggers. You have two options to apply to your filters: All Monitored Activity or Selected Activity. If you choose Selected Activity, you will have the same choices you had when creating activity alerts. There are hundreds of possible combinations, and you can have multiple filters that apply to your policy.

6. Once you're done creating the relevant activity filters, you must decide what risk factors you need. The anomaly engine monitors your selected activities and behavior in Office 365. You have the option of selecting All Monitored Activity or Selected Activity. For each activity selected, and for each activity that does not use the default of All Monitored Activity, you can configure further granularity for activities. Figure 8-9 shows some risk factors, and it also shows what your screen should look like when defining an activity for a specific risk factor.

> **TIP** When creating alerts, it's useful to track your selections in an Excel spreadsheet. As shown here, the selection possibilities are extensive and you can easily lose your place in the policy and filter options hierarchy.

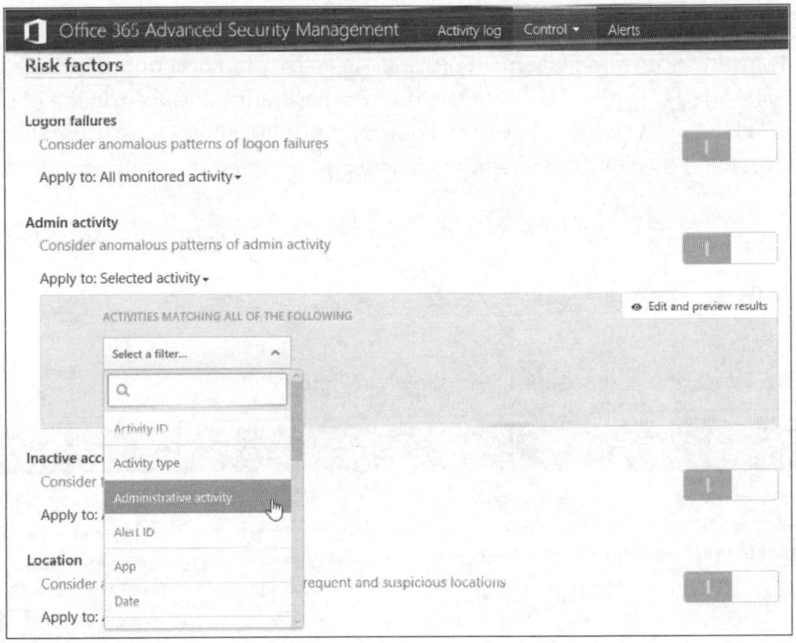

FIGURE 8-9 Applying a specific activity to be filtered for in relation to the Administrative Activity risk factor

7. The finishing step is choosing how email alerts are handled when an anomaly is detected. In the last section of the configuration page, shown in Figure 8-10, you can define a daily alert limit (the default is five) and specify whether alerts are sent via email and text message. Depending on your selection, you enter an email address, a phone number, or both for alerts to be sent to.

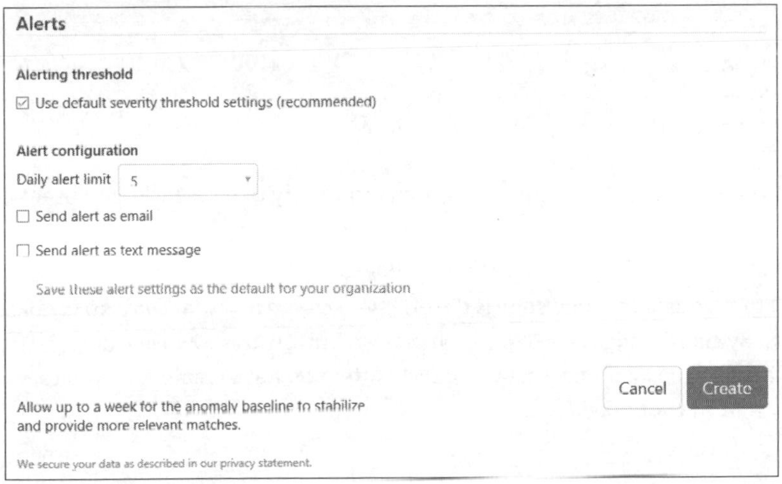

FIGURE 8-10 Choose email, text messaging, or both for policy alerts

Activity logging

Office 365 Advanced Security Management provides an activity log dashboard you can use to easily view your logged activities. There are two options: Basic and Advanced. In the basic view of activity logs, as shown in Figure 8-11, you can quickly find a log entry by selecting the app you want to target and then one or more of the following:

- User
- IP Address
- Activity Type
- Location

You can also select one or more apps, also shown in Figure 8-11.

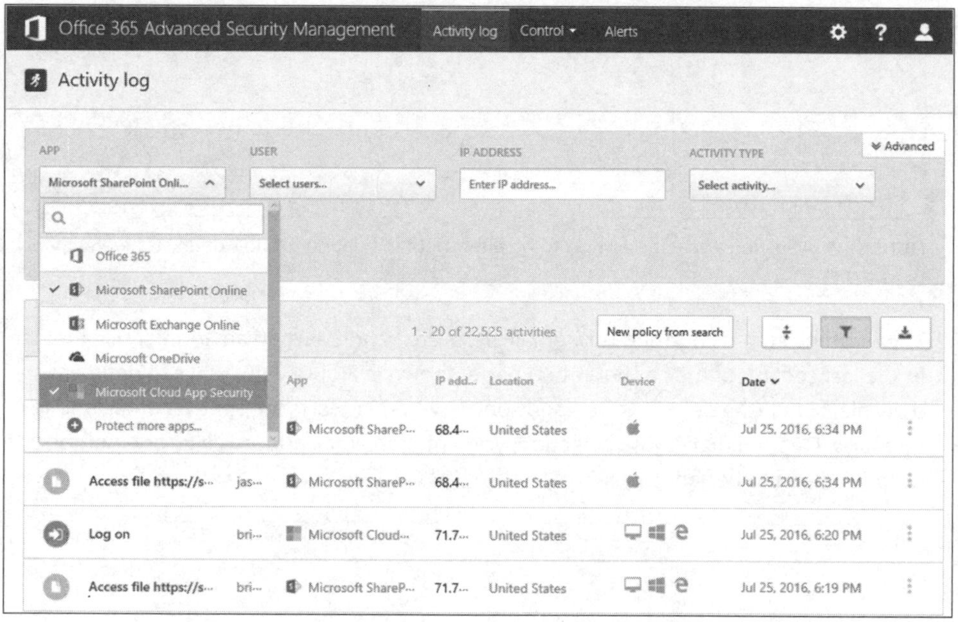

FIGURE 8-11 Select one or more apps from the drop-down menu

Depending on the activity type, the popup display a variety of data, including user name, date, location, IP address, source, organizational unit, device type, IP tags, activity ID, user groups, user agent tags, matched policies, target object, type, and ISP.

A recent feature you might find useful is the ability to create a new activity policy based on a log search. By clicking the New Policy From Search button, as shown in Figure 8-11, the log query will be inserted into a new activity policy. After you have created the policy, you can further modify it to suit your needs.

Governance

Some IT Pros do not like the topic of governance, nor do they like writing governance plans. However, the cloud makes governance a mandatory topic, even for those who once overlooked it. The benefits of Office 365 are commonly stated as anywhere, anytime, any device access to data. However, those same features can also be security risks. Data can be accessed from anywhere a user is, anytime a hacker chooses, and on any device from which the hacker happens to initiate a compromise. The accessibility of Office 365 mandates a strong governance plan and the execution of that plan.

Planning

We hear a lot about governance planning. It has been our experience, however, that governance plans are rarely followed. The two primary reasons that we see for why governance plans are built and forgotten is that they are large, unwieldly, and unenforceable. In fact, a good idea is to use a SharePoint Online site and make your governance plan a dynamic and useful place to visit. We practice Governance Through Osmosis when possible. We create a site where users can get training, where the governance working group (GWG) can make decisions and meet virtually, and where we can include fun games that reinforce your governance strategy. This approach will help keep your governance from being an unpracticed discipline.

> **TIP** Governance is mostly about mitigating organizational risk, and a governance plan should include only enforceable items. Technical control items, such as folder names and file names, are often included in governance plans and they're rarely enforced. In fact, including unenforceable items in your governance plan weakens the plan under scrutiny.
>
> Likewise, items that directly mitigate organizational risk, such as intellectual property or compliance, are often ignored when the plan includes a lot of fluff. When you introduce a few unenforceable items into your governance plan, you set yourself up for a result of no governance at all. Keep it small, keep it simple, and keep it aligned with risks that your executives will understand.

No two governance plans are the same. In fact, if you ask 10 different professionals to define governance, you'll get 10 different answers. Our experience with SharePoint Online governance is to keep it relevant and clearly define the application governance boundaries. A good starting outline is covered in the rest of this chapter. Note the headings and know that the content might vary greatly in your organization.

Identifying plan scope is very important for useable governance. When allowed, we address tenant governance in multiple layers. Each layer does not equate to a unique plan, but each layer does have interactions with the other layers in this model. Of the six listed in Figure 8-12, this chapter is focused on layers one through three: Tenant, SharePoint Online (SharePoint Online, including OneDrive for Business and related products), and Sites and Services. In some

IT organizations, the scope will go as far as layer five, Sites, but such a plan is doomed for failure in all but the largest and most well-staffed organizations. SharePoint Online is built for users and power users to control their destiny within the platform, and that occurs in layers four through six.

Level four, Site Collections, is the largest point of contention in most organizations. However, it's a simple problem to solve. If IT staffs the business professionals (*Biz Pros*), sometimes known as IT business analysts (BAs), it's reasonable for site collection governance to fall under IT. In the cloud, Biz Pros are the BAs/MBAs who also understand the user interface (UI), user experience (UX), services, and process engine in Office 365. They are the professionals who interface between the business and IT. If the Biz Pros are not in IT and are spread throughout the organization, IT simply won't have the time or resources to manage at the site collection layer.

> **TIP** We often create a Team or Department governance template. This is a 2-page or 3-page document that details the most important governance items to the business. We provide this to the site collection administrators as a starting point for their governance. We delegate some governance to the people who own the processes and content.

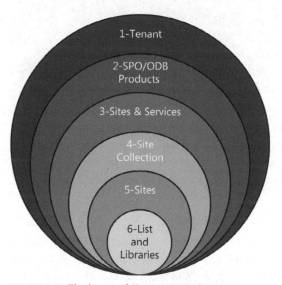

FIGURE 8-12 The layers of SharePoint Online governance

The layers in Figure 8-12 are derived from the platform's architecture itself. It's a reasonable approach to align platform governance with the platform's architecture. Inherent within the tenant and product layers is the management of products, such as SharePoint Online, Yammer, and Exchange Online. Inherent within the Sites & Services layer is the need for a solid information architecture and governance plan, because "where stuff goes" and "who can see it" are really parts of a URL taxonomy and service application permissions discussion. It's impossible to have a good SharePoint Online governance plan without a solid information architecture. (I would repeat that, but the editors probably wouldn't let me.)

There's a wealth of content available on information architecture, but one of the best starting places is the Information Architect Institute, *http://www.iainstitute.org*. This fact, coupled with the fact it's unique to each organization, precludes us from trying to discuss it in this book. Just know that without having a good idea of how you'll bucket information and then clearly define who owns those buckets, you'll find it difficult to enforce governance or security.

Governance roles

For Office 365, we successfully used five swim lanes to express the tasks and responsibilities of the five interested parties within the process:

- Business users
- Office 365 liaison
- Office 365 administrators
- Office 365 developers
- Governance working group

The process expressed in this document is less detailed than a full-blown task list. The process described is meant to give you some ideas of how you can create an agile, yet comprehensive, governance master process. The two roles that might be new to you are the governance working group and the Office 365 liaison. They are described in the following sections.

Governance working group

The term *governance working group* (GWG) was mentioned already because it's the critical hub in practical governance. In some organizations, this is called a *governance committee*. We find that the term *working group* makes governance friendlier and allows us some flexibility as we architect the stakeholders and approvers. The GWG uses and enforces the agreed-upon change-control processes.

Office 365 liaison

The Office 365 liaison is usually a member of the business group. This individual plays a major role in this change-control process. This person must have excellent written and verbal communication skills and, sometimes, significant patience. The liaison is responsible for communicating back and forth between the business group she represents, the GWG, and the parties responsible for implementing changes. The liaison also serves on the GWG. This individual's role is illustrated in Figure 8-13.

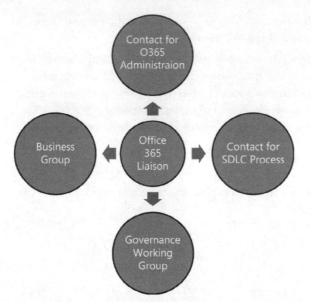

FIGURE 8-13 The Office 365 liaison interacts with the Office 365 administrator and the business group. This person also is part of the GWG and works with the lead for software development.

Change control

Change control is important for the stability of any system. In some organizations, this topic is included in configuration management. We largely agree with that. However, we include it here for organizations without rigid configuration management practices. Including it in your governance plan is better than not having it at all! There are three primary focus areas regarding tenant change control: the site collection creation process, site collection governance changes, and site collection feature changes.

Site collection creation process

Site collections are the primary security boundaries in SharePoint Online (as well as being storage quota boundaries). We minimize site collection creation, unless needed for security or to better manage size. A new site collection complicates many enterprise deployments because it's another configuration set that must be managed. The challenges that come with managing lots of site collections include a lack of navigation inheritance, limited branding inheritance, new site-scoped content types, new site-scoped columns, and a new permissions-inheritance structure.

We recommend you define and document a site collection creation process. Figure 8-14 shows an example of a site collection creation process flowchart.

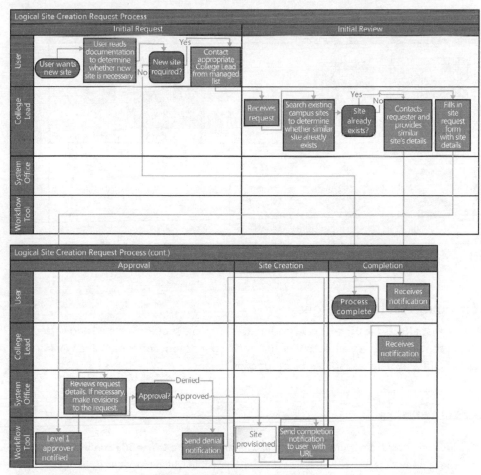

FIGURE 8-14 Example site collection creation workflow for a college

Site collection governance changes

Changes to the site collection template provided to departments and teams should be approved by the GWG. Figure 8-15 shows an example of a governance-changes-approval flowchart. While you delegate governance to the site collection administrators, you need to verify that the changes don't affect the platform. Large app purchases, third-party software, and custom branding are examples that can affect the usability of the platform by visiting users.

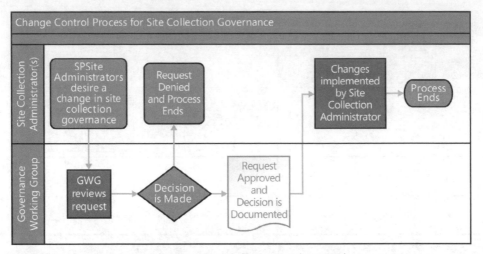

FIGURE 8-15 Governance site collection–scoped changes need approval

Site collection feature changes

Any feature that affects the user experience and user interface should be tested and vetted. This testing should be done in a test tenant and not in your production tenant. Many early adopters of Office 365 are testing in their production tenant.

Real World

Speaking of test environments, the many members of the Office 365 admin and development teams must have a safe environment in which to test new changes before implementing them in production. We recommend a tenant in which the team can test changes, third-party products, and custom solutions. As part of the change control governance for Office 365, it's required that the test environment be adequately similar to the production environment so that certain quality assurance tests can be run on new updates and changes before they are implemented in production.

Remember, this is a cloud service and, as such, many configuration changes are managed by Microsoft that we cannot control. The product roadmap can be seen at *http://fasttrack.microsoft.com/roadmap*. While Microsoft does release regular updates, it does not reduce the importance of approving configurations that we can control. For a development environment, most MSDN licenses will include a development tenant. In short, developers use an MSDN tenant; integration and staging requires a small, dedicated enterprise tenant; and production is not used for development or testing.

Ben Curry, Office 365 MVP

The level of testing and approvals vary greatly depending on your organization, but in some organizations IT needs to completely control feature deployment to ensure compatibility with customizations and third-party products. The right answer is somewhere between no feature-change management and comprehensive feature-change management. Figure 8-16 shows a basic feature-change-approval flowchart.

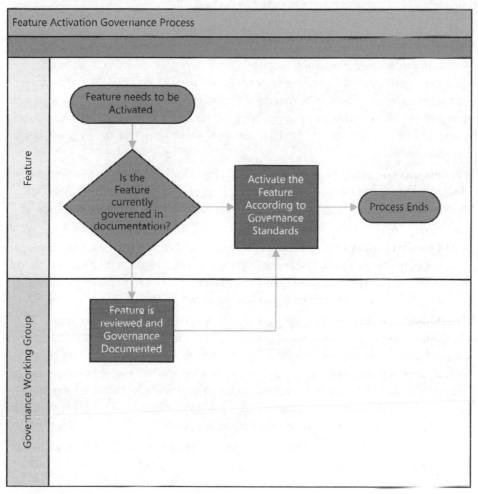

FIGURE 8-16 Features that affect the usability of the platform should be approved.

Tenant governance

Governance is primarily about mitigating risk. You must first understand the risks your organization is facing, both technical and nontechnical, and then work to mitigate those risks. Office 365 can both increase risk and mitigate risk.

Office 365 can mitigate risk through the thoughtful implementation of features such as DLP, activity alerting, SPSite auditing, anomaly detection alerting, rights management, and mobile data management. Conversely, some data that was previously stored on-premises in virtual vaults might now be vulnerable. Moving data from on-premises solutions to the cloud broadens the possible audience for that data, and you need to ensure you have the controls in place and features enabled to keep that data as secure as possible.

Site security monitoring

Much of this chapter focused on security monitoring and alerting. However, there are still many areas that need to be monitored within SharePoint Online SPSites that cannot be done from a centralized console. Site security monitoring is usually delegated to the SPSite administrators and SPWeb owners. This is a major decision to make: How will you accomplish site monitoring and who is responsible for it? The following is a starting list for you to build your SPSite monitoring tasks:

- **Permissions and group changes**   Many security incidents happen as mistakes and not just intentional attacks. Site permissions should be at the top of your auditing list. Accidental inclusion of an external group in a confidential site could have catastrophic consequences.

- **Audit policy changes**   All audit policy changes should be treated as suspect. They should be approved by the governance working group. Be aware of numerous audit log entries that appear to be inconsequential. Sometimes this is intentional white noise that is created to hide a single, unfriendly, audit log policy change.

- **Check-in/check-out**   Your known, confidential, and high-risk data repositories should be monitored for who checks in and checks out a file. Data integrity is a key to good governance and security. Whether intentional or unintentional, changes to critical corporate documents that are unapproved can have negative consequences. Examples we have seen are employee performance reviews being modified, executive salary information being changed or leaked, website copy-approved content being overwritten, and legal contracts being erroneously updated.

- **List and site modifications**   There are numerous list and site modifications a user can do. Depending on your organizational risk, you might need to track modifications. We usually divide sites into three categories: confidential, internal-use only, and publicly available. These three are good starting points for segmenting information and implementing governance that is aligned with that segmentation.

- **Searches**   On multiple occasions, we have seen threats surface in user searches. This risk is always a concern when sharing data with external collaborators. People looking for more information that they should not have access to often use search as the first tool to find confidential data. We recommend monitoring the sites that you know host confidential content.

TIP   We usually prohibit anonymous access to the tenant unless it's approved by the GWG, a secure location is created, and security controls are implemented for auditing and monitoring access.

Secure store service

The secure store service provides the capability to store login information securely in Share-Point Online and associate it with a specific identity or group of identities. For example, this service manages authentication and authorization for Access Apps. The passphrase used to generate keys in the secure store service is not retained within the platform itself, so it should be recorded and kept in a safe place. Be careful about who is given access to the secure store, and ensure there's a process in place to track changes.

Managed Metadata Service service application governance

Most of the SharePoint Online technologies have been covered in this book. However, a possible governance issue for many organizations is the Managed Metadata Service service application (MMS). The MMS has two primary parts, the Content Type Hub and the Term Store. The Content Type Hub is an SPSite hosting content types that are published throughout your tenant. The Term Store is a database that hosts your noun taxonomy. Your noun taxonomy consists of term groups, term sets, and terms.

See Also   For more information on the MMS, browse to *https://technet.microsoft.com /library/ee424402.aspx.*

We have seen instances where external sharing was turned on for SPSites, yet confidential terms within the MMS could be seen through those external sites. This is a good example of how service application data can leak into seemingly secured sites. To understand how to govern the MMS, you must understand the following MMS security roles and boundaries.

MMS TITLES AND ROLES

The *term store administrator* is the individual who manages the term store at the tenant layer. The *local term store manager* refers to the individual or individuals who manage term sets for a given site collection through the administration interfaces at the site layer.

TERM STORE ADMINISTRATOR RESPONSIBILITIES

The first line of governance for this service application is to assign those with taxonomy or library sciences experience permissions to administrate MMS. You do this by browsing to the SharePoint Online Admin Center, as shown in Figure 8-17, selecting Term Store in the left navigation pane, and then adding these individuals to the Term Store Administrators field. Click the Save button when you're ready.

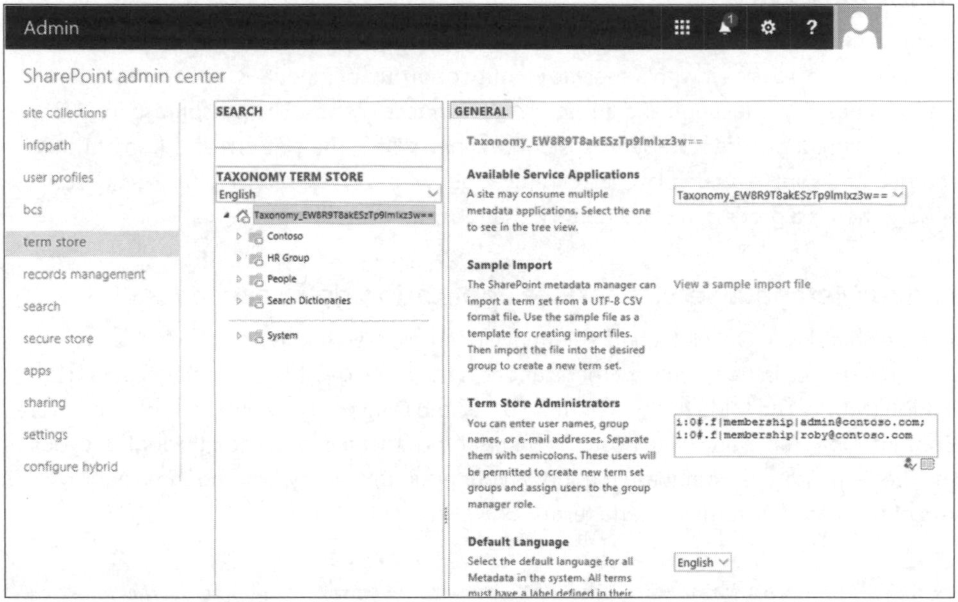

FIGURE 8-17 Add qualified individuals to administer the term store

The term store administrator is responsible for managing keywords, orphaned terms, and hashtags to ensure no term violates any acceptable use or harassment policies in the organization. In addition, this position is responsible for managing appropriate terms in a global term set. The person in this role also creates and deprecates term sets and term groups, as well as assigning management permissions to term groups.

> **TIP** If term store administrators also manage items in the Content Type Hub, they need to be site collection administrators for the Content Type Hub SPSite. To find the Content Type Hub for your tenant, replace <tenant> with your tenant name and browse to *https://<tenant>.sharepoint.com/sites/contenttypehub*.

The term store administrator is responsible for the management of content types in the Content Type Hub. The hub should be quarantined and not used for other purposes. Restricting access reduces the potential that changes, intentional or unintentional, will be made to content types that are then syndicated throughout the tenant. A simple quarantine action virtually eliminates this risk.

TIP You should expect that term conflicts will arise. If the term store administrator cannot resolve conflicts between groups in the organization regarding the use of same or similar terms, the issue should be escalated to the GWG for their decision.

Additional service governance

The secure store service and managed metadata service are only two examples of aspects of Office 365 to be managed and governed. There are, however, many more, including search, SharePoint Online user profiles, Yammer, Exchange Online, Skype for Business, Azure AD and identity sync, licensing, mobile device management (MDM), monitoring and support, the video portal, eDiscovery, and data loss prevention (DLP). Each of these should be included in your governance plan as well.

If nothing else, define who owns each of these and who is the administrative lead, even if it's the same person for each one. You also should designate a backup administrator. In some cases, the ownership of the service can be enforced through a technical control such as delegated administrators. In other cases, it will need to be a logical ownership. For those with technical controls, we highly recommend that access be removed for those without responsibility.

Additionally, capture some key decisions and strategies around each service to guide their management going forward. Some of these key decisions include

- How are users and groups managed? Where can they be created?
- How is security enforced?
- How is licensing managed?
- What is the workflow for making a change to the service?
- Which changes are common enough to be exempt from the change workflow?
- What is the service's application lifecycle model (ALM)?
- Who is responsible for monitoring the service? How does somebody get help if it's needed?
- How does the service handle sensitive data? Should it?
- What about external interactions, like external sharing?
- Are there any compliance or retention requirements?
- How is the service audited?

Finally, as with the rest of the governance plan, take the time to occasionally audit these additional services. Is the defined ownership still correct and relevant? Is any additional governance needed as a result of changes in the services? Are any changes being made that are inconsistent with the change control policy? Rely upon the audit tools available in the platform or, if these are insufficient, consider implementing a third-party solution.

CHAPTER 9

Migrating content to SharePoint Online

You might have been told that your company is migrating to Microsoft Office 365. You might even be the one tasked to make it happen. Sure, you now know how to administer the services, and you know how they can be used to make your users more productive—but migrations? That's an entirely different story.

Migrations are less technical. They require a lot of the soft skills we discussed back in Chapter 1, "Getting started as an Office 365 Cloud Pro." In a migration project, the technology is usually the easiest part.

If you're like most IT Pros, you're probably daunted by the prospect of a migration project. However, migrations are an important part of the Cloud Pro's duties. There's a lot of on-premises data, and quite often a company looks to save costs and increase its return on investment (ROI) in the cloud by moving its data there. Over time, we expect the need to migrate to the cloud to decrease (although cloud-to-cloud migrations will increase). In the meantime, though, you need to understand the factors involved with migrating to the cloud.

We don't have space in this book to go into a lot of technical depth about migrations. Additionally, an entire book could be written on the raw, technical migration activities. By the time this book is published, much of that content would already be outdated. Our experience also shows the technical details of a migration are often the simplest part of the migration. To that end, this chapter discusses migration strategies and how you might run a migration project. Our focus is on equipping you to think holistically about migrations because, again, the technology will be the easy part. Migration is primarily a process exercise, not a technological one.

NOTE We do not cover Microsoft Exchange Online and Skype for Business migrations specifically in this chapter. Many planning and communication sections in this chapter are applicable to those types of migrations, but this chapter is targeted at Microsoft SharePoint Online.

Browse to *https://support.office.com/article/Decide-on-a-migration-path-0d4f2396-9cef-43b8-9bd6-306d01df1e27* to begin planning your Exchange Server Migration. In short, you'll create an Exchange hybrid environment, fully configure that environment, and then migrate mailboxes to the cloud.

Skype for Business migrations are usually straightforward, assuming a solid hybrid environment is built first. Browse to *https://technet.microsoft.com/library/jj204669.aspx* to learn more about creating a hybrid Skype for Business implementation and then moving users to the cloud.

Use a methodology

As you enter a migration effort, you really should have a defined methodology in hand. A *methodology* injects discipline and order into a process, and it helps ensure you're being deliberate as you move forward. If nothing else, a methodology is beneficial in demonstrating and proving that your approach is well planned and communicated.

Any methodology you use should include a minimal set of phases, sometimes called *gates*. Gates ensure that everyone involved in the migration agrees on what's being migrated, the fidelity of the migration, and the timelines. Instead of focusing on any one methodology, this section outlines the required gates and activities for a successful migration. There are four gates you should use, at a minimum, as illustrated in Figure 9-1. You can add gates for your organization and project scope. Just know that gates are a powerful tool in your arsenal to bring together multiple stakeholders and begin the early phases of communication.

As you can see, a solid methodology is cyclical. It can be iterated upon. Although you can do the entire migration in one iteration through one set of gates (a *Big Bang* migration), this doesn't have to be the case. Instead, you can be more agile and migrate separate pieces of the whole until everything has been moved. The methodology ensures that each of these iterations is done consistently and completely, regardless of the migration's scope.

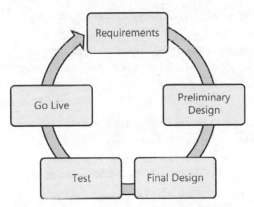

FIGURE 9-1 Basic migration design methodology

The following sections cover each phase of the methodology illustrated in Figure 9-1.

Requirements phase

Requirements are gathered during discovery. The better your discovery is, the better your requirements are. Requirements can be technical in nature, such as minimum operating specifications. Requirements can also be business-related, such as a business unit mandating that migrations take place only on weekends and holidays. Technical requirements aren't more important than business requirements, and both can equally affect your migration design. Requirements are important for all project types, but we believe they're critical for a successful migration.

Because migrations take a fair amount of test iterations, being forced to assume a new requirement, because it was missed in discovery, can cause significant project delays and budget overruns. Some requirements might not seem obvious for a migration because they aren't present in a system implementation project. The most important example is content to be migrated. Don't assume all content will be migrated, and don't assume all content should be treated with the same level of care. There's likely data that can be bulk migrated without retaining 100 percent fidelity. We use the term *fidelity* when discussing migrations as how close to the source content the eventual destination content is.

For a migration, you don't perform deep content discovery during the Requirements phase. Instead, you need to focus on what data repositories need to be dived into deeply when you're in the Design phase. It's in the Design phase where you go through content with a fine-toothed comb. In addition to data repositories, you need to understand any critical processes that might have in-flight data, such as workflows. *In-flight processes* refers to processes that might be paused for any number of reasons, such as an approval, or content that might be routed to third-party applications. These are commonly overlooked

It's possible that not all data will be in lists and libraries, so that's why you need to meet with the business stakeholders and understand how they use their data and what might be under the hood. It's common to see third-party widgets installed by the business, dodgy scripts inside of Web parts, and .htm pages stored in document libraries to bypass web content management governance. These are only examples, and we're sure you'll find more during your migration.

Discovery, and the resulting requirements, should also be considered your first step toward risk mitigation. You shouldn't be held responsible for omission by the business. Likewise, insufficient resources to migrate as the business requires should be called out as a project risk. Don't be afraid to call out risks in your project reviews. We have often had requirements reviews in which we didn't get past the risks slides in our presentation! The more risks you can identify in the Requirements phase, the easier your job will be getting the resourcing and buy-in as the project continues.

> **TIP** During the Discovery phase, be sure to address the need to research dead sites, rarely used sites, and old content. For the Preliminary Design phase, we usually recommend unused and abandoned sites be archived and deleted. This doesn't mean a deep discovery for unused content during the requirements phase; this means a cursory check to see what sites haven't been used in over a year or more. Often, IT Pros will already have a good idea of what sites aren't being used.

During the Requirements phase, focus on the big buckets of content and customizations you need to migrate, and then get agreement from stakeholders on which items should be included in the migration and to what level of fidelity. All stakeholders will want 100 percent fidelity, of course, but you have to define the costs and let the funding stakeholders make the final decisions. An enterprise-scoped migration is rarely funded at 100 percent fidelity across the board. SharePoint is not Exchange Server; it's significantly more complex to migrate. You don't have to capture every single nuance of your migration in the Requirements phase, because you'll do more research and content discovery in later phases. Do the best you can, and push the business for good content requirements. After deciding what content you'll migrate, you next must decide if you'll re-architect data during migration.

A lot of your organization's content will need to be touched during migration. So, if you're looking to re-architect, the migration process might be the perfect time to change data structures. You can even re-architect components altogether, such as moving from InfoPath forms to another form solution. Although doing this will be more challenging than just moving data, it can prevent your users from seeing new URLs twice: once for migration and another time for data restructuring. Although this aspect should be covered as you move into your migration design, having it documented helps communicate your plans to all stakeholders. Try to set all the data-migration requirements in the Requirements phase, because adding requirements in later phases introduces project risk and complicates the project.

Real World

One of the most common mistakes in discovery is making assumptions. It reminds me of the analogy of a fish gathering requirements for a new aquarium. He asked his tank-mates, "How warm do you like your water?" They responded with, "What's water?"

The lesson learned is to not make assumptions about requirements. Your users leverage features continually and often do not know what they are or what to name them. Try to speak the language your users speak. They often don't know the difference between a site and a list, so find out what they call items and use the same terms.

When it comes to migrations, details matter. Our motto for migration discovery is "Know. Don't guess." Nothing replaces understanding the users' needs and combing through the data to be migrated. It's really important to understand what won't migrate easily and what might not migrate at all. Our experience shows the majority of hours spent on migrations are spent on discovery and testing. The actual migration is usually the smallest part of the project.

Ben Curry, Microsoft MVP

Preliminary Design phase

The most important part of migration preliminary design is inventorying all content to be migrated. Many organizations overlook, and under commit resources to this phase because it's time-consuming. To help reduce the level of effort, consider breaking up your data into critical and noncritical sets. Then spend extra effort ensuring that critical data and processes will function after migration.

Another method to reduce the shock of a large migration is to do it in waves. Because your URL will change for all SharePoint Online content anyway, you might consider breaking your migration into multiple chunks, thus giving you more time to perform a proper inventory and conduct adequate testing. Remember that testing isn't just examining the raw upgrade of the content, it also looks at the usability of the final experience. Ultimately, you need to make sure you're leaving the customer and stakeholders with a system that's in a more usable state than when you started.

> **TIP** Verify your existing data boundaries are within SharePoint Online limits, such as list-view size, file size, and site-collection sizes. Otherwise, some items might fail during migrations. The latest SharePoint Online boundaries are very gracious, so you'll encounter fewer issues than you might have in the past. For more information, see "SharePoint Online software boundaries and limits" at *https://support.office.com/article/SharePoint-Online-software-boundaries-and-limits-8f34ff47-b749-408b-abc0-b605e1f6d498*.

During your migration design, consolidate redundant sites, lists, or libraries. Frequently, you'll see duplicate and triplicate data sets, and the less you have to migrate, the easier your migration becomes. Archive and delete content that's considered stale and that's outside any document-management retention period.

> **TIP** Some boundaries, such as maximum site quota, are determined by your license type. Be sure to verify your license types before beginning migration.

Next, create a connections map for any repositories you'll migrate to Office 365. To ensure full functionality after the migration, you must identify all connections in and out of the farms and any connections between SPSites. Common examples of connections are third-party software solutions, line-of-business (LOB) integration, antivirus systems, custom code, workflows, and document-capture processes. All connections must be re-engineered for Office 365 or they will likely break.

> **TIP** When migrating, remember not all of your on-premises settings are available in Office 365. Examples are file-size limits, view-limit thresholds, and web application policies.

Common design challenges include

- Undefined content owners
- Branding elements that will not migrate and must be re-created
- A large volume of content
- The complexity of content
- A lack of technical resources
- Oversimplification by management and stakeholders
- Getting time from business users for requirements
- Getting time from business users for testing and acceptance
- Metadata items (such as created by, created date, last modified date, and custom)
- Workflow definitions
- The workflow history
- The workflow state
- Audit logs
- Alerts
- The Recycle Bin
- Lookup lists that have problems because of GUID remapping
- Scale limitations
- Content throttling during migration

NOTE Be cautious when migrating in phases. Processes often span workloads and sites, and what seems like a simple migration can quickly snowball into a large, complicated, high-risk effort.

Final Design phase

The Final Design gate should be a combination of your Preliminary Design phase plus changes by stakeholders. Additionally, often you can perform feasibility testing in the Final Design phase. Feasibility testing ensures that the migration method or tool works the way you need it to and that the items can actually be migrated the way you expect. The outcome of this testing often alters the final design. The final design you come up with shouldn't constitute a huge change, but it should review all activities, lessons learned, political challenges, task status, roadblocks, go-live plans, issues, and risks.

Test phase

Testing should be a two-fold process. First, it should address the technical migration aspects, and, second, it should address the usability for the user. Ultimately, your focus for the project is not just performing a migration for the sake of a migration, but producing a migration that results in user experiences that are at least equal to, if not greater, than the one before the migration took place.

When testing, you'll find it's best to divide your migration test plan into these two aspects. Your migration test plan should make sure the following questions are answered:

- Does the migration actually work?
- Did any of the migrations fail?
- Are all features and apps running?

This last question is critical. Keep in mind that although a system can show signs of being healthy and running, the business applications might not actually be functioning as needed by the users. Ensure your test plan includes your workflows, forms, custom applications, and any customizations made to the environment prior to the migration.

Go Live phase

Going live should be the easiest part of the project if design and testing was done well. Make sure your communications have been clear, expectations were set, and escalation paths have been documented. If possible, have a rollback plan.

Migration scenarios and scope

In this section, we discuss various topics related to migration. These strategies and considerations largely apply to any migration, not just to a SharePoint Online migration. Deciding what you'll migrate, the level of data fidelity you'll target, and prioritizing your migration are the first steps.

Start with an information architecture

You might be tempted just to lift and shift content from SharePoint or file shares directly into a SharePoint Online site. There's something to be said for just getting the migration over with, because simply getting all content into the cloud is a significant hurdle to clear. However, we highly recommend you pause and first develop an information architecture for Office 365. In fact, we'd go so far as to say you shouldn't migrate without one.

Information architecture is a broad topic. Just as a technical architecture describes all the technical components of a system, information architecture describes everything about how information is structured, accessed, controlled, and maintained. It includes everything from the site structures to the metadata and navigation. Taxonomy, content types, permissions—all of these should be addressed in a comprehensive information architecture. We can't stress highly enough how important defining your information architecture is to performing a successful migration.

If nothing else, at least think through how the data should be organized. What are the major buckets in which the data *should* live? Just because data was stored in a certain way in the past doesn't mean it needs to be that way in the future. Data should be stored in a way that not only makes logical sense but also is findable to users. It should also be stored in a hierarchy that's secured naturally and simply. Broken permissions inheritance is a primary marker of a poor information architecture.

A well-designed and well-implemented information architecture can enhance the value of the system, decrease ongoing maintenance, maximize opportunities for innovation and improvements, protect the data, drive users to the correct location for their work, and simply make good sense. As such, the value of an information architecture, even if it's just a site structure, is extremely high.

You at least need to know where the data is going before you can move it there.

The easiest migration is no migration

When starting a migration effort, it's an extremely good idea to first review the data with the data owners to classify the data. Just because you can migrate something doesn't mean you should. Is there still value to it? Is it still being used?

Quite often, users create data and don't look back after its use has ended. Very rarely are file shares or other data systems actually maintained by the users or data owners. They frequently won't know why something is there or whether or not it's being used, so they just leave it. A migration project provides an excellent opportunity (and an excuse) to finally get your users to perform some cleanup. The more you can leave behind, the faster and less complicated the migration will be.

If your data does not have an owner clearly defined, take advantage of system metadata to discover whether or not something is being used. File systems provide a variety of dates that can give you a clue. If, for example, you see that certain files haven't been modified in the last three years, you likely can leave them behind. Also, if you have the time and the system has the capability, consider implementing some kind of auditing solution and then wait to see what is and isn't being accessed. Doing so not only helps you identify what isn't being used, but it also tells you what data has the highest activity and thus needs the highest priority and care. In SharePoint, there are ways to determine the last time something was accessed. If you have auditing in place, you can use it to gain an understanding of data-access patterns.

Finally, as you categorize your data and identify what won't get migrated, make sure you consider what to do with the stuff that's left behind. Do you simply delete it? Doing so might enable you to decommission the system after the migration, but it's highly risky. What if someone needed that data after all? Instead, we recommend setting the data to read-only and then regularly auditing who accesses it. It'll probably be safe to remove after enough time has elapsed without it being accessed. The ROI might not be as quick or as high, but the risk is much lower.

Test migrations

As we said earlier in the "Use a methodology" section, when performing migrations, take the time to test. There are three primary reasons to test migrations:

- You need to test the tools selected and validate that they'll work as expected. The migration method should be updated and tweaked based on the lessons learned.

- Testing provides better data for estimating the time that will be needed to migrate content. This time can be variable because of network conditions, server utilization, and wide area network (WAN) bandwidth available. If you first test your migration plan, you can complete a realistic migration schedule that's based on actual metrics.

- Testing familiarizes the content owners with the final design. It puts flesh on the theoretical skeleton that existed up until that point and lets them get a sense of what the result will look like. This awareness on the part of stakeholders might result in tweaks to the structures and information architecture, and it might generate some additional excitement about the project.

Testing doesn't have to be done just once. In fact, it should be repeated until you reach the point that you're comfortable with the tool and the process and have a high level of confidence in both. If users are also involved in test migrations (and they should be), tests will provide you with real feedback. Migrations are important to get right the first time, and testing can help make this happen.

Use a Big Bang approach or migrate gradually?

What is the timeframe for the migration? Does it need to be a Big Bang migration and happen all at once over a single weekend, or can it be done gradually and in pieces? The volume of the data, WAN bandwidth, and migration complexities determine the answer to this question. The timeframe is an extremely important factor in the migration method chosen.

If it's possible to do, the Big Bang method of migration might be your best bet. It can be vastly easier to manage than other approaches, and it can be easier on the users. Instead of migrating pieces at a time, you migrate it all at once. This process can be difficult to accomplish with SharePoint Online, though, if you do not have significant bandwidth or you have a large amount of data.

You'll most likely be performing a gradual migration. This means migrating chunks of data as atomic units over time. A gradual migration can occur over the course of a couple of weeks or over an entire year. The pace at which the migration happens is dependent on the amount of data, the complexity of the data, and the schedule or cooperation of end users.

When performing a gradual migration, an important point to consider is what to do mid-migration when data is split across both locations. Users might find it confusing to have some sites or workloads in one place and other sites and workloads in another. If you're not careful, this division can lead to a kind of information chaos. The chaos can be limited by ensuring entire workloads are moved as an atomic unit. Everything related to a workload should be migrated together, because failing to do so adds a significant amount of confusion. It's better to wait to migrate than to split a workload between the cloud and on-premises installations. Adopting a search-first migration strategy can also help avoid the confusion, because search via the Cloud SSA, the hybrid service that provides a single index for both on-premises and cloud content, can present users with the information they're looking for regardless of where it's currently living. We'll discuss search-first migrations with the Cloud SSA in the upcoming sections.

Determining the right tools for the job

Something will need to actually move the data from one location to another. This movement can be as simple as a user dragging and dropping files or as complex (and expensive) as a major third-party migration tool. The tool you should choose is primarily driven by the migration method dictated by the requirements you determined. For lift-and-shift migrations, the SharePoint Online PowerShell migration cmdlets can be used effectively for quickly uploading file shares or sites in bulk. For gradual migrations, third-party tools will likely make the work much easier. If you're adopting a self-service migration, where users are responsible for migrating their own content, drag-and-drop in Windows Explorer is the way to go.

Data migration is one of the major development spaces for Microsoft partners. A good number of vendors provide products to migrate data to SharePoint Online and OneDrive for Business from file shares, on-premises SharePoint, and other document-management systems. Before evaluating a tool, you should first have your requirements clearly defined. This includes the overall migration strategy. Evaluate the tool with these requirements in mind. For example, if you're migrating a SharePoint site with workflow, make sure the product migrates workflow. Some tools are more geared toward centralized, IT-managed migrations, so they might not be the best choice if you're planning a self-service migration. Additionally, if you have a large amount of data, you might need a tool that can continually migrate changes from the source system to the cloud so that the final cutover can be done within the time allotted. Finally, consider costs. There's a wide range of prices for third-party tools, so make sure you know your budget going in.

Note that you don't need to purchase a third-party tool. They can solve a lot of problems and make the job easier, but they're not strictly necessary. Microsoft has made available an API for migrating file shares and on-premises SharePoint sites. Many third-party tools actually use this API on the back end. The process is entirely done using PowerShell (via the SharePoint Online Management Shell) and moves data in bulk. From a high level, the process involves first creating a content package that is essentially an export of the site or file share. You then upload the package to an Azure storage container that you own. Finally, you submit a migration job that takes the package from the Azure container and imports it into the site of your choice. This method can be much faster than moving content one file at a time, because Microsoft throttles operations in Office 365.

> **MORE INFO**   For more information about this API, see the "SharePoint Online Migration API User Guide" at *https://support.office.com/article/SharePoint-Online-Migration-API-User-Guide-555049c6-15ef-45a6-9a1f-a1ef673b867c*.

Migrating SharePoint and My Site content

Most likely, you'll need to migrate information from an on-premises SharePoint farm to SharePoint Online. This migration might also include personal sites (My Sites). The tried-and-true traditional migration method on-premises, database-attach, is not available with SharePoint Online, so you need to approach the migration a bit differently than you might have in the past. In this section, we look at some special and specific considerations that are unique to migrating from SharePoint to SharePoint Online.

> **TIP**   Microsoft is one of the largest users of SharePoint Server. In March, 2016, the company published a technical case study describing its project to move 185,000 SharePoint sites to SharePoint Online. The case study discusses how Microsoft approached the migration and the lessons the company learned while doing it. If you're considering migration from on-premises SharePoint to SharePoint Online, we highly recommend you read "SharePoint to the cloud: Learn how Microsoft ran its own migration" at *https://www.microsoft.com/itshowcase/Article/Content/691/SharePoint-to-the-cloud-Learn-how-Microsoft-ran-its-own-migration*.

What won't migrate?

Perhaps the most important technical thing to know about migrating from SharePoint Server to SharePoint Online is what *won't* migrate. The vast majority of content can migrate to SharePoint Online. Generally speaking, a list item is a list item and a document is a document. You can feel pretty confident that the content itself will not have a problem with the migration.

However, there are some elements or capabilities that absolutely will not migrate to SharePoint Online. One general thing to keep in mind is that Microsoft has basically just given us site collections to work in. If the stuff in your sites are dependent on anything outside of a site collection, chances are good it won't be a candidate for migration.

They've also told us that you can't have any code (other than JavaScript) running in SharePoint Online. This primarily includes farm solutions, although they also recently shut down the ability to use code in sandboxed solutions. A farm solution (a .WSP file) contains custom .NET code that is installed into the farm and runs on the servers. It can be something you purchased from a vendor, downloaded from the internet, or built yourself. Microsoft needs to make sure that SharePoint Online service is stable, consistent, and performing for all of its users. Remember the analogy of the apartment building back in Chapter 1? There's no way to guarantee this if Microsoft were to allow farm solutions. They're notorious for causing all kinds of problems in a SharePoint Server farm. So anything that requires a farm solution will not migrate as is.

The following are the solutions or components that will not migrate to SharePoint Online:

- Any kind of farm solution, including timer jobs
- Sandboxed solutions with custom code
- PerformancePoint
- External lists (via Business Connectivity Service)
- Anything at the SharePoint Server web-application level, such as user policies
- Managed paths other than Teams or Sites
- Running workflows (workflow instances)

Running workflows, also known as inflight workflows and technically called *workflow instances*, can be especially challenging. How do you migrate the state of a running workflow so that it can continue where it was after the migration? Unfortunately, you can't. To our knowledge, no tool supports migrating workflow state. Any running workflow must be stopped and, optionally, restarted as part of the migration. You need to make sure you have a plan for this. Can you simply stop them? Is the workflow safe to restart in SharePoint Online? The answer to the latter will likely take a solid analysis and understanding of the workflow. If possible, and if there's time, redesign the problematic workflow so that it can be restarted without concern. This can usually be done by using one or more columns to record the workflow's progress and state along with logic that uses these to move to the right step when the workflow starts.

Additionally, although technically it can be migrated, seriously consider not migrating your branding and master pages. Due to the incredibly fast pace of change in SharePoint Online, Microsoft highly recommends never modifying the master page. We agree. This does mean, though, that you'll have to test your pages to make sure they still work and make sense. They might be dependent upon a customization in a modified master page. If so, plan on reworking the pages so that they work with the default master page in SharePoint Online.

Finally, keep in mind that some functionality, like email-enabled libraries, will not be available after a migration. You can still migrate the content in the library like any other, but the email capability will no longer work. You'll either need to engineer a replacement solution or leave the capability behind.

What about My Sites?

As discussed in Chapter 5, "Managing the client: OneDrive for Business, Office Pro Plus, and Mobile Device Management for Office 365," My Sites are personalized site collections in SharePoint in which users can save their personal files. The on-premises OneDrive for Business is based out of the users' My Sites. As part of SharePoint, it's reasonable to assume that the My Sites will be migrated to Office 365 as well. However, this doesn't have to be the case. The question of what to do with My Sites during a migration can be a complicated one.

My Sites, just like personal file shares, are often either not used at all or are full of cruft that is not valuable. At the same time, they might be heavily used by some users. Many organizations actually opt *not* to migrate My Sites or personal file shares and start users fresh in the new system. Migrating them can result in a large amount of work that simply might not be worth the investment.

It can help, though, to have some data on how My Sites are used in your company. The following script can help you determine which My Sites have seen some activity. It loops through all potential My Sites and their non-system lists and libraries, looking for an item that has been created or modified in the past 365 days. If it finds an item, it will tell you in green where it was found and then move on to the next My Site. Unfortunately, the *LastItemModifiedDate* properties on the site and list objects are not accurate for this purpose. The goal is to give you a rough sense of activity in your My Sites. The script needs to be run from a SharePoint server in the farm:

```
Add-PSSnapin Microsoft.SharePoint.PowerShell -ErrorAction SilentlyContinue
$date = (Get-Date).AddDays(-365)
$mySiteHosts = Get-SPSite -Limit All | Get-SPWeb -Limit All |
        Where-Object {$_.WebTemplate -eq "SPSMSITEHOST"}
foreach($mySiteHost in $mySiteHosts)
{
    $mySiteHostUrl = $mySiteHost.Url
    $mySites = Get-SPSite -Limit All | Get-SPWeb -Limit All |
            Where-Object {$_.Url -like "$mySiteHostUrl/*"}
    foreach($mySite in $mySites)
```

```
{
    $foundUpdate = $false
    Write-Host "Now processing $($mySite.Url)"
    foreach ($list in $mySite.Lists |
            Where-Object {$_.IsCatalog -eq $false -and $_.Hidden -eq $false})
    {
        foreach($item in $list.Items)
        {
            if(($item["Modified"] -ge $date -or $item["Created"] -ge $date) `
                -and ($item["Created"] -gt $mysite.Created.AddMinutes(5)))
                # Avoid false positives by giving a 5-minute buffer since
                # the My Site was initially created
            {
                Write-Host "`tFound update in ""$($list.Title)."" Modified = `
$($item["Modified"]). Created = $($item["Created"])" -ForegroundColor Green
                $foundUpdate = $true
                break    # Stop looping through items
            }
        }
        if($foundUpdate)
        {
            break  # Stop looping through lists
        }
    }
    $mySite.Dispose()
}
$mySiteHost.Dispose()
}
```

After you determine whether or not you're going to migrate users' My Sites, you then need to determine the method. If they're to migrate their own content, you'll need to provide them with information on how to do so (such as drag-and-drop). Self-service My Site migrations can decrease the complexity of the migrations, but it simply might not be doable by some users. If you will be migrating their content for them, then the SharePoint Online Migration API might be an excellent choice because each My Site will be self-contained and the process can be automated via PowerShell. Third-party migration tools should be able to migrate My Sites as well.

Migration gotchas

As you consider migrating your SharePoint sites to SharePoint Online, you should be mindful of several gotchas:

- **URL changes** When you migrate to SharePoint Online, you must change your URL. Unfortunately, there's no way to customize the SharePoint Online URL, let alone maintain the existing on-premises URL. Plus, only the /sites and /teams managed paths are available. What this means is that anything that uses a hardcoded URL will need to be updated as part of the migration. This could include pages, workflow definitions, navigation elements, InfoPath forms, and so on. After the migration, plan on having users go through all of the pages, links, and functionality in order to validate them all. If you're able, take time before a migration to find all hardcoded URLs and either change them into relative URLs or record them so that they can be updated as part of the migration process.

- **InfoPath forms** InfoPath web forms are still supported in SharePoint Online (unless they're disabled in the SharePoint Online Admin Center). Therefore, InfoPath forms can be successfully migrated along with lists and libraries. However, you should analyze the forms to make sure they will still work in SharePoint Online. Examine the data sources and make sure they only reference lists local to the site collection by way of relative paths. Any data source used in the form must be accessible from SharePoint Online (the internet), so any that rely upon on-premises sources will either need to be redesigned or have the data source exposed to the internet. Additionally, it's quite common to see InfoPath forms calling the SharePoint user profile web service to get information about a user. These will either need to be removed or re-engineered to use the hidden User Information List instead. Finally, be on the lookout for any hardcoded URLs.

- **Old web parts** Chances are very good that SharePoint pages will be migrated along with the lists and libraries. Some of these might use web parts that are available in SharePoint Server but that aren't in SharePoint Online. These pages will need to be redone using web parts that work in SharePoint Online. Almost every web part that is in SharePoint 2013 is also in SharePoint Online, so this isn't a large concern if you're on SharePoint 2013. The only ones missing are the four PerformancePoint web parts, because the service is not available in SharePoint Online. If you're migrating from SharePoint 2010, then you'll need to look out for the following web parts that aren't in SharePoint Online (thanks to *www.collabshow.com* for the reference):

  - Chart
  - Exchange-related
    - My Calendar
    - My Contacts
    - My Inbox
    - My Mail Folder
    - My Tasks
  - PerformancePoint-related
    - PerformancePoint Filter
    - PerformancePoint Report Viewer
    - PerformancePoint Scorecard
    - PerformancePoint Stack Selector
  - Search-related

- Advanced Search Box
- Dual Chinese Search
- Federated Results
- People Refinement Panel
- People Search Box
- People Search Core Results
- Refinement Panel
- Related Queries
- Search Action Links
- Search Best Bets
- Search Box
- Search Core Results
- Search Paging
- Search Statistics
- Search Summary
- Search Visual Best Bet
- Top Federated Results
- SQL Server Reporting Services Report Viewer
- What's New
- What's Popular
- Whereabouts

- **Permissions**   It's extremely unlikely that the exact same permissions (ACLs) on the on-premises content will work as-is in SharePoint Online. As such, plan on having to redo some permissions. Most third-party tools provide the ability to map accounts and groups, so take advantage of the feature if you have it.

- **Sandboxed solutions**   If your site uses sandboxed solutions, it's possible that it can be migrated as is. However, only declarative sandboxed solutions will work in SharePoint Online. If your sandboxed solution has custom code, it will not work in SharePoint Online and thus you need to find a replacement solution (or abandon it altogether).

- **Checked-out documents**   Most migration tools are unable to migrate checked-out documents. They're locked and inaccessible by anyone other than the person who checked it out. It's a very good idea to go through all of your document libraries to make sure all of the content is checked in.

Migrating file shares: Should I or shouldn't I?

It's likely that you're considering migrating files in your file shares to Office 365. There are a good number of reasons why you might want to migrate files in such a way, including the following:

- Office 365 can provide nearly unlimited storage simply, without the need to provision additional hardware.

- If the amount of storage needed is less than the amount of storage already available in the tenant through existing licensing, the storage comes at no additional cost.

- Eventually, the file-share system and servers will need to be upgraded and replaced. This upgrading process will not be required for Office 365.

- Content in Office 365 is potentially available from any web browser anywhere on the planet without requiring access to the internal network.

- Content stored in SharePoint Online and OneDrive for Business can take advantage of all the benefits of SharePoint Online, such as the following ones:

  - Versioning with rollback

  - Real-time collaboration in most Office file formats

  - Workflow (business process automation)

  - Audit and document policies

  - Data loss prevention (DLP)

  - Online document previews

  - External sharing

  - In-place holds

- All data in Office 365 is protected from disaster (although making backups is still advisable).

- The file server infrastructure possibly can be retired, reducing costs.

- File-share data can easily be discoverable via eDiscovery (and search as a whole).

The following are some of the negatives of or challenges to migrating file-share contents to Office 365:

- Your current file shares and servers represent a sunken cost. If the amount of storage needed is more than what's already available through current Office 365 licensing, your organization will incur an additional monthly cost to provision the extra storage.

- Content in Office 365 is potentially available from any web browser anywhere on the planet. This flexibility increases the chance of data leakage.

- Data in SharePoint Online is generally not available directly from Windows Explorer. You can open a document library in Windows Explorer and even map it as a drive, but doing this is generally discouraged.

- Users probably know where their information is now. Migrating to a new platform will require significant adaptation on their part.

- There might be processes and workflows that use the file shares. Moving the files into Office 365 necessitates a change in those processes and workflows.

Although you and users of your system will experience some pain in adapting to Office 365 (as in any move to another system), users eventually will learn to use the new locations and methods. Given time and proper internal marketing and training, users very likely will recognize the benefits of moving content into Office 365.

You'll find that it's best to not include migrating file shares in the scope of your SharePoint migration. File shares can be personal to groups, organizations, and people. Migrating file shares can be a lot like moving antique furniture—an item might or might not be valuable. Something that might not appear to be valuable to you, might be valuable to the user—even if it has only sentimental value. However, because file-share migrations often involve many files and large amounts of content, you should ensure your file-share migration approach is complemented by a solid file-share migration methodology.

Dealing with source material after a migration

After data has been moved to the new location, what should be done with the data in the old location? There are multiple schools of thought on this.

It might be quickest and easiest to simply "rip off the bandage" and remove the old location altogether. This approach guarantees there's no confusion about where to go for the content. However, it can cause confusion for users as they learn to adapt. It can also break unknown and unexpected processes that rely upon the location. If this method is chosen, expect many frustrated and angry help desk calls. Their duration will likely be short, though.

The least-disruptive option is to simply leave the location exactly as is and direct users to the new location. This strategy allows processes to continue as is and gives users time to adapt. However, it's extremely likely that this approach will result in a split-brained system, with changes being made in both locations. If the same document is modified in both locations, which one will win? In this scenario, one location should be declared the master of the content.

A more realistic option is to keep the data in the original location, except you set all of it to read-only. This approach allows casual read usage to continue unchanged for a time, but it prevents data conflicts and forces changes to be made in the proper location. The old location should be monitored to determine who still continues to use it. These individuals can then be directed to the right place. After the monitoring shows that users have stopped using the old location, it can be removed entirely.

Search-first migrations

Most people know how to use search. Although they might not know how to search *well*, they have experience using Bing or Google. You can take advantage of this user familiarity with search when migrating to Office 365. SharePoint Online has an excellent search engine that uses complicated algorithms and analysis to surface to users information that's specifically relevant to them. The more they search and click on results, the more tuned to them the search function becomes.

Because of the high-quality search engine in SharePoint Online, you can rely on search to surface the data your users need, regardless of where it lives in the service. Instead of relying on memory or site navigation, you can train your users to start with a search to find the content they need. You can also use pages with search-based web parts in SharePoint Online to give them what you think they want. If you then marry this concept to hybrid search, users can find their data even if it's on-premises data. This approach is considered a *search-first migration*.

When migrating on-premises SharePoint, we sometimes start by building the search capability into the new farm and then federating it with the old farm or farms. The search function crawls those old farms in addition to the new farm, giving us a single index with results from all systems. The old farm taps into the new farm's search service as well, giving the user the same results regardless of which farm she's searching from. As data is migrated from one farm to another, whether you chose to use a Big Bang or gradual approach, the search index is updated as the farms are crawled and the new data locations are found. If, for example, a site is moved from an old farm to a new farm over a weekend, a query that ran on Friday that returned results from the old farm returns the same results on Monday, except the results are from the new farm. Thus, a search-first migration can be used to abstract away from the user the storage location of the data, even going so far as hiding from the user that a migration happened at all.

Because you don't have the same capabilities with SharePoint Online as you do with on-premises SharePoint, you need to rely on hybrid search to accomplish this. You can perform a hybrid search either by using *classic hybrid* and query federation or, better yet, by using the new hybrid cloud search service application (SSA). See Chapter 6, "Hybrid Office 365," for more information about hybrid search. The new cloud SSA can present a single set of results to the user, regardless of whether the data is in SharePoint Online, in an on-premises SharePoint site, or on a file share. By deploying the cloud SSA, you can have a search-first migration as you did with the on-premises system.

Note that a search-first migration is not itself a migration method. It does not move data for you. However, it can be used alongside the other migration methods to smooth out the user experience. Regardless of whether or not they use search first, users can be instructed to use it as a fallback option if they're struggling to find their data.

Change management and communication

Change is risky. Change is usually disruptive. Change is certainly uncomfortable, and to many it's even scary. A migration to Office 365 is change—big change. The user interface, the methods of accessing data, and the locations of data will all change. Bookmarks will break, as will processes that haven't been updated. There's no way around it—migrating to Office 365 will be disruptive.

You need to manage this change thoughtfully, taking care to consider its impact on your users. When implementing a change of this magnitude, you need to do it with as much user buy-in as possible. Ultimately, you'll need support from all levels in the organization, because it might end up affecting everyone at some point in time. The amount of support you need will be directly related to the scope of the migration and its pace. A full, company-wide migration of all file shares will require significant support, because it will affect everyone. However, smaller, targeted migrations of individual sites, folders, or workloads requires less support up front; thus, the support likely will be easier to obtain. In addition, you won't find anything much more powerful in garnering support than proven success. It's far easier to achieve success on a smaller migration than on a huge one.

Therefore, we recommend that when you approach a migration project and attempt to manage its resulting change, you start small with a specific site or workload that's manageable. Ideally, pick one that has the support of one of your end-user champions. This small migration can be a pilot or proof of concept. It will serve not only to get you ready for bigger and riskier migrations, but it also will give you an easy win. The win then gives you momentum you can carry forward into a second targeted migration. As you continue to build on your wins, other users will begin to see the successes and want to know more. The ultimate goal is that content or process owners will naturally be drawn into the platform and become willing participants as they see the success of their peers and want a piece of the action.

Communication is a critical part of this change management. As successes are realized, you need to advertise or market them inside the organization. Find some way to share what you're doing. Your best advocate should be your user champion or the content owner who benefited from the migration. It's more likely that others will listen to their story if it comes from that person than if it comes from you. So if at all possible, enlist the end users in your communications so that you can sell the benefits of migration more effectively.

Communication

Creating effective buy-in from users is necessary for any platform or solution to be adopted. Effective communication can help spur adoption of the platform and help users change. If they don't understand the why and how of impending changes, there will be a lack of confidence in the migration and the direction being pursued.

Proper communication bolsters confidence and brings about encouragement and enthusiasm for process and technological changes. Communication and training are the keys to a successful migration and growing user adoption. The ADKAR principles can help you manage the change. *ADKAR* (the acronym is spelled out in the following list) is a methodology that satisfies the raw nature of human need for successful adoption of organizational and technological change:

- **Awareness**   Users need to be aware of the need for change. The more they know what to expect (and when), the more they can prepare for the change.

- **Desire**   There needs to be a desire for change within the culture in order for change to be supported or accepted. Communicate the new possibilities made available through the migration to foster desire in the organization.

- **Knowledge**   Knowledge in the migration process is two-fold. Knowing how and why the migration will be done increases the willingness to bring about successful change. Access to a knowledge base or a training center assists you in making the users aware of the upcoming migrations and provides them with the tools to assist in the change.

- **Ability**   Training needs to be in place to facilitate the transfer of knowledge to the users. A lack of knowledge among the users stymies adoption of the new system or process.

- **Retention**   After users are trained, sustain their ability to function in the new context through regular touch points. Avoid training six months ahead of schedule. Instead make it just-in-time training. Also, incentives can enable reinforcement during and even after the initial migration begins. Showcasing wins within the new system acknowledges success, creates more awareness of the new system's capabilities, and bolsters the desire for change.

As you start a migration project, we recommend you create a communications plan that uses the ADKAR principles just described. Communication must be ongoing and regular; it's not something that you can get away with doing just once. Your users have other work to do, and your migration project is not their focus, so you can't expect them to keep your one or two email messages always in mind. At the same time, you need to be careful not to overwhelm or pester your users. If you communicate too frequently or too broadly, your communication just becomes noise that the users will tune out. Targeted, just-in-time communication can help avoid this problem. Communicating well requires judgement and experience, and it might be one of the more challenging aspects to a project.

We recommend you create a site with information about the migration. This site can be a one-stop shop for all things related to the migration, including schedules, training, contact information, and post-migration help. You can use it to publish the expected migration mappings and as a forum to highlight successes. Realistically, only people who care about the migration will visit this site, so keep them in mind and do what you can to equip them and support your partnerships.

Additionally, we recommend you establish a Yammer group (or even a SharePoint social community) for two-way communications throughout the migration. Not only can you use it to provide updates to your users, but it can be a powerful tool to receive feedback as well. If you use it well, end users who have gone through migrations will be able to support their peers, thus distributing the support work. After the migration is complete, you can either remove the site or, if it proved to be successful, keep it going (and updated) as your training and learning center. Because of the latter possibility, we recommend you name the site something that makes sense to users after the migration project is closed. So "/sites/MigrationSupport" might not be the best name or URL.

Running a migration project

We discussed many topics with regard to migration throughout this chapter. In summary, we can say that, at its root, *every* migration project must have a plan. It's not advisable to embark on a migration project without a plan—that type of spontaneity is best reserved for weekend getaways. There's always a goal and a purpose to the project. The plan helps you reach that goal.

One of the most difficult parts of every migration is the actual management and facilitation of the migration project itself. It's common for people to want to quickly make use of new technology and features; however, this quickness can increase risk and shift expectations in a way that cannot be supported easily by the organization. Ensure that each migration plan has a documented purpose and objective. From there, identify and specify the migration approach and methodology you will use.

When developing a migration plan, the following are primary components that should be included:

- Migration project foundation, organization, and enablement
- Discovery and requirements
- Premigration evaluation
- Feasibility testing
- Communication plan
- Data categorization and cleanup
- Data map from existing structures to the destination information architecture
- Communication, communication, communication
- Migration testing
- Risk management plan
- End-user training
- Production migration
- Post-migration support
- Old content and system disposal

Always, always, always make sure you understand your licensing and ensure you have the proper installation of apps before the migration. Also, check with your software company for all third-party products to ensure you have a migration license so that you can perhaps run two production instances for a short migration window.

In summary, always have a solid strategy for technology, but focus on the processes that drive the business, especially on the people who will be leading the change and working with the portal. Planning is key—we cannot emphasize this fact enough. Ensure there's a specific, documented understanding of the post-migration user needs and expectations. Remember, sometimes the best migrations are the ones where few people notice it actually happened. Just keep the following tips in mind:

- Take small steps, and use familiar tools.
- Focus on the people—end users and change agents.
- Understand the culture of the organization.
- Find and support standards; don't chase broken processes.

The technology is expensive and complicated, but it's the cheapest and easiest ingredient.

Index

Symbols and Numbers

A

R

S

Video Portal
- configuring of, 228–229
- disabling of, 230
- management of, 229–230
- overview of, 87, 226–228
- video file formats, 228

View Group Permissions, SharePoint Online, 100–101

virtual machines (VMs)
- Azure Active Directory Domain Services (Azure AD DS), 57
- Azure AD Connect availability and, 72–73

Visio, Office ProPlus deployment, 138–139

Visitors, SharePoint Online sites, 100–102

Visual Studio, Cloud Pro skills, 3

W

waffle, extensible app launcher, 180–181

Where-Object, PowerShell, 18, 32

Windows 10 for Office Mobile apps, 124

Windows Active Directory, 54–57

Windows Authentication, publishing on-premises applications, 188–191

Windows Azure Active Directory Module for Windows PowerShell, 21–22

Windows Intune, 88

Windows Mobile, Office 365 support for, 124

Windows PowerShell. See PowerShell

Windows Task Scheduler, 22

wizards, Add Domain Wizard, 58–60

Word. See Office ProPlus

workflow instances, data migration and, 272

workloads, hybrid environment decisions, 166–168

WS-Fed, Cloud Pro skills, 3

X

XML
- Cloud Pro skills, 4
- Office ProPlus, configuration XML files, 140–142

Y

Yammer
- add-ins, 206–207
- admin center URL, 12
- hybrid options, 165
- overview of, 203–205
- updating social feeds, 205–206
- Video Portal settings, 229

Your time, Delve Analytics, 219–220

About the authors

 **BEN CURRY** is founding partner, principal architect, and technology strategist at Summit 7 Systems, a Microsoft Gold Partner in cloud productivity, collaboration, and content management. He is a 10-time Microsoft MVP in SharePoint and Office 365 technologies.

 BRIAN LAWS is a Cloud Architect at Summit 7 Systems, a Microsoft Gold Partner in cloud productivity, collaboration, and content management. He has been deep in SharePoint since the 2007 version and has worn the infrastructure, developer, and architecture hats. His head is usually in the Cloud, dreaming about PowerShell and automation. Outside of work, Brian tries to spend as much as he can with his wife and kids. Whenever he gets the opportunity, he enjoys reading comics, playing video games, and keeping up with his favorite shows. He's a geek through-and-through.

Now that you've read the book...

Tell us what you think!

Was it useful?
Did it teach you what you wanted to learn?
Was there room for improvement?

Let us know at http://aka.ms/tellpress

Your feedback goes directly to the staff at Microsoft Press,
and we read every one of your responses. Thanks in advance!